COOLA

The true story of the Pearson executions

an incident in the Irish War of Independence

By

Paddy Heaney
Pat Muldowney
and others

Edited by

Philip O'Connor

Aubane Historical Society 2008

> This book is dedicated to the
> IRA Volunteers and
> Cumann na mBan
> of the Cadamstown area
> who risked their lives for
> Irish independence

© **The authors and Aubane Historical Society**

The moral right of the authors to be identified as the authors of this work has been asserted

All rights reserved

Aubane Historical Society
ISBN 978 1 903497 48 7
2008

Aubane Historical Society
Aubane, Millstreet, Co. Cork, Ireland
www.aubane.org
Orders: jacklaneaubane@hotmail.com

Contents

Acknowledgements	4
Foreword	
– *Jack Lane*	5
1. The True Story of the Events at Coolacrease	
– *Paddy Heaney and Pat Muldowney*	7
2. The Cadamstown IRA in the War of Independence	
– *Paddy Heaney*	71
3. The British Army and the War in South Offaly	
– *Philip O'Connor*	86
4. Land Grab?—What the Documents Say	
– *Philip O'Connor*	97
5. "Amish-type Farmers"?—Pacifism and the Cooneyites	
– *Pat Muldowney*	144
6. An Extraordinary Set-Up: The Irish Grants Committee	
– *Philip O'Connor*	152
7. Poisoning the Well or Publishing the Truth?	
– *Brian P. Murphy osb*	159
8. Academic Evasions: Revisionists & the War of Independence	
– *Brendan Clifford*	182
9. Exposing Propaganda	
– *Pat Muldowney*	217
10. RTÉ and the Holy Grail of Revisionism	
– *Nick Folley*	233
11. Defending their Own: the Broadcasting Complaints Commission	
– *John Martin*	258
Documentation	**279**
Appendix 1 Photographs	279
Appendix 2 Irish Army Reports on the Pearson Execution	297
Appendix 3 Location Maps of the Events at Coolacrease	302
Appendix 4 Proceedings of British Military Court of Inquiry	305
Appendix 5 Selected Land Documents	322

Appendix 6	Pearson Claims before "Irish Grants Committee"	**347**
Appendix 7	On Executions by Popular Resistance Movements: Extract from *The Gadfly* by E.L. Voynich	**383**
Appendix 8	A Note on the Debate in the Press	**388**
Appendix 9	Transcript of the RTÉ film 'The Killings at Coolacrease' (by *Malachi Lawless*, with annotations by *Pat Muldowney*)	**407**
Appendix 10	List of documents	**452**

Index   **456**

Cover design by Barrie Kidd, BK Graphics

The cover illustration incorporates a photograph of the Slieve Bloom Mountains and a watercolour impression inspired by a scene from the film *The Wind that Shakes the Barley*. Used by kind permission of the director, Ken Loach, © Sixteen Films/Joss Barratt

Acknowledgements:

The authors would like to thank Jack Lane of the Aubane Society for proposing this book and supporting it throughout its production; Simon Comer, Nick Folley, Niall Guerin, and Claire McGrath-Guerin for valuable additional information; Philip McConway for new information from his current research into the War of Independence in Offaly; Seán McGouran for accessing the records of the Irish Grants Committee; Malachi Lawless for compiling the transcripts of the RTÉ programmes; the Offaly Historical and Archaeological Society, Paddy Heaney, Philip McConway and others for sourcing photographs; the staffs of the Military Archives, the National Archive, the Records Branch of the Department of Agriculture, the Land Registry and the Land Valuation Offices (Dublin) and the British National Archives, Kew (London), for their cooperation and, most of all, a special thanks to the people of the Cadamstown area for consenting to information on their families being published in this book.

Foreword

This is two stories in one. It deals with the actual facts of an execution during the War of Independence at Coolacrease in Co. Offaly and then describes how this story was dealt with by RTÉ before, during and after its *"Hidden History"* programme on the incident was broadcast on 23rd October 2007 and again on 13th May 2008.

This incident in the War was not hidden history in any sense. The facts are long known and well known in the locality. It was not so well known nationally simply because it was not a national event. Paddy Heaney and others have written about it in detail over the years. Paddy has a close family connection with the incident. A relative of his died from shots fired at him by the Pearson brothers.

He and his colleagues were defending the democratic and legitimate Irish Government established by the 1918 election against which Britain had launched a war. The Irish Government elected overwhelmingly in that election had made its position crystal clear: *"We solemnly declare foreign government to be an invasion of our national rights which we will never tolerate, and we demand the evacuation of our country by the English Garrison"* (Declaration of Independence, 21st January 1919). Instead, the Garrison was strengthened and went on the offensive against the newly elected Government. The Pearsons chose to assist the Garrison in a paramilitary capacity.

The Cadamstown roadblock was part of the IRA's preparation for a major attack on Crown forces in Birr (where the Crinkle military base was located) and an Offaly-wide mobilisation was planned for this action. It was a rehearsal for taking control of the county's roads and bringing the other side's mobility to a standstill. The Pearson brothers attacked those preparing the roadblock. On the orders of the senior IRA command the brothers were executed directly as a result of this attack.

There is nothing at all unusual in this. It was a military event in a military conflict. But RTÉ sought by *"every trick in the book"* to make it into something else. They made this local incident into a national issue and endorsed the claim that it was a sectarian killing. The Pearsons were members of the 'Cooneyites', a minority Protestant community. The national broadcaster was in no way (as it claimed) a neutral facilitator of two sides of a validly contested historical argument. RTÉ was fully complicit in the programme's claim that the executions were murder, part of a sectarian land grab and ethnic cleansing.

The programme tarred the people of the Cadamstown area as sectarian land-grabbers, implicated the army of Dáil Éireann in the alleged atrocity and even inferred that the officials of the Irish Land Commission were complicit in it.

The programme further insinuated strongly that sectarianism and ethnic cleansing were a general characteristic of the War of Independence itself and the legitimacy and morality of that war were thereby challenged.

That challenge was taken up by Paddy Heaney, Pat Muldowney and others and this book records how they successfully met that challenge. They have proven conclusively the military nature of the incident, the absence of sectarianism in the war in Offaly and the absence of any land grab arising from it.

It is an extraordinary situation that the national broadcaster of a State seeks to misinform its audience and discredit legitimate actions that were necessary to establish the very State it serves! Yet this is the situation we are in here in Ireland at the present time.

There is an ideological campaign against the legitimacy—and the basic facts—of the War of Independence, and that campaign has now been given official sanction by RTÉ.

It is essential to counter this malicious campaign and this book is an attempt to remind ourselves again of the actual facts of that war; the why and the how of it and hopefully it will help set the record straight.

Jack Lane
Aubane Historical Society
August 2008

Chapter 1

The True Story of the Events at Coolacrease

By
Paddy Heaney and Pat Muldowney

Basic Facts

On 30th June 1921, a party of about thirty members of the Irish Republican Army arrested two young farming brothers called Richard and Abraham Pearson while they were making hay in a field near their house in Coolacrease, near Cadamstown in County Offaly. They were brought back to the house which was set ablaze, and the two brothers, aged 24 and 19, were shot by a firing squad.

The rest of the Pearson family left the area, eventually emigrating to Australia. Two years later the Pearsons sold their Coolacrease farm of 341 acres (142 hectares) to the Land Commission, a government land reform agency. The Land Commission divided up the farm into fifteen portions, which were allocated to local people.

The Controversy

The Pearsons belonged to a religious grouping called Cooneyites or Christian Conventions. As far as we know, every member of the IRA party involved in the shootings was Catholic. Each of the families who received part of the Coolacrease land in 1923 was Catholic.

Was this a sectarian murder of innocent farmers? Was it a land grab carried out under cover of the War of Independence just before it ended eleven days later? Does this incident provide evidence of an ethnic cleansing agenda directed by a Catholic, separatist, anti-British majority against a Protestant minority of British settler ancestry?

Controversy has been further fuelled by other aspects of the shootings. It is claimed that the brothers were deliberately shot in the genitals for the purpose of torture and mutilation. The two brothers were shot at about 4.30 p.m., but survived the shootings. However Richard Pearson died from his injuries about 10 p.m. that evening, and Abraham died about 6 a.m. the following morning. As their deaths were not instant, it is claimed that the shootings were deliberately intended to cause agonising, lingering and prolonged suffering.

It is claimed that, to heighten the terror, their mother, three sisters, younger brother, and two female cousins were forced to witness the shootings while their house and possessions were consumed by flames.

After the shootings, it is claimed that harassment, boycott and squatting made it impossible for the surviving Pearsons to try to return and rebuild their shattered life in Coolacrease; so that they were eventually forced to cut their losses, dispose of their property at a fraction of its value, and cast themselves adrift in the world before finally settling in Australia.

A television programme ("*The Killings at Coolacrease*") broadcast by the Irish broadcaster RTÉ on 23rd October 2007 and repeated on 13th May 2008 portrayed the Coolacrease shootings in this light.

But, as this book shows, the reality was very different from what was portrayed in the RTÉ programme.

The Background

The Slieve Bloom mountains straddle the county boundary between Laois and Offaly (formerly Queen's and King's Counties) in the Irish midlands. To the west of Slieve Bloom the townland of Coolacrease adjoins the village of Cadamstown, four miles to the north east of Kinnitty, and about half way between Birr and Tullamore.

The British conquests of Ireland in the sixteenth and seventeenth centuries had been followed by plantation of British Protestant settlers on the expropriated lands of conquered and displaced native Catholic Irish. This was the historic background of the Protestant Pearsons.

Through the nineteenth century the Catholic Irish gradually won a measure of citizenship rights in the United Kingdom of Great Britain and Ireland. In the 1880's a struggle for agricultural tenant rights was fought against a mainly Protestant landlord class, culminating in a number of British Government schemes for Irish farmers to purchase their tenancies from their landlords. This transferred ownership of most of the land back to the native Irish.

The Pearsons lived in the Aghaboe area of County Laois, about thirty miles from Coolacrease. They were not landlords. And, as tenants themselves, they benefited like everybody else from the general land reform movement in Ireland at the end of the 19th century.

In 1911 the Protestant Benwells sold their 341 acre farm at Coolacrease to the Pearsons for £2000. The Pearsons moved across the county boundary from County Laois to their new farm in the Cadamstown area in Offaly. They settled into the neighbourhood successfully and, by all accounts, established good neighbourly relations with the majority local Catholics, and with the Protestant families of the area—the Droughts, Biddulphs, Jacksons, McAllisters, Ashtons.

Though formerly belonging to the Anglican Church of Ireland, at this stage the Pearsons were, in strictly doctrinal terms, not Protestant.

Cooneyism

About 1900 a new religious movement started in County Fermanagh. The inspiration of the movement was in the Faith Missions, which conducted summer-time prayer and preaching meetings on a Protestant inter-church basis. One of the founding members was Edward Cooney from Enniskillen.

The adherents of the new movement rejected church hierarchy, formal ministry and organisation, in favour of a more purely spiritual zeal, and in favour of a relatively unstructured form of religious practice similar to the Faith Missions. It was possible to argue that sincere faith was more likely to be found in this than in the more worldly routines of the mainstream Protestant religious congregations.

Along with adult baptism, the movement espoused preaching as the most important religious activity. They had specific points of similarity with sixteenth century Anabaptists and their successor faiths, who, like the Cooneyites four centuries later, broke away from the Protestant Reformation churches.

Members of the new movement were recruited from existing Protestant congregations by itinerant Cooneyite preachers, and there was occasional conflict because of proselytising.

By the time they settled in Coolacrease in 1911, the Pearsons had joined the Cooneyite movement, and William and Sidney Pearson, at least, were actively involved as there is a record of their participation in religious functions in Tipperary and Mountmellick.

Life in Coolacrease

The family consisted of father and mother William and Susan Pearson; eldest son Richard, sons Abraham, Sidney and David; and daughters Matilda, Ethel and Emily.

The children attended the local Catholic school in Cadamstown village, about a mile from their house. Why not a Protestant school? The reason can only be surmised. In general, there was some degree of tension between the Protestant denominations and Cooneyism in those days because of active proselytising by Cooneyites from the Protestant congregations.

There is no report of any bad feeling between the Pearson family and local Protestants, initially. But a school within a mile of their house would have been very convenient for a busy, hard-working farming family like the Pearsons.

When the Pearsons took over Coolacrease from the Benwells, a couple called Maher who kept house for the Benwells stayed on for a very brief period with the Pearsons. This couple had lived in the coach-house which, with the main dwelling house formed two sides of an enclosed yard or inner courtyard, the other two sides consisting of farm buildings.

The Pearsons did not employ local workmen for farm labour. In a farm of 341 acres this would have been very unusual in those days when farm work was largely unmechanised. But the Pearsons with their large family of four boys and three girls could themselves do the work of mixed farming—tillage, cattle, dairy, poultry, turf cutting.

The Pearsons became part of the community. Coming from neighbouring Co. Laois, the Pearsons and their neighbours were likely to have had many mutual acquaintances. As a farming community, there would have been much routine interaction, borrowing and lending, and the normal cut and thrust of wheeling and dealing in stock, horses and the like. The Pearsons with their 341 acre farm were relatively mechanised and progressive. They were regarded as good neighbours, generous and helpful in emergencies.

As a child, the eldest son Richard played for the school hurling team. Later on, the Pearsons participated in the social life of the area, interacting with their neighbours, attending the house parties and dances, and generally functioning as part of the community.

In 1919 William Pearson, with other local farmers including a strongly Republican one, canvassed door-to-door on behalf of the King's County Farmers' Association, in which he was subsequently elected to a representative position for the Kinnitty area. This is an indication of the extent to which the Pearsons were integrated into an accepting and welcoming community.

On the Pearson side, there is every indication that they were putting down roots in this community, and that they were there for the long haul.

The Cadamstown Community

The Pearsons were not initially hostile to their neighbours. The Pearsons were not really outsiders; they came from a rural area not too far away (about three hours by bicycle) where life was very similar, with many mutual points of reference—good and bad harvests; sporting events; talk of horses which, in those days, were companions and practically family members; fair days; the doings of mutual acquaintances; and the myriad aspects of everyday life.

At the same time, the integration of the Pearsons into the community indicates that the community was open and welcoming towards them. A merely religious difference seems to have been no barrier to acceptance by the majority-Catholic, minority-Protestant locals; even though Cooneyism had an early twentieth century track record of religious conflict, mostly with the established Protestant congregations from which they drew new members. (There is no record of the Pearsons ever engaging in any such purely doctrinal conflict, or conflict unrelated to politics, at that time.)

So what kind of community did the Pearsons encounter when they moved to Coolacrease in 1911?

Historically, this area of the Irish Midlands is a great cross-roads between North, South, East and West. The ancient roads known as the *Slí Dála* and *Slí Mumhan* run close by. It is close to the ancient line of division between *Leath Mhogha* (south) and *Leath Choinn* (north). The Grand Canal runs through the county, from Dublin to the River Shannon. In modern terms, it is close to the cross-country east-west motorway which forms part of the Dublin-Galway link, and to the main north-south routes.

In the middle ages, the English part of Ireland was bottled up in an area called the Pale around Dublin, where it was kept under pressure by the surrounding inhabitants—the native Irish and the earlier English colonists and settlers who had adapted to the native Irish way of life.

By the sixteenth century the English state had resolved its internal dynastic quarrels and its long wars in France, and began its overseas adventures which were to lead to expansion across the Atlantic, and ultimately to conquest and extermination of indigenous peoples around the globe.

The first such adventure was the conquest of the Irish and hibernicised English around the Pale. In the 1550's the Catholic, half-Spanish Queen Mary (eldest daughter of Henry the Eighth) and her husband King Philip of Spain, conquered, expropriated and displaced the native Irish in Offaly and the surrounding area. The resulting English and mainly Protestant colonisation gave the area the names Queen's County (Laois), King's County (Offaly), Maryborough (Port Laoise) and Philipstown (Daingean). There are a great many other colonial residues of the Laois-Offaly conquest.

This conquest was followed by the Elizabethan war of extermination in Munster, which set a precedent and example for the directly-following extermination and colonisation along the eastern seaboard of America as the English state extended further into the western hemisphere.

Offaly was on the north-south route for the armies of O'Neill and

O'Donnell seeking to join up with a Spanish expedition to Ireland, resulting in the 1601 Battle of Kinsale. On the return journey, some of the Irish soldiers settled in this area. This is reflected to this day in the many Catholic Ulster surnames from this time common in the area.

Several centuries of brutal conquest, expropriation, colonisation and suppression followed.

In the course of the nineteenth century the Irish Catholics won recognition as British subjects where previously they had been the targets of a strict penal legal code; and they began their long recovery from their historic defeats and disasters.

Thus the area around Cadamstown had many historic remnants; including settlement by native Irish, mostly Catholic, and a Protestant minority, mostly of English extraction. A degree of accommodation and inter-mingling had been arrived at, and the community that the Pearsons joined in 1911 was mutually accepting, tolerant and harmonious, even if not fully integrated.

What specifically was the situation surrounding the Pearsons in Coolacrease from the time of their arrival in 1911?

The Pearsons' Neighbours

The Pearsons' 341 acre farm at Coolacrease was bounded on the one side by the lower slopes of Slieve Bloom, a low mountainous area straddling the boundary between Co.'s Laois and Offaly; and on the other side by flood-prone and boggy lowland plain.

A near neighbour was Albert Jackson of Kilnaparson, who farmed 900 acres in a situation similar to Coolacrease, but lying higher up the hillside. Unlike the Pearsons, Jackson employed a number of locals and had, in addition, an efficient system of summoning local assistance, by means of a whistle, for common emergencies such as straying cattle, difficult calving and the like. The Protestant Ashtons also farmed 250 acres nearby.

The other adjoining and close-by farms were: J.J. Horan (105 acres), Din Deegan (80 acres), Brian Donnelly (330 acres), Tom Donnelly (80 acres), John and Mick McRedmond (140 acres), Joe O'Carroll (80 acres), Tim Nolan (100 acres), and Tom Horan (4 acres adjoining Pearsons, plus 27 acres in nearby Deerpark). Horan's was the only small farm adjoining Pearsons.

Jackson was Protestant, and the other Pearson close neighbours were Catholic. The Pearsons' nearest neighbour was Tim Nolan who farmed 100 acres. Many families lived in more harsh and difficult circumstances higher up the slopes of Slieve Bloom; an area which is now afforested, with few inhabitants.

The village or hamlet of Cadamstown, about a mile from Coolacrease, had a school, a few dwelling houses, and a post office which was run by the Protestant McAllister family. Other Protestant families in the neighbourhood were the Droughts and Biddulphs.

At one time Cadamstown had a police station (Royal Irish Constabulary or RIC), but by the beginning of the twentieth century, the nearest police station was in the larger village of Kinnitty, about four miles away in the direction of Birr, which was a further ten miles or so from Kinnitty. Birr had a large British Army barracks in Crinkle. Fifteen miles in the opposite direction was the town of Tullamore, which had a British military garrison during the War of Independence.

The Political Situation

The Anglican Church of Ireland was the main Protestant denomination in Ireland. As a minority religion, its status as the state religion in Ireland, funded by the population as a whole, was removed in 1870.

Centuries of conquest and colonisation meant that ownership of land was mostly in Protestant landlord hands, in a system which, in practice, produced endemic poverty and hardship and frequent famine. The problem was not that the big landlords were mainly Protestant. The problem was that the economic system was based on renting, by layer upon layer of Protestant and Catholic property owners, tenants and sub-tenants sub-letting and renting to one another and to other clients beneath them. The productive, or working, or wealth-producing members of society were inadequately rewarded for their efforts. After paying rent to the strata which were leeching off them, they had, in good times, just enough to survive. In bad times they died like flies.

It was a bedraggled, conflicted, poverty-ridden, catastrophe-prone system. It produced squalor on an incredible scale. It degraded most of the population and corrupted the rest. And it bore down especially on the native Irish Catholics in whose conquest the system originated. Millions starved in genocidal conditions. Millions more were driven off in ethnic cleansing of unparalleled scale.

This was welcomed by the British rulers of Ireland. In an editorial of 2nd January 1852, the *Times* said:

> "The pure Irish Celt is more than 1,000 years behind the civilization of this age. ... The native Irish ... defy all ordinary attempts to tame them into agricultural labourers, such as are the staple of the British agricultural population. ... Hence that miserable and helpless being the Irish cottier ... [Its] condition and character has been so often described ... that we need not prove the existence of such a class incompatible with civilization. ... Calamitous as are the events [the Great Famine] by which it has come to pass, we now thank Heaven that we have lived to speak of the class as a class that has been. ... We resign ourselves without reserve ... to [Ireland's] continued depopulation until only a half or a third of the nine millions claimed for her by [Daniel] O'Connell remain. We may possibly live to see the day when her chief produce will be cattle, and English and Scotch the majority in her population."

In yet another illustration of how the Empire dealt with unnecessary and inconvenient human garbage around the world, from the initial conquest of Laois-Offaly until the mid-twentieth century, we read how:

> "In 1830 Tasmania was put under martial law, a line of armed beaters was formed across the island, and an attempt was made to drive the aborigines into a cul-de-sac" (Moorehead, *The Fatal Impact*);
>
> "The final extermination [of the Tasmanians] was a large-scale event, undertaken with the co-operation of the military and judiciary. ... Soldiers of the Fortieth Regiment drove the natives between two great rock formations, shot all the men and dragged the women and children out of fissures in the rocks to knock their brains out" (Ziehr, *Hell in Paradise*).

Not surprisingly, British government in Ireland did not acquire legitimacy in the form of popular support, despite having had centuries of unchallenged supremacy in which it could have sought to earn such legitimacy and support as a reward for good government. As a consequence, Irish submission to British rule was produced and maintained by force, not consent.

The chief instrument for this was the Royal Irish Constabulary, a militarised police force, recruited from the Irish, whose higher ranks were Protestant Irish, English or Scottish; along with strategic garrisons of the British Army in the main centres of population, including places like Birr in Co. Offaly. These were the defences in Ireland of the world's greatest military power. Resistance was futile, though that did not deter some attempts. These rebellions involved many Catholics who by the nineteenth century were sufficiently confident to assert themselves, and some Protestants who saw no future in a rotten system. Between rebellions there was sullen acknowledgement of the invincibility of British power.

Irish Home Rule

The winter and spring of 1879-80 produced yet another near-famine crisis in many parts of Ireland. But this time, instead of meekly submitting to yet more starvation and ethnic cleansing, the population organised itself to overthrow the landlord system. The struggle which followed is called the Land War. In the course of it, the shape of modern Irish society crystallised.

The struggle was successful. Seeing that its position in Ireland was at risk in the face of Irish organisation and determination, the British government forced its supporters in Ireland to accept the new reality, and ownership of land was transferred to the farmers by means of land purchase schemes. A government land reform agency called the Land Commission expedited the transfer.

These changes were not granted by a benign government intent on improving conditions in Ireland. Instead they were wrested, at great cost, by hard struggle against a government and its supporters in Ireland who resisted every step of the way. So the victory did not produce warm feelings towards the government for conceding. On the contrary, it strengthened a movement for Irish self-government because the reforms had to be wrested from an unwilling power.

It was not that self-government under British sovereignty was regarded as preferable to full independence. The Irish had no reason to want second-best. But in the Land War, they did not make the mistake of attempting to take over the land by force, in the manner in which it was seized from them in the Conquests. It was obvious that they were no match for the force that could be deployed against them. Instead, they demanded reforms that subjects of the Crown were entitled to strive for, and they won them by determinedly non-violent policies involving disciplined organisation and political representation.

Keeping Ireland within the British Empire was non-negotiable on the British side. It was absolutely clear that any movement towards independence would be met by overwhelming force. In case the previous centuries of Irish experience left any doubt, the Boer Wars provided new proof.

But Home Rule under the Crown and within the Empire was another matter, and, with the non-violent and successful land struggle under their belt, the Irish organised for that.

By 1911 when the Pearsons moved into Coolacrease this political strategy was about to bear fruit. The landlords had been paid off peacefully, in effect undoing the Conquests. The confident new landowners such as the Pearsons had their destinies in their own hands. With security of tenure, these farmers were creating, through co-operative investment in dairies, a food-processing industry which was the pre-cursor and foundation of modern Irish industry. There were many other signs of recovery.

A political compromise on Irish self-government under the Crown was on the cards. This was expected to satisfy British Imperial policy, after the manner of the self-governing, but loyal, British South Africa under new arrangements following the Boer War conquests. It was expected to satisfy the British-minded people in Ireland (some Catholic, but mainly Protestant) who would remain securely under the Union Jack and within the Empire. And it was expected to satisfy Irish aspirations to govern themselves after centuries of British rule.

Irish Independence

Irish Home Rule was enacted in 1912, the year after the Pearsons arrived and settled down in Coolacrease. The prospects looked promising.

But an armed revolt by Unionists against the Home Rule Bill took place in Protestant Ulster, and Home Rule was shelved. This threw the Home Rule movement into crisis. It seemed to prove that the British government responded to force rather than parliamentary methods. It indicated that British Imperial rule had not, after all, changed into a commonwealth enterprise in which all subjects were equal, but that the racist, supremacist attitudes expressed in the 1852 *Times* editorial, quoted above, were still alive and flourishing.

Worse still, the Irish Home Rule leadership, in a bid to trump the Ulster Unionist revolt, threw itself behind Britain's intervention in the European War, helping to turn it into a world-scale catastrophe. On the British side, the reasons for fighting the war were stated to be democracy and the rights of small nations. But a massive extension of the British Empire emerged from the war, in which many thousands of Irish people, both Protestant and Catholic, were involved, often for conflicting and incompatible reasons. Millions were killed on all sides of the War.

In April 1916 armed separatist Irish Volunteers took possession of some buildings in Dublin, and made a formal declaration that Ireland was an independent Republic. Britain responded by laying waste Dublin city centre using artillery, with considerable loss of civilian life; and by executing the leaders and interning the rest when the Republicans surrendered after a few days' resistance.

Irish public opinion shifted even further away from Home Rule under the Crown, and towards complete independence outside the Empire. The Republican internees were gradually released over the following couple of years. Hostilities continued, with occasionally violent confrontation and renewed imprisonment. British threats of conscription of Irishmen into the Great War were resisted, in an atmosphere of political excitement and impending change.

Following the end of the Great War in November 1918, general elections to the British Parliament were held throughout the United Kingdom of Great Britain and Ireland on December 18, the first such elections in which a majority of the adult population could vote.

The Irish independence movement contested these elections on a manifesto of recognition of the Irish Republic declared in 1916, abstaining from the British Parliament, setting up an independent Irish Parliament, and use of *"any and every means available to render impotent the power of England to hold Ireland in subjection by military force or otherwise"*.

The independence candidates won an overwhelming majority of the Irish constituencies and implemented their manifesto by setting up an Irish parliament called Dáil Éireann, and by creating an Irish Government. The British Government, which had fought and won the Great War on the supposed grounds of democracy and the rights of small nations, did not win any Irish constituencies, or even contest them. Yet it did not acknowledge the results of the elections, and continued as the nominal government of Ireland without entering into discussions with the elected representatives. It refused representation to the elected government in the Versailles Conference where its Great War propaganda about democracy and the rights of small nations were supposed to be put into effect.

The electoral mandate of the independence movement was renewed and strengthened in further elections held in January and June 1920, and in May 1921.

Armed conflict between the Irish Volunteers (IRA) and Crown Forces (Royal Irish Constabulary, Auxiliaries, Black-and-Tans and regular British Army forces) increased during 1919, 1920 and 1921.

A Truce between the two sides came into force on 11th July 1921.

Less than two weeks earlier, the two Pearson brothers, Richard and Abraham, were shot and their house burnt. How did this come about?

The IRA in Cadamstown

The Volunteer forces formed in reaction to the Ulster Volunteer Force found recruits in the Cadamstown area, and after 1916 a local unit was formed. The first members were Jimmy Delahunty, Tom Donnelly and Mick Heaney. (After the 1918 election of the Irish government, the Irish Volunteers became known as the Irish Republican Army or IRA.)

By August 1917 the unit consisted of twenty four men: Michael McRedmond, Joseph Manifold, John Manifold, Martin Guinan,

Michael Guinan, Thomas Donnelly, John McRedmond, John O'Connor, Patrick Carroll, James Delahunty, Joseph O'Carroll, John Dillon, William Glenn, Joseph Heaney, Michael McDonnell, Joseph Honan, Michael Heaney, Thomas Horan, John Joe Horan, Jack Dooley, Jack Brophy, Luke Daly, Patrick Honan, and William Heaney.

These were local farmers, farm workers and labourers. Several of them owned large farms adjoining Pearsons (the McRedmonds, Joe O'Carroll, Tom Donnelly, J.J. Horan). Tom Horan owned a small farm adjoining Pearsons. The unit's quartermaster, Jimmy Delahunty, was the son of the former Cadamstown postman, and made a living by labouring. He grazed a cow on the roadside ("the long acre"). Bill Glenn was a labourer, the son of a Scottish soldier killed in the Battle of the Somme in 1916. The Manifolds were descended from English settlers in the area. Mick Heaney was a son of Bernard Heaney who had a large farm in Glenleiter, a hillside area outside Cadamstown.

All of these were Catholic. In Offaly, some Protestants were members and leaders of the IRA. Walter Mitchell of Rahan is the most notable of these. His brother Vol. Herbert Mitchell served in a Flying Column in Co. Cork. A Protestant relative of theirs, Tom Mitchell of Roscomroe (near Kinnitty), had served in the British Army and provided military training and a safe house for the Cadamstown IRA.

The Cadamstown IRA obtained arms by requisitioning them from people of the area. Most of their arms were obtained from the arsenal of Captain Drought, who subsequently requested the return of the rifle of their son who had been killed in the Great War. This weapon was returned in person by Vol. Mick Heaney.

The Pearsons were asked by Vols. John Dillon and John Joe Horan, who owned large farms close to Pearsons, to hand over their guns to the IRA. They refused, and the two Volunteers withdrew without delay and without any further challenge to the Pearsons, having observed that one of the Pearson girls left the farm on a bicycle—to report them to the Kinnitty RIC, they suspected. On her return through Cadamstown the bicycle was seized and broken by a girl of Cumann na mBan, the women's organisation in the independence movement.

What were the local loyalties and affiliations? By the end of 1918 the independence movement had secured an overwhelming electoral mandate, and could reasonably expect that its independence mandate should be acknowledged by all citizens, on democratic grounds— grounds for which Britain had supposedly fought and won the Great War at the cost of millions of lives.

Of course that did not mean that independence was preferred and supported by everyone. Some Catholics in the Cadamstown area had made a big commitment to the British cause, including in the Great War, and were loyal to the point of flying the Union Jack on occasion. Protestants in Ireland traditionally identified with Britain, though a significant minority of them had pioneered and inspired the independence movement, for the purpose of producing better government.

The political ferment produced within the Protestant community an attraction or alternative to their traditional allegiance. Similarly, within the Catholic community the attractions of an Irish identity based on citizenship rather than ethnic origins reduced the influence of clericalism to the extent that, for instance, excommunication of activists did not deter them. It is notable that during the 1920's there was a resurgence of clericalism when the independence movement was temporarily shelved in favour of Dominion status under the Crown and within the Empire.

The War of Independence in Offaly

The Offaly area was strategically important, and it was a hub or crossroads between other strategic areas. It is not far from the Curragh (Co.Kildare) where British military power was based and from where imprisoned independence activists sought to escape to rejoin the struggle in Munster and in the west and north west. The Slieve Bloom wilderness was an escape route and place of refuge.

Though previously relatively quiet, as elsewhere fighting intensified in Co. Offaly in 1921, and the local IRA was placed under new leadership.

The IRA Chief of Staff Richard Mulcahy was to become Minister for Defence in the Free State government formed in 1922 under the terms of the Treaty with Britain which gave Southern Ireland Dominion status within the British Empire. In 1921 Mulcahy, under the authority of the elected government in Dáil Éireann, appointed IRA organiser Thomas Burke as OC (Officer in Command) of No. 2 Brigade of the Offaly IRA. Thomas Burke was born in Portumna, Co. Galway, and had been studying medicine in Dublin. Burke's commission was to step up military resistance to the war waged by Crown forces in Offaly against the elected Government and its defence forces, and to take action against collaborators, spies and informers who were seriously damaging the resistance.

Under Burke's orders, several Catholic spies and informers were executed. A successful engagement took place in Kinnitty, four miles south west of Cadamstown, and two Catholic RIC men were killed there. Across Offaly there was similar intensification of the war.

In June 1921 the Cadamstown unit of the IRA was ordered to block the Birr-Tullamore road as part of county-wide manoeuvres. Around midnight the roadblock party came under attack and three IRA men were wounded, one of them very seriously.

In the official investigation by the Officers' Battalion Council of the IRA, the identity of the attackers was given as brothers Richard, Abraham and Sidney Pearson of Coolacrease. Burke ordered that the three men be executed and their house burnt. This order was carried out on 30th June 1921, and Richard and Abraham Pearson were shot.

The Pearsons in the War of Independence

How did this come about? After such a promising start in the area, how did the Pearsons end up in armed confrontation with their neighbours, in opposition to the Irish democracy? In what way, if any, were they different from the majority of Protestants and Catholics, who, even when some of them were not enamoured of what the electorate had voted for, kept clear of involvement in the military conflict caused by the British Government's over-ruling of the democratic decision?

In addition to the attack on democracy, the British campaign was lawless and anarchic, employing tactics of reprisal, torture and murder of prisoners and the indiscriminate burning out and shooting of uninvolved civilians; even loyalist civilians were sometimes on the receiving end of these terror tactics. In contrast, on the Irish side, the Dáil's courts and defence forces were accessible to all citizens and tended to the support of civil order and, as far as possible, the maintenance of infrastructure and services through branches of government such as the Corporations and County Councils.

What in particular, above and beyond their loyalist background, might have motivated the Pearsons to violently oppose this; to challenge the democratic forces of law and order; and to espouse the anarchy, terror and thuggery of the Imperial forces?

Thomas Burke's investigation of the Pearsons reported that, in addition to their attack on the roadblock party, they were suspected of passing information to the British side, and of having links with the Ulster Volunteer Force, the loyalist army formed to oppose the Irish Home Rule Bill of the British Parliament.

The Pearsons had grown increasingly hostile to the local community and expressed aggression and supremacist contempt in various ways. They came into open, and armed, confrontation with local people when they tried to block a path on the boundary of their farm which had been traditionally used by church-goers coming down the hillside of Slieve Bloom. After two local IRA men, John Dillon and J.J. Horan, intervened to keep the peace, they were arrested and jailed within twenty four hours of the confrontation. The people most likely to have reported them to the RIC were the Pearsons.

Their house was under IRA observation and the Pearsons' suspicious involvement with Crown forces was reported. For instance, Vol. John Manifold (aged 19) was ordered to keep the Pearsons under surveillance from a vantage point in a beech tree in the grounds of the house. Their mail was intercepted and they were found to be passing information to the British side. An English soldier called Charlie Chidley was driver for British staff officers in Crinkle Military Barracks outside Birr. Chidley deserted to the IRA, and his reports of driving British staff officers to Coolacrease House confirmed suspicions about the Pearsons' intelligence role.

The Pearsons were well placed for this work since they had become part of the local community, had attended school with local independence activists, knew the community intimately, and maintained active social connections in the area. But no local people were employed by the Pearsons, so it was not easy to find out what was going on in Coolacrease.

These are the facts, but not the explanation. They do not fully explain the mind-set or motivation which brought about this state of affairs, when other loyalists, both Catholic and Protestant, kept out of the local conflict.

The Planters of Luggacurran

A book (*I met Murder on the Way: the Story of the Pearsons of Coolacrease*) published by Alan Stanley in 2005 gives further insight into the outlook of the Pearsons.

The Stanleys' recorded connections with the Pearsons date back at least to the 1870's, when Alan Stanley's grandfather Henry went to work in Australia with William Pearson's brother, returning to Ireland in 1885 where he became a member of the Orange Order. The two families also established a connection by marriage.

In the country to which Stanley and Pearson returned in the 1880's, the Land War was raging. In Counties Laois and Kilkenny, Henry Charles Petty-Fitzmaurice, fifth Marquis of Lansdowne, owned 9,000 acres, one of many estates in Ireland and England. Lansdowne held important positions in the Liberal Government of Gladstone and became Governor-General of Canada and Viceroy of India.

Lord Lansdowne disagreed with Gladstone's concessions to tenant farmers and sought to break his tenants by the tried and trusted methods alluded to in the 1852 Times editorial referred to earlier. By 1889 Lansdowne had evicted about 300 people from their homes and livelihoods in nearly 100 farms in Luggacurran, Co. Laois.

In their place, Lansdowne installed Protestant tenants recruited locally from the ranks of bailiffs and estate workers, and from Ulster and Scotland by advertisement. These became known as the Planters of Luggacurran. Among the Planters were several families of the Stanleys, including Alan Stanley's grandfather Henry Stanley.

But this time the people who were evicted did not tamely embark for America to submit to ethnic cleansing as previous generations had done. Instead they remained in the area in emergency housing provided by the tenants' organisation, and campaigned vigorously for reinstatement in their farms.

The Land War was ended by tenant purchase of their farms, with reinstatement of evicted tenants. The evicted farms had been kept vacant by a policy of social solidarity which, by preventing land grabbing, broke the power of the landlords.

But reinstatement in Luggacurran was problematic, since the land had in this instance been "grabbed"—by the Planters. The Luggacurran problem seemed intractable, and remained a sensitive issue for decades. Over a period of time, most of the evicted tenants found other land to farm.

But some tensions remained, and the Planters experienced insecurity and fear. They had grabbed their farms from people who did not conveniently disappear. There was some moral question over their position. Was there not a danger that their farms would be seized from them by the people they had displaced, especially if there was some outbreak of trouble or instability? These were circumstances conducive to suspicion, hostility and paranoia.

In fact, that did not happen—except in 1922, in the period before the outbreak of civil war when it was uncertain which side, Republican or Treatyite, was in control. Both sides had resisted extra-legal or direct action on any outstanding land tenure issues. Both sides stood essentially for law and order.

Earlier, in 1921, Alan Stanley's grandfather had already sold his Luggacurran farm to a relative and moved to Wales. In early 1922, a local "land committee", taking advantage of the power vacuum, initiated direct action and seized several Planter farms. The Free State government restored the Planters to their farms within a few months.

These events have some bearing on what happened to the Pearsons.

Alan Stanley on the Pearsons

In his 2005 book ("*I met Murder on the Way*"), Alan Stanley describes the involvement of his father and grandfather in Luggacurran, and how what happened there among the Planters impacted on the Pearsons across the county boundary in Coolacrease.

Stanley says that during 1920-21 the sons of the Planters, his father William among them, formed themselves into an armed group which colluded with the notorious Auxiliaries (British military sent to Ireland to wage war on the elected government and its defence forces) in a plot to "lift" a local IRA Volunteer.

> "My father [William Stanley] used to keep company with a number of young men in the [Luggacurran] area. Like him, they were all sons of 'planters'. ... All were in possession of a pistol of one kind or other. ... They liked to play at soldiers. ... The ringleader was [James] Kavanagh. ... Kavanagh's mother ... espied two handsome young Englishmen [at Sunday Matins], auxiliary Police Cadets, and invited them home for lunch. They were in Ireland to boost the Royal Irish Constabulary ... It seems there was more than a social element to their visits to the Kavanagh household. Violet Stanley ... told me she overheard them discuss plans to 'lift' a young man of the area who was an active IRA member. ... If the local brigade (IRA) had tolerated playing at soldiers [i.e. Kavanagh & Co.'s paramilitary antics], fraternising with the enemy was a different matter altogether, one that in many cases exacted the extreme penalty. It was not long until ... they got notice to leave. ... Frank [Stanley, Alan Stanley's informant] believed it was the decency of the Luggacurran people that enabled them to get off so lightly." (*I met Murder on the wa*y, 2nd edition, pages 103-107.)

The plot was discovered and the members of the armed loyalist gang were ordered to leave the area. Alan Stanley paints this affair as little more than youthful excess, but acknowledges they were lucky to get off so lightly.

As a result of this crisis, William Stanley's father sold his farm to a relative and bought another one in Wales. But instead of accompanying his family there, William himself went to live with his friends and relatives the Pearsons across the county boundary at Coolacrease, posing as their workman. From local information in Cadamstown we know that William adopted the assumed name Jimmy Bradley.

In his report to IRA Headquarters about the decision to execute the Pearsons, the Offaly commander Thomas Burke said that the Pearsons *"had been active in promoting the Ulster Volunteers movement in their district in which there are a number of 'Planters'"*. William Stanley was one of these Luggacurran Planters. Burke's wording suggests that he had information that William Stanley may not have been the only one.

In his application of 14th April 1927 to the British government's compensation agency for loyalists (the Irish Grants Committee) William Pearson stated: *"I was always known as a staunch Loyalist and upholder of the Crown. I assisted the Crown Forces on every occasion, and I helped those who were persecuted around me at all times."* What help, what persecution did he have in mind, if any? There is no evidence that he helped the Ashtons, Jacksons, Droughts, Biddulphs or McAllisters; nor that they were persecuted. But Pearson did help William Stanley by taking him in when he was ordered out of Luggacurran. There was no shortage of accommodation in the Coolacrease farm complex. For instance, the coach house had been used as a dwelling, and was brought back into use.

Did William Stanley arrive in Coolacrease unaccompanied by any other would-be paramilitaries from Luggacurran? What about the Luggacurran weapons described in Alan Stanley's book? All that was known locally was that there were numbers of strangers coming and going in Coolacrease. The true identity of "Jimmy Bradley" was not known in Cadamstown until Alan Stanley's book was published in 2005.

The local newspapers report that a mere two years before this, in early 1919 when the democratically elected Irish government was in its early stages, William Pearson along with other farmers including one of strong Republican bent, had been involved in door-to-door canvassing to obtain support for the King's County Farmers' Association of which he was subsequently elected an office holder in the Kinnitty branch. So Pearson, though a loyalist, was held in sufficient esteem in the community to be elected to a representative position.

But in 1921, the on-the-run loyalist paramilitary William Stanley arrived in Coolacrease, perhaps accompanied by other militant loyalists from the beleaguered Luggacurran Planter community; while on the IRA side a vigorous new leadership from outside the area was put in place by IRA headquarters in Dublin. The scene was set for confrontation.

William Stanley passed on to his son Alan an account of what happened prior to the 30th June shootings. A week or so beforehand, while William Pearson was absent from Coolacrease, his son Richard challenged a group of rebels sawing down a tree on their land for a roadblock, according to Alan Stanley. He challenged them but they warned him off with dire threats. Richard continued to trade words, then went back to the house, fetched a shotgun and fired it over the heads of the rebels, according to the version relayed by Alan Stanley in his book.

Alan Stanley says that he heard another version of this from his father's cousin, Oliver Stanley, who told him that the IRA roadblock party were attacked by "security people", a patrol of police and Auxiliaries who shot two of them. But, said Oliver, the IRA thought, mistakenly, that they had been attacked by the Pearsons. (It is not really believable that, with IRA roadblocks across the county, British forces would have fought their way through to Cadamstown at night for such a minor objective.)

A week or so later William Pearson was again absent, along with Sidney, one of his sons. Alan Stanley says that the family was warned that they were going to be attacked by the IRA, but, after talking it over decided this was just a ruse to frighten them away so that others could take possession of their property.

That afternoon brothers Richard and Abraham Pearson were making hay in a field, helped by William Stanley. About 4 p.m. a party of armed men approached them. William Stanley shouted *"Run for your lives"* and ran off. Despite being shot at he made his escape across the countryside. He was picked up by the IRA, but escaped again the following day, according to Alan Stanley's account.

William then fled to Tullamore RIC station. From there he made his way to relatives in Northern Ireland, where he stayed for about six months. Then he rejoined his family in Wales where they had moved after selling their place in Luggacurran, following their son's paramilitary involvement with the Auxiliary plot against the IRA.

The warning mentioned by Alan Stanley is puzzling. He makes reference (deleted from the third edition of his book) to a postman called Delahunty who was a member of the IRA. But Jimmy Delahunty, who became postman two years later (1923) was imprisoned since the week before the executions, having been picked up the morning after the roadblock attack. Delahunty's father had been postman, but died some years earlier. So Stanley's reference to Delahunty is not credible.

On the other hand, this information coming from William Stanley is corroborated by David Pearson in his 1983 letter.

It is possible, after they separated in the hayfield on 30th June 1921, that William Stanley and David Pearson came into contact again six months or more later in Wales or England. But William Stanley died in 1981, and David Pearson's letter was written in 1983, and the two had not been in contact since, at the latest, about 1928, or even perhaps since 30th June 1921, the day on which they say the warning was received. Therefore the confirmation by David Pearson of William Stanley's story of the warning, is almost as good as independent corroboration.

The explanation may be as follows. In that period, the post was brought from Birr to Cadamstown by pony and trap driven by an ex-British soldier from Birr, who may have been in a position to have heard about Thomas Burke's execution order. The McAllisters ran the post office in Cadamstown, and by this route the Pearsons may have got word of the impending attack.

The "Atrocity"

Alan Stanley provides an account of the shooting of the Pearsons, but these details cannot have been provided by his father, since he had made his escape prior to the shootings and, as far as we know, never again set foot in the area. Alan's account is taken mainly from the local newspapers of the time. In addition, he received a letter in 1983 from David Pearson in Australia.

Here is a summary of Alan Stanley's account, drawn from the local press reports that week—particularly the unionist *Kings County Chronicle*. The two brothers were taken back to the house. The house was searched and prepared for burning. The two brothers, Richard and Abraham, were taken to the yard and shot within view of their mother Susan, three sisters Matilda, Ethel and Emily, younger brother David, and two female cousins.

Alan Stanley adds an idea of his own, that the bullets used were dum-dum (designed to cause massive trauma), and that the shots were aimed to the groin and buttocks. In the third edition (2007) of his book, the dum-dum allegation is absent.

The two brothers did not die immediately but were put on a mattress in an adjoining field, where, about three hours later at 7.30 p.m., their wounds were dressed by a local doctor. Richard died of haemorrhage and shock after about a further three hours or so. Abraham was taken to the military hospital in Birr and died there some hours later from the same cause.

David Pearson's 1983 letter confirms some of these details. Aged fourteen years, he cycled to Tullamore (about fifteen miles away) to summon help immediately after the shootings, and returned in a military lorry with police and army, but by then the family had been removed by the Birr police and army to Crinkle military barracks fifteen miles in the Birr direction.

Alan Stanley reports that the two brothers were buried hastily and unceremoniously in Killermogh graveyard in County Laois, in the area where they had lived before Coolacrease. Cooneyites did not have their own church buildings and cemeteries. The bodies were brought to the cemetery by the British military on a Crossley Tender, accompanied by the women of the family.

Alan Stanley says that Mrs. Susan Pearson, her son Sidney and daughter Emily then went to live with Alan's grandfather Henry in his newly purchased farm in Wales after his hasty exit from Luggacurran following the exposure of William Stanley's collusion with the Auxiliaries. Later they were joined in Wales by the same William Stanley after his six months' refuge in Northern Ireland following his expulsion from Luggacurran and flight from Coolacrease.

Alan Stanley thinks that William Pearson stayed with a family called Blakemore across the border in England, along with his son David and daughters Ethel and Matilda.

The "Land Grab"

William Pearson made frequent visits to Coolacrease to settle his affairs. In his 1983 letter, David Pearson said that, with the main house burnt out, they used to stay in the coach house which had previously been used as a dwelling by the Mahers.

Alan Stanley's book reports that, prior to the shootings, the Pearsons had a sense, mentioned above, of an impending land grab of their farm by locals. Stanley says that there was local disappointment when the Benwells sold Coolacrease to the Pearsons in 1911, that the Land Commission did not step in to purchase it for allocation to landless people locally.

In his 1983 letter to Alan Stanley, David Pearson implies that the executions were in pursuance of a land grab:

> "When Syd [his brother Sidney Pearson] came back to the farm 12 months later and started ploughing, next morning he found a note on the plough, advising him to stop, or he would be shot. So it is evident their main object was to take over our land."

This letter also says that:

> "The Rebels came back next day [after the executions] and stole cattle, horses and harness. ... We then lived in the coach house on the farm and were often intimidated by rebels marching through the ruins with revolvers drawn."

On the "land grab" issue, Alan Stanley Stanley says:

> "In the end, of course, the Land Commission, under the new Irish Government [of 1923], did take control and in what amounted to an uti possidetis, vested the freehold in the peoples who had moved in on the lands."

What Alan Stanley is saying here is that the Pearson farm was squatted by locals, and the Land Commission, under the authority of the Free State Government, colluded in the theft and granted the Pearsons' farm to the squatters.

The "land grab" allegation was the thesis of a documentary ("*The Killings at Coolacrease*") first broadcast by the Irish broadcaster RTÉ on 23rd October 2007, which expressed in broad terms the theory put forward by Alan Stanley.

What became of the Pearsons afterwards?

Alan Stanley describes in his book the compensation awarded to William Pearson by the Birr County Court in October 1921, and the purchase of the Pearson farm by the Land Commission in 1923. He does not mention the further compensation paid to William Pearson in 1928 and 1929 by the Irish Grants Committee, a British Government agency for awarding compensation to loyalists.

Before the latter payment, William Pearson had purchased a 163 acre farm in Suffolk in the English Home Counties. After receiving the Grants Committee award, most of the Pearsons emigrated to Australia where, according to Alan Stanley, they purchased a number of other farms and businesses which they operated successfully.

Alan Stanley's father William Stanley returned to Ireland in 1928 to a farm in Co. Carlow, not far from Luggacurran, which was purchased for him by Alan's grandfather Henry.

The Pearson and Stanley families then lost contact for a while, according to Alan, except for a 1950's letter to William Stanley from Emily Pearson, except for a 1950's letter to William Stanley from Emily Pearson living in England, and the 1983 letter to Hilary Stanley (Alan's sister) from David Pearson in Australia.

William Stanley lived out his life in Co. Carlow, where, according to Alan he supported the Treatyite party Cumann na nGaedhal/Fine Gael until it declared the Free State to be a Republic in 1948, whereupon he became disenchanted with it.

Alan gives the impression in his book that he found his father to be difficult and moody. After he died in 1981, a sense of curiosity and filial obligation motivated Alan to find out more about his father's Coolacrease stories. He says his father never disclosed to him his loyalist paramilitary collusion with Auxiliaries in Luggacurran. This information was given to him by a relative of his father.

The first published account of the execution of the Pearson brothers appeared in Paddy Heaney's book *"At the Foot of Slieve Bloom"* first published in year 2000. The information for this account was gathered over a long period from the various participants in the actual events, and it describes the Pearsons' involvement with Crown forces and their attack on the Cadamstown roadblock. The account is objective and unsensational and occupies about one and a half pages out of three hundred and sixty nine.

This publication seems to be the incentive which motivated Alan Stanley to write and publish "*I met Murder on the way*". A further influence may have been Peter Hart's book "*The IRA and its Enemies*"

(Oxford University Press 1998) which alleged that innocent Protestants were murdered by the IRA in West Cork, an allegation which has been further construed by Eoghan Harris and others into a story of ethnic cleansing. Alan Stanley regularly refers to Hart's book in his account.

Some Comments on Alan Stanley's Story

Alan Stanley takes an unabashedly imperialist position. He regrets that British people in Ireland were deprived of their British identity and heritage by the Irish independence movement. He makes no acknowledgement that the independence movement had an overwhelming electoral mandate, confirmed and reinforced in a series of elections, and put into effect in 1938 with the adoption of the Constitution proposed by the De Valera Government; accompanied by the ending of the British military presence in the southern jurisdiction, ten years before the formal declaration of a Republic by a Government led by the Treatyite Fine Gael party. Stanley regrets that the unelected power, in its war of suppression of the elected Irish government, did not employ the kind of extreme military measures used to end the 1916 occupation of buildings in Dublin by independence activists.

The Pearsons' close neighbour, the Protestant Albert Jackson, had a farm nearly three times the size of Coolacrease. Yet he experienced no upset or trouble during the British assault on the democracy, and lived out his life there in peace and harmony and prosperity. The other Protestant families nearby—Droughts, Biddulphs, Ashtons and McAllisters—also experienced no trouble.

When fourteen year old David Pearson was looking for help after the shootings, before cycling on to the RIC barracks in Tullamore he called in to Jackson's, and was told to go away, that they had "*brought it on themselves*". Alan Stanley says in his book that more than sixty years later he still encountered these words and this attitude among Protestants when he enquired about the shootings.

Nonetheless, Alan Stanley's account provides some possible explanation of how the Pearsons, having first enjoyed mutually harmonious relations with both Catholics and Protestants, ended up in a position of extreme alienation and hostility to the local community.

The Pearsons had a close relationship with the Luggacurran Planter Stanley family and through this and other connections may have shared their sense of fear and threat resulting from the Luggacurran history of land grabbing and attempted ethnic cleansing. So that, as instability took hold when Britain sought to break Irish democracy, and when the outlook of the 1852 *Times* editorial reasserted itself, the Pearsons may have felt increasingly paranoid and hostile, like white settlers under threat from restive natives.

William Stanley fled from Coolacrease to take refuge with relatives in Ulster. His father Henry Stanley was a member of the Orange Order. It may be that the Ulster and Orange connections can explain the supremacist attitudes exhibited by the Pearsons in interfering with mass-goers, and other similar sectarian, triumphalist conduct.

A significant element in the 1912 Ulster armed revolt against the British Parliament was a sense that they could never share power in a Home Rule government with an inferior race. The attitudes towards subject peoples expressed in the 1852 *Times* editorial were ones which inspired the British Empire for centuries. They did not disappear overnight when the democratic era dawned.

Alan Stanley says that, in addition to his father William Stanley, a number of *"sons of Luggacurran Planters"* were involved in an armed loyalist group. These included Francis Mullins (whose family had come over from Scotland, presumably in response to Lord Lansdowne's advertisement for Protestant settlers), James Kavanagh, George Sythes and Edward Stanley, a cousin of his father's.

Coolacrease and Luggacurran

"The Planters of Luggacurran" (Leigh-Ann Coffey, Four Courts Press, 2006) describes that period. On 31st March 1922, another Planter farmer called Stanley was ordered out when his farm was seized by a group of armed men unconnected to either Free Staters or Republicans. Two days later, a Planter called Stone and his tenant David Mullins had their farms taken over. On 19th April Philip Stone and Joseph Stone were evicted in the same way. All were re-instated by the Free State government when the power vacuum was filled.

Coffey connects these events to the specific local history of land grabbing by the Luggacurran Planters, the fact that they had obtained the land from the people before them as part of an attempt to ethnically cleanse the area. There is no mention in Coffey's book of the loyalist paramilitary episode of the previous year. Neither Free Staters nor Republicans condoned direct action on any outstanding land tenure issues. But the local situation in 1922 must have been aggravated by the loyalist paramilitary collusion with Auxiliaries in 1921.

According to Coffey's book, a Luggacurran Stanley family sent their children for safety to Durrow, Co. Laois, where the Coolacrease Pearsons lived before 1911. The Luggacurran Planters were interrelated and close-knit, and had well-established connections with the Pearsons.

Offaly IRA commander Thomas Burke reported that the Pearsons *"had been active in promoting the Ulster Volunteers movement in their district in which there are a number of 'Planters'"*. The only one of these Planters that there is information about at present is William Stanley.

In the RTÉ Hidden History documentary "*The Killings at Coolacrease*", a Pearson relative called Cecil Pearson was said to be "*around at the time*". This could mean that he was residing in Coolacrease. Cecil Pearson was said in the documentary to have related an account of how Richard Pearson reporting straying cattle to the RIC, and how he may have been falsely accused of passing information about an IRA operation. (Straying cattle is a routine matter between neighbours, and only very rarely a police matter—least of all in the middle of a war in which the police were active. This story does not ring true.)

These circumstances indicate that there is nothing outlandish about the notion that Coolacrease House was a centre for militant loyalists and Crown forces.

So a variety of circumstantial evidence supports Thomas Burke's report about the suspicious activities of the Pearsons. Local people were aware of the presence of strangers in Coolacrease, but since no locals were ever employed there they did not have the normal social means of establishing the credentials of strangers turning up there in the course of a war. The Pearsons, on the other hand, having grown up, played with and attended school with the local people, had continuing social connections in the neighbourhood and were very well placed to know about local comings and goings.

All of this indicates that, in addition to ordering the execution of the Pearson brothers for their attack on the roadblock, there was military justification for Thomas Burke to order that the Pearsons' house be burnt down, so that they could not continue to live there. (The adjoining outhouses were not burnt, including the coach house which had previously been used as a residence and was used again as a residence by William Pearson. This oversight could be because no local Volunteers were involved.)

The Cadamstown Story

The first overt clash between the Pearsons and the Cadamstown IRA was when Vols. John Dillon and J.J. Horan intervened to restore order when the Pearsons provoked sectarian conflict with church-goers over a traditional mass path. The Pearsons blocked the right of way by felling a large beech tree across it. On another occasion latrine waste was dumped on the stile used by families on their way to church. This seems to indicate that an extreme and aggressive sectarianism had entered the Pearsons' souls after opting for the UVF side.

On the day following their efforts to restore peace, Dillon and Horan were arrested by the RIC and imprisoned. J.J. Horan owned a large farm adjoining Pearsons. Dillon's farm, also large, was close to Pearsons'.

The roadblock orders received in late June were part of County Offaly-wide manoeuvres which were intended to build up towards a major attack on Crown forces in Birr. The Cadamstown roadblock party consisted of Volunteers Mick Heaney, Tom Donnelly, Bill Glenn, Mick McRedmond, Tom Horan, Joe Carroll, Jimmy Delahunty, John Manifold, and Jack Brophy.

The tree selected for the roadblock was about halfway between the Pearsons' house and Cadamstown village, at a point on the roadside where Pearsons' land adjoined Tom Horan's.

The first two, Mick Heaney and Tom Donnelly, were on sentry duty on either side of the proposed roadblock; Mick Heaney on the Coolacrease side, and Tom Donnelly on the Cadamstown side. The other seven were engaged in cutting down the tree, starting at about 11.30 p.m.

The Roadblock Volunteers

Here is an account of the IRA men on roadblock duty:

1. Mick Heaney was from Glenleitir, 5 miles south of Cadamstown, 6 miles from Coolacrease His father had 40 acres of mountain land, plus a share of 1,433 acres mountain commonage.

2. Tom Donnelly who owned 87 acres close to the Pearsons.

3. Bill Glenn was the son of British soldier from Scotland who was killed at the Battle of the Somme. A labourer, Bill supported his mother Mary Glenn. His brother worked in England. He obtained land in Coolacrease about six months after the Land Commission allocated the first of the farms. He lived with his mother in the coach house. Bill Glenn survived until fairly recently.

4. Mick McRedmond had 140 acres adjoining Pearsons, with his brother John Joe, also in IRA but not at roadblock. Both brothers were arrested the day after the Pearson attack on the roadblock.

5. Tom Horan had 4 acres adjoining Pearsons (including the tree used for the roadblock), plus 27 acres in nearby Deerpark.

6. Joe Carroll farmed 80 acres adjoining Pearsons. When the Pearsons opened fire he tried to find his coat which he had set down on the ground with a revolver in the pocket. But he couldn't locate it. Joe Carroll's mother was a member of Cumann na mBan and a teacher in Cadamstown school, so she probably was teacher to the young Pearsons.

7. Jimmy Delahunty was a labourer. His father had been the Cadamstown postman. Jimmy became postman in Cadamstown in 1923, and obtained a portion of land in Coolacrease when Jack Fehery (ex-British soldier) gave up his Coolacrease allocation.

8. John Manifold was a farmer's son. This large family, related to the Heaneys, farmed 140 acres in Magherabawn near Cadamstown. John Manifold was six and a half foot tall and became one of the first members of the Civic Guards, the Free State police force.

9. Jack Brophy was a local man who worked a farm with his brother. He later took the Free State side in the Civil War. In the 1920s he was allocated a farm by the Land Commission near Kinnity.

In addition to these members of the Cadamstown unit, a number of other Volunteers were posted on guard, at a distance from the roadblock. Vols. Jim English and Frank Doyle from Kinnitty were deployed on guard along the Old Coach Road. This is a parallel road into Cadamstown, and the Pearsons' house lay between these two roads.

The Pearson Attack on the Roadblock

Before midnight, the roadblock party detained Bert Hogg, a retired RIC man who was making his way to the Pearsons' house. At about midnight, sentry Mick Heaney heard footsteps approaching along the road from Pearsons. He called out: *"Halt. Who goes there?"*, received no answer, and repeated the call. A volley of shots was fired at him. He was shot in the stomach, a rifle bullet passed through his left side, a shotgun was discharged at close range and he received pellets in the face and arms. He managed to return fire.

The other sentry, Tom Donnelly, ran to his assistance and also returned fire, and thought he hit one of the attackers. Bert Hogg was shot in the back and legs by the attackers as he ran away from the engagement in the direction of Cadamstown. Tom Donnelly was lightly wounded in the head.

A fourth man, Jack Brophy, was also wounded, suffering gunshot wounds to the wrist and upper arms. He carried the scars to the end of his life and later recalled that there had been "a lot of firing that night".

Mick Heaney was seriously injured and was taken to Tim Nolan's house on the Old Coach Road, close to Pearsons', where he received first aid from a Cumann na mBan member. From there he was taken by pony and trap to Dr. Brown of Kilcormac, and then to Tullamore hospital where he secretly received medical treatment. His life was saved but he did not make a full recovery and he died a few years later.

The following morning all other members of the roadblock party were rounded up by RIC and soldiers and imprisoned. Later the Pearsons came into Cadamstown village and erected white flags as a triumphalist gesture. This was consistent with the way they had been conducting themselves.

At Officers' Battalion Council, Thomas Burke (OC Offaly No. 2 Brigade) investigated the roadblock attack and it was established that the attackers were Richard, Sidney and Abraham Pearson. Burke ordered that the three be shot and their house burnt.

Burke's report to headquarters includes the following: *"[The Pearsons] had been active in promoting the Ulster Volunteers movement in their district in which there are a number of 'Planters'"*. The word 'Planter' did not refer to Protestant farmers generally, but was used in connection with the recent Protestant land grabbing in Luggacurran. The phrasing suggests that Burke was aware of the Pearsons' connection with Luggacurran. Perhaps William Stanley was not the only one of the Luggacurran loyalist would-be paramilitaries to frequent Coolacrease, and perhaps these militant young Queen's County loyalists were seeking another contest with the IRA, this time in adjoining King's County (Offaly).

The Attack on Pearsons

The Pearsons and their allies were a force to be reckoned with. Just a week earlier in a daring attack and follow-up arrests, they had wounded several volunteers, prevented the establishment of a roadblock and practically destroyed the Cadamstown IRA. There was widespread local suspicion concerning their paramilitary connections. Offaly Brigade IRA had what it considered hard evidence of the collaboration of the Pearson brothers with the British military and intelligence campaign in the county. A member of the Planter Luggacurran would-be paramilitary outfit was consorting with them. Their close involvement with the Crown forces meant that any operation against them was risky. Offaly Brigade held a formal enquiry and ordered the execution of the brothers and the burning of the house.

On 30th June 1921 as the Flying Column of the Offaly Brigade was in a training at Dowras in Eglish parish near Birr, the O.C.

(Officer Commanding) selected nine men and told them to be ready in one hour. In the meantime two cars arrived. The men boarded the cars and the O.C. rode in front on a motorcycle. On arriving in Kilcormac the men dismounted and some of them smoked or walked around. They then headed up the road for Lackaroe. They crossed the Silver River at the weir above Cadamstown and moved across the bog on foot. John Grogan who was working on Cush Bog described the scene:

"At about 10.30 I saw a motor bike and two cars traveling up the road for Lackaroe just opposite where I was working. The convoy halted and the first car stalled. The men dismounted. After some time the second car hauled the first car away, with the motor bike positioned behind one of the cars. The men came across the bog. There were nine men and an officer in front. All the men had rifles slung over their shoulders. The officer carried a revolver. The officer was dressed in a green jacket, knee breeches and leggings, and all the men wore ordinary coats, collars and ties ..."

The flying column of ten men were unknown in the immediate area, and at least two were from North Tipperary Brigade, which formed part of 3rd Southern Division.

The party came prepared for armed resistance, as it was thought that firing points had been cut through the walls of the Pearsons' dwelling house in preparation for a possible siege. About twenty men from local IRA units were deployed in the surrounding area to provide look-out and cover for the Flying Column operation. The commanding officer of the flying column later recalled to Paddy Heaney: *"We were informed that the Pearsons were making hay in a field, not far from the house. We approached and observed two men making hay. They were Dick and Abe Pearson, and another man was working a horse. He was known locally as Jimmy Bradley."* His real name, as we know only since 2005, was William Stanley. Stanley was operating a horse-rake to gather the hay. All three were barefoot, as was the custom when making hay. It was about 4 pm. When Stanley saw the column entering the field he began running towards a stile, a hundred yards away. The O.C. fired as he ran in a stooped zigzag fashion, and he was shot in the arm. Several shots were fired at him as he ran, but he did not halt and made good his escape.

While Stanley got away, Richard and Abraham made no attempt

to escape. They stuck their hay-forks in the ground and struck an attitude of defiance. They were taken back to the house and held, with the family, in the dining room while the house was prepared for burning. The men from local IRA units acting as lookouts and keeping guard on the approaches to the house did not go onto the Pearson property. The O.C. read out the court martial verdict to the Pearson sons. They made no comment nor did they protest in any way. At about 4.30 pm the other members of the family were moved to a grove of trees about 300 yards from the enclosed farmyard, where they were held under guard. Here, according to one of the daughters, they were told by one of the men guarding them: *"Don't think that we are doing this because you are Protestants. It is not being done on that account"*. The house and its contents were then burned.

Richard and Abraham Pearson were brought back into the enclosed yard adjoining the dwelling house where they were stood up against the inner wall of the yard. They faced the ten-man firing squad bravely. The brothers threw themselves to the ground as the firing started. Their demeanour to the end was that their attackers were bluffing; and that that they could not, or would not dare, act against them.

The firing was inaccurate and many of the shots hit the barn wall. As the house went up in flames there were heavy explosions, thought to be ammunition stores blowing up in the flames. The flames and explosions sent out a signal detectable for many miles.

The IRA party was on foot and had to move quickly.

Later that day, William Stanley was arrested near Mountbolus, about five miles from Coolacrease. He was detained overnight in Mahons' house there. Though he was a suspicious character his Luggacurran background was probably not known, and his execution had not been ordered. He was released the following day.

From Alan Stanley's account he then made his way to the Tullamore RIC; from there to relatives in the North; and after a further six months to his family's new home in Wales where they had settled after selling up in Luggacurran because of William's paramilitary exploits there.

The Aftermath

An idea of what happened in Coolacrease following the shootings can be gleaned from various sources. In his 1983 letter David Pearson said he went by bicycle to Tullamore to get help, and when he returned with police and army that evening the family had already been taken to Birr by the police and army there.

Though the attitude of the younger Pearsons was defiant, Mrs Susan Pearson had fainted when the IRA party arrived, and she had to be carried to the grove of trees, on a mattress, by Richard and Abraham. In his 1983 letter, David Pearson said that the family were taken to an "*outer yard*". At that point, according to Ethel Pearson's testimony to the Court of Inquiry, "*Six of the raiders, two or three of whom were masked, ordered my brothers down into the yard*", from the Grove.

The configuration was that the dwelling house formed one side of a quadrangle enclosing an inner yard or courtyard, while other farm buildings, structures and outer yards or working areas adjoined this quadrangle with its enclosed courtyard where the shootings took place. The grove of trees was on the perimeter of this farm complex, as can be seen in ordnance survey maps of the time (see maps in the Appendix). Though the Pearson sisters later claimed to have witnessed the shooting of their brothers, the interior of the enclosed courtyard would not have been visible from the grove of trees.

The brothers were still alive when the IRA party left. The question arises, how or why did the officer in charge of the executions fail to carry out his orders, and leave the Pearson brothers alive? The armaments available to the IRA were often low calibre, and there were many instances of targets standing up and walking away after they had been shot.

Also it seems that the Pearson brothers never lost their nerve. They took evasive action as they were fired on. The inaccuracy of the shooting can perhaps be explained by the well-known psychological inhibitions experienced in the firing squad mode of execution. The medical reports say the men's wounds were extensive and serious but not mortal. As the adjoining dwelling house went up in flames with unanticipated explosions, the whole countryside for miles around was alerted to the military action.

And who was to know that there would not be other, bigger explosions, potentially devastating to the execution party trapped in the confines of the courtyard adjoining the blazing dwelling house?

The officer in charge, in urgent need to get his men rapidly out of the area, on foot, may have been sufficiently distracted not to notice that the brothers were still alive, especially if they had the presence of mind to keep still and pretend to be dead.

When the IRA party left in the direction of Kilcormac, the brothers were moved out of the yard into an adjoining field and placed on a mattress, possibly the same mattress that they themselves had just used to carry their mother to the grove of trees. David Pearson set off by bicycle to Tullamore, first calling into Jackson's, who refused to help him. Ethel Pearson rode a horse into Cadamstown village to look for help.

About two hours later, the dispensary doctor in Kinnitty, four miles away, received a message to go to Coolacrease. He arrived there by bicycle a half hour later at 7.30 p.m., found the two brothers in the field alive but bleeding, dressed their wounds, and left. He was summoned again at about 10.40 p.m., and when he arrived Richard Pearson was dead. One of the newspaper reports says that a Dr. Morton also examined them that afternoon.

By this time the Birr police and military had arrived, and the family was moved to Crinkle Military Barracks near Birr. Word was sent to Mountmellick RIC to contact William and Sidney Pearson at a religious meeting which they were attending, and to prevent them from returning to Coolacrease in ignorance of the shootings.

The wounded Abraham Pearson was put in the Crinkle military hospital, and a military doctor was called to attend to him at 2 a.m. This doctor dressed his wounds and went back to bed. When he was called again at 6 a.m. Abraham Pearson was dead.

William and Sidney Pearson were brought to Crinkle Barracks, Birr, from Mountmellick. The following morning William Pearson was brought back to Coolacrease by the military. Local women were rounded up to milk Pearsons' cows, who had probably not been milked the previous evening and so would have been in considerable pain.

Local men and boys were rounded up and lined up on the bridge in Cadamstown village. Mrs. Susan Pearson was asked to identify from them any of the IRA party which attacked them. None was identified, though one uninvolved man, John Carroll, was arrested and jailed because a hat found at the scene of the shootings fitted him.

The Pearson women were moved out of the military barracks to stay in the house of a relative in Birr.

Military Courts of Enquiry in Lieu of Inquests

The following day, 2nd July, British Military Courts of Enquiry were held on Richard and Abraham Pearson. The British Military Courts in Lieu of Inquests replaced the civil Coroners' Courts which were suppressed by the British as they tended to give verdicts of murder against Crown forces.

In this case, the Court records provide us with more details of what happened. Here is the medical evidence on Richard Pearson:

> "The Court having assembled pursuant to order, proceed to view the body and take evidence.
> 1st Witness: Frederick William Woods civilian medical Practitioner of Kinnity Kings County having been duly sworn in states:-
> At Kinnitty on the 30th June 1921 I was leaving the dispensary in the village at about 18.55 hours. A civilian informed me that he was sent in to ask me to go out to attend to two of the PEARSON boys who had been shot. I at once proceeded to COOLACREASE house where the PEARSONS live, arriving there about 1930 hours and found RICHARD H PEARSON lying on a mattress in a field at the back of the house. I examined him and found a superficial wound in the left shoulder, a deep wound in the right groin and right buttock, the entrance (?) of the latter being in front. In addition there were wounds in the left lower leg of a superficial nature and about six in the back which were glancing (?) wounds. In my opinion these wounds were all caused by either revolver or rifle bullets, and were fired at close quarters. I dressed the wounds anti-septically and after attending to his brother ABRAHAM PEARSON I returned to KINNITTY at about 20.45 hours. At about 22.40 hours the Police came to my house and asked me to come to COOLACREASE House I found RICHARD H PEARSON dead. In my opinion the cause of death was shock and sudden haemorrhage as a result of gunshot wounds. The fatal wound in my opinion was that on the groin.

Cross-examining by the Court

Q No. 1 Do you not consider a groin wound to be a serious one?
A 1   I do if such a wound implicates the blood vessels.
Q2   Did the groin wound of the deceased implicate the principal blood vessels?
A2   It did not
Q3   Did any of the other wounds implicate any of the principal blood vessels?
A3   None that I saw.
Q4   When you first saw the deceased was he losing much blood?
A4   He had apparently lost a considerable amount of blood.
Q5   In view of this loss of blood was the deceased's condition precarious?
A5   It was.
Q6   On being called by the Police to examine the deceased for the second time did you find any wounds which you had not previously discovered?
A6   I did find one.
Q7   Was this wound a dangerous one?
A7   It was.

Fredk Wm Woods LRCP+SI"

Here is the medical evidence on Abraham Pearson:

"The Court having assembled pursuant to order, proceed to view the body and take evidence.

1st Witness. Lt. Colonel C.R. Woods R.A.M.C. (retired) in medical charge of CRINKLE BARRACKS, BIRR, having been duly sworn states:-

At 0200 hrs on 1 July 1921 I was called to the MILITARY HOSPITAL, BIRR. I found the deceased lying there suffering from gunshot wounds. His wounds were dressed by me. I examined his wounds and found extensive wounds on left cheek, left shoulder, left thigh and lower third of left leg. In addition there was a wound through the abdomen. The latter wound had an entrance at the front and appeared to have its exit at the lower part of the back, fracturing the lower part of the spinal column. In my opinion death resulted from shock due to gunshot wounds.

(Signed) C.R.Woods Lt. Col. RAMC Retired."

The other recorded evidence is the following:

"2nd witness:- ETHEL MAY PEARSON having been duly sworn

states:-

I am the sister of the deceased. About 4 p.m. on the 30th June 1921 I came into the hall at COOLACREASE house and found it full of armed men, some of them in masks. My mother, my two sisters and my two girl cousins were with me in the hall and we were all ordered into the dining room. My mother fainted and we asked for water but we were not given any for twenty minutes and then we were given dirty water. During this time some of the raiders were searching the house, and I heard them breaking things up, while others were bringing in petrol and hay. We were then ordered outside and went out by the back door where I saw my two brothers surrounded by the raiders. The deceased was one of the two. I saw the flames burst out. I heard a raider say to another, "Am I much burnt". My mother who was in a fainting condition was carried by my two brothers into a little wood we call the Grove and we all went with her by the order of the raiders. Six of the raiders, two or three of whom were masked, ordered my brothers down into the yard. I saw the raiders search my brothers and place them against the wall of the barn and shoot them. There were about six or eight who shot and they used rifles and shotguns. At this moment there were about 35 raiders in the yard. Within two or three minutes after the shooting the raiders all disappeared. I got on a horse and proceeded to CADAMSTOWN to fetch a Doctor. On the way I saw the raiders proceeding over the bog land towards FRANKFORD. I have seen the deceased in the Military Barracks Mortuary at CRINKLE and I identify the body as that of my brother [Richard / Abraham]. He was [24 / 19] years old last birthday. He was not a member of any political organisation. I could identify the man who appeared to be the leader, and some of the others. (Signed)

3rd witness Susan Matilda Pearson, having been duly sworn in states:-

I am the sister of the deceased. At about 4 p.m. on the 30.6.21 I was lying on the sofa in the kitchen at Coolacrease Ho. when armed and masked men came to our house. Some had service rifles, others shotguns and revolvers. They pointed rifles at us and ordered us into the dining room where we were kept for about an hour. During this time the raiders searched the house and took away five bicycles, my brothers' suits and the girls' clothes. Then they scattered hay about the house and sprinkled petrol over it, ordering us out of the house before setting fire to it. They placed my brothers, shortly afterwards, against the wall of the barn and shot them. When they fell they shot them again. The raiders almost immediately started off in the direction of FRANKFORD. I could identify some of the raiders as I have seen them in KINNITTY. I identify the body which I have seen in the Mortuary of the Barracks at CRINKLE as that of the deceased. Susan M. Pearson."

Interpretations of Court of Inquiry Reports

It has been argued that the shots were deliberately aimed at the genitals. This is a reference to the single wound to the right groin (the place where the right thigh meets the torso) of one of the men. The medical evidence shows that the men experienced wounds from face to lower leg. A Dublin Castle propaganda statement issued on 9th July 1921 interprets the right groin wound as a wound to the thigh.

It is also argued that the fact that the men did not die immediately was the result of a deliberate intention to inflict torture before death. The actual medical evidence indicates that the manner of the shooting was such that, if the slow but steady bleeding had been arrested (no major blood vessels were damaged), the men's lives might have been saved. The IRA sentry Mick Heaney, seriously wounded by the Pearsons at the roadblock, also received an abdominal wound from which he made a partial recovery because he received adequate medical treatment from the nearby Nolan family, from Dr Brown, and in Tullamore hospital.

It is said that the Pearson women were forced to witness the executions in the enclosed courtyard as a further act of terror and atrocity. The IRA Quartermaster Michael Cordial was present at the executions, and in his witness statement of 1957 he says that the family were removed from the scene before the executions.

The courtyard is relatively small. As a working farm area it would not then have been the open, empty space that it is now. If the women had been allowed, or forced, to remain in it during the shootings, it is most likely that in such a tense and emotional situation, with ten or so men and officers of the firing squad, and the seven Pearsons and two cousins, all milling around at close quarters, a panic-stricken, disorderly riot could have ensued. The officer in charge could hardly have allowed such a situation.

Taken at face value, the Pearson sisters' testimony to the British Military Court of Inquiry implies they were taken first to the safety of the Grove, and then brought back into the courtyard where they could witness the shootings. This makes no practical sense.

RIC Investigation of the Roadblock Shootings

Attached to the Court of Inquiry reports is the following, appended at British Army headquarters in the Curragh:

> "*The COOLACREASE Murders—30.6.21.*
> Possible motives.-
> 1. The acquisition of Pearson's land which is very rich. In support of this, Pearson was driving through KINNITY in a Police lorry on the morning after his sons murder when Father Houlahan, a local Priest, asked him what he was going to do with his farm now.
>
> 2. Revenge by Sinn Fein. It is said by the C.I. Queens County that the two Pearson boys a few days previously had seen two men felling a tree on their land adjoining the road. Had told the men concerned to go away, and when they refused had fetched two guns and fired and wounded two Sinn Feiners, one of whom it is believed died. It is further rumoured when the Farm house was burning, two guns fell out of the roof.
>
> Para. 1 above is the substance of a story told by Miss Pearson the daughter to Major Browne, Royal Scots Fus. Stationed at BIRR. 25/7/21"

Regarding item 1, it is unlikely that the Kinnitty curate Fr. Houlahan would have addressed a remark to William Pearson in a spirit of antagonism or threat. Fr. Houlahan was notoriously anti-Republican. Earlier that year he personally attempted to stop the IRA burning down Kinnitty RIC barracks. When William Pearson was canvassing the area for the King's County Farmers' Association in 1919, it is likely that he had the endorsement, explicit or implicit, of Fr. Houlahan or other local Catholic clergy, because that is how such things were done at that time.

Though some members of the Catholic clergy were actively pro-independence, a church-state conflict had broken out during the War of Independence, when some elements in the Catholic Church applied the extreme clerical sanction of excommunication against members of the independence movement. Clerical power suffered a major setback when this sanction was ignored.

In mid-1922 Republican and Free State soldiers fought for control of the Kinnitty area. During the fight, Fr. Houlahan was detained at gun-point by the Republican side. The Free State side won Catholic

Church endorsement in the Treaty War, at the cost of institutionalising a clerical power which then took several generations to reduce.

So the relationship between Catholic clergy and independence activists was not simple or uncomplicated. The Pearsons were already paranoid about land seizure, even before the trauma of the shooting of their brothers and the burning of their home. These factors provide the context for item 1.

The meaning of item 2 above is contested. It appears to report a statement by the Queen's County (Laois) RIC County Inspector that the Pearsons had shot two men at the roadblock a few days prior to their execution. So it appears to provide RIC confirmation of the findings of Thomas Burke in IRA Officers Battalion Council.

But the sentence following it reports a rumour about guns in the Pearsons' house, so some commentators interpret the first sentence as an RIC report of a local rumour. But it is most unlikely that the Queen's County RIC had to rely on mere rumour to find out what the Pearsons were up to in the week before the shootings.

On the morning of the shootings, William Pearson and his son Sidney Pearson had cycled to a religious meeting in Mountmellick, Queen's County (Laois), where they were picked up by the RIC to prevent them from returning to Coolacrease in ignorance of the shootings. The Queen's County RIC had the Pearsons in their custody and had every motive and opportunity to interrogate the Pearsons about what had been happening in Coolacrease, especially since one of their retired colleagues, Bert Hogg, had been shot and seriously injured there.

We can be reasonably certain that the RIC were well-informed about the roadblock attack.

The Pearsons' Explanation of the Executions

We know the official Irish position on the executions as stated by Thomas Burke. We also know the Harris/RTÉ position. But what reasons did the Pearsons themselves give for the executions?

According to the *King's County Chronicle* of 7th July 1921, one of the Pearson sisters said: *"There was some trouble about a pathway last year, but this was settled long ago, the path having being given to those who claimed a passage through it. I don't think that has*

49

anything to do with this occurrence." In the British Court of Inquiry documents, under the heading 'Possible Motives', one of the Miss Pearsons is reported as saying to Major Browne of the Royal Scots Fusiliers that the reason was *"The acquisition of Pearson's land which is very rich".*

In his 1926 application to the Irish Grants Committee, Sidney Pearson said: *"We were accused of the I.R.A. of giving information to Government Officials of their movements."*

In his 1927 application to the Irish Grants Committee, William Pearson said: *"The Republicans were determined to drive me out and get possession of what was always known as one of the best farms in Ireland".*

David Pearson's 1983 letter to Hilary Stanley, quoted in Alan Stanley's book, says:

> "[Alan Stanley] wants to know why we were subjected to such treatment. ... (J. White) told us that the IRA had allotted a quota for each district to be eliminated by a certain date. This may have applied to us. ... Your father [William Stanley] was correct in saying they were murdered for no reason. ... It is evident their main object was to take over our land."

In these explanations, the roadblock incident is the elephant in the room.

Whether one believes that the Pearsons fired their weapons to kill or to miss, the shot or shots they fired at the roadblock were the immediate reason for the execution order against them. A violent incident on this scale, a matter of days prior to the executions, is not something that can be excused or rationalised away like the mass path incident.

Why was such a dramatic and public incident not explained in any of the Pearson accounts of the executions? Why was it not even mentioned?

Could it be for the same reason that William Stanley never disclosed his Luggacurran loyalist exploits? It is practically impossible to think of any innocent interpretation of these events that is in any way realistic. And that is why they cannot even be mentioned by the Pearson side.

But the discreet veil drawn by William Stanley and the Pearsons was rudely lifted by Alan Stanley in his book *I Met Murder on the Way: the Story of the Pearsons of Coolacrease*. That is why this book is so important, as it blurts out, from the Pearson side, the unmentionable facts of what really happened.

Witnessing the Executions

Were the women allowed, or forced, to witness the shootings from an outer yard? David Pearson wrote in 1983 that he and his mother and sisters were taken to an outer yard. To get to the Grove from the dwelling house they would have had to pass through an outer yard.

But David does not say they witnessed the shootings, even though he mentions some much lesser matters such as damage to a tractor. To the eyes of a 14 or 15 year old boy in 1921, this may have loomed large even in relation to the scale of the wider calamity. Likewise, testimony from the girls, some of them teenagers, mentions the loss of clothes, musical instruments and a bicycle.

The evidence above of Ethel Pearson has her two brothers carrying their mother to the Grove, a considerable distance from the house and inner yard, and a location from which the inside of that courtyard would be invisible. Then she says her two brothers were ordered back down to the yard. There is no dispute that the shootings took place in the inner courtyard.

Ethel Pearson says: "*I saw the raiders search my brothers and place them against the wall of the barn and shoot them*". She does not say she was forced to watch, or that anybody else saw the shootings. Her mother was in a faint. The family could not have been left unguarded in the Grove, free to wander around, because that would have enabled them to seek help, posing a threat to the IRA party.

So Ethel Pearson's evidence is contradictory on this point. Why is there a contradiction in this evidence? We can speculate that one of the first questions asked of the Pearson family was whether they actually saw the executions, and we can speculate that the implications of this quickly became apparent to them.

There is no doubt that the Pearsons were peddling atrocity stories to gain sympathy and other advantages, having previously alienated the whole community, both Protestant and Catholic, by their conduct.

By 1927 William Pearson brought these atrocity stories to a level where all credibility is lost. In a written statement to the Irish Grants Committee he said that there were five hundred IRA raiders, that his daughter too was shot, that he was present that day and went for help, and he said many other things known to be false. (The Irish Grants Committee was an agency of Irish loyalists under the auspices of the British government for awarding compensation to those on the loyalist side who suffered damages in the War of Independence.)

His statement of 14th April 1927 to the Grants Committee says: *"For the burning of my haggard, yard, stable, storehouses, forge, wool, hay, straw, haylifters, machinery, turf, tractor, tools, etc., valued at £1000, I received £300* [damages from Judge Fleming in Birr County Court on October 12 1921]". But the only thing that was burned was the dwelling house, in accordance with Tomas Burke's orders. The yard, storehouses, machinery etc. were not touched. The coach house (part of the complex of buildings adjoining the dwelling house) was subsequently used as a dwelling. Nearly a century later, part of the roof of an outhouse adjoining the burnt out dwelling house is still in place. David Pearson's 1983 letter says that a tractor was damaged, not by burning but by gunfire. But if the tractor was parked in the inner yard, the highly inaccurate shooting of the firing squad may have damaged it.

William Pearson made these false statements in a successful bid to maximise compensation payment from the Committee. In other words, mere truth could take a back seat when advantage could be gained by lying.

The Pearson story of having witnessed the executions started in a relatively small way two days later (2nd July) in the Military Court of Inquiry with Ethel Pearson's statement: *"I* [not 'we'] *saw the raiders search my brothers and place them against the wall of the barn and shoot them"*. A few days later (7th July) the *King's County Chronicle* reported that *"The shooting was witnessed by their sisters and two other ladies"*.

And in the Dublin Castle statement of 9th July, we get: *"They were placed on a little hill just outside the back of the house. The two eldest sons were then taken, and in full view of the rest of the family were put up against a wall and shot, meanwhile the Sinn Feiners played ragtime music, on the piano and one of the sons' violins".* (Never mind that the inner courtyard where the shootings took place was enclosed by housing on four sides, with only a small gateway as opening to the outer yards, and from the hillside further up the inside of the courtyard would have been practically invisible. The Grove was even further away and surrounded by high hedging.)

By 14th April 1927 (William Pearson's Application to the Irish Grants Committee), this had become:

> "We [William and son Sidney] returned home to find the house completely burnt out, two of my sons lying dead in the yard having been murdered in the presence of my wife and other children. These sons were grown up and worked on my land. There were about 500 men engaged in the outrage and the boys were put up against a wall, compelled to watch their home being burnt, and were then riddled with bullets by a squad of 10 men. One of their sisters tried to save them and a volley was fired at her and the hair was cut away from her scalp by bullets".

In fact William Pearson did not arrive home until the following day. The Pearsons earlier reported about 30 attackers, not 500. None of his daughters was fired on, because otherwise it would have been reported at the time.

Suppose we assume that the Pearson family members were actually removed from the scene, as Michael Cordial testified, and as the Pearson sisters themselves testified when they said they were taken to the Grove, some distance from the house. How then might the Pearsons' story have developed? Out of natural curiosity, horrified sympathisers (police, military, Birr townspeople, Pearson relatives, newspaper reporters) would have asked them again and again: *"Did you actually see the two boys being shot?"*

Well, the family certainly saw them immediately after the shootings. The brothers were almost certainly conscious, at least from time to time, and probably able to relate something of what happened to their sisters. A lame (even if truthful) response such as *"Well, we were actually out in the Grove. But we did hear the shots, and when we came down into the courtyard we saw what had happened"* might have been a disappointment of heightened expectations. The temptation to give the anticipated shocking response, and the payoff in terms of extra horror and sympathy to be gleaned by it, may have been too much to resist.

Slowly Bleeding to Death

The medical reports on the two brothers give haemorrhage and shock as the causes of death. The Crinkle Barracks hospital doctor was a retired military doctor, and no doubt had vast experience of gunshot wounds from the Great War. The wounds reported were mostly not serious, but the multiplicity of such light wounds, in conjunction with a more serious wound, must have been quite serious. A single cut may not be fatal, but a thousand cuts can kill. Each of the brothers had a serious wound (but not a mortal wound, according to the medical reports); Richard to the right groin, and Abraham to the abdomen.

Shock is the physiological response to trauma, reducing sensations of pain and protecting life by restricting the supply of blood in favour of the more essential parts of the body's systems. So victims feel cold and may drift in and out of consciousness. First aid advice for treatment of shock is to wrap the patient warmly.

Would the two brothers have been able to stand up and walk unaided? Probably not. According to the medical report Richard was *"lying on a mattress in a field at the back of the house"* at 7.30 p.m. The house and its contents were destroyed, so this was probably the same mattress used to carry their mother to the Grove. Blankets and other clothing were destroyed in the fire.

Would the brothers have been able to take food and drink to sustain them in their trauma? Maybe, but their house and its contents were destroyed, and it seems their neighbours did not come to their assistance. Albert Jackson sent young David Pearson packing when he called in for help. Their nearest neighbour was Tim Nolan, and Nolans' was the house to which Vol. Mick Heaney was brought a week earlier after being shot in the abdomen, arm and neck by the Pearsons. So it is not likely that the Nolans gave any assistance.

It was three hours before the Kinnitty doctor arrived on his bicycle, and by then the brothers must have been considerably weakened by blood loss. According to the medical reports, no major blood vessels were damaged, so bleeding, though extensive, was probably not intensive. Death comes quite quickly from intensive bleeding if there is damage to a major blood vessel. But people who cut their wrists in a "cry for help" often do not injure themselves too severely, and, if caught in time, the bleeding can be stopped and their life saved.

Apart from cleaning and dressing their wounds, the medical attention received by the brothers seems to have been very limited. Earlier they had exhibited stoicism in the face of mortal danger. If they continued this stoic behaviour during the afternoon, perhaps telling people they were not feeling all that bad, then this might explain why the many hours during which they might have been saved by emergency medical care were frittered away and wasted.

How much pain were they in as they slowly bled to death over six hours and fourteen hours? Just like the pain endured by Mick Heaney and the other people they shot, it must have been considerable, even if they did not complain of it. But shock was also reported. And a feature and a function of shock is that sensations of pain may be reduced.

As the investigations of Philip McConway show, other war deaths of IRA and RIC in Offaly in that period were much more gruesome, painful and shocking.

The horrors of war spare nobody, not even uninvolved civilians. The Pearsons could have remained uninvolved. Instead they chose to engage as combatants against the elected government. But though they got involved, the responsibility for starting the war does not lie with the Pearsons, nor with anybody else in Ireland. The war was the responsibility of the unelected power which, instead of negotiating with the elected representatives, chose a military response.

The Land Issue

Some of the Pearson women went to live with the Stanleys in Wales, where, according to Alan Stanley's book, Mrs Pearson posed as the widowed sister-in-law of Alan's grandfather Henry Stanley. According to his Irish Grants Committee statement, William Pearson spent a couple of years tending to his affairs and travelling back and forth between Offaly, Wales and England.

He said he was looking for land to buy in England, and eventually bought a 163-acre farm in the Home Counties area (Suffolk, which was farmed by his son Sidney, according to Sidney's 1926 Grants Committee statement).

David Pearson's 1983 letter says that the rebels came back to Coolacrease the day after the shootings and stole cattle, horses and horse harness. But from the evening of the shootings, Coolacrease was occupied by the British military. William Pearson came back to Coolacrease the following morning. The Cadamstown IRA had been devastated by the Pearsons' roadblock attack and the resulting arrests. The execution party did not come from the local area and was long gone.

William Pearson said in his 1927 Grants Committee statement says that he was boycotted, squatted, intimidated, and prevented from selling his property. Some of the obvious lies in this statement have already been pointed out; such as his claim that 500 IRA men were involved in the attack, that his daughter was shot, and that he sought help earlier that day.

The Irish Grants Committee records of the Pearsons' applications for compensation show that a high proportion of his compensation claims were rejected as bogus or inflated. These documents state that he held auctions of his property and received fair prices for it. The local press reports that he put his farm up for public auction, but rejected the highest bid.

From the Truce of 11th July 1921 into the first half of 1922, Republicans were in control of this part of Offaly. In that period, William Pearson used the Republican Courts to obtain compensation for a stolen gate, and to obtain return of some stolen pigs. So a system of law and order was available, and William Pearson availed of it.

In October 1921, William Pearson received compensation award from Judge Fleming K.C. in Birr Quarter Sessions for loss of property and for the death of his sons. In 1923 he sold the farm to the Land Commission for £4,817, about £14 per acre.

The biggest single issue in the Grants Committee papers of 1927 is the sale of the Pearson farm. The 341 acre farm had cost £2,000 in the politically promising year of 1911, just under £6 per acre. The agricultural boom of the Great War was over, and Civil War had followed the turmoil of the War of Independence. Land values were discounted. In this period, good land was worth about £10 per acre, while inferior land like the mixed hillside and bog of Coolacrease was worth about £5 per acre.

But Pearson claimed it was worth £15,000, or £44 per acre. He produced a letter claiming that a would-be purchaser wanted to pay him £10,000 (£30 per acre), and an auctioneer's valuation of £17,000 (£50 per acre). There is neither rhyme nor reason to these wildly different valuations.

Tellingly, while the Irish Grants Committee submitted Pearson's valuations of small items (such as losses due to alleged boycott and trespass) to tight scrutiny and rejection, it merely noted, without evaluation or assessment, the ludicrous valuations of the farm presented by Pearson. And the Grants Committee paid out around £7,440 of further compensation. Most of this (£5,183) was the calculation for the alleged loss on the sale price.

It would seem that the Grants Committee was impressed by Pearson's tale of atrocity, boycott, squatting and persecution, including the wrecking of his own and his wife's health. (William Pearson never enjoyed very good health, but he lived to 74, dying in 1939. His wife Susan died in 1947, aged 76 years.)

The Committee went through the motions of rigour in regard to small items claimed for. But this may have been cover for its real purpose of paying Pearson generously. The Committee was under the control of Irish Loyalists, and following protests about it in the British Parliament, the Grants Committee gravy-train was wound up shortly after this.

But, by hook or by crook, Pearson got the money which he held out so doggedly and pushed so hard for.

What Happened Afterwards

It is said that the Pearson brothers' graves in Killermogh graveyard were unmarked. If this is true, it was primarily the responsibility of William Pearson who was sufficiently wealthy to erect proper headstones on his sons' graves. Alan Stanley reports that the Pearson family never talked about the executions. If it weren't for Alan's book we would have no information at all from the Pearson side about their attack on the roadblock. His book gives the game away.

David Pearson's 1983 letter to Alan Stanley makes a perfunctory reference to the notion of a land grab, says nothing at all about the roadblock attack, and concludes as follows: *"After 62 years I would like to forget about this sordid affair"*.

At some fundamental level, did the Pearsons themselves feel that *"they had brought it on themselves"*? In neglecting a proper graveyard memorial to his two sons, was William Pearson reflecting some inner conflict about the mayhem that his sons and their Luggacurran Planter associate had caused? Was there any sense that, having survived the shootings, the brothers' lives were then lost because of insufficient care and attention?

Alan Stanley's grandfather Henry had to leave Luggacurran hurriedly because of his son William Stanley. This man provided a refuge in Wales to the Pearson women when they were in a similar predicament.

But strangely, despite this intimacy and the earlier generations of close friendship and inter-marriage, contact between the Pearsons and the Stanleys was broken for several decades, according to Alan Stanley. It was only renewed by later generations to whom those tragic events were practically a closed book. Could this be because headstrong elements in both families brought down such great trouble on everyone?

Another straw in the wind is reported in Alan Stanley's book, where he says that the Pearsons did not talk about the 1921 events, not even among themselves. On the RTÉ radio Liveline broadcast of November 5 2007, the grandson of Sidney Pearson confirmed this.

And on those occasions where we have directly reported statements from the Pearsons themselves (in the local newspapers following the executions, in the Irish Grants Committee applications, and in David Pearson's 1983 letter), there is not a single reference to the roadblock incident.

This suggests that the Pearsons may have been privately embarrassed and ashamed of their conduct at that time. But what the Pearsons themselves kept very quiet about was blurted out in Alan Stanley's book. Without Alan Stanley's book the only published account of Coolacrease would be one and a half pages by Paddy Heaney. There would have been no Hidden History documentary and no controversy.

And without Stanley's book we would not have had confirmation from the Pearson side about their attack on the roadblock, nor would we know about their Luggacurran paramilitary connection. Such things happen in the heat of war. There are many indications that the Pearsons wanted to put the past behind them and forget about it all.

According to Alan Stanley, the Pearsons bought farms and businesses in Australia where they were prosperous and successful. Emily Pearson lived in England and was equally successful. In 1975 brothers Sidney and David Pearson made a brief visit to Coolacrease.

The shooting of the Pearsons can be traced directly to the intervention of Richard Mulcahy in the war in Offaly, and was carried out by his authority. With Cathal Brugha and Michael Collins, Mulcahy directed the course of the War of Independence. He became Minister for Defence in the Free State government formed in 1922 under the terms of the Treaty or Articles of Agreement, by which Britain gave Southern Ireland Dominion status within the British Empire. Mulcahy went on to become Minister for Education and leader of the Fine Gael party.

It is said that the reason why he did not become Taoiseach in the 1948 Fine Gael-led Coalition government was because of his Civil War record. There were questions about his leadership position because of his role in enforcing the 1922 Treaty which was acceded to in Ireland under a British threat of "immediate and terrible war". In 1938 the British military presence was finally removed from the area subject to the Treaty. Then, under different leadership, the Fine Gael-led coalition government was able in 1948 to declare the Irish State to be an independent Republic outside the British Commonwealth, a status which has proved durable.

According to Alan Stanley, William Stanley ("Jimmy Bradley") was politically active in support of the Fine Gael party of which Mulcahy was leader.

Two other names are known to be connected to the Pearson execution party. These are Thomas Burke and Michael Cordial.

Thomas Burke, the IRA commander who issued the execution order, was a Republican prisoner in Portlaoise Jail when he was visited there by Michael Collins, on his way to Cork where the latter met his death on August 22 1922. Burke became a farmer in his native Portumna in Co. Galway.

Michael Cordial, the IRA Quartermaster who described the executions in his 1957 Witness Statement, became an officer in the Free State army. Cordial's Witness Statement about the Pearson executions was written in 1957. Cordial may have been one of the men who fired on William Stanley as he fled from the hayfield where the Pearson brothers were arrested. But ten years later he and Stanley were in the same political camp.

What about the members of the roadblock party?

Tom Donnelly continued to farm in the area and his relatives still live there. Joe Carroll, whose mother was the Pearsons' schoolteacher, took a neutral position in the Civil War and his family continued on in the area. John Manifold was six and a half foot tall, and became one of the first members of the Free State police force. He was an easily recognisable figure directing traffic in O'Connell Street in Dublin. The Manifold brothers did not get involved on either side of the Treaty War.

Jimmy Delahunty became the postman in Cadamstown after he was released from the Curragh in 1923. After an ex-British soldier gave up the portion of Coolacrease land allotted to him by the Land Commission in 1923, Jimmy Delahunty, who was grazing a cow on the "long acre" (the roadside), received part of this land. Delahunty lived to age 95, and, as one of the founding members of the Cadamstown IRA, was a significant source of information about those events. Bill Glenn, son of a Scottish Somme casualty, similarly received some of this land from the Land Commission. Bill Glenn was the youngest of the roadblock party and died fairly recently. Jack Brophy, who suffered gunshot wounds in the Pearson attack, took the Free State side in the Civil War and later was allocated a farm of about 25 acres from the Land Commission in the Kinnity area.

Mick Heaney, the sentry shot by the Pearsons, took the Republican side in the Civil war. After the Free State side captured Kinnitty in mid-1922, Heaney, with Mick Carroll (who was not in the roadblock party) faced the stark options confronting defeated Republicans—

join the Free State forces or get out.

A number of these defeated Republicans, including Heaney and Carroll, felt unable to make such an accommodation with the new regime and left for Australia in 1922. But Mick Heaney never fully recovered from injuries inflicted by the Pearsons and he died soon afterwards.

The Division of the Pearson Farm

The message of the Niamh Sammon/Eoghan Harris documentary *The Killings at Coolacrease,* broadcast on RTÉ television on 23rd October 2007 and again on 23rd May 2008, was that the Pearsons were innocent victims of sectarian murder in pursuance of a land grab and ethnic cleansing. This was the message contained in preliminary announcements by RTÉ.

In case the public did not get the message it was hammered home in newspaper articles and radio programmes just before the progranmme was broadcast:

> "Some believe the Pearsons were innocent victims targeted purely for their land. The two boys had been killed at a time of great land hunger and that hunger was keenly felt in Offaly where good farmland was hard to come by. The attack on the family was, some argue, merely a land grab, perpetrated by men desperate to get their strike in before the war came to an end" (Niamh Sammon, *The Irish Times,* 20.10.07).

In an interview with Niamh Sammon, Ryan Tubridy (RTÉ Radio 1, 22nd October 2007) referred to it as a case of ethnic cleansing and Ms Sammon concurred. On the 'Hidden History' programme itself, Dr. Terence Dooley stated:

> "The revolutionary situation was used essentially as a pretext for running the Protestant farmers and landlords out of the community, to take up their land." On the Pearsons he said: "William Pearson ... moves into an area, he takes up a 340 acre farm that is surrounded by a multitude of small uneconomic holdings, where the local people—and they tend to be Nationalist farmers—are looking for access to this land themselves. ... [He] had lost his two eldest sons who he had used to run the farm. He couldn't get others from the local community to work for him. Raids continued on his property, and his attempts to sell his cattle were boycotted by the locals. He couldn't sell his farm because

any potential buyer was put off. William Percy: "The price I offered was 10,000 pounds and I might have gone higher only the people would not allow any outsider to purchase the land. I was not allowed to close the bargain." So he was becoming squeezed all the time. What he attempted to do was cut his losses by selling the land to the Land Commission for around 5,000 pounds."

This line is repeated by Alan Stanley (Author, *"I Met Murder on the Way"*, 2004) and backed up by two other academics, Professor Richard English (Author: *"Irish Freedom: A History of Nationalism in Ireland"*, 2007) and Dr. William Murphy (Mater Dei Institute of Education).

No evidence of any substance was offered by the academic trio in support of the land grab theory, and the statements presented as facts are false.

William Pearson's farm at Coolacrease was surrounded, not by small farms as asserted by Dr. Dooley, but by relatively large ones.

The farms adjacent to Pearsons' were: J.J. Horan (105 acres), Din Deegan (80 acres), Brian Donnelly (330 acres), Tom Donnelly (80 acres), John and Mick McRedmond (140 acres), Joe O'Carroll (80 acres), Tim Nolan (100 acres), and Tom Horan (4 acres adjoining Pearsons, plus 27 acres in nearby Deerpark). Horan's was the only small farm adjoining Pearsons. The largest farm near Pearsons' was 900 acres owned by the Protestant Albert Jackson of Kilnaparson. The Protestant Ashtons farmed 250 acres nearby.

William Pearson did not employ local labour. According to the *King's County Chronicle* of 13th October 1921, William Pearson is reported as saying that his two boys spared the expense of employing a lot of workmen every year, as "*one man interested in the work would be worth six who were not*".

Pearson was not prevented from selling his property. The *Midlands Tribune* of 27th August 1921 reported that, at a public auction of his farm held on 21st August, he refused the highest bid. According to his application to the Irish Grants Committee dated 14th April 1927, he successfully auctioned his farm equipment and received fair prices for it.

The William Percy letter quoted by Terence Dooley is an obvious price-boosting fraud. Dr. Dooley said in the documentary that the

Land Commission's price of £5,000 represented a loss. This is nonsense. A mere ten years earlier, and with a dwelling house in good condition, William Pearson bought the farm for £2,000. In the post-Great War agricultural slump and in the worsening political climate, and with the dwelling house burnt out, the most that could reasonably be expected for the farm on the open market was about the same. Therefore £5,000 was a more than generous offer.

Which raises the question, why did the Land Commission pay such a high price for William Pearson's farm? In doing so, the Land Commission saddled the subsequent owners with financial encumbrance and crippling annuity payments.

Pearson would not work the land at Coolacrease, or rent it out, or sell it on the open market. He could afford not to, because, in addition to Great War agricultural profits free of labour costs, he received substantial compensation from Birr County Court in 1921. By 1926, after buying a 163 acre farm in Suffolk he still had £6,000 in the bank, according to the Irish Grants Committee documents.

Pearson put the squeeze on the Land Commission, which was ultimately responsible for economic use of the land and getting it back into production. The biggest single component of the Land Commission file on the Pearson farm is the extensive correspondence with him concerning the purchase price.

Which brings us back to the issue of the evidence for the land grab theory of the Hidden History documentary, since RTÉ and programme producer Niamh Sammon claim that their theory is proved by evidence in the Land Commission file on Coolacrease.

Here is what they claimed in published correspondence with the Broadcasting Complaints Commission.

RTÉ said:

"The theory that the Pearson killings were the result of a land grab was also examined by the programme makers. Documentation from the Land Registry office and the Land Commission was made available to Dr. Terence Dooley, a highly respected historian and author of 'The Land for the People'. Dr. Dooley used the contents of these files as the basis for his comments."

And the programme Producer/Director Niamh Sammon said:

"The production team was given access to these original [Land Commission] files."

But when Philip McConway, a credited researcher in the documentary, telephoned Ms. Sammon about accessing these files in the course of programme production, she told him that they were confidential.

This was confirmed by the Archivist of the Land Commission files, who has declared that: *"I can find no record that RTÉ has had access to the former Irish Land Commission documents, stored in the Records Branch of the Department of Agriculture, Fisheries and Food, relating to the townland of Coolacrease (Pearson Farm)"* (Letter to Pat Muldowney, 13th March 2008).

So, on the one hand, we have programme producer Niamh Sammon and RTÉ saying they had access to, and made use of, the relevant Land Commission files; while on the other hand we have the Archivist of those files saying there is no record of such access. They cannot both be telling the truth. What conclusion must we draw from this?

Paddy Heaney was informed by the Department of Agriculture that, as the owner of a portion of the land once owned by the Pearsons, he was entitled to access these documents; or that he could appoint a representative to access them on his behalf. Accordingly he appointed Philip O'Connor as his representative and obtained, through him, copies of the relevant documents.

The documents confirmed the information Paddy Heaney had already garnered from his father, Brian Heaney, and from other people involved at the time. This information proved that there was no land grab in Coolacrease. Paddy Heaney provided this information to the documentary. But on the basis of no evidence at all, they went ahead and broadcast their bizarre tale of a land grab.

Despite such a glaring inconsistency they continue to insist that their broadcast propaganda was supported by evidence from Land Commission documents—documents which they had never even seen! No evidence at all was put forward in the documentary to support their bogus theory, because there is no such evidence.

In the course of production Paddy Heaney explained to Ms Sammon what actually happened when the Land Commission divided the Pearsons' farm in Coolacrease in 1923. He obtained much of this information in the first instance from his father, Brian Heaney, who returned from the USA in 1921. What he was told by him was corroborated by what he was told by the other people concerned, and subsequently by the Land Registry, Valuation Office and Land Commission records.

In dividing Coolacrease, the purpose of the Land Commission was to provide land to landless people, or to people who had only very small amounts of land. Dividing the 341 acres into 15 portions meant that the average amount was less than 23 acres each of relatively poor land. This was not sufficient to make a living. But the idea was that this small amount of land would improve the position of people who had little or no property.

Unfortunately, this was a miscalculation in many cases, since the land was encumbered by the exorbitant price paid by the Land Commission to William Pearson. The annuity charges payable by the new owners to the Land Commission made these relatively insignificant patches of land uneconomic, even in conjunction with employment as labourer or tradesman.

The division and allocation was done by T.H. Blackall, a senior official who had served the previous regime. Inspector Blackall worked alongside the Kinnitty curate Fr. Houlahan who provided local knowledge. One would have hoped that politics would have been kept out of it, and that social and economic considerations would have been the primary considerations.

But this was far from the case. Most of the Cadamstown IRA supported the anti-Treaty cause, and most of these, including all the members of the roadblock party, were interned at the time of the division of Pearsons. Almost all of them were already landholders, and were not involved in receiving land at Coolacrease. A founding member of the Cadamstown IRA was the landless labourer Jimmy Delahunty who received a portion of the land initially allotted to ex-British soldier Jack Fehery. But Jimmy Delahunty received this only after Jack Fehery had rejected the land because of the high costs. At the time of the initial allocation Jimmy Delahunty was still in jail. Priority in allocation was given to ex-British soldiers. Fr. Houlahan was virulently anti-Republican, and elements in the church used the post-Treaty situation to recover social influence which had been lost to some degree in the great democratic ferment which characterized the struggle for independence. In Coolacrease Fr. Houlahan gave preferential treatment to his own favourites.

The people who were selected for allocation received letters from the Land Commission inviting them to meet Mr. Blackall and Fr. Houlahan in the house of local man, Dan Downey. A firm supporter of the Treaty, Dan Downey was a single man and a labourer by occupation. Through the influence of Fr. Houlahan, Dan Downey was contracted to organize the repair the fencing in Coolacrease. This was a major commission as the land had become practically derelict since the shootings of June 1921. Later Dan Downey married Jimmy Delahunty's sister.

The first three people to receive these letters of allocation were ex-British soldiers. These three attended on the first day of the land division process which continued for days, and intermittently over weeks and months. The three were Johnny Grogan, Jack Multany and Jack Fehery. The Land Commission records of the allocation note that Grogan was an ex-serviceman who served three years in France and was badly wounded, that Multany was an ex-serviceman who served three and a half years in France, and that Fehery was ex-Irish Guards and served three and a half years in France. As an ex-British soldier, Jack Multany had a house built for him. He was a former employee of Albert Jackson of Kilnaparson. He did not work for the Pearsons, who did not employ any local labour.

Brian Heaney had purchased a small piece of land near Cadamstown when he returned from the United States in 1921. He was assured by Fr Houlahan that he could expect some land from the division of Coolacrease. But he did not receive a Land Commission letter at that point.

Nonetheless, he attended at Dan Downey's house on the first day of the land division, and observed the three initial allocations. The fact that the three were ex-British soldiers smacked of discrimination. His second cousin, Bernard Heaney, who owned a large farm in Glenleiter attended, with others, on the second day to protest at this discrimination. Brian Heaney was not present on the second day.

Bernard Heaney was the father of a large family, including Mick Heaney, the roadblock sentry shot and seriously injured in the stomach by the Pearsons in their attack on the IRA roadblock. Mick

Heaney was active on the anti-Treaty side. At this time he had already left for Australia with other Republicans whose principles did not allow them to make an accommodation with the victorious Free State.

Though he was ineligible on account of his own comparatively large landholding, Bernard Heaney of Glenleitir was allocated sixteen acres of cutaway bog. It seems that the Land Commission letter addressed to Brian Heaney, whose first name was Bernard (though he went by the name Brian), came into the possession of his relative Bernard Heaney of Glenleitir. That is how Bernard acquired the title to this portion of land. Fr. Houlahan advised Brian to write to the Land Commission about this, which he did. Eventually, Bernard Heaney settled with Brian Heaney, who bought the sixteen acres from him.

Jack Fehery did not succeed with his twenty nine acres, and this land reverted to the Land Commission. It was then divided further and allocated to Brian Heaney and to Jimmy Delahunty after his release from internment. Other members of the Delahunty family were on friendly terms with Fr. Houlahan. Jimmy's mother and sister looked after the local Cadamstown chapel of St. Lughna. The case made on his behalf to the Land Commission included the fact that he grazed a cow on the "long acre" (the roadside). Also, about this time Delahunty got the job of postman in Cadamstown.

Another allocation which failed was the thirty acres given to Tom Dillon, who had twelve children. This was re-allocated to Patrick Rowe of Clonaslee, across the county boundary in Laois. The transfer took place four years later. The fact that a recipient for this piece of land came from some distance, in another county, indicates that there was no great local demand for it; nor indeed any special zeal shown by Fr. Houlahan in seeking out local people to take it on. The idea that there was a local Republican conspiracy to grab this land is simply a fantasy, unsupported by the recorded facts.

Dan Downey himself received twenty eight acres. Another labourer, Martin Egan of Glenleiter, received thirty three acres which he had to relinquish after ten years as he was unable meet the annuity payments to the Land Commission.

Mick "the Yank" Carroll, who also returned from USA in 1921, was allocated sixteen acres along Silver River, and he named this patch "Coney Island". His namesake, IRA man Mick Carroll had departed for Australia with Mick Heaney and other Republicans.

The apolitical Thomas O'Brien was the owner of a small piece of mountain and received a small allocation in Coolacrease. After 20 years he sold his six acres in Coolacrease to Elizabeth Byrne. James McCormack, blacksmith, also non-political, received eighteen acres.

John Carroll received nineteen acres. He is pictured in the Curragh internment camp photograph of Cadamstown IRA members but was not an IRA man. He was arrested in the line-up of locals on Cadamstown bridge the morning after the Pearson executions. A hat lost by a member of the execution party was found to fit him. In his book "*I Met Murder on the May*" Alan Stanley mentions this line-up and says it was inspected by Mrs. Susan Pearson, but mistakenly locates it in Kinnitty. Bernard Scully of Cadamstown village, a boy of 14 or 15, was in the line-up until the British Army officer in charge ordered him to be released. The Scully's door was kicked down in the raid.

Bernard's mother Margaret Scully, widow of a labourer who lived in Cadamstown village, received eleven acres which Bernard sold to local farmer Joe Young in about 1970.

James Coughlan received thirteen acres. He was a carpenter who worked for Captain Drought. His father was in the British Army, and their sympathies at that time were anti-Republican.

In September 1923 portions of land were allocated to Brian Heaney, and to John Walsh, a labourer from Kinnitty. John Walsh declined the offer.

There was a distinct lack of enthusiasm for taking on these costly and not very productive pieces of land. Active Republicans were detested by Fr. Houlahan. But, as in the case of Jimmy Delahunty, accommodations were made, and in the end a few former Republicans eventually received allocations in Coolacrease. Considering that Cadamstown was overwhelmingly Republican in sympathy, it is surprising how few of these were involved, and what lengths Fr. Houlahan was prepared to go to before they were considered.

Bill Glenn, a member of the IRA roadblock attacked by the Pearsons, was interned at the time of division of Coolacrease. After his release, with his mother, a Somme widow, he received thirty acres. He lived with his mother in the coach house in Coolacrease. Bill had worked as a labourer, and his brother worked in England. Former IRA man John Joe McRedmond received thirty acres including the ruins of Coolacrease House. The presence of farm buildings made this land, along with the Glenns' portion, especially costly, so it was extremely difficult to get anybody at all to take it on. These were the problems caused by the exorbitant settlement that William Pearson extorted from the Land Commission.

McRedmond's and Glenn's portions were subsequently sold to their present owner.

The new landholders were expected to make twice-yearly repayments to the Land Commission. The repayments books show that the amount charged for the Pearson land was double the amount charged for other comparable land in the area. The reason for this is that the Land Commission bought the land from the Pearsons for at least double its real value.

Also the Land Commission had to carry out a great deal of expensive infrastructural work on the land in order to make the place workable by new landholders. For instance, Fr. Houlahan's friend Dan Downey got the contract for fencing. This work was completed to a high standard. Some of the oak stakes used are still visible after nearly a century. Local people were employed to draw gravel, by horse and cart, to construct a roadway down to the Silver River which ran through Pearsons' land.

The twice-yearly repayments on this land only came to an end about ten years ago; whereas a large proportion of land purchase annuity repayments terminated more than forty years ago, in the mid-1960's. The Coolacrease land was so costly that more than one lifetime was needed to pay it off.

This is the account of the disposal of Coolacrease which Paddy Heaney heard from his father and from the other people involved. It is confirmed in detail by the Land Registry, Valuation Office and Land Commission records. It is the account which he gave to the makers of the Hidden History documentary.

But, on the basis of no firm evidence at all, Niamh Sammon, Eoghan Harris, along with Professors Dooley, English and Murphy, concocted a story of a sectarian land grab. And RTÉ backed up this propagandist concoction with bluster and lies about Land Commission documents—documents to which they were never permitted access.

Conclusion

The Pearsons arrived in Coolacrease in 1911 and established their credentials as good neighbours in a welcoming and broad-minded community. Political developments caused a divergence in sympathy and outlook between the Pearsons and the local community. The Pearsons had strong personal and family connections with loyalists in nearby Luggacurran, where a lingering dispute over 1880's land grabbing and attempted ethnic cleansing fostered an atmosphere of suspicion and hostility over land and political affiliation, and a loyalist armed group came into confrontation with the Irish forces there. The Pearsons themselves attacked the IRA in the course of a roadblock operation, and their execution was ordered because of that. There was no sectarian atrocity against the Pearsons.

The Pearsons decided to move out and sought to sell the farm in August 1921, one month after the execution of Richard and Abraham and the burning of the house. However, despite offers for the farm, it was removed from sale when the reserve price was not achieved. William Pearson subsequently commuted between England and Offaly, maintaining the farm, and selling off stock and machinery. Claims by Alan Stanley that the farm was squatted and plundered have been proven untrue. When the opportunity arose, William sold the farm to the Land Commission for more than double what he had originally paid for it. The Land Commission divided and allocated the land to local small holders and landless men on the basis of strict Land Commission procedures, if anything favouring former British Army servicemen.

There was no land grab, sectarian or otherwise, and no preference for Republicans in the allocation of the land.

The claims of the 'Hidden History' film in these regards are at best greatly wide of the mark and at worst a tissue of lies and untruths in pursuit of a 'hidden agenda' of trying to characterise the Irish War of Independence as a process of sectarian ethnic cleansing.

Chapter 2

The Cadamstown IRA in the War of Independence

By

Paddy Heaney

Since the days of the dispossessions and the Great O'Neill a strong spirit of resistance remained alive in the Slieve Bloom area. Throughout the 17th and 18th century Raparees—descendants of dispossessed families—were active and secret societies flourished up to the mid-19th century in response to the arbitrary power of landlord and magistrate. Resistance was mounted to the enclosure of land and other developments which threatened the people's subsistence.

In the 1790s an active branch of the United Irish Society developed in Cadamstown and volunteers from the area took part in the 1798 rebellion in Wexford, suffering great losses. A mass hanging of prisoners took place at Birr and fugitives were hunted down and killed by the Yeomanry in the surrounding district. In the early 19th century there were various acts of resistance which were reported as *"agrarian outrages"* and these were met with hangings and transportation. The Famine also hit the Cadamstown townland hard, with the population falling through famine and emigration from 1,560 in 1841 to just half of that a decade later. In Kinnitty Parish the population fell from 2,562 in 1841 to 1,598 in 1851 and 776 in 1881.

An active branch of the Fenian movement was established in Cadamstown. This became known as the Irish Republican Brotherhood (I.R.B.). Many local men were associated with it, and the core I.R.B. group consisted of Mick Egan, Mick Purcell, Jimmy Ryan (a blacksmith and pub owner in Cadamstown) and Tommy Davis.

The period of the Land Wars saw the formation of a branch of the Irish Land League, and there were several clashes between the people and the military authorities. Serious confrontations occurred down to as late as the early 1900s, although, despite aggressive retaliation by landlords and their agents, both the clergy and the enlightened local magistrates—the Droughts—played a positive role in dissipating local tensions. The area was staunchly in support of Home Rule and its Irish Party MP in Westminster vociferously represented the people of the area and their interests.

A branch of the Gaelic League, which had been founded in Dublin in 1893, was formed in the village of Cadamstown on 16th March 1903. Mrs. Carroll the local school teacher was the chief organiser; twenty locals attended that first meeting. This soon swelled to over forty. The branch continued its activities up to the War of Independence when many of its members played an active and noble role in the struggle for freedom.

The G.A.A., founded in Thurles in 1884, developed as a very strong movement throughout Offaly, not least as hurling had already been a popular sport in the Cadamstown area for over a hundred years. Local matches were often organised, later even under the patronage of local landlords like the Manifolds and Bernards. Cadamstown had one of the first local branches of the G.A.A. in Offaly and the local team (known as the "Home Rulers") won the county championship in 1889. Ten members of the 1900 Offaly hurling team were men from Cadamstown.

G.A.A. matches received scant media coverage, with the *Kings County Chronicle* ignoring the 1889 county championship altogether. A local newspaper was created to fill the gap, the monthly *Cadamstown Scarifier,* which, with the backing of the local I.R.B., had a marked nationalist tone (images of Parnell and Wolfe Tone featured in the masthead). It provided a lively source of alternative news until suppressed under the Sedition Acts. Its editor mocked the lack of G.A.A. coverage in the *Chronicle* in verse: *"For that rotten rag the Chronicle, Our game would not report".*

The G.A.A. was a well spring of the political revival in Cadamstown as elsewhere, and many members of the Volunteers and later the IRA came through its ranks. In 1918 the British authorities prohibited the playing of games except under permit. In an act of defiance, on 4th August 1918, close to one thousand matches were played throughout Ireland. Two games of hurling were played at different locations in Cadamstown that day, and both were raided by the R.I.C. and British military.

When the National Volunteers were formed in 1913 in response to the Ulster rebellion against Home Rule, many from the Cadamstown area joined their ranks. They drilled openly with hurls in the village until arms were obtained. After the 1916 Rising a branch of the anti-Redmondite Irish Volunteers was formed in Cadamstown, and the first three men sworn in on 1st March 1917 were James Delahunty, Tom Donnelly and Mick Heaney. They took the oath from Lar Langton at the ruins of the ancient and historic Carrolls' Castle. A descendant of the Carrolls, who had been dispatched to Maryland during the dispossessions, had been one of the signatories of the American Declaration of Independence.

In August 1917 the second half company of the Offaly Brigade was formed in Cadamstown, comprising twenty four men: Michael McRedmond, Joseph Manifold, John Manifold, Martin Guinan, Michael Guinan, Thomas Donnelly, John McRedmond, John O'Connor, Patrick Carroll, James Delahunty, Joseph Carroll, John Dillon, William Glenn, Joseph Heaney, Michael McDonnell, Joseph Honan, Michael Heaney, Thomas Horan, John Joe Horan, Jack Dooley, Jack Brophy, Luke Daly, Patrick Honan and William Heaney.

The quartermaster was James Delahunty. His job was to look after the arms, see that they were properly stored and catered for, and also to receive and pass on dispatches. The secret hiding place was near the Bow Meadow. Dispatches were relayed through the network of companies throughout the midlands and passed efficiently from townland to townland. Though most of these men were Catholics, there were also Protestants in the IRA. The best known was Walter Mitchell of Rahan, a Protestant volunteer with the Offaly IRA. His brother Herbert (known as Seán) fought with the IRA in Cork. A relative, Tom Mitchell of Roscomroe, a former British Army soldier, provided military training and a safe house for the Cadamstown IRA.

Soon after the Volunteers were formed, a branch of Cumann na mBan was established in each parish of the district. A committee was formed in Cadamstown village in 1915 and my mother was present along with her sister Mary Ellen Dillon, Katie Brophy, Sis Donnelly, Johanna Horan, Ann Manifold, Nellie O'Brien, Kate Guinan and Mrs. Carroll, the school teacher. Classes were held for first aid, home nursing drill, signalling and in the care and use of arms. For military matters Lar Langton came once a month. Lectures were arranged, with Irish dancing and the Irish language at the top of the agenda. When wholesale arrests of Volunteers followed the suppression of the 1916 rising, the Cumann na mBan began collecting for the Volunteer Dependents Fund and organising prison visits.

When the War of Independence started in 1919 following British rejection of the 1918 election result, the IRA in the area went on a war footing. The wild mountain area of the Slieve Bloom above Cadamstown village provided safety for the men of the company. There were many safe houses in this district. Horans of Deerpark, Dillons of Seskin, Ryans of Seskin, Nolans of Deerpark, Dalys of Glenlitter and Heaneys of Glenlitter. Many men from Cloghan found refuge in the mountain area, for instance, the Geraghtys, the Grogans and the McIntyres. The Slieve Bloom Mountains were a prime route southwards to the main centres of the struggle for men escaping from internment at the nearby Curragh Camp in Kildare and the network of escape routes and safe houses played a critical role in this.

There was a major breakout of prisoners from the Curragh Camp early in 1920. Ten of the escaped prisoners were guided to the safety of the Slieve Bloom Mountains. They were brought to Dillons of Seskin on a night in May by a volunteer from the Clonaslee Company. There they were fed and had a good night's sleep. The following day they made preparations to continue their journey in the direction of Tipperary. They hailed from different counties in Munster and one particular man came from an island off the Kerry coast. The local company guarded them during their stay at Dillons. They left Dillons on the summer's night and were guided across the mountain by my mother and her brother, Pat Dillon. They arrived at Maloneys of Ballybritt near Roscrea the following morning. A volunteer from Cashel was awaiting their arrival and, after a brief rest at Maloney's, they continued on their way to the safety of the

Tipperary hills.

The girls in the Cumann na mBan were active in delivering dispatches. Sis Donnelly and my mother often travelled all night. They never travelled in pairs and their footwear was specially made with hollowed out heels to conceal dispatches. In 1920 when the IRA from South Offaly and North Tipperary were to attack Birr Police Barracks, every item was finalised the previous week. It was Sis Donnelly who kept information flowing between North Tipperary Divisional Headquarters and the South Offaly Brigade. My mother delivered a dispatch to Jim Carroll of Ross the previous day, saying that all was ready. The attack was to coincide with the fair at Birr, as strangers would not be noticed.

Tom Donnelly delivered a consignment of gelignite by horse and cart that morning at 6.30. Other horses and cars came in from Nenagh, Rathcabbin and Roscrea with car loads of sheep and suck pigs with rifles concealed in the cars. There were almost 100 volunteers in the fair, fully armed. A scouting party was sent in from Cadamstown, included were John Dillon and Lar Langton. They met Jim Carroll at Syngfield and proceeded towards the town of Birr. They were alarmed to find armed soldiers stationed all along Bridge Street. The town was completely saturated with troops, Black and Tans and R.I.C. As my Uncle John told me afterwards, there was no time to turn back. As all three were armed, they turned up the Roscrea road. People were assembling for early mass. They decided they would go into the church as a patrol was approaching behind them.

As they were about to dismount a party of R.I.C. came up a side street and they were immediately recognised by Sgt. Watson who was stationed at Birr. He shouted at Lar Langton, *"We have you now, Lar"*. Watson ordered the R.I.C. to open fire and Lar Langton fell seriously wounded. Jim Carroll and John Dillon sped up the Roscrea road under a hail of bullets. Just as Lar fell, a young curate rushed to his side. While attending him he removed Lar's revolver and concealed it on his person. A party of Auxiliaries arrived and they attempted to shoot Lar as he lay on the ground. The Auxiliaries and the R.I.C. were debating who would shoot him when a party of Leinsters who were stationed in Crinkle Barracks arrived on the scene with rifles at the ready. They scattered the mob and brought Lar to Crinkle Barracks. The Leinsters mounted a guard on Lar through the night as the R.I.C. and Auxiliaries were howling for his blood. He was put under the care of an English doctor. The bullets were extracted and Lar was nursed back to life. The doctor wrote a letter to Lar's mother that he was a brave soldier and a gentleman. Lar was later transferred to Spike Island.

The incident in Birr and the shooting of Lar Langton urged the South Offaly Brigade to become more active. The Cadamstown Company were on the move almost every night, providing safe houses for the flying column, blocking roads and digging trenches. In May 1920, a series of raids took place by police in the area. This was an attempt by the R.I.C. to intimidate local people. Two R.I.C. officers came on bicycles from Kinnitty to attend Mass at Cadamstown on two successive Sundays. They sat at the back of the church to observe any strangers. The second Sunday they arrived, the back seats were full. The police tried to force a man out of his seat and this was resented by a crowd who were standing at the back of the church. They forced the two policemen to leave. It was decided to ambush the police the following Sunday outside the village, but this was turned down by the O.C. for various reasons.

In August 1920, many R.I.C. barracks were vacated, including Kinnitty, Kilcormac and Rath. In order to prevent the burning of the buildings, the R.I.C. usually left the wife of the sergeant in the barracks. However, the local IRA was not put off by this and within three days the three barracks and courthouses were destroyed. In Kinnitty the wife of Sgt. Byrne was given five minutes to leave the building and then it was demolished.

The men of Cadamstown IRA worked closely with the new underground institutions of the Irish Republic. Sessions of the Republican Courts were held at Birr, Tullamore and in the local districts. Taxes were raised and the population was overwhelming in its support for the new government. In Cadamstown contact to the underground institutions and courts was through Tim Nolan, and also through J.J. Horan, who was elected a Sinn Féin District Councillor for Kinnitty.

The small Cadamstown Company was hard pressed for ammunition and explosives. Heaney's house at Coolcreen was used as an ammunition factory where box bombs and cartridge shot were manufactured. The local blacksmith, Jim McCormack, though not involved in the IRA, showed the men how to make explosives. The box bomb consisted of an iron box of a horse's car sealed at one end. It was filled with powder and a fuse attached. Sometimes gelignite was used when available. This when placed against a barrack wall or bridge could have a devastating effect. The cartridges were emptied of the small shot and replaced with home made shot, which was much larger. Jim Delahunty, who acted as quartermaster, told me the local men often worked all night and into the early morning preparing for some action.

Arms were always a problem. On orders from GHQ in Dublin in 1920 guns were collected from local farmers who had them, and houses with military connections were particularly targeted. The Biddulph home was visited and two or three guns were found, which the family handed over.

The home of the Droughts in Lettybrook was also visited. Captain Drought often entertained visitors from England, especially retired army officers, who would spend a week grouse shooting on the mountains. The local Company had a Cumann na mBan member working part-time during the summer to watch strangers coming and going and supply information. She duly informed the company that preparations were in progress for a dinner party to receive a group of visitors from England. The company held a meeting to plan a raid for weapons. Twenty men were involved.

Two sentries were placed one mile each side of Droughts. Jack ("The Warrior") Dooley took up position near the village of Cadamstown, armed with a double-barrelled shotgun. If enemy lorries came from either the Birr or Tullamore direction, he was to fire two barrels in the air to warn the sentry at Droughts. Joe Carroll was in command of eight men guarding the entrance to Droughts. Mick Heaney, with ten men approached the house and Mick Heaney demanded to see Captain Drought and explained his mission. Captain Drought invited them inside and told them to search the house, but asked that they not disturb the visitors. The house was searched but nothing was found. Mick then led his men into the dining room. As he entered, the young girl who was serving the table nodded her head towards the French windows. Tom Donnelly and Pat Carroll investigated and found a compartment beneath the window where twenty rifles, ten revolvers and a quantity of ammunition were stored. When the visitors were searched, each had a loaded revolver ready for use. They took the arms with them and the company then thanked Captain Drought and apologised for disturbing the visitors and their entertainment! The Droughts later requested the return of one of the guns, which had belonged to their son who had been killed in the Great War. Mick Heaney returned the rifle to them in person, and they were very grateful for this. Captain Drought also let it be known that there were additional weapons in the house, and these were duly collected from him.

The Pearson home was also targeted. The Pearsons were known to be active on the loyalist side, so the approach was made very cautiously. John Dillon and John Joe Horan, who owned large farms close to Pearsons, called to Coolacrease House and asked the Pearsons to hand over their guns to the IRA. They refused, and the two Volunteers withdrew without delay and without any further challenge to the Pearsons. But they observed one of the Pearson girls leaving the farm on a bicycle—to report them to the Kinnitty RIC, they suspected. On her return through Cadamstown the bicycle was seized and broken by a girl of Cumann na mBan, the women's organisation in the independence movement.

The study by Fergal O'Brien of Kinnitty, *Aspects of the War of Independence in South Offaly,* brought to light many interesting details of the fight in the area, including the activities of the Drumcullen Company IRA. O'Brien also recounts the hostility of the local clergy in both Kilcormac and Kinnitty to the IRA. Fr Houlahan, for example, attempted to stop the IRA from burning Kinnitty Barracks and at Mass the Sunday after the raid he said that those who destroyed the barracks and courthouse would be better off suppressing intemperance in the village!

The movement also targeted the postal system to try to establish what information was being forwarded to Dublin Castle from the area. On 14th August 1920 letters delivered at Birr for the first time were marked "censored" by the IRA. Earlier the same year, on 10th May, E.H. Brown, agent for the Castlebernard and Drought Estates, was held up by three masked men and relieved of £400 in half yearly rents from tenants.

In spring 1921, activity was stepped up. Cadamstown was the only area in Offaly declared a no-go area and a curfew was imposed. The meeting place for the two half companies—Cadamstown and Drumcullen—was Drumcullen graveyard. Training increased, including undercover work.

Joe Connolly, from the South Offaly Brigade command, often travelled to Dublin to meet with Cathal Brugha to negotiate the procurement of arms supplies. Word came through that a supply was on the way. The Drumcullen Company was detailed to block the road at Killyon. The Clareen Company was to make the roads leading to Kinnitty impassable. The Killoughey and Kilcormac Companies had the task of sealing off the roads leading from that area. The Clonaslee Company had the difficult task of transporting the arms to the required place. They arrived in six motorcars, one arriving every hour to allay suspicion. The local company was about to carry the arms to a safe place when word arrived that the military had been alerted and a large column had broken through the blockade at Killyon. According to the scouts who were posted on nearby hills, the column consisted of six lorries and a Crossley tender. To make matters worse, four military lorries had crossed the barriers on the Curragh Togher although a trench had been dug across the road. The previous night the military obtained planks and drove the lorries across the trench. The Cadamstown area was now saturated with troops. They were closing in on the Sisken area where the arms were being unloaded. Two riflemen were dispatched to fire on the troops and draw them away from the area. They positioned themselves on Spink Hill and kept a steady fire on the advancing troops. Then they retreated across Barlahan. This gave the men time to dump the arms in furze and head for home. The following day, a British raid led to the arrest of two volunteers, who were transferred to Tullamore Jail. Joe Connolly of Brigade command sought to make contact with the prisoners to find out the location of the dumped arms, and organised two nuns, Sisters Donnelly and Deegan, to visit them to get the information. The following night the arms were transferred to Poll an tSagairt and safety. The thorough search of the area by the military the next day failed to uncover the stash of rifles, ammunition and gelignite.

On Tuesday, 17th May 1921 an attack took place on an R.I.C. patrol in Kinnitty village. This ambush was to have taken place at Cadamstown but the plan was changed at the last moment. The cycle patrol of seven constables left Birr at 9.30 in the morning and travelled to Cadamstown to serve notice on jurors for Birr quarter sessions. When the R.I.C. party was returning through Kinnitty at 4 o'clock they divided, with three taking the direct road to Birr and four taking the Kilcormac road. As the party of four was passing the burned out barracks in the village the local flying column of the IRA opened fire on them. All four policemen, Constables Fitzgerald, Doran, Connors and Dunne, were seriously injured having been shot numerous times. The injured policemen attempted to get to the safety of the public house. However, Constable Dunne, a twenty-two year old from Tuam, did not make it and died. The injured men were brought to Birr Military Hospital where Constable Doran, a 26 year old from Kildare, died. The flying column that carried out the ambush consisted of men from the immediate neighbourhood. The area was saturated with British troops but only two arrests were made.

The local company knew that there were Dublin Castle agents in the area so they had to be very careful. A suspicious stranger in the area was arrested by local volunteers and found with a map with certain houses marked with red ink. He was handed over to the Killoughey Company where he was court-martialled and shot on the Corrigeen Road. The IRA locally kept a watchful eye in particular on the Pearson house at Coolacrease which was suspected of being the local contact point for the active loyalist movement in the area. The Pearsons had previously refused to hand over weapons to the local resistance and the British military were observed coming and going from the house. The Pearson sons had also started acting aggressively towards local people, with Richard (Dick) in particular being regarded as a "hot head". John Dillon warned him on two occasions with regard to his conduct. Dick responded by threatening to have his house burned. During that period there was IRA intelligence to the effect that six local houses were planned to be burned by the police and the military: Donnellys of Curragh, Nolans of Deerpark, Dillons, Ryans and Dalys of Seskin, Heaneys of Glenlitter. Two RIC officers used to come on their bicycles from Birr on alternate Sundays, to attend Mass in Cadamstown Church. After mass they proceeded to Pearsons. They received a warning that they would be shot. They never came afterwards.

The first major incident involving the Pearsons concerned a Mass path leading from the Deerpark in the direction of the village of Cadamstown. It ran along the boundary of the Pearsons' land on their side of the ditch. The path had been used by locals since the village church was built in 1842. The confrontation at the Mass path between the Pearsons and local people, which took place in the first week of June 1921, is related in Chapter 1. The day following the incident, a group of police and Auxiliaries appeared in the village and proceeded up the Coach Road, inquiring after the way to Dillon's. Pat Purcell, who was living nearby, decided to contact Dillons. He walked up the road carrying a horse's winkers to allay suspicion. The police demanded to be brought to Dillons. This he refused to do. He was assaulted with rifles and left unconscious on the road. They later arrested Denis Deegan, a young boy, and under threat he led the party to Dillons where John Dillon was arrested. That day, the two volunteers who had intervened to restore order at the mass path—John Dillon and J.J. Horan—were arrested by the RIC and imprisoned, denounced presumably by the Pearsons.

Later in June 1921, shortly after this incident, the local company received word to block the Birr-Tullamore road on the Coolacrease side of Cadamstown, as part of manoeuvres in support of a planned ambush on the military at Birr. The local company mobilised and marched to Coolacrease where at around midnight they selected a large beech tree to use to block the roadway. The armed confrontation which ensued with the Pearsons at the road block is recounted in detail in Chapter 1. Three volunteers—Tom Donnelly, Mick Heaney and Jack Brophy—were shot and wounded. A fourth man, Bert Hogg, an ex-RIC man who had been visiting the Pearsons and had been apprehended by the volunteers, was also wounded by their gunfire. Mick Heaney, who was badly wounded, was thought by the British military at the time to have been killed.

The day after the roadblock attack, British troops swooped on Cadamstown. The village was surrounded. Houses were searched and every able-bodied man was placed along the bridge. The local police from Kinnitty and Birr walked up and down the line picking out people for questioning. One group of police was dispatched to the Curragh near the village. After a short time they returned with Tom Donnelly and John McRedmond. An English officer remarked: *"Did it take 20 police to arrest two teenage boys?"* Eight members of the local company (four had been arrested previously) who had been involved at the roadblock attacked by the Pearsons were arrested that day though others escaped to the mountains. In addition to John Joe Horan and John Dillon who were already arrested, the men taken into custody that day were Joe Carroll, John Carroll, Tom Horan, Jim Delahunty, John Joe McRedmond and Tom Donnelly. They were transported by lorry to Birr, whence they were taken to Tullamore. As the convoy passed through Eglish, they came under heavy rifle fire from various positions at a place called Ballincard. It was later known that the Drumcullen Company had prepared an ambush, not knowing there were Cadamstown prisoners on the lorries.

The men were lodged in Tullamore Jail where they were given nothing to eat for three days and were subjected to beatings by British soldiers. The prisoners were interrogated by a detective from Dublin Castle. After one week they were transported to the Curragh of Kildare and interned at Hare Park where they were to be held until November 1921. The round up had shattered the strength of the Cadamstown IRA.

Hare Park was a prisoner of war camp where IRA men and their sympathisers were interned. At one point there were seven or eight hundred prisoners from all over Ireland there. The republican prisoners ran the camp in a military fashion and officers were appointed to take charge of each hut. Drill sessions took place daily and exercises, football and other sports kept the prisoners fit and healthy. The huts were inspected daily by the camp authorities and the food was not so bad.

The roadblock attack and the multiple arrests alarmed Offaly Brigade headquarters who carried out an investigation which decided that for the attack on the IRA roadblock and the passing of information to the enemy, the three Pearson brothers were to be executed and the house burned. This operation was carried out on 30th June 1921 by the Flying Column of the Kilcormac Battalion, with volunteers from surrounding units deployed in the surrounding area to provide lookout and cover for the Column. The two Pearson brothers arrested were executed by a firing squad of the flying column. None were local men. The brothers faced the firing squad bravely and the house and its contents were burned.

The day following the executions there was a further raid on the village by R.I.C. and British military. My mother was caught up in this, just as she was going to bring the cows in for milking for her brother, John Dillon, who was imprisoned. As a party of R.I.C., Black and Tans and British soldiers approached the house she heard commands and English voices calling, and started running down the boreen. There was then a crack of rifles. She felt something strike her head and fell and passed out. A medical officer was bending over her as she came around. He said it was a bad graze and that she was lucky. He then addressed the R.I.C. and called them cowards and murderers. My mother told me that the young officer wrote to her years after.

The Slieve Bloom mountains saw much action in the War. Jim Tormey's flying column based in County Westmeath consisted of thirty men who took part in many ambushes throughout Westmeath and County Longford. British troops poured into that area to curb Tormey's Column. The column was hard pressed so they retired to the safety of the Slieve Bloom Mountains. As the song says, *"And to the Slieve Bloom Mountains came Jim Tormey's flying column"*. The Cadamstown Company had the honour of guarding Tormey's Flying Column for three weeks as they rested in the mountain. The flying column then returned to Westmeath where they engaged British troops at the famous ambush at Park outside Athlone. This proved fatal for them as they lost their great leader. He was killed as he led his men into action on that day. There is a cross erected to his memory at the spot where he was killed.

My mother travelled with Mrs. Carroll in a pony and trap to visit the Cadamstown prisoners at the Curragh. Mrs. Carroll had two sons in the camp while my mother's brother, John Dillon, was interned there. On another occasion, Mrs. Carroll and my mother travelled with Tim Brophy by motor car to the Curragh. Cars were scarce at that period. They arrived safely and visited the prisoners, giving them fresh clothes and food parcels. When they set out to return home the car wouldn't start. Two British officers offered their help and suggested pushing the car to try to get it along. Mrs. Carroll refused, saying she would not accept help from representatives of the British Empire. Eventually Tim got the car going again.

There were men from all over Ireland in the camp at that stage and the Cadamstown prisoners had the honour of meeting some of the great leaders of the IRA. One such leader was Ernie O'Malley who was a national organiser and who wrote a special account of that period called *On Another Man's Wound*. He was one of the great freedom fighters of his time.

Following the Truce in July 1921, all prisoners were released and the Cadamstown men arrived home to their native parish on 10th November 1921. A huge bonfire was lit on the Park Hill which could be seen all over the county. They were welcomed as heroes. They returned to their homes only for a short time and, because they believed the Truce would not last, they began to muster the local company. The first training camp for officers was set up at Leitir Lugna Abbey during the Truce. IRA officers from all over Offaly attended. A training camp for volunteers was established on the slopes of Knockhill, and this was also attended by men from all over the county.

My information on the fight of the Cadamstown IRA in the War of Independence was gleaned from the men and women who took part in it, and who gave their information willingly to me. I was fortunate to have met and interviewed many of the men and women before they passed away, including the man in command of the flying column of the South Offaly Brigade on the day of the Pearson execution. I would like to stress that people never liked to talk about that period in our history. But, like their comrades elsewhere in Ireland, they played a noble part in that struggle. Offaly did not witness the intensity of warfare that was experienced in Munster and to some extent in Dublin. But it played a role and the resistance in South Offaly was considered by the enemy an effective and brave force. The movements of the British Army were severely restricted and their intelligence operations in the county were effectively countered.

Shortly before my mother died, she told me a great deal of the exploits of that period. She ended by saying: *"I look back on it now with pride and pleasure, with my association with these great people of that period. My contacts with the men on the run, the people who sheltered them and fed them from their scanty fare. I saw wounded men with smiling faces. I never observed a sign of cowardice in any of the men before any engagement. All worked for the cause, giving everything they had."*

When the Treaty was signed and the tragic Civil War began, men who had fought together now fought one another. Of the Cadamstown IRA only three men did not remain with the Republican side, and of these only one joined the Free State forces. The whole of the Cadamstown Cumann na mBan remained with the Republican side. A bitter struggle was fought in South Offaly, and many men were again interned. This will go down as the blackest period in our history. But time is a great healer and we will look back with pride on that great struggle for Irish freedom. We can recall that when Ireland needed men, Cadamstown did not let her down. Their names will go down in history and, like the men of '98 and the Fenians of '67, their deeds will be recalled around the firesides on the slopes of the Slieve Bloom Mountains.

Chapter 3

The British Army in the War in South Offaly

By

Philip O'Connor

At the height of the War of Independence, *The Irish Times*—which has recently again been referring to the Famine as *"natural disaster"* [1]—thundered in an editorial that a *"hideous conspiracy of murder exists with the object of establishing an independent Irish Republic"*. Countering this conspiracy of murder, the *"gallant ranks"* of the R.I.C. had been augmented by *"new troops and new police ... As a body, the new forces have done their difficult and dangerous work with careful regard for the lives of the civilian population."* [2] The *"new troops and new police"* mobilised by the British State to prevent implementation of the 1918 Election result consisted of the militarised R.I.C., filled out with British recruits ("Black and Tans") and Auxiliaries, with massive back-up from the regular British Army. The First Dáil had offered an amnesty to all R.I.C. men who resigned from the force and promised that their full pension entitlements would be honoured (which they were). The elements of the R.I.C. which chose to remain and continue the war against the Irish democracy consisted of a much reduced but hardened rump. The "Auxiliaries" (R.I.C. Auxiliary Division) was a force of former British officers raised following a British Cabinet decision proposed by Winston Churchill, Secretary for War. They were distributed in

---

[1] 'Irish Famine Victims to be Commemorated', *The Irish Times,* 22nd July 2008.

[2] *The Irish Times,* Editorial, 22nd February 1922. On the position of *The Irish Times* on Irish Independence see John Martin, *The Irish Times Past and Present*, Belfast Historical & Educational Society (2008).

company-sized units throughout the country, attached to local R.I.C. divisions and under the overall command of the buccaneering General F.P. Crozier. He had been a key British officer in the organising of the U.V.F. to counter the threat of Home Rule in 1912 and, following the Great War in which he served, had fought both against and alongside *Freikorps* militias in the Baltics. The business of the Auxiliaries was what Crozier called *"revolution quelling"*.[3] Contrary to the *Irish Times* view of the Irish resistance to the military force sent to suppress the Irish democracy, the terrorism in the war that ensued was not supplied by the Irish side.

The British Army in the Birr-Tullamore area was represented by a depot unit of the Leinster Regiment ("The Prince of Wales Own Leinster Regiment") which, as we will see, proved very luke-warm in a counter-insurgency role. With the British military "surge" of January 1921 the serious end of the British Army in the area was provided by 1st Battalion, Royal Scots Fusiliers (1./RSF). The Court of Inquiry in lieu of Inquest into the deaths of the Pearson brothers was held at Crinkle Barracks, a home base of the Leinsters, but was presided over by Major G.W. Browne, commander, 3rd Coy, 1./ RSF, stationed in Crinkle. The other members of the Court were Captn. D.M.W. Beak of the Royal Scots and Lieut. J.J. Kingston of the depot unit of the Leinsters. The barracks had been built in 1805 to house up to 2,000 soldiers during the massive garrisoning of Ireland which followed the 1798 Rebellion.

The Royal Scots, who first arrived at the Curragh from Britain on 4th January 1921, were headquartered when moved to Offaly in the R.I.C. Barracks at Tullamore Jail, with individual companies posted to towns and outposts around Laois and Offaly.

The Leinsters had a history going back to 1805. It was in action in a litany of British wars and colonial policing operations: Britain's war against America, against France, against Russia in the Crimea, in the slaughter of the "Indian Mutiny", and then as a garrison force in the colonial outposts of Gibraltar and Malta. After a spell in Ireland in the early 1870s, it was again off on a "tour of duty" in India

---

[3] General F.P. Crozier, *The Men I Killed,* Athol Books, 2002.

from 1877 to 1894. Thereafter it was split between India and garrisoning duties in Tipperary Town.

In the strange interlude represented by the "Great War", the Leinsters suddenly found themselves fighting for freedom, democracy and the rights of small nations. When John Redmond committed the Irish Party to the British cause in the war, many men—including from Offaly—joined up. The Leinsters fought in France and in Churchill's failed attempted invasion of Turkey at Gallipoli.

At the end of the "Great War" the British mass army raised to fight it was demobilised and reduced to its so-called "peace-time" strength. About 15,000 Irishmen opted to stay in service. For the Leinsters, it was back to business as usual, with elements being sent to Egypt and Palestine to suppress nationalist movements.

But events in Ireland had an impact on the remaining Irish forces in the British Army. In June 1920, 400 men and NCOs of the Connaught Rangers (88th Regiment) stationed in India refused to obey orders after hearing of Black and Tan atrocities in Ireland. They demanded the withdrawal of British troops from Ireland. Non-Irish regiments were brought in to quell this mutiny with lethal force. Two Irish soldiers were killed and another seriously wounded. Eventually a court martial tried the men involved and 19 were sentenced to death while others were given prison sentences ranging up to 20 years. In the end, only one man was executed as it was felt executions on a major scale would have the same negative effect on Irish troops as had the 1916 executions. Around the same time the British Ambassador in Berlin urged Sir Henry Wilson to withdraw the Royal Irish Regiment from the occupation force in East Prussia because it was *"full of Sinn Fein and cannot be relied on"*. Wilson agreed and asked the Foreign Secretary, Lord Curzon, for approval to withdraw the Royal Irish adding: *"it is urgent in every sense"*. No Irish regiments were sent to Ireland during the 1919-21 period (except for depot units already stationed there) and in July 1921 Field Marshal Wilson admitted that Irish soldiers throughout the British Army in significant numbers had sought exemption from serving in Ireland.[4]

---

[4] Peter Beresford Ellis, *'Anois agus arís'* (2006) on http://www.Irish abroad.com/news/

In 1919-20 the Leinsters and the other "Irish" regiments had much *"revolution quelling"* to do:

> "Sending Irish regiments to Ireland was politically unsound and militarily inadvisable. Irish units were therefore despatched to other parts of the empire. Five of the Irish battalions went to India to form part of the colonial garrison. The Leinsters (100th Regt) were involved in putting down an uprising in June 1920 among the Moplahs, in Malabar, in south west India ... In November 1919 the 2nd Battalion of the Munsters arrived in Egypt and were used as aid to the civil power putting down nationalist demonstrations and countering insurgent activity until in mid-1921 Britain announced that it was recognising Egyptian independence. The 2nd Dublins (102nd Regt) were sent to garrison Istanbul in 1919 and were involved fighting the Turkish nationalists. The nationalists won and in November 1920 the Dublins embarked for India. The 2nd Royal Irish Rifles and 1st Royal Irish Fusiliers went to Iraq, and were initially stationed in Baghdad. They were soon fighting Iraqi insurgents between Baghdad and Basra. Then as now, the fighting was tough and casualties high..." [5]

Under the terms of the 1921 Treaty, the ten "Irish" regiments of the British Army—with the exception of the Irish Guards and two Ulster regiments—were disbanded with effect from 11th June 1922, though individuals could opt to continue to serve in other units of the British Army.

Many young men from South Offaly joined the British Army in the "Great War" and served mostly in the Leinster Regiment, though also in an array of other units. In his book, *At the Foot of Slieve Bloom*, Paddy Heaney recounts the good relations that existed between the local population and the soldiers of the Leinsters at Crinkle Barracks, a relationship which maintained even during the War of Independence. As elsewhere in Ireland, there was no antagonism whatsoever to men who had joined up. Paddy Heaney recounts the awe with which people in Cadamstown listened down the years to the adventure stories of the veterans of Britain's wars throughout the world.[6] In addition, not a few returning veterans also became active in the IRA.

---

[5] Ibid.
[6] For example, *At the Foot of Slieve Bloom,* pp. 53 ff.

During the War of Independence the small depot unit of the Leinsters stationed at Birr played an apparently luke-warm supporting role to the R.I.C. Given the local connections referred to above, relations between the Leinsters and the local population remained good, and Paddy Heaney relates an incident where soldiers from the Leinsters intervened to prevent a group of R.I.C. and Auxiliaries from killing a wounded IRA man (Lar Langton) taken prisoner during a shoot out in Birr in 1920. He also recounts that they generally treated prisoners well, in contrast to some other British units:

> "It should be pointed out that during this period the Leinster Regiment was stationed at Crinkle Barracks, Birr. Prisoners arrived in Birr where they were handed over to the Leinsters who treated them very kindly. They removed their handcuffs before they were taken to their cells. On the following morning, before they were handed over to the British soldiers, they soaped their wrists so that the handcuffs would not bite into the skin." [7]

As the Leinsters were not proving a particularly enthusiastic *"rebellion quelling"* force, other reinforcements were drafted in from Britain.

The Royal Scots Fusiliers (RSF) were one of the premier units of the British Army, participating since the 17th century in a dizzying array of battles against Britain's enemies and colonial policing actions against various *"native"* populations throughout the Empire. In the "Great War" no fewer than 100,000 men passed through its ranks as cannon fodder. At the end of the War for Democracy and the Freedom of Small Nations, things returned to normal for the Royal Scots too. Between Britain's two *"World Wars"*—i.e. during the *"peace"*—the Royal Scots were kept busy. In September 1919, one Battalion was off on *"imperial service"* in Rangoon, and in early 1920 two further Battalions were sent to the Crimea to try to save Deniken's White Army then in headlong retreat before Marshal Budenny's Red Cavalry. Meanwhile, the home battalions in Scotland were mobilised in 1921 to break the miners' strike. In 1922 the

---

[7] Ibid., pp. 301-5.

Battalion in Rangoon was moved to Secunderabad, then on to Aden in 1925, seeing *"action"* at every turn. They finally returned to Britain in 1926 and, barracked at Maryhill in Glasgow, *"saw duty"* in the General Strike. In January 1926 the 2nd Battalion was sent to Egypt, then on to China in 1928. In 1930 they were moved to Quetta, then in 1934 to Lahore (India), and finally, in January 1938, to Hong Kong. At the same time, the 1st Battalion was moved to the Middle East to suppress what was officially called the *"Palestine Insurgency"*, where it was kept busy until January 1939. All of this activity constituted what in those days was called the "peacetime" role of the British Army.

The 1st Battalion RSF (220 men and 86 officers) was sent to Ireland at the end of 1920 to *"aid the civil power"*, arriving at the Curragh on 4th January 1921 where it was accommodated in huts at Rath Camp—where republican prisoners from Cadamstown were later interned. It was then moved to King's and Queen's Counties (Offaly and Laois), where it formed part of the British 14th Brigade commanded by Colonel-Commandant P.C.B. Skinner. Its headquarters were at Tullamore Jail, with various companies posted to centres around the two counties, including 3rd Company at Birr under Major G. W. Browne, who later presided at the Court of Inquiry into the Pearson deaths. Browne compiled the note on *"possible motives"* based on Ethel Pearson's story of local land hunger, and on the R.I.C. County Inspector's report on the Pearson attack on the IRA roadblock and weaponry hidden in the roof of the Pearson house.

When the Scots arrived in Offaly they were confronted by the stepped up campaign in the County under IRA Commandant Thomas Burke's leadership, which in turn was a response to the major escalation of the war on the British side since the official *"reprisals"* policy launched in the New Year (it had been *"unofficial"* previously). The official History of the Royal Scots Fusiliers has interesting things to say about what it calls the regiment's involvement *"in the situation in Ireland which ultimately led to the creation of the republican state of Eire"*. Besides reinforcing and supporting the R.I.C., it was regularly called upon by the military command for armoured patrolling, rounding up suspects and undercover *"intelligence"* work. In stark contrast to the Harris/Sammon documentary, the official history betrays a sense of respect for the effectiveness of the Irish resistance in Offaly:

> "[military tasks consisted of] the guarding of roads to keep communications open; the forestalling of raids by the Irish Republican Army; the rounding-up of suspects. The initiative was always with the rebels and the defence inevitably a step behind in its measures ... The only counter-measures consisted of maintaining strong garrisons at selected points in the two counties, and frequent patrolling in box-bodied Ford cars, Crossley 18-cwt. tenders and 3-ton lorries. Two Peerless armoured cars each mounting two Hotchkiss guns were also available for assistance, but proved clumsy and unreliable. The flying squads held in readiness to deal with "incidents" were always absurdly late in their arrival on the scene; the quarry had struck long since and melted away, to re-appear elsewhere at some unguarded spot .." [8]

The Scots felt restricted in the *"counter-measures"* they were allowed to undertake: *"No attempt could be made to clear an area, since that would have been impossible without evacuating the civilian population and so admitting a state of war..."*

The War of Independence was fought at its most intense in Munster and to some extent in Dublin. While less intense, operations in other counties were also critical. In Offaly the resistance effectively tied down British forces and restricted their movements to armoured convoys. The Birr area was heavily garrisoned and was the foremost unionist stronghold in Co. Offaly. In early 1921 Richard Mulcahy sought to have efforts intensified, and had Seán Mahon, the then O/C South Offaly No. 2 Brigade, replaced by Tom Burke, a Galway man who as a student in Dublin was active on the staff of G Company, 3rd Battalion of the Dublin IRA. Burke was not well known, but Mulcahy interviewed him and decided to send him first

---

[8] Colonel J. C. Kemp, *The History of the Royal Scots Fusiliers 1919-1959*, University Press Glasgow, 1963. Kemp was a former officer of the Regiment, and the forward to the book is provided by Field Marshal Sir Francis W. Festing C.C.B., K.B.E., D.S.O., "late The Royal Scots Fusiliers". The book—commissioned by the Regiment itself—can be read online (hence the absence of page references here, though all quotations are from Chapter 1).

as an organiser and then as brigade commander to South Offaly. The Offaly IRA—which had no more than 40 rifles available to it (16 in the South Offaly Brigade)—was poorly armed and had limited training. But it proved an effective force, particularly at sabotage and the harassing of British military mobility. The monthly report of the Birr Battalion for June 1921 contained a summary of military operations. The sabotage tactics it described were encouraged and applauded by GHQ. An extract from a military report from the Clara Battalion was published in *An tÓglach,* the IRA Journal, under the heading 'A Model Harassing Week'. *An tÓglach* commented:

> "There is nothing desperately heroic about it—just inflicting on the enemy a thousand pounds worth of damage in one week at no loss to ourselves. In fact it's an example how to win a war....This minor raiding activity is not as spectacular as a big ambush but it is a real and valuable help to the units who are fighting in the big ambushes. It means that the Enemy can transfer no forces from Offaly to Cork... It cannot be too forcibly pointed out that the added value of numerous small 'jobs' is enormous, and rots the Enemy like anything."

The effectiveness of these tactics was acknowledged also by the RIC County Inspector in Co. Offaly. In June 1921 he made a desperate plea for more resources and sterner measures, otherwise *"the IRA will win"*.[9]

That the British war strategy in seeking to counter the resistance in Offaly was a counter-insurgency terror is spelt out in the Royal Scots' own *'official history'*:

> "When the Scots Fusiliers arrived there in 1921 the situation was chaotic. On New Year's Day 1921 "authorised" reprisals had begun. The inhabitants of districts where outrages had occurred were held collectively responsible, on the assumption that the outrages could not have taken place without connivance. The punishments were burning and demolition of property. Fortunately the Scots Fusiliers were not involved in this repugnant role ..."

---

[9] Thanks to Philip McConway for this additional information from his forthcoming study of the South Offaly IRA.

Paddy Heaney's account of the war in the Cadamstown district includes several incidents where officers of the regiment intervened to stop acts of thuggery and even murder by members of the R.I.C. and Auxiliaries. Soldiers disliked their "policing" role. Once in August 1920 four lorry loads of soldiers descended on Cadamstown with orders to comb through every house. After "raiding" Jim McCormack's home (the blacksmith), a well tended and comfortable thatched cottage, a soldier asked him—*"Pat"*—if he could take some of his roses from his garden back to his family, as he'd *"be leaving this hell hole of a country tomorrow"*, to which he received the answer: *"You can have them all, with a heart and a half, so long as you leave me in peace"*.[10] But the policing role of the Scots was not always so benign. Though the *"official history"* claims that the regiment did not become involved in reprisal atrocities (*"this repugnant role"*), members of the regiment did participate in aspects of the "dirty war":

> "Officers of the Scots Fusiliers were sent out to discover and study the tricks and booby-traps used by the I.R.A. As the Adjutant observes: "This was a tricky job and very efficiently done by Lieutenant Grant-Taylor, O.B.E., M.C., and 2nd-Lieutenant Strong, who were employed on intelligence duties. They were dressed as civilians and moved among the local inhabitants, picking up information as to the whereabouts of I.R.A. bands" …"

Stationed in Hunston House in Moystown, Lieutenant Kenneth Strong travelled on a motor cycle throughout the south Offaly area, frequently in various disguises, for his intelligence gathering activities. The regiment was also involved in the execution of Republican spies identified to it.[11] The sanitised official history touches directly on some of the activities of the Royal Scots stationed with the R.I.C. and Auxiliaries at Tullamore Jail:

> "During the 'Troubles' the majority of the Battalion was billeted in the gaol at Tullamore. The adjoining courthouse served as the officers'

---

[10] *At the Foot of Slieve Bloom*, pp. 304, 59.

[11] Information from Philip McConway. Uniformed officers did not travel alone in this area. It is interesting that Alan Stanley (*I Met Murder*...) refers to a lone British officer on a motorcycle calling to the Pearson house "for petrol".

mess. One wing of the gaol and the exercise yard were retained by the Royal Irish Constabulary for their prisoners. During the first twelve months of the Battalion's stay more than 80 Sinn Feiners captured by the Scots Fusiliers were detained there, all of whom had been identified by the R.I.C. as persons liable for trial on major criminal charges such as murder, arson and the like. Throughout its stay, the Battalion received the utmost support from the R.I.C. under their County Inspector, Mr. Ross, who was made a member of the officers' mess."

Paddy Heaney gives an account of the experience of Republican prisoners at Tullamore Barracks in late June 1921 following the Pearson attack on the IRA roadblock party at Coolacrease and denunciation of local Republicans to the R.I.C. This includes the involvement of members of the Royal Scots Regiment in the torture and mistreatment of prisoners:

> "The village was surrounded. Houses were searched and every able-bodied man was placed along the bridge. The local police from Kinnitty and Birr walked up and down the line picking out people for questioning... One group of police and auxiliaries proceeded up the Coach Road and inquired the way to Dillons. Pat Purcell, who was living nearby, decided to contact Dillons. He walked up the road carrying a horse's winkers to allay suspicion. The police demanded to be brought to Dillons. This he refused to do. He was assaulted with rifles and left unconscious on the road... Eight were arrested that day and many more escaped to the mountains ... [The eight men] were transferred to Tullamore Jail where a detective from Dublin Castle interrogated them ... They got nothing to eat for three days."

In addition to four men rounded up a few days earlier, these further arrests broke the strength of the Cadamstown Company of the IRA. The captured men were starved and badly beaten by British soldiers at Tullamore Barracks, before being moved to Hare Camp on the Curragh.[12]

There are other interesting connections between the Royal Scots and the business of *"revolution quelling"* in Ireland. The father of

---

[12] *At the Foot of Slieve Bloom*, pp. 301-309.

General Crozier, commander of the Auxiliaries until his resignation in February 1921 in protest at the official policy of reprisals which he regarded as counter-productive, had been an officer in the Royal Scots and during the Land War had been attached to the military force stationed in Birr to assist R.I.C. eviction parties. Another officer of the Royal Scots who played a role in Ireland was Captain William Darling. A war hero, he was posted to Dublin Castle in 1920 as editor of the principal R.I.C. propaganda sheet, the infamous *Weekly Summary,* which was responsible for inciting the police and military to undertake acts of terror and revenge.[13]

The Royal Scots left Ireland in early 1922 after the signing of the Treaty and were the last British unit to evacuate Rath Camp on the Curragh. As related above, they moved on to the business of rebellion quelling elsewhere across the globe, a role that kept them busy until 1939 when rebellion quelling was again momentarily replaced by a war for democracy etc.

The British war in Ireland as described even by the official history of the Royal Scots Regiment was one where terror, spies and agents played a major and deadly role. This was the war in which the Pearsons chose to become military participants on one side, a choice for which they paid the price.

---

[13] See Brian P. Murphy, *The Origins and Organisation of British Propaganda in Ireland 1920,* Aubane, 2006, pp. 21 ff.

Chapter 4

"Land Grab"?
What The Land Documents Say

A review of the relevant documentation in the archives
of the Irish Land Commission, the Land Registry,
the Valuation Office (Dublin) and
the British Public Record Office (London)

By

Philip O'Connor

"Ethnic Cleansing in the Midlands"?

One of the central aspects of the Sammon/Harris 'Hidden History' documentary and the media propaganda supporting its thesis which appeared on RTÉ Radio and in the *Irish Times* and *Sunday Independent* is the allegation that a sectarian 'land grab' occurred at Coolacrease and lay at the basis of the IRA action against the Pearson brothers.[1] In the Pearsons' later claims to the London based compensation body, the "Irish Grants Committee", they claimed that, through *"boycott and persecution"* they were forced to abandon the farm, and *"compelled to sell the land to the Land Commission"* for *"about 1/4 of its value"*.

At Clontarf Castle on 30th May 2007, Niamh Sammon's documentary was initially announced by Kevin Dawson, RTÉ's "Commissioning Editor for Factual Programmes", under the working title 'Atonement: Ethnic Cleansing in the Midlands'. An opinion piece in the *Sunday Independent* two days before the eventual

---

[1] See transcripts and list of articles in Appendix 8, 'A Note on the Debate in the Press'. On RTÉ Radio see the Chapter by Nick Folley, 'RTÉ and the Holy Grail of Revisionism'.

broadcast on 23rd October 2007 of The Killings at Coolacrease was entitled 'Speak it in a Whisper: Irish Ethnic Cleansing'. A few days previously, in *The Irish Times* (20th October), Sammon herself wrote: *"The attack on the family was, some argue, merely a land grab, perpetrated by men desperate to get their strike in before the war came to an end"*. Again, on the morning before the programme was broadcast, Ryan Tubridy on RTÉ Radio put it to Sammon regarding what had happened at Coolacrease: *"That's known nowadays as ethnic cleansing isn't it, I mean, it's the language of the time?"* She replied: *"At a local level, these things were happening, ... This obviously was more than an agrarian outrage."* [2]

On the programme itself, Alan Stanley, son of the loyalist paramilitary and Luggacurran fugitive William Stanley, and author of *I Met Murder on the Way,* set out the basic claim:

> "It's very hard not to wonder if somebody who knew that a Truce was imminent did not decide, "Well look lads, there's some nice pickings here, let's go for it". I know it's very dangerous to say that... but the land... of course... the land... of Ireland for the people of Ireland."

Stanley's speculation is backed up by various academics. Dr. Terence Dooley (Department of History at NUI Maynooth and author of *The Land for the People*): *"The Revolutionary period was used essentially as a pretext to run many of these Protestant farmers and landlords out of the local community, for locals to take up their land"*. With regard to the Pearsons he states:

> "William Pearson purchased the farm at Coolacrease in 1911. So, he moves into an area, he takes up a 340 acre farm that is surrounded by a multitude of small uneconomic holdings, where the local people—and they tend to be Catholic and Nationalist farmers—are looking for access to this land themselves. There is the added tinge of sectarianism, in the sense that Protestant land remains in Protestant hands."

Professor Richard English (Queen's University Belfast) adds his twopence worth:

> "So in that sense it was seen as an alien incursion. It was small

---

[2] Ibid. For transcript of the Tubridy Show see http://docs.indymedia.org/view/Main/CoolaCrease

scale, it was only the family, but in the sense that they were seen as aliens, people that didn't genuinely belong, weren't genuinely integrated into the community, and indeed were taking land from the rightful possession of the community, as locals would have seen it."

English speculates further that the Army of the Dáil shared these resentments:

"Looked at from the IRA's point of view, a family that was outside their own community, that had taken land that the IRA's community would have seen as rightfully theirs, that was fraternising with what they would have seen as the enemy. All of that would have been added together and seen as the Pearsons not only being outside the community, but as potentially targets that were legitimate."

For English this allows for some conclusions:

"You can justify killing someone on the grounds that they are an enemy of the war for freedom. But it could also be that in this case they own a large farm ...as in this case... it becomes divided up amongst the local people."

And Dr. William Murphy (Mater Dei Institute of Education) adds:

"It [the roadblock incident] allowed the local IRA to express the fears they had about the Pearsons. It justified their paranoia. It justified their social resentment at their landholding. And now they had a reason."

Dr. Dooley completes the thesis:

"William Pearson had lost his two eldest sons who he had used to run the farm. Essentially he couldn't get others from the local community to work for him. Raids continued on his property, and his attempts to sell...his cattle were boycotted by the locals. He couldn't sell his farm because any potential buyer was put off, e.g. William Percy, "The price I offered was 10,000 and I might have gone higher only the people would not allow any outsider to purchase the land. I was not allowed to close the bargain." So he was becoming squeezed all the time. What he attempted to do was cut his losses by actually selling the land to the Land Commission for around 5000 pounds..." [3]

The Pearsons' claims to the Irish Grants Committee that the execution of the brothers and the burning of the house were motivated

---

[3] A full annotated transcript of the programme is given in Appendix 9.

by a land grab by the local IRA, that following these incidents they were boycotted and their land raided, and finally that they had been compelled to sell their land to the Land Commission at a price greatly below its value are thus accepted at face value and without qualification by the programme makers and the academic experts interviewed on the programme.

The 'Hidden History' programme thus tars the people of the Cadamstown area—and specifically the people who received land from the division of the farm—as sectarian land grabbers, implicates the Army of the Dáil as actively complicit in this, and infers that the Land Commission officials who carried out the purchase of the farm and its sub-division were at worst complicit in this, and at best weak in the face of malign forces.

Niamh Sammon's Mysterious "Documents"

So what evidence did the programme produce for this? In the programme itself two pieces of evidence are referred to—the claims by the Pearsons to the Irish Grants Committee regarding boycott, the trampling of crops, property stolen from the farm, intimidation etc. and a note from William Percy of Frankford (i.e. Kilcormac) that he had been prepared to pay £10,000 for the farm and "*might have gone higher*" but had been prevented from doing so by local boycott. This note in fact is part of the Pearson claim to the Irish Grants Committee. In other words, the Pearsons' unsubstantiated claims to that British compensation body are accepted as proven, documented facts. It is significant that Dr. Dooley on the programme refers only to this source of evidence in giving his version of events.

It was only in the succeeding dispute before the Broadcasting Complaints Commission that Niamh Sammon introduced a new source for her claims. In her reply to Paddy Heaney's complaint about the programme she stated: "*The programme team was given access to the Land Commission records. Mr Heaney has not viewed these files*". And she responded to Pat Muldowney's complaint with the statement:

> "The theory that the Pearson killings were the result of a land grab was also examined by the programme makers. Documentation from

the Land Registry office and the Land Commission was made available to Dr. Terence Dooley, a highly respected historian and author of 'The Land for the People'. Dr. Dooley used the contents of these files as the basis for his comments." [4]

In the programme itself, however, Dr. Dooley, who makes several appearances on screen, makes no such claim to Land Commission documents as the basis of his statements. Not a single piece of evidence he cites is taken from the Land Commission or Land Registry records. His evidence comes exclusively from the claims of Sidney and William Pearson to the Irish Grants Committee. His interview snippets are accompanied by pictures of documents, mostly from the Irish Grants Committee file. Only two Irish land documents are shown—an extract from the Land Registry title of deed for the farm recording the Pearson purchase in 1911 and its sale to the Land Commission in 1923 (*"Folio 1863"*) and a copy of the Land Commission map of the Pearson farm (*"Estate of William Pearson, 11th August 1923, Record No. 10307"*).

The records of the Land Registry office are publicly available from its office in Dublin Castle. The records of the Land Commission, however, are not so readily available. The Commission itself ceased to exist in 1992 under the Irish Land Commission (Dissolution) Act 1992 and its records were transferred to the Records Branch of the Land Services Division of the Department of Agriculture & Food. This office is located on Bishop's Street in Dublin, in the same building as the National Archives, but separate from and not forming part of them. Land Commission records are not generally available to the public or to researchers as they have not yet been transferred to the National Archives and are also not available under the Freedom of Information Acts as they pre-date them.

---

[4] Broadcasting Complaints Commission, Producer's response to Paddy Heaney's complaint, January 2008, and Producer's response to Pat Muldowney's complaint, January 2008. The records of this complaint process have not been posted on the BCC website. However, they are published in full on http://docs.indymedia.org/view/Main/CoolaCrease. See also Chapter 11, 'Defending their Own: the Broadcasting Complaints Commission'. It is interesting that during the making of the programme Niamh Sammon in correspondence with Pat Muldowney referred to the archival sources accessed for the programme—these included the Land Registry but not the Land Commission (letter N. Sammon to P. Muldowney, 9th July 2007).

But, given Niamh Sammon's dramatic claim, we contacted the Department of Agriculture. The archivist of the Records Branch which holds the Land Commission records replied to us, outlining the policy of the Land Services Division on the personal records of the former Land Commission in their archives as follows:

> "The title documents form part of the root of title of those allotted land on the Estate and are not available to the general public for research etc.... The other files in this office are files on private individuals who sold land to the Land Commission and those who applied for and were allotted land by the former Commission. These files contain private and personal information on the individuals concerned and are not generally available for public inspection. The Department considers them to be day to day working documents that are often consulted in land ownership matters. Owners/purchasers and/or their personal/legal representatives are allowed access to relevant documents/maps by prior consultation with this office." [5]

In other words, title documents and records are only available to actual land holders. On this basis, Paddy Heaney, a landholder in Coolacrease, was given access to documents relating to the division of the estate, and in particular to the allocation to his father, and we reproduce some of these below. Dr. Dooley in the past has had access to former Land Commission archives. In his book *The Land for the People* he lists them as a general source used, but nowhere refers to files relating to specific title.[6]

At first sight it seems astounding that Dr. Dooley would allow himself to be used for such a crude propaganda purpose. In the

---

[5] Letter, Melanie Hall, Keeper of Records, Land Services Division to Philip O'Connor, 25th Feb. 2008.

[6] It is interesting that a work by one of Dr. Dooley's research students at Maynooth on the evictions and planting by Lord Lansdowne of his Luggacurran estate and the trouble there in 1922 (see the account in Chapter 1 above) also makes no reference to Land Commission records and again relies heavily on compensation claims made to the "Irish Grants Committee" in London. On this committee and its workings see the chapter below, 'An Extraordinary Set-Up: The Irish Grants Committee'. The thesis in question—which is used to support a generalised theory of Catholic land-grabbing—was published as Leigh-Ann Coffey, *The Planters of Luggacurran, County Laois, A Protestant community, 1879-1927*, Dublin, 2006. Coffey's inadequate study makes no reference to the loyalist paramilitary cell which operated at Luggacurran in 1920-21 and in which Pearson relatives (including William Stanley) were involved.

'Hidden History' programme Dooley mainly generalises on the role of "land hunger" in the "Irish revolution" and what he says specifically about the Pearson case is merely an uncritical regurgitating of their claims to the Irish Grants Committee. No other proof of any kind is offered for his statements.

Following the programme, I revisited his book. And there it is again: "*In a climate where land-hunger prevailed, taking land from so-called 'Protestant colonists' merely acted as a form of self-justification for taking land without having to pay for it*".[7] He refers for this among other cases to two of his favourite "examples"— events in 1922 on the Cosby and Lansdowne Estates at Rathdowney and Luggacurran respectively in Co. Laois (then Queen's County). But neither of these cases involved land-grabbing in any meaningful sense. The term "colonists" or "planters" was never a reference in rural Ireland to Protestant farmers in general (despite insinuations in the programme—and in Dooley's recent writings—to the contrary). It was an exact description—the people concerned were actually "planters": in the 1880s (i.e. just thirty years before the events examined here) the landlords concerned had evicted sitting Catholic tenants who were up to date in rent payments and installed Protestant tenants from the area or from Ulster and Scotland in a conscious attempt to replace a Catholic community with a Protestant one. But by the 1880s Catholics evicted from their tenancies were no longer sleeking off defeated to make a new home in America. Instead, through Davitt's 'Plan of Campaign', they stayed put, housed and supported by their neighbours, resolutely determined to get their land back. In the case of the people evicted from the Cosby and Lansdowne estates, some of them tried during the "inter-regnum" of 1922 to reverse the attempted ethnic cleansing of the 1890s and repossess their farms. It is not irrelevant to our story that the Pearsons counted several relatives among these very "planters." As Dr. Dooley himself relates in his book, however, this attempt at repossession of stolen farms was not supported by either the Free State forces or the IRA, and the new Free State authorities confirmed the Protestant settlers in the possession of the farms and found

---

[7] Terence Dooley, *The Land for the People. The Land Question in Independent Ireland,* Dublin, 2004, p. 44.

alternative holdings for the evicted Catholic families.[8]

The small scale planting on the Cosby Estate near Rathdowney and the much larger one on the Lansdowne Estate at Luggacurran were not typical of anything. They were throw-backs on the part of the landlords concerned to practices of an earlier period. Attempted sectarian plantations at this stage were rare indeed. One has to wonder at an academic like Dooley raising such obviously anomalous cases to the status of the general experience of either landlord or tenant, Catholic or Protestant farmer, at this time.

If the 'Hidden History' team had access to personal records from the distribution of the Pearson estate, this was with the express consent of the Records Branch of the Department of Agriculture and in breach of its own rules. Following Sammon's alarming claim to the Broadcasting Complaints Commission, we therefore approached the Land Records Branch again, and received the following reply:

> "I can find no record that RTÉ has had access to the former Irish Land Commission documents, stored in the Records Branch of the Department of Agriculture, Fisheries and Food, relating to the townland of Coolacrease (Pearson Farm). It is not possible to say if access to the documents was granted to Dr. Dooley at some stage by the former Commission." [9]

In other words, no access was granted to the records, unless prior to 1992! To clarify this anomaly I wrote to Dr. Dooley on 16th July 2008 and he rang me back on 5th September (!)—as we were going to press. He said he had seen the Land Commission file but would not state if he had examined all the records it contained. He also would not confirm whether or not it contained anything to substantiate Niamh Sammon's claims. I had examined files of the subdivision of the farm released on the application of Paddy Heaney (as a local landholder) and had several meetings with staff of the Records Branch and other Department of Agriculture offices which have authority over them. In addition much local information on the sub-division was available from Paddy Heaney's own researches.

---

[8] Ibid.

[9] Letter, Melanie Hall, Keeper of Records, Records Branch, Land Services Division to Pat Muldowney, 13th March 2008. Reprinted in Appendix 5.

But Dr. Dooley's statements meant that an accusation of complicity in a sectarian land grab by officials of the Land Commission had now to be answered. Such an accusation had never before been made as far as I was aware. I was therefore given additional detailed information on the sub-division of the farm without breaching the confidentiality of the personal title records. The correspondence of the relevant Department of Agriculture offices was again examined, and no trace of correspondence from Dr. Dooley or in relation to the Pearson farm could be found. Even the receipt books (for charges for photocopying etc.) showed no trace of such documentation being released. I was assured again that neither RTÉ nor anyone else had had access to the personal title records of the division of the estate. The map of the estate used on the programme could be available from several sources, but the Records Branch were adamant they had not released it.

If Dr. Dooley had examined the Pearson Estate records he would have found nothing to support the Sammon/Harris claims of a sectarian land grab. If any such evidence was held by the programme makers it would have featured in the programme, or been made available in the subsequent controversy. It wasn't. As we will see, the records of the division of the farm in 1923 provide no evidence for the theory of a sectarian land grab (in fact quite the opposite). The only basis for such a theory are the Pearsons' unsupported claims to the British "Irish Grants Committee" in 1926-8, which is why these form the only "evidence" presented in the 'Hidden History' programme.

A final word on Niamh Sammon's claims. The programme—unusually—did not employ a Historical Consultant, but it did employ two historical researchers, Philip McConway and Paul Rouse. Because of Sammon's claims regarding Land Commission documents, Pat Muldowney spoke with Paul Rouse, and asked if he had seen the Land Commission records which Sammon claimed verified the assertions of the programme. His defensive reply was that he "*wasn't the only researcher on the programme*". So we asked the other researcher, Philip McConway if he had seen them. He replied that he had been disturbed by the claims being made regarding "land-grabbing" (his own evidence contradicted the thesis), but when he asked Sammon—repeatedly—to allow him view the mysterious documents supporting this, she refused outright, claiming that the Land Commission documents were *"confidential"*. So even the historical researchers on the programme were never given access to the alleged documents! Finally, the credits at the end of the programme list the archives consulted in its making—the Records Branch of the Department of Agriculture which holds the Land Commission archives is not included.

We secured some key documentation from the Land Commission records on the division of the Pearson farm, and also held extensive talks with Records Branch staff regarding the process of the division of the estate.

Let us examine what the documents actually do tell us.

The Pearsons Move to Coolacrease

The Land Registry office contains all extant land registration records. "Folios" in the Land Registry are the records of ownership title to specific, mapped, registered areas of land since the 1890s. *"Folio 1863"* is the Land Registry record for what became the Pearson farm from the 1890s down to its purchase by the Land Commission in August 1923 and its subsequent sub-division, and it provides some interesting background to this story.[10]

The long term landlords over this land until 1909 had been the family of l'Estrange Malone (descended from the Lestronge family of the plantation era). This explains why, despite the subsequent sale of the land to the sitting tenants, the Benwells, and then to the Pearsons, the land was still being identified in Valuation Office records in the 1920s as the "Malone Estate". The land area in 1909 is given as 339 acres, 2 roods and 2 perches in the townland of Coolacrease, King's County, with a further 1 acre, 2 roods and 35 perches *"or thereabouts"* in the townland of Cadamstown, King's County. In total a farm of about 341 acres (= 142 Hectares).

In 1909 the Benwells, long-term Protestant tenants of the L'Estrange Malones, bought out their tenancy through the Land

---

[10] *County: King's. Folio 1863. Local Registration of Title (Ireland) Act, 1891. Register of Freeholders.* Land Registry Office, Dublin.

Commission under the Land Acts. On transfer of the lands to the Benwells the "*sporting rights*" on the lands remained with their former landlord and his son and successors for life. The Benwell sisters—Mary Hannah Benwell and Rhoda Banwell—took up full ownership in April 1909 at an annuity to the Land Commission of £90-13-6 "*until an advance of £2,790 has been repaid*" (i.e. until redemption of the purchase price). The ownership structure changed in February 1911 through the involvement of several additional owners, young English relatives of the elderly Benwell sisters, resident in England. The Benwells were a modestly well connected family with long roots in Ireland. The father of the house, Samuel John Benwell, had died around the turn of the century and, in 1918, the only daughter of the house was to marry the son of a General in Southern Rhodesia.[11] The Benwells were also a well liked and highly regarded family locally, and Paddy Heaney has collected many anecdotes about them. They employed local people on the farm, both before and after they changed from tenants to owners under the land reform acts. One local who worked on the farm did so not for payment, but in return for being allowed graze cattle on the farm. One of the elderly sisters liked to joke that they owned the farm but Mahon had the cattle. This was typical of the easy going relationships which existed with the Benwells.

Two years later, one of the elderly sisters died, and the farm, its ownership restructured for inheritance purposes to include younger relatives in England, was sold on again through the Land Commission. The new owners were the Pearsons. When the Benwells sold the farm to the Pearsons in 1911 they achieved a substantially lower price (£2,000)—of about 25%—than they had paid for it (£2,790). This represented a decline from £7-19s per acre in 1909 to £5-18s per acre in 1911 (the price included the house and farm buildings) and would appear to contradict the claims in the RTÉ programme that there was major upward market pressure on land prices in this area driven by what Dr Dooley called "*land hunger*".

As regards the new registered owner (as of 29th June 1911), William Pearson, he is described as a "*farmer*" of Derrylea,

---

[11] *The Times,* 22nd July 1918.

Monasterevin, Co. Kildare. This in itself is revealing, as this was not where the Pearsons actually lived before moving to Coolacrease. They had been living with their then young family in a house shared with another family near Rathdowney in the Aghaboe area in Co. Laois, about 30 miles south east of Cadamstown.[12] Monasterevin, in Co. Kildare, the address given by William Pearson (possibly his parent's address), is even further away, about 45 miles east of Cadamstown. It is, in fact, quite close to Luggacurran, the scene of Lord Lansdowne's infamous mass eviction and planting of Protestant farmers with Orange Order links from Ulster and Scotland just twenty years previously. The history of this event is related in Chapter 1 above. Luggacurran was known as a hotbed of loyalist activism, including of the militant type. It was from here, during the War of Independence, that William Stanley—father of Alan Stanley (author of *I Met Murder on the Way*) and relative of William Pearson—was to flee due to his paramilitary activity and go into hiding under the alias "Jimmy Bradley" on the Pearson farm in Coolacrease.

The Pearsons took possession of the Benwell farm "*in fee simple*" (i.e. paying cash) for the sum of £2,000. On the same date a bank charge of £900 was registered on the land in favour of the Bank of Ireland, repayable on demand in half yearly instalments at the then standard interest rate of "*five pounds per cent per annum*". This was presumably a loan towards the cost of purchasing the land, but may also have included amounts for investment in improvements and new machinery, as the Pearsons subsequently ran a modern mechanised farm and later auctioned off farm machinery.

These facts indicate that the Pearsons were buying into a substantial farm—incurring a long term loan in the process—with the intention of remaining for the long haul. William Pearson and his family were members of the Cooneyite faith, a radical sect more in the spirit of the Anabaptists than the Amish. The Cooneyites repudiated

---

[12] This was possibly the farm of 400 acres rented there by cousin Richard Pearson, a relative of William's, who was temporarily ejected in 1922 during a conflict over planted land as one of four farmers on the Cosby estate who had taken over "evicted farms" in the 1880s. They were re-instated by a Free State Land Court and their descendants are there to this day. According to Dooley (*Land for the People*, p. 44), the evicted Catholic families were given alternative land.

mainstream Protestantism and, like the Anabaptists, regarded the bible—on which considerable store is placed in mainstream Protestantism—as the "*paper pope*". Nevertheless, their Cooneyism did not interfere overmuch. While the Pearsons, unlike the Benwells before them, never employed local labour on their farm, they mingled with and were accepted by the local community. That their estrangement from the local community did not come about until the height of the War of Independence is shown by the fact that in 1919 William was elected by his neighbours to represent the Kinnitty area on the County Executive of the Farmers' Association.

The True Value of the Pearson lands

Much is made in the 'Hidden History' programme of the fine quality of the Pearson lands, allegedly much coveted by small holders around Cadamstown. Claims by the Pearsons that it was "*one of the first farms in Ireland*" and "*probably the best farm in King's County*" played a major role in their later claims to the Irish Grants Committee for compensation. So how good was it?

Until the mid-19th century, land valuations in Ireland were carried out under the Grand Jury Act (1634) which gave grand juries the right to raise taxes on the basis of the land values they set locally. This was the basis for what became known as the Poor Law Valuation. The first modern valuation process was carried out between 1830 and 1846 by Mr (later Sir) Richard Griffiths, with the process being completed in two further valuations in 1846-52 and 1852-65. This was a very thorough process, involving extensive collecting of evidence and the use of existing indices such as market prices, the Poor Law Valuation, etc.[13] Regardless of market price increases over the following century, the valuation amount remained the same, serving as a base figure. Rents and rates were set on the basis of it, as were later also the annuities repayable to the Land Commission for land purchases under the Land Acts. It also enables reasonable judgements to be made regarding comparative land values. The records of the Valuation Office also enable the sequence of ownership

---

[13] Raymond Crotty, *Irish Agricultural Production, Its Volume and Structure*, 1966, p. 298f.

of holdings in the Cadamstown-Coolacrease area to be traced for the period 1869-1934.

Valuation rates in the wider immediate area of Coolacrease range in this period between 8s and over £1 per acre (the latter being exceptional).[14] The rates for the Coolacrease area in 1909 on a per-acre basis were as follows: 11s per acre for Saville L'Estrange Malone's own farm (130 acres), 18s per acre for the Deegan farm (37 acres) and, for the largest farm, the 339-acre Benwell tenancy, a rateable valuation of £232, i.e. 13s per acre.[15] An additional small patch of land, between 1-2 acres, was outside the townland boundary, which explains why the farm is given as 339 instead of 441 acres. Updates to the list for 1912 record some changes of ownership, including the transfer of the Benwell farm to William Pearson (Coolacrease, holding 3), with the valuation remaining constant.[16]

What became the Pearson farm was listed therefore throughout the period 1880-1914 at an average valuation of 13s per acre in an area where valuations ranged from 8s to over £1 per acre. It was clearly a fairly good farm, but by local standards it was not exceptional, with a rateable valuation around average value. Valuation rates for Offaly farmland in turn were around the national average and notably less than the prime lands of Meath or Cork.

The valuation of the individual parcels into which the Pearson farm was divided in 1923 gives further information on its quality. The record for 1914-34 includes a margin note to the Pearson farm added in 1923: "*House burned*", and reducing the rateable valuation for the house and buildings, but not the land. The same record book contains a list of new entries for Coolacrease for the period 1923-4, i.e. following the sub-division of the Pearson farm by the Land Commission.[17] A further record gives valuations for 1935.[18] Combining these records gives the following picture (farm size rounded to nearest acre; p.a. = per acre):

---

[14] Valuation Office, Dublin, *Valuation Birr 1, 1857-1934,* Book A, sheet 18.

[15] Ibid., *Valuation Birr 1 1857-1934*, Book B, Sheets 11ff., and Book C, Sheet 14.

[16] Ibid., *Valuation Birr 1 1857-1934*, Book D, Sheet 17.

[17] Ibid., Sheets 17, 35-6.

[18] Ibid.,*Valuation Birr I 1934-69, Book No. 23, Co. Offaly, R.D. Birr No. 1*, Sheets 22ff.

Map ref	Land holder 1925	Acres	Val. £/s	Val. p.a.	Owner 1930s, etc.
3-4	John J. MacRedmond	30	23/10	15s	Inc. farm buildings, val. reduced £7->£3
6-7	M. Carroll	16	6/15	8s	Later Michael Carroll
8	Bernard Heaney	11	9/00	16s	Later Patrick Heaney
9-10	Jas. Delahunty	18	14/10	16s	Reverts to L.C., then James Dillon
11-12	Martin Egan	23	22/05	19s	Reverts to L.C. then to others
13-14	Wm. Glenn	30	20/10	14s	Later William McRedmond
15-16	John Grogan	27	21/10	16s	Later to Patrick McGunn
7-18	Thomas Dillon	29	21/00	14s	Later Patrick Rowe
19-20	John Multany	27	23/15	18s	Plus "house" with val. £3
21	Jas McCormack	18	13/05	15s	Later Patrick Haydon
22	John Carroll	19	11/10	12s	
23	Thos O'Brien	6	4/05	14s	
24	Bernard Heaney	16	8/05	10s	Later Brian and then Patrick Heaney
25	James Coughlan	13	7/15	12s	Later James Coughlan
26	Margaret Scully	11	6/10	12s	
27	Marie Anne Horan	0.2	0/15	N/a	Th. O'Brien (incl. "house—no value")

Valuations for full holdings range from 10s to 19s per acre. The final entry (Marie Anne Horan) is a minute parcel (2 roods) including valueless outbuildings. The house recorded for John Multany was built by the British Government under the scheme for war veterans. The Pearson farm as we know from its topography and also from these valuation records included quite good quality land around the road and house, and much poorer, wet and boggy land around the River Silver which was prone to flooding. While the total valuation of the Pearson farm remained constant, the valuation range when broken into 15 smaller parcels is notable, indicating a wide spectrum of land quality.

Here it should also be borne in mind of course that 341 acres worked as a unit, with the full resources of outhouses, farmyards and machinery, was a very different proposition from the 15 micro-farms on small bits of land into which it was divided, some of it bogland. The Glenns and McRedmonds who received Pearson land in the 1923 sub-division had the added cost (in Land Commission annuities or rates) of those buildings but not enough land to make this additional cost economic.

The rateable valuation of the Pearson land was thus consistent with very average values for land locally in 1890-1914, and was not among the more highly valued farms in the district. The sub-division of the land shows a range of valuations for the individual parcels, indicating the varying quality of the resulting parcels.

The Pearson farm was not only not the best land in the district, it was also not the only large Protestant owned farm in the immediate area. As is pointed out elsewhere in this book, Albert Jackson of Kilnaparson farmed 900 acres and the Ashtons 250 acres nearby. The Droughts and Biddulphs also farmed several hundred acres each. There were also large Catholic owned farms adjoining the Pearsons, such as J.J. Horan (105 acres), Din Deegan (80 acres), Brian Donnelly (330 acres), Tom Donnelly (80 acres), John and Mick McRedmond (140 acres), Joe O'Carroll (80 acres), and Tim Nolan (100 acres),

The Pearson farm was one of several large farms in the area, including four large Protestant owned farms. None of these other holdings suffered in any way during the War of Independence. In addition, the land of the Pearson farm was average to modestly good, and included much poor quality land.

The Alleged Squatting and Raiding of the Pearson Farm

Following the burning of Coolacrease House on 30th June 1921 and the family's move to England, the Pearsons, in their claims to the Irish Grants Committee, maintained they had been subject to "*boycott & terrorism*" and were "*compelled to sell it* [the farm] *to the Irish Land Commission*" for "*about 1/4 of its value*".[19] In Alan Stanley's book it is also claimed that the land was squatted and: *"In the end, of*

---

[19] Sidney Pearson, Application to the Irish Grants Committee, 28th October 1926. Appendix 6 below.

course, the Land Commission, under the new Irish Government [of 1923], *did take control and in what amounted to an* uti possidetis, *vested the freehold in the people who had moved in on the lands".*[20] They also claimed that following the executions the land had been raided, property stolen, and attempts to sell the farm, stock and machinery boycotted. These claims are repeated uncritically in the 'Hidden History' programme.

In fact, on the evening of the execution of the two Pearson brothers and the burning of Coolacrease House on 30th June 1921, British troops from Crinkle Barracks moved in and occupied the farm. Under their supervision, local women were drafted in to milk the cows. William Stanley fled to Northern Ireland and from there to England. William Pearson moved his family out. Mrs Susan Pearson, Sidney and Emily went to live with Henry Stanley (father of William Stanley) on his newly purchased farm in Wales after his hasty exit from Luggacurran following the exposure of William's collusion with the Auxiliaries. William Pearson himself stayed with a family called Blakemore in England, along with his son David and daughters Ethel and Matilda. William Pearson made frequent visits to Coolacrease to settle his affairs, staying when there in the coach house which had not been burned.[21]

And what of the local IRA during this period? Two key members, John Dillon and J.J. Horan, who were neighbours of the Pearsons and owners of substantial farms, had been arrested the day after the mass path incident in the first week in June and, following brutal treatment at the hands of the British military at Tullamore Jail, had been interned at the Curragh.[22] The week before the execution of the Pearson brothers, following their attack on the IRA roadblock on about 23rd June,[23] most of the IRA men involved had been arrested

---

[20] *I met murder on the way*, 3rd ed. (2007), p. 66.
[21] See Chapter 1.
[22] See Chapter 2. The internment at this time of the two men is confirmed by the *King's County Chronicle*, 9th and 16th June 1921. J.J. Horan was also a District Councillor for Kinnity.
[23] The exact date of the incident has not been recorded. Thomas Burke, o/c Offaly No. 2 Brigade IRA, in his report on the Pearson execution, recorded that *"C. Coy. (Kinnity) 3rd Battalion reported to me on 26/6/21 that some of their men have been fired on a few nights previously, whilst engaged in a road blockade operation"* ('Preliminary Report of execution of the two brothers Pearson of Cadamstown, Kinnity'—See Appendix 3).

in a major raid by the British military on Cadamstown. The roadblock volunteers were Mick Heaney, Tom Donnelly, Bill Glenn, Mick McRedmond, Tom Horan, Joe Carroll, Jimmy Delahunty, John Manifold, and Jack Brophy. In early July more men were rounded up and interned.[24] The interned prisoners—who included two of the three men who later received land at Coolacrease, Jimmy Delahunty and John J. McRedmond—only returned from internment on 10th November 1921.[25] Many of these men also fought on the Republican side in the Civil War and were interned again in 1922 and held until late 1923, including two of the three IRA men who later received land—Jimmy Delahunty and Bill Glenn—as well as Mick Heaney, who had been badly injured in the roadblock attack and whose father later received a small piece of land at Coolacrease.[26] So not only were many of the Cadamstown IRA interned following the roadblock attack and held throughout the months during which the Pearsons claim the boycott and raids occurred on their property, but the small number of IRA men who actually later received land were also interned throughout much of 1922-23 and hardly in a position to engage in land "*squatting*".

The 'Hidden History' programme gave a picture of near anarchic conditions in relation to land seizures and occupations during the War of Independence. But, according to Dr. Dooley himself, in his book *The Land for the People,* the Republican Arbitration Courts established in May 1920 to deal with land disputes and disturbances were highly successful and their rulings "*mostly accepted".* Where land seizures did occur the land was promptly restored to its legal owners by the Courts and these decisions were enforced by the IRA. While the majority of "*agrarian outrages* " reported were confined to the "*congested districts"* of the western counties, the system of Republican Courts operated throughout the country. Dooley summarizes: "*Land courts were remarkably successful in bringing*

---

[24] Some of these are identified in a report in the *Midland Tribune,* 9th July 1921. A photograph of Cadamstown prisoners in Hare Camp, Curragh, is included in Appendix 1.

[25] As we went to press a further roadblock volunteer—Jack Brophy—was identified. He was a fourth man wounded by the Pearsons. See Chapter 1.

[26] The events of the Civil War in this area are recounted in Paddy Heaney, *At the foot of Slieve Bloom.*

stability to threatening circumstances", and even quotes Paul Bew as accepting that the courts dealt promptly and fairly with land disputes and seizures.[27] The role of these courts and their approach to preserving order—including in relation to land and property—is well dramatised in Ken Loach's film, *The Wind That Shakes the Barley*. Throughout the same period, the British system also continued to operate through the RIC and the District and County Courts.

Offaly was not a *"congested district"* but Republican land courts did meet in the midlands, presided over by Judge Kevin O'Sheil, including at sittings in Birr and Tullamore. At one stage the Pearsons appealed to the Republican Courts regarding a small amount of property that had been stolen, and the court promptly ordered this to be returned to the family. But the evidence available contradicts the other claims by the Pearsons of extensive theft, boycott and squatting. Up to December 1921, RIC County Inspectors' *Monthly Reports* regularly included accounts of alleged *"agrarian outrages"* and of incidents of alleged land *"grabbing"* and *"squatting"*. The RIC County Inspector's reports for King's County includes several such *"agrarian outrages"* in Co. Offaly, but none in the Cadamstown-Coolacrease area. The *King's County Chronicle*, the principal unionist newspaper in Co. Offaly, also reported such news—including the executions and burning of Coolacrease House—but it too never refers to any incidents of *"agrarian outrage"* at Cadamstown or Coolacrease.

A Dublin Castle press report claimed that after the burning of the house 10 horses, 10 cows, 1 bull, 88 young cattle, 51 sheep and lambs, 3 rams and 3 fat pigs, a dray and creel and a set of harness had been stolen,[28] and William Pearson did lodge a claim with the County Court for a lengthy list of property. But, acting on information supplied by the RIC, the Court confirmed that only three pigs, a gate and a harness had been taken (the ones ordered returned by the Republican Court) and awarded compensation for these items.[29] He also claimed compensation for the burning of the house and contents,

---

[27] Dooley, *Land for the People*, pp. 47-50.
[28] Dublin Castle Statement, 9th July 1921, Code 1029. Reprinted in Appendix 4.
[29] Philip McConway, 'The Pearsons of Coolacrease', *Tullamore Tribune*, 7th and 14th Nov 2007. These issues are dealt with in greater detail in Chapter 1.

other buildings damaged, and the loss of his two sons, and Judge Fleming K.C. in Birr Quarter Sessions on 12th October 1921 awarded compensation totalling £3,840 for the burning of the house and the death of his sons.[30] The records of the Land Commission on the Pearson farm also contain no reference to land squatting or grabbing at any time during 1921-23.

The only contemporary "record" that anything of the horrendous persecution and land squatting alleged by the Pearsons occurred following the events of 30th June are the Pearsons' own later allegations to the "Irish Grants Committee". Alan Stanley's outlandish claims of the grabbing and squatting of Pearson land during in 1921-22 are a flight of fantasy. It never happened.

Also, Pearson's later claim that he had been offered £10,000 for his farm, but that the potential buyer, a William Percy of Frankford (Kilcormac), had been refused permission by the priest to buy it has no credibility. Aside from the absurd notion that local clergy had to give permission for the sale of property (as claimed by Pearson), the farm was in fact put up for auction on 21st August 1921 but, according to both the nationalist *Midlands Tribune* and the unionist *King's County Chronicle* of 27th August 1921, had been withdrawn when the highest bid—by a Mr. Finnamore of Kilcormac—failed to reach the reserved price. There is no doubt that in both the economic and political conditions then pertaining, it was a difficult time to sell land. Pearson also later claimed that when he sought to auction off stock and machinery from the farm, local boycott had forced him to nearly give them away at prices far below their true value. As we will see, even the valuer operating for the Irish Grants Committee dismissed these claims, however, and judged that he had received a "*fair price*" for them. This further undermines the claim of a boycott.

Following the sale of the stock and machinery, the farm was no longer worked. The Pearsons settled where they had moved in England and Sidney soon after purchased and was operating a 163-acre farm in the Home Counties. Following the political division over the Treaty, the local IRA remained on the republican side and occupied Crinkle Barracks. Although the Cadamstown area was

---

[30] 'Schedule Showing Value of Losses and Compensation Claimed and Received'. See Appendix 6.

strongly republican and later largely supportive of Fianna Fáil, at the start of the Civil War the Free State forces rapidly secured control of the area. Many local republicans were soon again interned.[31] The farm itself was secured by the local establishment—Fr. Houlahan commissioned Dan Downey, a local labourer, to repair and maintain the boundaries and fencing of the farm which were becoming derelict. As soon as the opportunity arose, William Pearson, through his legal representatives, opened negotiations with the Land Commission on the purchase of the farm.

The claims of land grabbing and squatting and of major property theft from the farm in the period after the burning of the house were later fabricated by the Pearsons to embellish their compensation claims to the Irish Grants Committee in London. Considering that that body never sought nor heard any contradicting evidence, it is little wonder that the Pearsons sought to maximise their case to it and hence the compensation they would receive. This is some excuse for the exaggerated stories of the Pearsons to the Irish Grants Committee. It is difficult to see any comparable excuse for the unqualified parroting of these stories by Dr. Dooley and the 'Hidden History' programme.

The Land Commission Purchase of the Pearson Farm

The Irish Land Commission was created as a rent fixing commission by the Land Law (Ireland) Act 1881. 'Fair rents' were set on the basis of the Griffiths Valuation described above. Following the Land Acts of 1885 (Ashbourne), 1891 (Balfour), and especially 1903 (Wyndham) and 1909, which effectively ended the system of colonial landlordism in Ireland, the Commission either assisted land transfers and land sales, or took over estates scheduled for dissolution and oversaw full reimbursement of the sale price to the landlord and the allocation by sale of the land to former tenants, small landowners and landless people, repayable by annual "annuities". The 1909 Act introduced the principle of compulsory sale of landlord estates. It further oversaw the subdivision of other lands which came into its

---

[31] See Paddy Heaney, *At the foot of Slieve Bloom*, pp.311 ff.

ownership and took land back into possession where new owners returned the properties due to inability to pay or other reasons. The Land Acts of 1903-09 finally reversed the process of colonisation and re-settlement. Land was not given back, of course, but purchased from the existing landlords at market prices. Land purchased was then vested in the Land Commission for repurchase by tenant farmers or new landholders on the basis of the price paid. While the annuity re-payments were based on the Griffiths Valuation, as previously rents had been, the full purchase price was to be recouped over time. This was so as to keep annuities at a level which could be met by land-holders. The greater the purchase price, therefore, the longer it would take to clear it. It should be noted that the annuities were generally a lot lower than the previous (exorbitant) rents had been, by as much as 25% to 50% according to Raymond Crotty.[32] On 31st March 1923 the Land Commission transferred to the authority of the Irish Free State and continued the process of land purchase and division.

When Fianna Fáil came to power in 1932 it did so with a promise to end the system of neo-colonial financial drain represented by the payment to the British State of the annuities collected by the Irish State, totalling the then very large amount of nearly £3.2m per annum (the weekly wage of an agricultural labourer at this time was about £1.25). This was in a context of total Irish GNP of something like £140m, total exchequer receipts available to the Free State of about £24m and an annual budget of about £22m. The annuities being transferred to England therefore represented the equivalent of a seventh of the total national budget by the late 1920s. Ireland was a poor country—total British GNP at the time was over two hundred times the Irish value.[33] While annuities were henceforth retained by the Irish State, the land holders continued to pay them. In 1938, under the Anglo-Irish Agreement ending the "Economic War" through which Britain had blockaded Irish exports in response to the withholding of the annuities, a final payment by the Irish State of

---

[32] Crotty, *Irish Agricultural Production,* p. 89.
[33] Figures from Department of Industry and Commerce, *Ireland—Statistical Abstract 1931* pp. 35, 126 ff. and http://en.wikipedia.org/wiki/The World Economy: Historical_Statistics.

£10m was agreed. De Valera later halved the cost of the annuities payable by Irish landholders. Annuities continued to be paid to the Irish Government by landholders in exceptional cases down to the 1970s.

In 1983 the Commission ceased acquiring land and this marked the beginning of the end of the Commission's reform of Irish land ownership. It was dissolved on 31st March 1992 by the Irish Land Commission (Dissolution) Act, 1992, and most of its remaining liabilities and assets transferred to the Minister for Agriculture and Food.

On the issue of the sale of the farm to the Land Commission in 1923, the Pearsons later claimed to the Irish Grants Committee that they had been forced to sell it to the Commission at a price way below its value. Sidney Pearson stated that they had been "*compelled to sell it to the Irish Land Commission in 1922* [sic] *for about 1/4 of its value ... The value of the farm before the burning would be £17,000.*" [34] William Pearson stated: "*In normal times I could have sold the farm at £15,000*" but "*as a result of subsequent persecutions and destruction of property I had to sell the land—one of the best farms in Ireland—for a quarter of the value to the Land Commission*".[35] To support this he enclosed the note from William Percy with the claim that he would have paid £10,000 for it and a note from the auctioneers Telford of Birr that the best of the land was worth £10 per acre (i.e. a maximum total value of £3,410) but that with the "*interest in the holding previous to the burning*" the total value would be £17,000. These figures are nonsense. Niamh Sammon went a step further: "*We have Land Commission documents that show the sale was forced*".[36] But the records of the Land Commission refute that: the transaction was a voluntary purchase with no compulsion involved.

Following the sale of the machinery and stock, the farm fell derelict. As soon as the opportunity arose, William Pearson, through

---

[34] Sidney Pearson, Application to the Irish Grants Committee, 28th October 1926 (see Appendix 6).

[35] William Pearson, Application to the Irish Grants Committee, 14th April 1927 (see Appendix 6).

[36] Interview for 'Hidden History' programme with Pat Muldowney, 28th July 2007: http://docs.indymedia.org/view/Main/CoolaCrease

his legal representatives in Dublin, opened negotiations with the Land Commission on its purchase. The largest file in the Land Commission archives on the farm is the correspondence negotiating the purchase price. The records of this file centre on the value of the farm, its buildings and the improvements made to it, with no references to squatting or grabbing of land. Finally the farm, which the Pearsons had bought for £2,000 in 1911, was purchased by the Land Commission on 23rd August 1923 for £4,817 (i.e. nearly two-and-a-half times the price they had paid for it).[37] This, as will be seen below, was a good price.

Alan Stanley states in his book: "*In the end, of course, the Land Commission, under the new Irish Government, did take control and in what amounted to an u*ti possidetis, *vested the freehold in the peoples who had moved in on the lands*".[38] We have seen that the notion that the Pearson farm was "squatted" is nonsense. But the idea that the Land Commission would have accepted the claims of "squatters" and have vested ownership of land in people who had "grabbed" it is even more far fetched. The 'Hidden History' programme nevertheless adopts this view and paints a picture of Land Commission distribution taking place in an atmosphere of land grabbing and sectarian violence, and capitulating to it. Land distribution is a highly sensitive issue, and the authority and respect of the Land Commission and its officials rested on its reputation for scrupulous adherence to procedure. In his book, *The Land for the People,* Dr. Dooley himself shows that squatted land was never accepted by either the Sinn Féin authorities of 1919-21 or the Free State authorities of 1922-23. The scrupulousness of Land Commission officials in undertaking the mammoth task of land sub-division and allocation in Ireland has never before been called into question as far as I am aware. Indeed, the records of Dáil debates on the Land Commission in the 1920s contain regular declarations by deputies across all parties praising the integrity of Land Commission officials

---

[37] Irish Land Commission, Record No. E.C. 10307, *Estate of William Pearson, King's County, Order vesting lands in the Irish Land Commission*, 2nd August 1923. See Appendix 5. Additional information from Department of Agriculture, Records Branch.

[38] *I Met Murder on the Way,* p. 67 (2nd ed.).

in the sub-division of estates and their resistance to party pressures.[39] This is yet another reputation which the Harris/Sammon 'team' have sought to drag in the mud to feed their own sectarian fantasies.

The Division of the Pearson Farm by the Land Commission

Does anything in the Land Commission records on the division of the farm support the claims of a sectarian land-grab countenanced by the Land Commission made by the 'Hidden History' programme? Besides the records examined, I had several conversations with Land Records Branch staff on this issue. This information was given to me without breaking the confidentiality of personal records and only as relevant to my enquiries. The records contain nothing which corroborated the sectarian '*land grab*' theory. Even the Pearsons in their efforts to inflate the price being negotiated with the Commission never made any such claims in their correspondence with the Commission. The records do contain claims of pressures from 'irregulars' and other 'outsiders' which the local curate, Fr. Houlahan, urged should be rejected. Throughout the sub-division process Fr. Houlahan continually intervened to seek to prevent land being made available to known Republicans. These pressures were ultimately disregarded by the inspectors concerned, who carried out the process in strict adherence to procedure.

The purchase and re-allocation of the Pearson farm in 1923 was overseen and minutely managed by inspectors of the Commission, under the supervision of a senior official, Mr. T.H. Blackall, a man who had loyally served the Commission under the British Administration and continued to do so under the new Free State regime. There were of course disputes over boundaries, eligibility and other issues, and also special pleading on behalf of particular individuals, notably by Fr. Houlahan. Houlahan despised Republicans and, as a staunch Redmondite, was particularly supportive of claims on behalf of former British ex-servicemen who had *"served King and Country"*. This was not as outlandish then at it may seem now, and

---

[39] E.g. in the debates on the Land Commission budget, Dáil Éireann, 'In Committee on Finance' (Vote 54), March 1928. Available online at http://historical-debates.oireachtas.ie/en.toc.dail.html.

Land Commission officials, who were civil servants, were receptive to such arguments. In June 1918, following the national movement which led to the abandonment of British plans to introduce conscription in Ireland, Lord Lieutenant French issued a new enticement to enlist in the form of a declaration promising land to war veterans: "*Steps are, therefore, being taken to ensure, as far as possible, that land shall be available for men who have fought for their country.*" In December 1919 the British Government passed an Act to provide land to Irish war veterans. By March 1921 the Land Commission, acting under this Act, had purchased 5,046 acres of untenanted land for this purpose and were negotiating on an additional 10,000 acres.[40] This was the context for Fr. Houlahan's endeavours and for the special consideration expected to be shown by the Commission to former British Army soldiers in the sub-division of the Pearson estate.

In the *Schedule giving Particulars of Division of Untenanted Land* of the Land Commission relating to the Pearson farm (reproduced in Appendix 5), the British Army war records of individuals are specifically noted opposite their allocation details. In one case only did Fr. Houlahan make a representation on behalf of a former IRA man, Jimmy Delahunty. As Paddy Heaney has related, Jimmy Delahunty's sister and mother were involved in cleaning and maintaining the local Catholic church building. This was why Houlahan intervened on Delahunty's behalf while he would not do so for other Republicans. In fact he intervened on several occasions to try to prevent allocations of land to republicans. In other words, it was despite rather than because of his republicanism that Houlahan appears to have assisted Delahunty's application. In the case of Paddy Heaney's own father, a Republican though not a member of the IRA, Houlahan refused to assist his claim, except to suggest he write himself to the Land Commission, which he promptly did.

The allocation of various parcels of the Pearson farm after its purchase by the Land Commission is related in detail in Chapter 1 above, based on local knowledge. Immediately following the purchase of the farm by the Land Commission from the Pearsons on 23rd August 1923, Fr. Houlahan organised a meeting of interested local people with Commission inspectors in the house of Dan Downey, a

---

[40] Dooley, *Land for the People*, p. 37.

Free State supporter. People not informed of this meeting later protested at their exclusion and sought a hearing. Their claims were then also heard by the inspectors. In the initial proposed allocations, the first allocations were made to three men with British war records, and offers of land were turned down by several people because of the high price. The records show that in fact not a great many people were interested in the land. Over the following months, and following much correspondence and alterations, the inspectors completed their proposed sub-division of the estate.

In Appendix 5 we reproduce the map entitled *Irish Land Commission (Estates Commissioners)—Estate of William Pearson, King's County*, signed by the senior inspector, T. H. Blackall and dated 11th August 1923 (LC Record No. 10307). It records the boundaries of the estate purchased, using Ordnance Survey Maps 31, 32 and 37, and the parcels into which it was subdivided (a version of this map with the same document number is the only Land Commission document—with the farm area coloured in—to feature in the 'Hidden History' programme). The division into parcels occurred before the decisions were made on allocations to particular individuals, and the creation of parcels was carried out on the basis of a variety of criteria and received practice. Allocation to individuals only occurred afterwards. The numbers on each parcel of land on the estate can be noted. These run in two series: 1-15 and 1a-9a. Where there are two parcels with the same number, but with a letter attached to the second one (e.g. 1, 1a), these were usually allocated to the same person. This is where split parcels were allocated, consisting of a piece of relatively good land (higher land, nearer the road) and a piece of unproductive wet land (beside the Silver River, which included cutaway bog and is very prone to flooding). The Commission also oversaw the construction of a roadway through the farm (marked on the map) to enable access to the new parcels. This is further evidence of the meticulous approach adopted by the Commission in allocating land from the Pearson estate. Accompanying the map and carrying the same Record No. 10307 is the *Schedule of Area—Estate of W. Pearson,* a list giving the precise acreage of each numbered parcel.

Also accompanying the map and carrying the same Record No. 10307 is the *Estate of William Pearson—Schedule giving Particulars of Division* (the original is also reproduced in Appendix 5). In the few cases where original names are crossed out and replaced with new names, this is where ownership changed soon after or where the offer of purchase was turned down by the potential purchaser before actual allocation. We examine these particular cases below. This document also specifies the clause under Section 17 (1) of the Land Act 1909 under which the decision in relation to each allocation was made. Most allocations ("a") were what were called "direct allotments" to owners of existing near-by properties and, though two landless men did receive allocations, none were made specifically under the provision for landless labourers (see Column 5 of the 'Schedule'). As was often the case with untenanted land in non-congested districts, land which became available was allocated by the Land Commission to adjacent land holders to make their holdings more viable. It will be noted that the Estate being divided is referred to as the Malone Estate. This is a reference to the L'Estrange-Malones, the previous long-term landlords over the property. (The Benwells had bought out their tenancy in 1909 under the Land Acts and sold it on in 1911—again through the Land Commission—to the Pearsons).

Only two of those who received land did not have a holding already—Jim Delahunty and Bill Glenn. Delahunty was the son of the former local postman, and also grazed a cow or two on the "long acre" (i.e. the roadside). He was a Republican and founding member of Cadamstown IRA, and was interned following the roadblock attack. As explained above, although a staunch Republican—which he remained—Fr. Houlahan supported his claim despite rather than because of this.

The other landless man, Bill Glenn, had also been in the IRA. Both had been interned during the Civil War and had therefore not been around during any of the intimidation alleged by Pearson. But Glenn's case too was not straightforward. His father had been a British Army soldier, posted to Birr in the 1880s with a Scottish Regiment. During the Land War, a local publican, Tommy Davis, was sentenced to three years in Mountjoy for refusing to provide his cart for use by an RIC party headed for the Clanrickard Estate outside Portumna in Co. Galway to "assist" in an eviction. He was welcomed home on his return from prison by bonfires and an outdoor party of the local community. Some of the Scottish soldiers sent from Birr to keep order in fact joined in the festivities, and at these Glenn's father had met and later married Mary Egan, the daughter of a local family. The friendly relationship of Scottish soldiers at Crinkle Barracks with the local community was a notable feature of the area. According to an article by Paul Rouse on the GAA website, *An fear rua,* Scottish soldiers from Crinkle were present as spectators and stewards at the first GAA All Ireland Hurling Final, which was held in Birr in 1888.[41] Bill's father was killed in action in the First World War, leaving his mother, who was to move onto the farm with him, a "Somme widow". In addition, Bill's brother, Tom, was also a British Army soldier in the "Great War", though he survived and went to live in England.

The only individuals with a note appended regarding their biographies are the three former British Army soldiers John Fehery [*"Ex-serviceman, Irish Guards, service 3 1/2 yrs France"*], John Grogan [*"Ex-serviceman xx? R.G?.A. Service in France badly wounded"*] and John Multany [*"Ex-serviceman Service 3 1/2 yrs France*]. In only one of these cases (John Fehery, a member of a family with several small farm holdings in the area) was the allocation not proceeded with. Paddy Heaney has established that Fehery turned down the offer of land because of its cost. The fact that neither the Land Valuation records (see above) nor the Land Registry[42] ever list him as having been an owner of the land in question would confirm that he never accepted it in the first place. Another recipient of land, James Coughlan (parcel no. 15), came from a previously pro-unionist family in the area. It is significant that there is no tradition locally of resentments at an unfair distribution or of there having been any unusual aspects to the sub-division—apart from the preferences for non-republicans promoted by Fr. Houlahan.

On the basis of Paddy Heaney's information combined with the Land Commission records, we have—very reluctantly—made the following breakdown regarding the affiliations of people who received land, as well as other relevant aspects:

---

[41] Cf. Paul Rouse, 'Original red-leather day for Thurles', *The Irish Times,* 2nd April 2008 and commentary on the 'Speak Out Page' of the G.A.A. website, www.anfearrua.com

[42] The Land Registry Office record for this title is *Folio 7399, King's County, Register of Freeholders.* This gives map references 2A and 2B and cites James Delahunty as owner.

Parcel	Name	*Allocation* (acres)	Basis*	Affiliations and other relevant information
1,1A	Michael Carroll	16	a	Known as Mick "the Yank" Carroll, on his return from USA he was allocated sixteen acres along Silver River, which he named "Coney Island". Not to be confused with his namesake, IRA man Mick Carroll, who did not receive land and emigrated to Melbourne, Australia with Mick Heaney and other Republicans after the Civil War.
2	Bernard Heaney [= Brian Heaney]	11	a	A Republican, but not in the IRA, he lived in the USA and helped to fundraise for Sinn Fein in New York. Heaney returned in late 1921 and bought a small piece of land at Cadamstown. Known as 'Brian', he was father of historian Paddy Heaney. He was also a relation of Mick Heaney, who was shot and wounded by the Pearsons at the roadblock (he died of his wounds some five years later, after taking the Republican side in the Civil War and emigrating to Australia). This land was initially allocated to Mick's father, Bernard, who had a farm in Glenlitter. On Fr. Houlahan's advice Brian Heaney wrote to the Commission about the mistake, "threatening" the Commission—that he would "*lay the matter before my member of parliament*"! (see documents in Appendix 5). The matter was later resolved, with Brian buying the land from Bernard Heaney.
2, 2A	John Fehery [*Name and allocation crossed out*]	29	d	Served with the Irish Guards in France throughout the war. One of the first allocations (29 acres), he turned it down due to the high price. On the Land Commission file here his name is crossed out, and in fact does not appear in the Land Registry or Valuation Office records as ever

* Basis of allocation under the 1903 and 1909 Land Acts

				having taken up ownership of this parcel in Coolacrease. John Walsh, a labourer in Kinnitty was also offered land in September 1923, but declined it. The Commission later gave part of the Fehery allocation to Brian Heaney, and another part to James Delahunty when he was released from Civil War internment (next entry).
2A, 2B	James Delahunty	18	d	Founding member of Cadamstown IRA. Interned at the time of the Pearson execution and again (by the Free State) at the time of land division. Landless labourer with a cow on the 'long acre'. Later postman. Family members—who looked after St. Lughna Church—were close to Fr. Houlahan, however, so, unusually, the PP intervened on his behalf to support a claim to some land. Received a small allocation (18 acres of poor, wet land), part of the allocation turned down for cost reasons by the former British soldier, Ferehy. The Delahunty holding reverted to the Land Commission in 1950.
3, 3A	Martin Egan	30	d	A labourer from Glenlitter, when he died in 1934 the land was invested in his widow, Kathleen. The annuities were revised downward from £20 to £12 in 1943 but were still not cleared when the land reverted to the Land Commission in 1947.
4, 4A1	John J. Redmond	30 3	d	IRA man interned after the Pearson executions. 30 acres including the ruins of Coolacrease House (3 roods). The addition of farm buildings made this land especially costly and difficult to allocate. The holding was later sold on to its present owners.
5, 5A	William Glenn	30	d	IRA member. Interned in Civil War, was interned at the time of the division of the farm. On his release, with his mother, a

					Somme widow, he received thirty acres. They moved in to the coach house in Coolacrease. Bill had worked as a labourer, and his brother Pat, like his father also a soldier in the British Army in the war, worked in England. The land was later sold on to its present owners.
6, 6A	John Grogan	27		a	Served with the British Army in France in the War, and was seriously wounded. Received first allocation (27 acres). As an ex-British soldier, had a house built for him by the British Government. He was a former employee of local farmer, Albert Jackson of Kilnaparson, and not the Pearsons, as later claimed by Niamh Sammon.
7, 7A 2	Daniel Downey	28 3		a d	Single man and a labourer, strong supporter of Treaty. Close to Fr Houlahan who secured him the job of repairing the fencing on Coolacrease farm in 1922-23. Initial division of the farm by the Land Commission was held in his house. He received 28 acres and some buildings (3 roods).
8, 8A	Thomas Dillon (crossed out), later Patrick Rowe	30		d	Thomas Dillon was not an IRA man. The farm later failed and in 1927 reverted to the Commission. Due to lack of local interest, the Commission re-allocated it in 1928 to Patrick Rowe from Clonaslee in Co. Laois (see valuation record).
9, 9A	John Multany	27		d	Served with British Army in France in the War. Allocation was among the first three. As an ex-soldier also had a house built by the British Government. Farm has remained in the family.
10	James McCormack	18		d	Local blacksmith, non-political, received 18 acres. The annuities were finally cleared in the mid-1970s.
11	John Carroll	19		a	Not IRA, though pictured in the internment camp photo of Cadamstown men in

				1921. He had been arrested in the line-up. of locals following the Pearson executions. A hat lost by a member of the execution party was found to fit him! He received 19 acres.
12	Thomas O'Brien	6	a	Apolitical. Owned a small mountainous holding. In the 1940s he sold his 6 acres to Elizabeth Byrne.
13	Bernard Heaney	16	a	Father of Mick Heaney, the IRA man wounded at the roadblock by the Pearsons. Mick emigrated to Australia after his release from Civil War internment. Bernard, who was confused with Bernard 'Brian' Heaney (see Plot 2 above), owned an adjacent farm and received this parcel of 16 acres in addition. As the valuation records show, it was very poor land.
14	James Coughlan	13	a	A carpenter, he worked for local Protestant farmer Captain Drought. Father was in the British Army and family was known as unionist sympathizers who on occasion flew the Union Jack. Record note "R.O. in Bank" (= "Receivable Order" lodged in bank).
15	Margaret Scully	11	a	Widow of a labourer who lived in Cadamstown village, she was the mother of Bernard Scully a boy of 14 who was in the line-up after the Pearson execution, but the British Army officer in charge ordered him to be released. Nearly fifty years later Bernard was to sell the 11-acre plot on to local farmer Joe Young.

In the division of a large farm by the Land Commission in the Cadamstown area it would have been strange if some active republicans were not amongst those who received land. In fact, if anything, local former IRA men are conspicuous by how few they were among those receiving allocations. Some who received land, while not IRA members, were republican supporters. But that is hardly surprising. There were also three former British Army men, others who were known to be Free State supporters or non-political, and one family that was formerly unionist in its allegiance. The Land Commission inspectors were sensitive to the need for local balance, and therefore ensured some Republicans were among those offered allocations.

To put things further in perspective: Paddy Heaney identifies the membership of the Cadamstown IRA in 1919-21 as follows: Michael McRedmond, Joseph Manifold, John Manifold, Martin Guinan, Michael Guinan, Thomas Donnelly, John McRedmond, John O'Connor, Patrick Carroll, James Delahunty, Joseph Carroll, John Dillon, William Glenn, Joseph Heaney, Michael McDonnell, Joseph Honan, Michael Heaney, Thomas Horan, John Joe Horan, Jack Dooley, Jack Brophy, Luke Daly, Patrick Honan and William Heaney.

Of these twenty three men, only three received land at Coolacrease: Bill Glen (a mixed allocation of 30 acres of poor and good land), Jimmy Delahunty (18 acres of mostly poor land), John J. McRedmond (a mixed allocation of 30 acres of poor and good land). Of these, only one (J.J. McRedmond) had a holding nearby. While all three had been active in the War of Independence, none can be regarded as among the leading figures of the Cadamstown IRA.

There simply was no sectarian or republican-led "land-grab" at the Pearson farm in Coolacrease.

The Question of Price

We have noted the extravagant claims later made by the Pearsons regarding the value of the farm, and also seen that under the Griffiths Valuation the assessed value of the Pearson land was fairly average for that area of Offaly.

The decade before Britain's "Great War"—when the Pearsons bought the farm—was one of rising agricultural prosperity in the wake of the Land Reform Acts, especially the 1903 Act which saw a major increase in the quantity of land transferred to tenant ownership. But for the same reason the open market for land experienced something of a glut. Raymond Crotty, the leading agricultural economist of twentieth century Ireland, found that under the Land

Acts, annuities (which averaged nationally about £1 per acre including interest) were about half what used to be paid in rent (in the mid-19th century rents in King's County averaged nearly £2). While this meant that the transfer of ownership led to a significant increase in disposable farm cash, competitive rents were replaced by uncompetitive land prices and the effect of the mass transfer to owner occupancy in the early 20th century was that "*it substantially destroyed the competitive market for land*". The greater impact of the transfer of land ownership was to increase farm incomes.[43] This might explain the loss made by the Benwells on the re-sale of their farm to the Pearsons in 1911.

The "Great War" changed all this, with a massive boom in demand for agricultural products to feed the British war economy. The boom however came to an abrupt end in 1920. Historian Louis Cullen:

> "The First World War, and especially the two years after it, were the most hectic period of agricultural prosperity in Ireland's history... Agricultural prices trebled from a base figure of 100 in 1911-13 to 288 in 1920... Prosperity was pronounced in the farming community... The great agricultural boom collapsed in 1920. Prices slumped. The index of agricultural prices fell from 288 in 1920 to 160 in 1924... Businessmen or farmers who had borrowed money were in great difficulties; the banks themselves were gravely embarrassed by the fall in the value of shares or land pledged as collateral for loans... The years 1921 to 1923 were years of economic contraction." [44]

So, apart from the war-induced boom in agricultural produce, which led to a trebling of prices, things rapidly deteriorated in 1920 and soon values were almost halved again. This was graphically illustrated by debates in the Dáil on the 1923 Land Bill, which sought to ameliorate excessive costs being borne by new landholders since the collapse of prices in late 1920.[45]

If the pre-war rise in on-farm prosperity was not necessarily reflected in rising land prices, this changed dramatically in the

---

[43] Crotty, *Irish Agricultural Production,* pp. 88-93. King's Co. rents, ibid. p.294.

[44] L. M. Cullen, *An Economic History of Ireland since 1660,* London, 1972, p. 171-2.

[45] Dáil Éireann, *Proceedings,* Vol. 4 (4 July, 1923), Land Bill 1923, pp. 125ff.

wartime boom. In 1928, questioned on high prices being paid to landlords for their land, the government told the Dáil:

> "Under the 1903 Act the average price paid per acre was 11.4 pounds; under the 1909 Act the price was 16.2 pounds and under the 1923 Act the average price paid per acre was 10.3 pounds These figures show conclusively that we are buying land to-day cheaper than it was bought under any of the earlier Acts." [46]

The high prices paid out under the 1909 Act related mainly to the boom years of 1914-19. After the boom period prices fell back to "normal" levels and stabilised. Between 1923 and 1944 the Land Commission paid out a total of a little under £4m for nearly half a million acres of land nationally, at an average price of less than £8 per acre. In the same period it purchased about 100,000 acres of tenanted land in Co. Offaly for £700,000, i.e. an average of £7-4s per acre.[47] According to Dr. Dooley himself, the average market price for land up to 1940 did not go beyond £10-£12 per acre.[48]

Purchase values for land were calculated by the Land Commission on the basis of the valuation and market price, and then negotiated with the vendor. The farm, which the Pearsons had bought for £2,000 in 1911, was finally purchased from them, following protracted negotiations on the price, by the Land Commission for £4,817, which was nearly two and half times the price they had paid for it in 1911. Their later claims that this represented just one quarter of the true value of the land, and that they had been compelled to sell at this price, are of a type with many of their other claims to the Irish Grants Committee. At an average of just under £14 per acre for a farm of average quality, the price represented a peak wartime value. The fall in post-war land prices noted by the Minister was not passed on to the Pearsons. By Offaly—and even national—prices, the Pearsons received more than a fair price from the Land Commission for their land in 1923.

---

[46] Dáil Éireann, *Proceedings*, Vol 22, pp. 993-4; Parl Sec., 8th March 1928, and Vol. 23, pp. 197-8, 19th April, 1928 [Vote 54—Land Commission].

[47] Department of Industry and Commerce, *Ireland—Statistical Abstract 1945*, pp. 84-86.

[48] Dooley, *Land for the People*, pp. 188-9.

How did this affect the people who received an allocation of Pearson land from the Land Commission in 1923? On 5th May 1924 the Land Registry recorded the Land Commission "*as full owners of the lands herein*", and the file was then stamped "*Folio closed*". A further entry records the subsequent transfer of the land to a series of new Folios representing the new holdings. These provide maps of the holdings as well as details of the ownership record, the annuities payable, the purchase cost of the land and other matters.[49]

Following the sub-division of the farm in 1923, the annuity payments ranged from 12 to 18 shillings per year per acre, averaging around 15 shillings (20 shillings = £1). This compares to the annuity costs of the Benwells in 1909 of just 7s per acre for the same land, i.e. purchase of the farm brought a doubling in annual annuity costs for the new owners. Later the annuities were revised downwards under the De Valera annuities relief scheme. The records show that in some cases the Land Commission repossessed or repurchased the land, occasionally as late as the 1950s. In some cases annuities were being paid until well into the 1970s. The reason for this was the price.

The actual purchase price to be redeemed by the new owners was high. One allocation of 28 acres cost £520 (i.e. nearly £19 per acre),[50] another was £345 for an allocation of 18 acres (i.e. just over £19 per acre)[51] and another again was £657 for 27 acres (i.e. £24 per acre).[52]

While the annuity charges were equivalent to typical local values, the cost of the land was not, which meant that it took considerably longer to clear. The price achieved by the Pearsons (£4,817) represented an average price of about £14 per acre. On the basis of the valuation records, each parcel involved in the sub-division of the land carried slightly different values according to the quality of the land. Examining all the folios it emerges that the cost passed on to the new owners was in a range of £13 to £24 per acre, and the annuities in the Coolacrease were to take long to clear.

---

[49] Land Registry, Folio Nos. 7391, 7392, 7399, 7400, 7401, 7402, 7403, 7404, 7405, 7406, 7407, 7722, 7723, 7911, 8074, 8076.

[50] Land Registry, Folio 7403, Plots 7 and 7a, land allocated to Dan Downey.

[51] Land Registry, Folio 7405, Plot 10, land allocated to James McCormack.

[52] Land Registry, Folio 7911, Plots 9 and 9a, land allocated to John Multany.

Securing a piece of Pearson land in 1923 was far from a juicy prospect for hungry land-grabbers! The people who "received" allocations paid through the nose for them!

The Irish Grants Committee

In Chapter 6 we provide a history of the Irish Grants Committee. Following the Treaty, various arrangements had been made to adjudicate on claims for compensation for damage suffered during the British war in Ireland. A joint Anglo-Irish body awarded a total of £7m by 1926, about half of it to claims from people from a unionist background.

In addition to this joint compensation body, in 1922 an Irish Distress Committee was established in London by the British Government to award compensation to "refugees" in Britain who had allegedly been compelled to leave Ireland. The Irish Government funded the awards of this body for a time under a reciprocal arrangement whereby Britain in return covered the claims of refugees in the area of the Free State who had been forced to flee from Northern Ireland. Awards made by the Irish Distress Committee were initially modest, amounting to less than £12,000. In 1923, however, and following intensive lobbying by loyalist interests, the mandate of the Irish Distress Committee—re-named the Irish Grants Committee—was extended and its awards, now funded by the British exchequer, reached over £50,000 by 1924.

In the same year a campaign in Britain led to the establishment of a Cabinet Committee to examine the case for a new compensation body. As a result, in 1926 the Irish Grants Committee was re-organised with a far reaching mandate. Applications would be accepted not only from refugees, but from "*all British subjects now or formerly residing or carrying on business in the area of the Irish Free State who, on account of their support of his Majesty's Government prior to July 11, 1921, sustained hardships and loss by personal injuries or by the malicious destruction of or injuries to their property in the area of the Irish Free State between July 1l, 1921, and May 12, 1923*".[53] Proposed awards were to be recommended

---

[53] *The Times*, 15th October 1926.

to the Dominions Office for approval "*taking into account the degree of hardship suffered by the claimant*" and regardless of whether compensation had already been received from other bodies. The new Committee started operations under this wide mandate in early 1927. The Government initially foresaw a budget of £480,000, but, despite the fact that of the 4,032 applications it had received, awards were recommended in only 2,237 cases, by March 1929 a total of £1,386,664 had already been paid out. In an attempt to curtail the escalating costs of its awards, Churchill in February 1928 announced amendments to how compensation would be paid out on recommendations of the Committee. In future claims in four figure sums would be met on the basis of the first full £1,000 and 60% on amounts above that. The storm of revolt that ensued in the Lords in 1928-29 led to a climb-down by the Government. On 1st March 1929 Amery announced that all recommendations of the Committee would be honoured in full. By the time the Committee finished its work and issued its final report in March 1930, the total cost of claims awarded had risen to £2,188,549.

The new members of the re-organised Committee of 1926 were Sir Alexander Wood Renton (Chairman), who had previously chaired the Anglo-Irish compensation commission described above, Sir James Brunyate K.C. S.I., C.I.E. from the India civil service, and Sir John Oakley. Major Alan Reid Jamieson continued on as Secretary. As the claims rolled in from early 1927, the only evidence sought or heard by the committee was from the Southern Irish Loyalist Relief Association. Experts on the ground in Ireland called in to substantiate or put a value on claimed losses were invariably members of the Association itself, including its 'Advisory Committee', and this was also to be the case in the Pearson case. The very close relations between the personnel of the Irish Grants Committee and the Southern Irish Loyalist Relief Association are outlined in Chapter 6. No attempt was even made to hear evidence from any Irish source that might contradict or challenge the claims made to it.

This was the body to which the Pearsons appealed in 1927 for compensation for their losses in Ireland. Their uncontested statements to the Irish Grants Committee are accepted uncritically as "evidence" by the Harris/Sammon documentary.

On the Pearson Claims to the Irish Grants Committee

Much of the basic script of the Harris/Sammon "documentary" for RTÉ is derived from Sidney and William Pearson's submissions to the Irish Grants Committee. We reproduce much of the documentation of this in Appendix 6.

Within two weeks of the re-structuring of the Irish Grants Committee, Sidney Pearson lodged an application on 28th October 1926 claiming losses of £20,000, made up of £10,000 for *"house, furniture clothing cash"* (including £8,000 for the house) and a further £10,000 for the land. One of his referees was Rev. Robert Weir of the Irish Land Finance Co. Ltd. in Montrath (i.e. Mountrath), a militant member of the Advisory Committee of the Southern Irish Loyalist Relief Association and known as an evangelical firebrand in the plantation area of Co. Laois.[54] Weir assured the Committee in a letter of 1st December 1926 that the Pearsons had *"had one of the best farms in King's Co."* The claim was rejected, with a note that Sidney Pearson's claims were *"not unamusing"*.

On 25th May 1927 Sidney's father, William Pearson, lodged a new claim through the Southern Irish Loyalist Relief Association, assisted by a King's Counsel, Mr. L.R. Lipsett K.C. who was also involved with the loyalist compensation lobby (see Chapter 6). This claim was far more sophisticated and well structured. With an eye to the new terms of reference of the Committee, it acknowledged the compensation already received from the Irish Court and sought compensation only for *"post-truce"* damage. He claimed the house had a value of £2,000—down from Sidney's £8,000—but still claimed an exorbitant value for the land: *"As a result of subsequent persecution and destruction of property I had to sell the land—one of the best farms in Ireland—for a quarter of the value to the Land Commission"*. At another point he claimed: *"The Republicans were determined to drive me out and get possession of what was always known as one of the first farms in Ireland"*.

---

[54] R.B. McDowell, *Crisis and Decline: The Fate of Southern Unionists*, Dublin, 1997, pp. 130-62.

He added an impressive list of claims for damage, lost crops, cattle sold below value etc. He claims he had been prevented from selling the farm at auction. Appealing to loyalist sectarian prejudices he says that the buyer who had wanted to pay him £10,000 for it was prevented from doing so, and attaches a hand written note from friend and fellow unionist William Percy, who lived near Kilcormac, to that effect: Pearson explained: "*He applied to the local priest for permission to buy and permission was refused*" and adds: "*In normal times I could have sold the farm at £15,000*". Asked if the losses were attributable to his allegiance to the UK Government he states: "*I was always known as a staunch Loyalist and upholder of the Crown. I assisted the Crown Forces on every occasion, and I helped those who were persecuted around me at all times.*"

His claim to the Committee was for £11,469 and he gave as his referees a neighbouring Protestant farmer in Cadamstown, Albert Jackson, as well as an acquaintance in Laois. But no references can be found among the papers that either of these men came forward with references to the Committee. Indeed it was Jackson who, in refusing to take in the wounded Pearson brothers after the shooting, had said "*You brought it on yourselves*". The largest portion of the claim was £5,183, which represented the difference between the spurious "offer" by Percy of £10,000 for the farm and the £4,817 received from the Land Commission.

It must be remembered that the only evidence collected or heard by the Grants Committee was from Irish loyalist sources, with no other Irish witnesses who might contradict such "evidence" ever being sought out or questioned. Even the British administration's own records—including for example the records of the 'Court of Inquiry' into the Pearson deaths which had circulated at the highest level in Dublin Castle—made no appearance at the Committee. This is interesting given that two of the four-member Grants Committee until 1926—Sturgis and Crutchley—had been very senior officials at Dublin Castle and closely involved in its black propaganda campaign (which included the statement of 9th July 1921 on the Coolacrease events). It is not conceivable that the Committee operated in ignorance of the Dublin Castle version of events in Ireland.

Given this context, it is hardly surprising that the Pearsons embellished their story with extravagant claims regarding losses and persecution suffered and regarding the value of the house and property. They were, after all, seeking to maximise a compensation claim before a body which they could be confident would not be hearing any contradictory evidence. The only thing that is extraordinary is the credibility which Irish academics give to "evidence" from such a source.

However, the credulity of the Irish Grants Committee did have limits. Its secretary, Alan Reid Jamieson, wrote to Major White of the Southern Irish Loyalists Relief Association (1st June 1927): "*The prices claimed under most heads appear on a preliminary survey to be very high*" and requested submission of evidence in support of them. Major White replied (11th June) that he had submitted "*2 or 3 letters generally supporting and confirming Mr. Pearson's statement*" (these are the letters from William Percy and Telfords of Birr) and, as regards providing additional evidence, added that "*This will be a matter of some difficulty, as nearly all the people who were intimately acquainted with Mr. Pearson have either been forced to leave the country or have left as life has become impossible*". This would tend to confirm that the Pearsons could expect no confirmation of their claims from any of their former Protestant neighbours and had become alienated from them. The Committee suggested (14th June) a meeting to discuss the issues involved. Following further correspondence it recommended a local valuer—Harry Franks, coincidentally a member of the 'Advisory Committee' of the Southern Irish Loyalists Relief Association—to review the Pearson claims (26th July) and this was gladly accepted by White.

The final submission to the Committee for its hearing on 2nd February 1928 consisted of William Pearson's statement and attached individualised claims, an assessment of these by the valuer, and the two letters in support of the claim. The note from William Percy of Frankford, King's Co., stated: "*Regarding the sale of Coolacrease after the burning. The price I offered was £10,000 and I might have gone higher only the people would not allow an outsider to purchase the lands. I was not allowed to close the bargain.*" This note features in several shots in the 'Hidden History' show. In fact, as we have seen, the farm had been put up for auction but had been withdrawn when it failed to reach the reserved price. The second letter, from Telford & Sons, auctioneers of Birr (6th October 1927), stated that the "*meadows on said lands*" (i.e. the best land of the farm) were worth £10 per acre in 1921-2 and "*the interest in the holding previous to the burning of the residence was value for (sic) £17,000 or thereabouts*". This makes no sense. Land in Ireland sold for its acre price, and £10 per acre for the Pearson farm would have given a price of no more than £3,410. Also enclosed was a medical certificate testifying to William Pearson's poor health.

The valuation of the claims made by Franks for the Committee was enclosed with a running commentary by Alan Reid Jamieson, Secretary of the Committee, including a special plea in the closing note:

> "These observations [on the itemised claims—PO'C] refer to the detailed claim presented only, but this is a case to which considerable history attaches. It is undoubtedly a case of quite exceptional hardship, and the claimant since 1920 has suffered terrible persecution and annoyance, his property being burnt and destroyed, and his two sons murdered. After an examination of the detailed items the Committee may wish to consider this general question of hardship, more especially as no claim is included in the detailed items in respect of loss of general profits since the claimant was driven from Ireland.
>
> It does not, however, appear that the claimant is suffering any acute financial hardship. He has a good farm in this country, and in addition has an income from a sum of £6,000 which he holds in the Bank.
>
> This is a type of case on which certain general considerations apply, and these can no doubt best be discussed when the case is presented."

Franks reduced the Pearsons' claims on many items, noting particularly that the cattle and machinery sold at auction had secured "*fair prices*", which gives the lie to the "boycott" theory. But, most importantly, and strangely, Franks simply repeated the £10,000 claim for the value of the farm stating his inability to judge it; he left it to the Committee to judge the difference of £5,183 sought between this sum and the amount paid by the Land Commission.

The Committee heard the case on 2nd February 1928, with William Pearson in attendance, accompanied by the lawyer Lipsett, Major White and Harry Franks. The proposal to accept the claim on account of the "*exceptional hardship*" of the case rather than on strict value criteria was accepted by the sympathetic Committee and an award of £7,440 was forwarded to the Dominions Secretary for approval. The opinion of the Grants Committee was accepted by the Under Secretary at the Dominions Office, Sir Harry Batterbee, who issued an order on 8th March 1928 for compensation of £4,864 to be paid, deleting the phrase *"in settlement of the claim"*. This sum represented acceptance of the full claim of £7,440, payable on the basis (under the Committee's terms of reference) of the first £1,000 in full and 60% of amounts above that, though it deleted the proviso that this was a final settlement.

The Grants Committee subsequently wrote to Major White on 8th March 1928 that when the Committee *"have completed its examination of all claims it may be possible to issue a further payment in cases exceeding £1,000"*. In other words, further amounts might be forthcoming. It retuned to the case to see what could be done regarding what Jamieson had described as the "*general question of hardship*". Notes by Committee members were added. One read: *"As the result of the numerous outrages applic's wife is now almost imbecile. The claimant himself is suffering from a complete breakdown and must leave England."* Another, dated November 1928: *"Committee consider that this is a case of exceptional hardship & should be noted as such. Case to be brought up later for spl consider."* Within the Dominions Office, an official sent a note to Assistant Secretary Harry Batterbee (later, as a member of the "Irish Situation Committee", a key negotiator on behalf of the British with the De Valera Government of the 1930s):

> "This is one of the most terrible cases of many bad ones which have come before the Dept. No summary would do justice to it. The case is fully presented on the application form. Applicant had for Ireland a large farm and claims that it was one of the best. Some compensation was received for pre-truce damage but nothing for his post-Truce sufferings and experiences.
>
> "The Committee regard it as a case of exceptional hardship and recommends £7,500 which includes £60 for costs and expenses…"

These deliberations coincided with the campaign in the Lords to have the payment formula reversed, and awards to be paid in full. As we have seen, Leo Amery, on behalf of the Government, relented on 1st March 1929. The following week the Committee wrote restoring the balance between the original value of the award and what had been paid (£4,817), i.e. £2,576, bringing the total paid to Pearson to £7,440. The bulk of this figure is accounted for by the amount claimed on the alleged value of the land (by now reduced to the figure of £10,000 mentioned by William Percy), which as we have seen was at least two-and-and-half times times its real value. But the Committee was not interested in such matters. Its major resolve was to compensate Pearson for the hardships he had endured arising from his loyalty, and which it had accepted without contradiction.

Conclusions

Niamh Sammon's claim that the evidence for her accusation of a forced sale of the farm to the Land Commission and of a sectarian land grab is present in the Land Commission and Land Registry records relating to the Pearson farm is false.

The Land Commission documentation we saw—as well as the additional information given to us orally—shows conclusively that the land was purchased voluntarily from the Pearsons and distributed by the Land Commission scrupulously and in accordance with procedure, overseen by a senior inspector of the Commission.

There is nothing in them—or in the documents of the Land Registry or Valuation Office which we also inspected—which contain a shred of evidence for her claims, or for those of her mentor, Senator Eoghan Harris, regarding a sectarian or any other type of land grab.

The Pearson lands were not of exceptionally high quality. Valuation records show them to have been modestly good by Offaly standards, with a mixture of quite good land in the higher areas near the road and poor wet bogland around the Silver River.

There was no forced sale of the Pearson farm to the Land Commission, in fact William Pearson received £4,817 for the farm under voluntary purchase by the Land Commission, which was nearly two-and-and-half times what he had paid for it in 1912, and a very good price compared to contemporary standards. There was no forced sale.

Despite claims that the farm was worth up to £17,000 all indications and comparisons with contemporary figures show that the price paid by the Land Commission in 1923—£4,817—was high, and in fact a burden on those who received allocations of it after its sale by the Pearsons. The Pearsons received a price representing nearly £14 per acre, when comparative national levels were about £10 and local values even somewhat less.

The "Irish Grants Committee" in London awarded money to southern Irish Loyalists who claimed to have suffered in the Irish War of Independence because of their "loyalty" to the Crown. It was staffed by representatives of the cream of the British and Anglo-Irish unionist establishment, including officials who had been involved at the very dirty end of the British war in Ireland. It did not take or hear any evidence from Irish sources other than from cronies of the Southern Irish Loyalist Relief Association. Its judgment of uncontested evidence has as little credibility as the evidence itself. It is not surprising that it received many exaggerated claims, or that the Pearsons would have greatly embellished their story to try to maximise the compensation they hoped to receive. What is extraordinary, however, is the willingness of Irish academics to accept such claims uncritically. Nevertheless even the Irish Grants Committee baulked at Pearson's claims and appointed a valuer (from Irish loyalist circles of course) who discounted most of them. In the end it recommended compensation based on the stories of hardship suffered rather than the material losses claimed.

Despite their involvement and traumatic experiences in the 1919-21 war, in material terms the Pearsons did well out of the period. Having bought the farm for £2,000 in 1911, they cultivated it intensively, earning well during the wartime record boom for crops, and a local valuer estimated the best of the farm (the "meadows") to have been worth £10 per acre by 1920-21. This would give a total value of £3,410. But Pearson received far more than this from the Land Commission—£4,817—in 1923. In addition, the County Court in Offaly had already awarded William Pearson compensation of £1,340 for property lost in the burning of the house, as well as £1,500 for the loss of his sons, and £1,000 for the burned house (total:

£3,840). Pearson admitted that he would have received further compensation (he says £4,000 but this is not credible) if he undertook to rebuild the house (this was under a special provision of the Compensation Acts), but, although so urged by the Court, he had declined to do so. In addition, in the case of the small amount of property actually stolen, a Republican Court had ordered that the people responsible return it to the family (this of course was not mentioned to the Grants Committee). When Pearson decided to leave Offaly, he received at auction a further amount for the stock and machinery of the farm, which the valuer appointed by the Irish Grants Committee regarded as a *"fair price"*. The Committee ultimately paid William Pearson a total of £7,440.

The documentation available from the Land Commission, the Land Registry Office, the Land Valuation Office and the "Irish Grants Committee" shows the reality of the value of the Pearson farm as of medium to good quality. The records contain not a shred of evidence to back up a case of Republican/sectarian land-grabbing or of a forced sale to the Land Commission. In fact they prove the opposite, in the sense that active Republicans were not those that "profited" from the division of the farm. The claims of the Harris/Sammon documentary defame the people of the Cadamstown area as bigoted land-grabbing terrorists and the officials of the Land Commission as complicit. The academic experts on the programme in condoning these claims have a case to answer.

Eoghan Harris, and the Reform Group generally, have been whipping up a false sectarian mythology about rural Ireland during the War of Independence, and spinning an interpretation of events that has provided ill-informed commentators, poorly educated "historians" and distant descendants with false history and an erroneous sense of grievance. While it is a house built on sand, this sectarian agenda needs to be challenged and rebutted.

The actual documentation confirms in full the researches of Paddy Heaney into the realities surrounding the sale of the farm to the Land Commission in 1923 and its consequent sub-division.

Chapter 5

'Amish-type farmers'?
Pacifism and the Cooneyites

By
Pat Muldowney

> "Think not that I am come to send peace on earth. I came not to send peace but a sword. The brother shall deliver up the brother to death, and the father the child. Ye shall be hated by all men for my name's sake, but he that endureth to the end shall be saved." *(Matthew 10)*

One of the central planks in the campaign by Senator Eoghan Harris and his followers on the issue of the Coolacrease executions was that the innocence of the Pearsons was underscored by their religious beliefs. They were members of a small sect known as the Cooneyites and there is ample evidence that, led by the father, William, they were very sincere and devoted members of that community. When Richard and Abraham Pearson were executed by Offaly No. 2 Brigade IRA on 30th June 1921, their brother Sidney escaped their fate as he was absent at the time of the execution with his father at a Cooneyite meeting or "Christian Convention" in Carrick House in North Tipperary.

Alan Stanley in his book, *I Met Murder on the Way—the Story of the Pearsons of Coolacrease,* compared the Cooneyites to the pacifist and anti-materialist Amish community of Pennsylvania, and Senator Harris took up the issue and made it a central feature of his keynote article on the issue of the Pearson execution in the *Sunday Independent* of 9th October 2005 (reprinted in this book) in which he focused on the peaceable nature of the Cooneyites. On cue, his line was taken up in the 'Hidden History' programme itself, where Dr.

Raymond Gillespie of Maynooth University said, regarding the Cooneyites: *"There are some similarities with the Amishes. There are some ideas that underly both groups. They conserve simplicity, they try to live out the word of the bible as they read it."* This is nonsense. The Cooneyites were an extreme sect whose disdain for Catholic and mainstream Protestant faiths would leave that of the most militant members of the Free Presbyterians in the shade.

The issue became ever more central and re-emerged in the RTÉ announcement in its Summer 2008 schedule of a re-showing of the programme on 13th May: *"The Killings at Coolacrease recounts in vivid detail the lead-up to this chilling event. It tells the story of how the Pearsons, members of a **small Amish-type sect** called the Cooneyites—came to buy a large farm in Offaly at a time of great land hunger"* (emphasis added).

Emmanuel Kehoe's TV review in the *Sunday Business Post*—entitled *'When History and Hearsay Collide'*—was the one exception to the mainstream media's wholesale swallowing of the Harris line pursued by RTÉ's *Hidden History*. Kehoe distrusted what he had seen and, while he did not access any of the documentary evidence that would have enabled him to dispute the Harris-Sammon version of the executions themselves, he did go to the trouble of investigating if there was any basis in fact for their claim that the Cooneyite religious beliefs of the gun-toting Pearsons were akin to those of the Amish—a pacifist community who take the injunction *"turn the other cheek"* so literally that they would not even raise a fist in self-defence.

As we learn from Kehoe, in 1909 the guiding light of the Pearsons, Edward Cooney himself, condemned to hell's everlasting holocaust every man, woman and child in Co. Fermanagh who was not a Cooneyite. In what he called "the Condemnation of Fermanagh" he specifically listed the damned as all those of the Calvinist, Methodist, Episcopalian, Plymouth Brethern, Salvation Army and Roman Catholic beliefs.

Kehoe writes:

> " *'The Pearsons'*, she [Niamh Sammon] wrote, were members of a *'peaceable, non-political, dissenting Protestant sect known as the Cooneyites'*. They were likened in the programme to Amish. But were

the Pearsons entirely peaceable? Locals accused them of harassing people who used a traditional Mass path over their land, of being spies and informers and perhaps, most outlandishly, of running a local militia. Finally there was an incident in which Richard Pearson shot at a group of local IRA men cutting down a tree on Pearson's land to block a road. *'The Pearsons are merely doing what they think any law abiding citizen should do and legally they are within their rights to defend their land and as they would see it to protect it against terrorist activity',* Professor Richard English of Queens University said. Within their rights maybe, but off their heads. When the two young men were shot it was alleged they were killed in front of their women relatives and shot in the genitals and the buttocks and left to die. Eoghan Harris said he wanted to see documentary evidence that Pearson had actually wounded an IRA man in the shooting over the tree, but viewers might have liked to see documentary evidence of this very peculiar, brutal method of execution presented here as fact.

"Harris wrote about the Coolacrease killings some time ago, and it appears to be one of those isolated incidents out of which he cuts a stick to beat a rather large drum. In the film Harris recalls that *"My father ran a small wholesale grocery business in the 50s"* and the Cooneyites used to come into him. *"They were terribly quiet, very, very gentle decent people. They were pretty much withdrawn from the world as a whole. I would say they found the whole world outside confusing. They were really husbandry people, you know, the land. Quiet evenings spent in reflection and meditation. These are the kind of people they were."* But were they entirely so? Founded by William Irvine, an evangelising Scot, in 1897 and Edward Cooney, the son of a Fermanagh magistrate, the Cooneyites still exist today, some in Ireland, some in the United States and in quite large numbers in Australia where the Pearsons moved after the killings and the burning of their home. Some today would regard them as a cult and their beliefs in 1921 would have set them apart from their mainstream, churchgoing Protestant neighbours.

"Whatever about the Cooneyites today, or when Harris met them, in 1909 they were creating a bit of a stir at their convention in Ballinamallard, Co. Fermanagh, so much so that the *New York Times* reported on 9th August under the heading 'Cooneyites Await the Millennium':

"It is the belief of the sect that the millennium may be ushered in at any moment, and prayer meetings are being held almost continuously. ... All the pilgrims are dressed in coarse, plain clothing. The men are unshaven and wear rubber collars. On the heads of the women are

straw sailor hats. All are busily engaged in manual labor or domestic duties milking, butter making, cooking, sewing, boot-making, carpentering, etc—every one being assigned to a daily task."

"Reporting on the same convention on 5th August 1909 the Fermanagh newspaper, *The Impartial Reporter*, was rather more hostile:

"Mr Cooney spoke for over two hours. It was not a Gospel address, or one of teaching; but one of condemnation of those who differed from his views. They were all going to hell. He knew all about it ... He repeated his denunciation of John Knox, Calvin, John Wesley; they had all gone to hell .. There was the usual torrent of abusive talk, bristling with denunciation and everlasting torment .. it was a repetition of former harangues .. One of the first points which would strike a listener to Mr Cooney's discourse, was the entire lack of charity and kindness. Mr Cooney is excellent as a spouter of damnation and hell fire, but when it comes to the love of God, and the tenderness of the Saviour for mankind, Mr Cooney appears to know nothing of it."

"'We are the light', he [Cooney] proceeded, 'and the condemnation of Fermanagh is, that they won't have the light, but choose the darkness, Methodist darkness, Episcopalian darkness, Plymouth brethren darkness, Salvation Army darkness, Roman Catholic darkness: you have been with the clergy, and supported them here, and you will be with them in hell. What would you think of the Rev Jesus, MA or BA, with £3 a week with an encouragement to get married with £12 a year or 'Father Jesus' hoping to die a Pope some day, or 'Rev Jesus' with his eye on the Archbishopric of Canterbury, or 'Lieutenant' Jesus hoping to become a Colonel or General some day in the Salvation Army? Would to God that this dirty devilish poison crammed into you at the Sunday school, took in through every bone of your body in the clergy house as the workings and doing of Christianity, were crushed out of your lives.' "

"Does this suggest that the Pearsons, not so long afterwards, might have been somewhat less benign and pacific than Harris or Sammon makes them out to be and that this, combined with a stiff-necked loyalism and their extensive lands may have made them more noticeable than other loyalist Protestants in the area? Is it conceivable that a group following Cooney's preaching could, for example, hassle local people over the sensitive issue of a right of way to Mass? Television histories have an odd habit of leaving the viewer wondering. This film, with its mixture of innuendo and hearsay, claim and counterclaim made me wonder what truth could be got out of the story at all and what wider reference it could have..."

Is Kehoe right in doubting whether the Cooneyite Pearsons were pacifist in the way the Amish and Quakers are?

Around 1900 the new religious movement was founded by Scotsman William Irvine in Fermanagh. Edward Cooney from Enniskillen was an early adherent and preacher. In an era of social change, questioning and challenge to old ways, the new movement grew and spread in Ireland, Scotland, England, France, Germany, Australia, Canada and the USA.

The movement viewed the religious bureaucracy of established Christian denominations as being destructive of true religion. They experimented with community property or Christian communism. In rejecting formal organisation, authority, clerical orders and church buildings, they also eschewed any formal title or designation for the movement, describing themselves only as Christian, and denoting their form of religious practice as the Way.

In practice this led to their being given many different names, such as Cooneyites, Go-Preachers, Tramp Preachers, Two-by-Twos, and many other, often uncomplimentary titles (e.g. 'Dippers'). Their central belief was that true Christianity was personally acquired by word of mouth from Jesus, and from then on, by person-to-person word-of-mouth transmission to individuals down to the present.

While they accepted the Christian bible in eclectic fashion, they eschewed any codification or written account of their religious beliefs and doctrine, so it is difficult for any outsider to fully understand their theology.

It is generally understood, though, that the origins of the movement lie in an acceptance of the literal truth of Matthew Ten (Chapter 10 of the Gospel according to Matthew), the most ferocious and violent passage in the New Testament. Here is an excerpt:

"... go, preach, saying the Kingdom of Heaven is at hand. Provide neither gold nor silver nor brass in your purses. Go not into the way of the gentiles, but rather to the lost sheep of the House of Israel. Beware of men, for they will deliver you up to their councils, and they will scourge you in their synagogues. Think not that I am come to send peace on earth. I came not to send peace but a sword. I am come to set a man at variance against his father and the daughter against her mother and the daughter in law against her mother in law. The brother shall deliver up the brother to death, and the father the child. And the children shall rise up against their parents and cause them to be put to death. Ye shall be hated by all men for my name's sake, but he that endureth to the end shall be saved."

The first two words of this ("Go, preach") gave them one of their many names. For practical or legal reasons they were obliged to give themselves a designation more specific than "Christian". Susan Pearson's death certificate (16 May 1947) gives her religious affiliation as "Christian Assemblies of Australia". "Christian Conventions" is another version of this. This name comes from their practice of an annual meeting of the faithful in the home or premises of a member. This is, or was, one of their most important religious events, and the meeting held in Carrick House, Mountmellick, Co. Laois (between Luggacurran and Rathdowney) on 30th June or 1st July 1921 may have been their annual Assembly or Convention. This might explain the absence of William and Sidney Pearson from Coolacrease at such a fraught time.

Were the Cooneyites/Christian Assemblies pacifist? In what way, if any, did they resemble Amish or Quakers?

Certainly their founding doctrine (Matthew 10) is anti-pacifist. It is said that their "workers" were exempted from military service because of their conscientious objector status; and that this implies that the movement as a whole was pacifist.

But just as the movement was, in practice, obliged to depart from strict adherence to their theology by accepting a formal name or designation ("Christian Conventions"), they also, in practice, had a form of membership ("workers" or "preachers") equivalent to the status of clergy—even though, strictly speaking, their doctrine did not permit any such elevated status. But the point is, clergy of all religious groups were exempt from military service. (These days, Cooneyite "workers" are sometimes called bishops.)

Were they similar to Amish or Quakers in any other way? The Amish can trace their descent from the 16th century Anabaptist movement in Germany. Just as the Anabaptists rejected the Lutheran Reformation in the 16th century, the Cooneyites rejected the mainstream Protestant denominations in the 20th century.

The Cooneyites practised adult baptism. In this way they resemble Anabaptists and present-day Baptists. Their eclectic approach to the bible means they are not, strictly speaking, evangelical. Likewise, the 16th century Anabaptists viewed the Lutheran embrace of the literal truth of the bible as a new form of religious authoritarianism— a *"paper Pope"* as they called it.

But there seem to be only a limited number of basic religious ideas which can be put together to give a dynamic to a religious movement. Like Roman Catholicism, Cooneyism differed from mainstream Protestantism by rejecting the notion that faith alone is sufficient for salvation. Catholicism requires also "good works" in the form of charitable action in the world; while Cooneyism required good works in the form of active preaching and conversion.

Like Cooneyism, Catholicism acknowledges the Holy Scripture (the bible essentially) as a source of religious truth, but not the only source. While Catholicism also acknowledges what it calls Tradition, for Cooneyism the person-to-person transmission of religious truth by word of mouth was central.

In the RTÉ documentary, Eoghan Harris described the Cooneyites, and by implication the Pearsons, as *".... really a husbandry people"*, given to *" ... quiet evenings spent in meditation and reflection"*. In other words they wouldn't hurt a fly so could never have shot Mick Heaney at the IRA roadblock. Is there any basis for this?

The religious extremism of the 16th century Anabaptists (precursors of the Amish) resulted in horrific fighting when they were opposed by the forces of the Protestant and Catholic German princes. In reaction to this most bloody and violent religious episode, a spirit of pacifism developed among the survivors, a spirit which has endured to the present among the Amish, Mennonite and Hutterite groupings.

Matthew 10-inspired zealotry and extremism characterised the early 20th century Cooneyite movement, making present-day Free Prebyterians look like New Age Buddhists in comparison.

The following accounts from the Fermanagh newspaper *The Impartial Reporter and Farmers' Journal* of 2nd June 1904 and 3rd September 1908, are given in Doug and Helen Parker's history of Cooneyism *(The Secret Sect)*:

> "[Cooneyite] Preachers were disliked because of their exclusive sectarianism and bigotry, and reports of the large demonstrations at Newtownards that took place when Edward Cooney preached there in

1904 provided evidence that a local clergyman conducted meetings to oppose the sect's activities, and that soon after an estimated crowd of three thousand people gathered, some to hear Cooney, others to disrupt his meetings with pipes and drums. A public baptismal ceremony that Cooney conducted in the same district was attended by a large crowd, some of whom scoffed at and antagonised the converts almost to the point of a fight, but the police intervened and kept the peace. Mourners and sectarians engaged in a scuffle at a church door and the lid of a coffin was knocked off when the sectarians attempted to bear the coffin away from the church for their own committal."

What comes across from these and many similar accounts of early 20th century Cooneyism is a picture of extremist religious intolerance and zealotry, and an attitude to physical violence which was much the same as other religious denominations.

And whatever about Cooneyism generally, the notion that the Pearsons in particular were pacifist is far-fetched.

More information on the Cooneyites can be found in:

Doug & Helen Parker, *The Secret Sect: the Nameless House Sect and Annual Conventions, the Cooneyites, also known as Two-by-Two Preachers, Die Namenlosen, Les Anonymes, the Way;* Macarthur Press, Sydney, Australia, 1982;

C. J. Jaenen, 'The Apostles' Doctrine and Fellowship: A documentary history of the early church and restorationist movements' *The Contemporary [Irish] Restoration Movement,* Ottawa: Legas Publishing, 2003, IX, 14, pp. 517-535;

Patricia Roberts, *The Life and Ministry of Edward Cooney 1867-1960*, Wm Trimble Ltd, Enniskillen, 1990.

Chapter 6

An Extraordinary Set-up: The "Irish Grants Committee"

By
Philip O'Connor

R.B. McDowell, now over ninety years of age, was for many years a respected historian and something of an iconic figure at Trinity College and, as he stated in a recent interview in *The Irish Times*, a life-long unionist who believed in maintaining the unionist perspective within southern Ireland. Like most unionists of his and the previous generation, he accepted the majority democratic decision establishing the Republic and believed that unionists should maintain a cultural perspective within it. His 1997 book, *Crisis and Decline: The Fate of Southern Unionists,* includes an account of the Irish Grants Committee, the body to which the Pearsons appealed for compensation in 1926-7 and on whose records the 'Hidden History' programme relied so heavily for evidence in reconstructing the events at Coolacrease in 1921.[1]

Following the Treaty, and in its spirit, a meeting was held of officials of the Free State and British Governments on the issue of compensation for damages and injuries sustained in the war. Despite the fact that the British government launched that war in flagrant contempt for the democratic decision of the Irish electorate, and despite the destructive nature of the war which it unleashed, the Free State agreed to the British proposal that each side mutually cover the costs of damage inflicted by their respective forces up to the Truce of July 1921. A Commission was then established composed of a

---

[1] R.B. McDowell, *Crisis and Decline: The Fate of Southern Unionists,* Dublin, 1997, pp. 130-162.

representative of each government and a Chairman. From November 1922 the chairman was Sir Alex Wood-Renton. The Commission functioned smoothly, according to McDowell, and by the time it concluded its business in March 1926 it had granted awards totalling over £7m to 17,792 claimants (out of 40,647 examined). About half of this sum was to claimants of a unionist background.

The issue of "refugees" was another matter. In May 1922 the British Government established the *Irish Distress Committee* to investigate claims from people who alleged they had been compelled to leave Ireland, and wrote to the Treaty Government, expressing the hope that the Irish side would agree to compensate *"these homeless and destitute refugees"*. The Irish Government responded that it would accept some responsibility in the case of *"law abiding citizens"* but added that it was *"common knowledge that a considerable number of persons have left Ireland on the plea of compulsion without any justification"*. If the British Government was to insist that unionist refugees in Britain receive compensation from the Free Sate, then Britain should reciprocate in relation to refugees from Northern Ireland in the Free State. In the event it was agreed that each Government would meet the costs of verified claims by refugees in each other's jurisdiction. By March 1923 the Colonial Office had met Irish costs of £17,651 for refugees from Northern Ireland in the Free State and the Free State paid £11,587 to meet sums awarded on the British side by the Irish Distress Committee.

The Committee from the start was shaped by leading imperial interests in close connection with Irish loyalist circles.[2] Lionel Curtis—a member of Lord Milner's imperialist insider group, the *Kindergarten* and *Round Table*—drew up its terms of reference and attended its first few meetings. It initially had four members. The first Chairman was Sir Samuel Hoare, soon replaced by Lord Eustace Percy (son of the Duke of Northumberland). The Secretary was Major Alan Reid Jamieson, a Colonial Office (former Irish Office) official. The third member was Mark Sturgis. A civil servant in the Irish Office he had been posted as Assistant Under Secretary to the

---

[2] A significant source for this chapter was provided by the pioneering work of Seán McGouran, 'Robin Bury's Faulty Witness', in *Church & State*, Cork, Autumn 2006.

new regime of Sir John Anderson brought in to Dublin Castle in 1920 to fight the war in Ireland. According to Charles Townshend, Sturgis was an advocate of a *"temporary military 'dictatorship' to meet the emergency"*.[3] Among other duties, Sturgis had also been connected with the propaganda work of the Castle, which involved the manufacture of atrocity stories, the white-washing of British atrocities and the construction of a falsified version of these events for the historical record.[4] Among this output was the tendentious story released about the Pearson execution two days before the Truce, entitled *Report on the Sinn Fein Outrage at Coolacrease Ho*[use], which we reproduce in the Appendix. The fourth member of the Irish Distress Committee was Ernest T. Crutchley, who had been a colleague of Sturgis' at Dublin Castle during the War of Independence (including at the time of the Pearson execution).

All in all, and to put it mildly, it was a grouping designed to view very sympathetically any claims by aggrieved southern Irish Loyalists, especially as another State was initially intended to foot the bill.

The British Government soon came under pressure from the well-connected loyalist lobby to extend the remit of the Distress Committee. In July 1922, the Cabinet Sub-Committee on Ireland recommended that while the Irish Government had a duty to meet post-Truce claims by Irish loyalists for losses and damage, the British Government should not be limited by this and should ensure that all claims were met *"adequately and promptly,"* i.e. it should meet costs of claims over and above what the Irish State would pay. On 31st March 1923 the Irish Distress Committee was re-named the *Irish Grants Committee* and continued dispensing awards. Following the approval of its terms of reference, the Colonial Secretary announced that the *"the Treasury had given the Committee carte blanche with certain limitations."* By 1924 up to 7,500 applications had come in and, of these, 4,300 received awards totalling £52,000. But this was still small change and the loyalist interest had set its sights on bigger things.

---

[3] Charles Townshend, 'The Irish Insurgency, 1918-21: the Military Problem', in R.D. Haycock, *Regular Armies and Insurgency,* London, 1979, p. 44.

[4] See the thorough study of these matters by Brian P. Murphy osb, *The Origins and Organisation of British Propaganda in Ireland 1920,* Aubane, 2006.

The main loyalist pressure group, the *Southern Irish Loyalists Relief Association,* was no ordinary group of colonial lobbyists. Its President was the Duke of Northumberland—whose son, Lord Eustace Percy MP, had been promptly made Chair of the Irish Distress Committee—and its Secretary was the Marquess of Salisbury. The only *'Mister'* on its list was Neville Chamberlain. Within 18 months of its establishment in 1922, the SILRA had interviewed 9,400 "refugees". Soon after the Treaty the Irish Unionist Alliance dissolved, realising its political future lay within the new State but, McDowell tells us, its Dublin Branch first organised an 'Advisory Committee' to support claims through the SILRA to the Irish Grants Committee. This grouping included Harry Franks, J.E. Walsh and the Rev. Robert Weir of Mountrath in Co. Laois. Franks and Weir, as related elsewhere in this book, later played central roles in backing up the Pearson claim. According to McDowell: *"Weir was particularly active. A fervent evangelical (he had started his clerical career in the Irish Church Missions, which carried on missionary work among Irish Catholics), he was a curate and then Rector in a very disturbed part of Queen's County."* In other words, in the recent plantation areas of the County.

The Association was supported in England by the 'Truth about Ireland League', founded by Mrs. Stuart-Menzies and supported by leading military figures, and Lady Bathurst, owner of the militantly imperialist *Morning Post.* Its supporters in the House of Lords raised its cause incessantly. Foremost among its champions in the Lords was the Marques of Lansdowne, the self same Lord Lansdowne who had implemented the ethnic cleansing and plantation of Luggacurran just over thirty years previously. There were extensive debates in the House, with an impressive array of well known friends of Ireland emotively pressing the case for compensation for Irish loyalists, notably Lansdowne, Danesfort, Haldane, Birkenhead, Northumberland, Carson, Birkenhead, Beauchamp, Salisbury, Mayo, Arran and Oranmore.[5]

---

[5] See *Hansard,* House of Lords, 20th March 1923; 5th March, 7th July, 16th July 1924; 17th June, 2nd July,15th July, 9th December 1925; 21st December, 22nd December 1927.

At the end of 1924 the Tories returned to power and the following year, after persistent lobbying and on the recommendation of the new Colonial Secretary, Leo Amery, the Government established a special committee to examine if all compensation claims had been adequately met, and, if not, whether further compensation should be funded additional to that already paid by the Free State or British Government. Amery was a leading imperialist (he had been a core member alongside Curtis in Lord Milner's imperialist insider group, the *Kindergarten* and *Round Table*) and later went on to become Secretary of State for India. After the Nazis came to power in Germany, he advocated joint British-German rule of the world and in 1937 founded the Empire Youth Movement to promote the racial purity of Britain. This was a mindset typical of British ruling class circles in the 1930s.[6] The Government committee consisted of two ministers (Lord Clarendon and Sir Eustace Percy MP), three representatives of the Southern Loyalists (Lord Northumberland, Lord Danesfort, and Sir Henry Wynne, the former Chief Crown Solicitor for Ireland) and the Scottish lawyer, Lord Dunedin. It met with the secretary of the Southern Irish Loyalists Relief Association, Major White, and the lawyer Mr. L.R. Lipsett of the Compensation Claims Commission, both of whom later played central roles in assessing the Pearson claim. Hardly surprisingly, the Government committee, in its report on 25th July, accepted that the Government had an obligation to meet these claims, which it said should be given *"a broad interpretation in terms of history rather than law."* The main requirement for claims was that claimants had suffered because of their loyalty to the Crown.[7]

The Irish Grants Committee accordingly was re-organised with a much wider mandate. On 15th October 1926 the Dominions Office (previously the Colonial Office) announced its acceptance of the Government committee's recommendations, with applications now being accepted not only from refugees, but from *"all British subjects now or formerly residing or carrying on business in the area of the Irish Free State who, on account of their support of his Majesty's*

---

[6] See Manuel Sarkisyanz, *Hitler's English Inspirers,* Athol Books, 2002.
[7] *The Times,* 14th October 1926.

Government prior to July 11, 1921, sustained hardships and loss by personal injuries or by the malicious destruction of or injuries to their property in the area of the Irish Free State between July 1l, 1921, and May 12, 1923". Proposed awards were to be recommended to the Dominions Office for approval *"taking into account the degree of hardship suffered by the claimant"* and regardless of compensation already received.[8]

The new members of the Committee were Sir Alexander Wood Renton (Chairman), who had previously chaired the Anglo-Irish compensation commission described above, Sir James Brunyate K.C. S.I., C.I.E. from the India civil service, and Sir John Oakley. Major Alan Reid Jamieson continued as Secretary. As the claims rolled in from early 1927, the only evidence sought or heard by the committee was that gathered by the Southern Irish Loyalists Relief Association. Experts on the ground in Ireland called in to substantiate or put a value on claimed losses were invariably members of the Association itself, including its 'Advisory Committee', and this was also to be the case in the Pearson claim. No attempt was even made to hear evidence from any Irish source that might contradict or challenge the claims made or the background stories provided, which surely should cast some doubt on the credibility of its gathering and assessment of evidence.

The Committee now became something of a gravy train. R.B. McDowell recounts in some detail the reputation it gained for outlandishly fraudulent claims. The Government initially foresaw a budget of £480,000 but, despite the fact that of the 4,032 applications it had received, awards were recommended in only 2,237 cases, by March 1929 a total of £1,386,664 had already been paid out. The Committee and its awards were becoming something of an embarrassment, not least as the British State was trying to shore up the Free State at this time against the threat from the republican agenda, re-invigorated since the entry of Fianna Fáil to the Dáil in 1927. In an attempt to curtail the escalating costs of its awards, Churchill in February 1928 announced amendments to how compensation would be paid out on recommendations of the

---

[8] *The Times*, 15th October 1926.

Committee. In future, he stated, claims in four figure sums would be met on the basis of the first £1,000 in full, and 60% of amounts conceded over and above that. The storm of revolt that ensued in the Lords in 1928-29 led to a climb-down by the Government. On 1st March 1929 Amery announced that all recommendations of the Committee would be honoured in full. By the time the Committee finished its work and issued its final report in March 1930, the total cost of claims awarded had risen to £2,188,549.

On 23rd January 1930 the Southern Irish Loyalists Relief Association wrote to the Committee asking that it destroy all letters on its files sent from people still resident in the Free State seeking financial compensation. The files of the Committee, after all, contained a mass of wild and unsubstantiated claims, nearly half of which had been rejected by the Committee. It was what amounted to a database of a hostile minority within the new Free State pleading its loyalty to the British government and claiming compensation for damages allegedly suffered for that loyalty. The mysterious request was complied with, nevertheless, and these letters were destroyed.

As the Committee completed its work, 144 members of the Southern Irish Loyalists Relief Association, whose Hon. Secretary was now W. M. Boland of Ballina, an ex-RIC man, signed a plea that the Irish Grants Committee not be disbanded. By this stage the President of the Association was the elderly William John Arthur Charles James Cavendish-Bentinck ("sixth Duke of Portland, Viscount Woodstock, Baron of Cirencester and Bolsover, and Lord Lieutenant of Nottingham"), who owned 180,000 acres and had the right to nominate two members to the Board of the British Museum.[9] But the gravy train had come to an end. In 1934 the British Government—now, to the consternation of Churchill, in "appeasement" mode towards the Irish, the Indians and the Germans— finally announced *"there is no penalization of Southern Irish Loyalists and hence no need of assistance"*.[10]

---

[9] According to *Time* magazine of New York, *"His predecessor as Duke had a molelike passion for tunneling under the lawns of his Welbeck estate, mile after mile, so that he could pop up and surprise his workmen."* 'Pensioners and Peers', *Time*, 1st October 1934.
[10] Ibid.

Chapter 7

Poisoning the Well or Publishing the Truth?

From Peter Hart's *The IRA and its Enemies* to RTÉ's *Hidden History* film on Coolacrease

By

Brian P. Murphy osb

Introduction: David Leeson on Poisoning the Well of the National Archives at Kew

At the end of last year, November 2007 to be precise, I became aware that David Leeson, Laurentian University, Canada, had made an extended critical reference about myself in his review of John Borgonovo's book, *Spies, Informers and the "Anti-Sinn Fein Society": the Intelligence War in Cork, 1920-1921* (Irish Academic Press, 2007). This review was written for 'Reviews in History,' the Institute of Historical Research's electronic reviews journal (see http://www.history.ac.uk/reviews/). At the same time, it was drawn to my attention that, in September 2005, Leeson had also commented critically about my use of sources on the Indymedia website. To address Leeson's review of Borgonovo's book first. In fact, in a review of some seventeen double-spaced pages that was supposedly devoted to Borgonovo's book, some two and half pages of footnote space had been devoted to a recent publication of mine, *The Origins and Organisation of British Propaganda in Ireland 1920* (Aubane, 2006) The comment in Leeson's text, which had served to introduce this footnote, was as follows: *"In fact, the UK's National Archive have preserved an enormous number of documents relating to the Irish War of Independence: and despite a recent effort by Brian Murphy and the Aubane Historical Society to poison this well, no*

159

historian can afford to ignore its contents".

Faced by remarks of this nature, I informed Dr. Jane Winters (Head of Publications, Institute of Historical Research, University of London) that they raised many questions: firstly, I stated, *"I am not a member of the Aubane Historical Society, although my book was published under its auspices; and, secondly, I have used the National Archives at Kew for over twenty years and have always acknowledged, with thanks, the value of the documents that are deposited there".*

Time, and space, prevented me from stating that the Aubane Historical Society, through the medium of Athol Books with which it is associated, has frequently reprinted original source material that is directly related to personalities whose names figure prominently in the records of the National Archives. For example, Major C.J.C.Street, *The Administration of Ireland 1920* (Athol, 2001); Lionel Curtis, *Ireland* (Athol, 2002); and General F.P.Crozier, *The Men I Killed* (Athol, 2002).

The publication of these works, all with important introductions, indicate a willingness to restore original source material into the historical narrative. Moreover, the publication by the Aubane Historical Society, itself, of Witness Statements for the years 1916-1921 that are held in the Military Archives, Cathal Brugha Barracks, Dublin, confirms the Society's commitment to making original records available. Indeed, *Sean Moylan in his own Words* (Aubane, 2004) was the first Witness Statement to be published and the book contained the first published list of all available Witness Statements, an invaluable facility for research students and the general public alike which is not available in any government publication.

Aware of my own, and the Aubane Society's, respect for the National Archives, both English and Irish, I concluded my observations to Dr. Winters with the comment that the views expressed by David Leeson *"raise questions as to his credibility as a reviewer. Clearly anyone"*, I continued, *"who makes remarks of that nature is not approaching the task at hand with the open mind that is the necessary prerequisite of a fair and objective review".* Dr. Winters responded to my concerns in an appropriate manner and the comments of Leeson were withdrawn from the review. However, the contents of his remarks about myself not only confirm a lack of objectivity but also betray a failure to read accurately the source material contained in the written text. At the centre of his error is his attribution to me of words and judgements that are essentially those of another, namely, Basil Clarke, Head of Publicity at Dublin Castle.

Leeson, having focussed on some letters and memoranda published in my book (Murphy, *British Propaganda in Ireland*, p.28), affirmed that:

> "the quality of Murphy's analysis can be fairly judged from his use of a memorandum on propaganda written by the Head of Dublin Castle's Department of Publicity, Basil Clarke. In this memorandum, Clarke defends the need for official press releases as part of a strategy of 'propaganda by news'. Murphy argues that by this, Clarke meant propaganda by false news—false official versions to combat the inconvenient truths of Irish Republican Propaganda: "Verisimilitude, a statement having the air of truth, while not, in fact, being so, was used by Clarke in order to deceive the assembled press correspondents"."

Leeson concluded that *"this argument is hard to sustain in the face of other passages from Clarke's own draft memoranda, such as 'propaganda then in my view should entail concentration on facts. Nor should one exclude even the unfavourable fact'"*.

If Leeson's analysis of Basil Clarke's memoranda was accurate and correct, then, indeed, my argument would be *"hard to sustain"*. However, the sentence about Clarke, for which I am taken to task, and beginning, *"verisimilitude, a statement having the air of truth, while not, in fact, being so..."* was purely a summary of Clarke's own memorandum. Even the word *"verisimilitude"* was Basil Clarke's and not mine! Immediately above my paraphrased conclusion one can read Clarke's own statement made to Andy Cope on 10 March 1921. It stated that *"about 20 Pressmen, Irish, British and foreign, visit the Castle twice daily, take our version of the facts—which I take care are as favourable to us as may be, in accordance with truth and verisimilitude—and they believe all I tell them. And they cannot afford to stay away. That is an advantage which no system of Press propaganda other than the news propaganda system, could win."*

In short, while it is correct to say that Clarke did include *"the unfavourable fact"*, he did so when it suited him. At other times he promulgated "our version of the facts" and, in particular, he made a very strong case for labelling this version of fact as *"official"*. He informed Cope, *"I would say that the labelling of the news in some way as official ("Dublin Castle," "GHQ," etc.) is the essence of the whole thing: the whole system of propaganda by news hangs on it".* Indeed, these extracts from the letter of Clarke to Cope, all of which are contained in my book, reveal a detailed, yet complex, system of propaganda by official news in which the facts of a case are either used or manipulated to achieve a specific purpose. For Leeson to argue otherwise is to misrepresent the contents of Clarke's letter.

Moreover, if Leeson had read the next page of my book, he would have found a letter of Major Street, Head of the Irish Office in London, which leaves no doubt that 'official' news was designed, when the occasion demanded, to deceive for propaganda purposes. Street wrote to Clarke on 12 March 1921 and declared that:

> "it seems to me that your critic (Andy Cope) does not understand the first principle of propaganda. In order that propaganda may be disseminated, in order that it may be rendered capable of being swallowed, it must be dissolved in some fluid which the patient will readily assimilate. Regarding the press as the patient, I know of only two solvents, advertisement and news, of which the latter is by far the most convincing and most economical."

From these words it is evident that the process to which Clarke and Street were committed was not simply the presentation of factual veracity: it was factual *"verisimilitude"*, Clarke's word, not mine, designed to serve a propaganda purpose. Far from poisoning the well of the National Archives, as Leeson claims, my reproduction of the material contained in their collections has, as far as humanly possible, faithfully attempted to let the contents speak for themselves. In this context many questions of academic capacity are raised in regard to Leeson's failure to read the contents of the National Archives with the diligence that they deserve. The same failure has manifested itself in his treatment of original documents that are central to the Indymedia debate about Peter Hart's, *The IRA and its Enemies* (Oxford, 1998).

David Leeson, Peter Hart
and Original Source Material Relating to the Kilmichael Ambush, 28 November 1920

In this debate Leeson stated that *"one reason I am not yet convinced that Hart is mistaken concerns the captured 1920 report to which his work refers".* This captured report relates to the Kilmichael Ambush, 28 November 1920, in which the Flying Column of the Third West Cork Brigade, under the command of Tom Barry, killed 17 members of the British Crown Forces. As the report is so central to the debate, it seems fitting to reproduce it here from the published account given by Peter Hart (Hart, *The IRA*, pp 25,26). Hart introduced the report by stating that it was Barry's *"original after-action report written for his superiors".*

The report reads:

"the column paraded at 3.15 a.m. on Sunday morning. It comprised 32 men armed with rifles, bayonets, five revolvers, and 100 rounds of ammunition per man. We marched for five hours, and reached a position on the Macroom-Dunmanway road ... We camped in that position until 4.15 p.m., and then decided that as the enemy searches were completed, that it would be safe to return to our camp. Accordingly, we started the return journey. About five minutes after the start we sighted two enemy lorries moving at a distance of about 1,900 yards from us. The country in that particular district is of a hilly and rocky nature, and, although suitable to fighting, it is not at all suitable to retiring without being seen. I decided to attack the lorries ... The action was carried out successfully. Sixteen of the enemy who were belonging to the Auxiliary Police from Macroom Castle being killed, one wounded and escaped, and is now missing ...

P.S. I attribute out casualties to the fact that those three men were too anxious to get into close quarters with the enemy. They were our best men, and did not know danger in this or any previous action. They discarded their cover, and it was not until the finish of the action that P.Deasy was killed by a revolver bullet from one of the enemy whom he thought dead."

This post-script concluded Peter Hart's published account of the *"captured report".*

It was in relation to this report that Leeson noted that "Meda Ryan and Brian Murphy have suggested that this report is not genuine" and stated that *"the report in question was reproduced in a printed document preserved in the Strickland Papers in the Imperial War Museum, entitled **The Irish Republican Army (From Captured Documents Only)*** (http://www.indymedia.ie/article/71352)." While these remarks of Leeson are correct, it is not correct to claim, that Peter Hart was referring to this source! The reference source to which Hart attributed the captured report was *The Irish Rebellion in the 6th Divisional Area from after 1916 Rebellion to December 1921*. This source is also to be found in the Strickland Papers, P.362, pp 63,64. I believe that I, myself, writing to the *Irish Times*, 10 August, 1998, was the first person to stress the significance of the contents of *The Irish Republican Army (From Captured Documents Only)*, to which Leeson now, late in the day, makes reference. Clearly it is of some academic significance that David Leeson incorrectly identified the source to which Hart made reference in his initial findings. Although the distinction may appear to be a fine one, it is, as will be clarified later, of some considerable moment in relation to the many claims that Peter Hart made about "the captured 1920 report".

The claims that Peter Hart has made about this report and his damning conclusion are to be found in the second chapter of his book, which is entitled, 'The Kilmichael Ambush'. To take the conclusion first: Hart stated that *"British information seems to have been remarkably accurate. Barry's history of Kilmichael on the other hand, is riddled with lies and evasions. There was no false surrender as he described it"*. The *"false surrender"* of the Auxiliaries, to which Hart makes mention here, formed an integral part of Tom Barry's accounts of the ambush. Basically, Hart is arguing from the presumption that the *"captured report"* is definitely Barry's; that silence in this report about a surrender of any sort proves that there was no *"false surrender"*; and, therefore, Barry's later accounts are *"riddled with lies and evasions"* by relating the *"false surrender"* story.

On these negative foundations Hart maintains that the traditional Irish nationalist version of the ambush cannot be maintained: the acclaimed heroic victory of a body of IRA freedom fighters, against their most feared opponents in the Crown Forces, is tarnished by the fact that they killed some of their opponents, in cold blood, after they had genuinely surrendered. Such is the argument of Peter Hart and it is made, it should be stressed, despite the fact that there is no mention of a surrender of any sort in the *"captured document"*.

This conclusion of Hart's is based on *"the captured 1920 report"* and the evidence of some anonymous witnesses, about whom a debate as to their reliability is ongoing. Hart maintained that the report was Barry's *"original after action report written for his superiors"*; that it was *"an authentic captured document"*; and that it *"was only printed in an unpublished and confidential history"*. Several observations may be made about these statements: firstly, the report was not *"written"*. As recorded in *The Irish Rebellion in the 6th Divisional Area*, it is a typed document; it is undated; and it is not signed. These facts would have been clear, if Hart had published the entire contents of the report. By omitting the final sentences, he has obscured the fact that the author is given, in typed format, as *"O.C. Flying Column, 3rd Cork Brigade"*. Secondly, and here the significance of Leeson's misreading of Hart's primary source becomes apparent, the report was not confined, as Hart claimed, to *"an unpublished and confidential history"*. It was published in *The Irish Republican Army (From Captured Documents Only)*. Although the circulation may have been limited, it was certainly published, clearly not confidential, and, presumably, used among military sources at the very least. I have, for example, found some pages of it in the files of the Dublin Castle civil administration.

Peter Hart, in reply to my letter of 10 August, was reluctant to accept the relevance of these points. Writing to the *Irish Times*, 1 September 1998, he still referred to the document as *"the first written account of the ambush"* and, in regard to *The Irish Republican Army (From Captured Documents Only)*, he maintained that it was *"a confidential printed (but not published) pamphlet issued to units by the Irish Command in 1921"*. All I can say is that the copy of *The Irish Republican Army* that I saw in the Imperial War Museum was a published document and that David Leeson viewed it in the same light, describing it as *"an official War Office publication"*. Refusing to acknowledge the points that I had made about the *"captured report"*, Hart stated, in his letter of 1 September 1998, that *"we must therefore ask the following questions: why would the British army forge a document which does not agree with its version of events, and then keep it secret except to mislead its own officers as to IRA methods?"*

At that time I did not reply to these questions for two reasons: firstly, it seemed to me that, having shown that the report lacked the authenticity of a signed, dated and hand-written document, it could not safely be used to justify the all-embracing conclusion that Hart had drawn; and, secondly, the contents of the *"captured report"* were so at variance with several known details of the ambush that it could not have been written by Tom Barry. Meda Ryan, in particular, drew attention to several issues over the contents of the "captured report": firstly, the number of men in the Flying Column was 36 not 32; the time of the ambush was closer to 4 p.m. than to 4.20 p.m.; thirdly, the Flying Column did not, at any time, retire from its planned ambush positions prior to the actual engagement; and, fourthly, P. Deasy was wounded, but not killed, during the action.

The views of Meda Ryan are of special importance because she interviewed, and recorded, several of those who had participated in the Kilmichael Ambush in the early 1970's (see Ryan, *Tom Barry, IRA Freedom Fighter*, Mercier/Cork, 2003; and her earlier book, *The Tom Barry Story*, Cork, 1982). Among these men were Ned Young (d.1989), the last survivor, and Paddy O'Brien (d.1979) both of whom spoke of a surrender call by the Auxiliaries. She also interviewed Pat O'Donovan and Tim O'Connell, both of whom fought in the same section of the ambush as Pat Deasy, one of the three members of the IRA who died as a result of the action. Indeed, the death of Deasy, and the manner of its recording by the "captured report" proves conclusively that it could not have been written by Tom Barry. It also provides a critical insight into Peter Hart's use of documents.

Three times, during the re-production of the report, Hart omits some of it contents. At the very end of the report, immediately prior to the post-script, one reads that a member of the Auxiliaries *"is now missing..."*. Among the sentences then omitted is the statement that *"our casualties were: one killed, and two who have subsequently died of wounds"*. In drawing attention to this selective omission, Meda Ryan observed that *"in reality it was the other way around: two Volunteers, Jim O'Sullivan and Michael McCarthy were killed and Pat Deasy died some hours later"*. Tom Barry, she concluded, *"would not have committed so glaring an error"*. Ryan's conclusion appears convincing and compelling. It is simply not credible that a commanding officer would have been unaware of the deaths under his command, especially as the wounded Pat Deasy was carried from the ambush site for several hours until his death and the Flying Column paid their respects to the two dead men on the field of battle. The real question that demands attention, after this brief consideration of the *"captured report"* is this: why did Peter Hart omit the significant sentence, *"our casualties were: one killed, and two who have subsequently died of wounds'"*?

The Issue of Forgery and Peter Hart's 'Honest Mistakes'

It was against this background that the question of forgery seemed secondary to the principal fact that the document, itself, could not be attributed to Tom Barry. Leeson, however, in his contribution to Indymedia, paid little attention to the considerations presented above, and repeated Hart's questions verbatim. He concluded that *"neither Murphy nor Ryan gave a satisfactory answer to that question"*. One cannot claim to have a definitive answer to this question, which, at this stage in the debate, would appear to be of only a speculative interest, but a possible response is to be found in the pages of the two British source documents. Ironically Hart, himself, in the very posing of the question, has indicated an answer to it by remarking that "the pamphlet's British author even comments that the Kilmichael report does not support the official version of the ambush, which claimed that the IRA mutilated the Auxiliaries bodies".

The pamphlet that Hart refers to here is *The Irish Republican Army (From Captured Documents Only)*. In other words, if I understand Peter Hart correctly, he is claiming that, if a forger was at work, he would have added the mutilation of the Auxiliaries to the forged report in order to blacken the reputation of the IRA. This argument might have some merit if both of the source documents that contain the Kilmichael *"captured report"*, *The Irish Republican Army (From Captured Documents Only)* and *The Irish Rebellion in the 6th Divisional Area*, had printed it without making any additional comments. However, both documents printed the *"captured report"* with comments that were taken, in large part, from the *"official version"* of the Kilmichael Ambush. In other words, the *"captured report"* was used as a peg on which to hang the *"official"* verdict on the ambush; and, with the word *"official"*, we are back in the world of Basil Clarke, *"verisimilitude"*, and distortion.

The effect is most clearly seen in the way in which the *"captured report"* is presented in *The Irish Rebellion in the 6th Divisional Area*, the document that Peter Hart cited originally. In that source, immediately following the *"captured report"*, it is stated that *"the true facts are as follows"*. The *"true facts"* recorded that the Auxiliaries were *"confronted by a man in British soldier's uniform, and wearing a steel helmet"*; that many of the IRA ambush party *"were dressed as British soldiers and wore steel helmets"*; that the dead and wounded Auxiliaries *"were indiscriminately hacked with axes and bayonets; shotguns were fired into their bodies, and many were mutilated after death"*. Similar *"true facts"*, although the list is not so comprehensive, were used to preface the *"captured report"* in *The Irish Republican Army (From Captured Documents Only)*.

The *"true facts"* were, in fact, composed by Basil Clarke, Head of Publicity, and his colleagues Captain H.B.C. Pollard of the Police Authority and Major Cecil Street of the Irish Office. Following the findings of the Military Court of Inquiry, held at Macroom on 30 November 1920, *"official"* press releases were made available, in early December, with such headlines as *"Mutilated Bodies"* and *"Mutilation with Axes"* (Murphy, *Propaganda*, pp 65-67). Although one Auxiliary, who had visited the ambush site, did inform the Court of Inquiry that *"all bodies were badly mutilated"*, the findings of Dr. Jeremiah Kelleher, while gruesome, did not endorse that finding. The only slight connection between the doctor's report and the *"official"* story was his evidence that a wound on one Auxiliary had been "inflicted after death by an axe or some similar weapon". In reality there were no IRA men in British uniforms and wearing steel helmets; there were no axes used in the ambush; and no bodies were mutilated.

At the time the *Irish Bulletin*, the organ of the Publicity Department of Dáil Éireann, attempted to correct the British version of the ambush. On 23 December 1920, under the heading, *Converting Acts of Warfare into Atrocities*, it stated that *"the English authorities prevented the examination of the bodies by any independent witnesses and spread... the reports that hatchets had been used to mutilate them"*. The *Irish Bulletin* then explained, with remarkable accuracy, the propaganda methods of Basil Clarke, even using the word *"verisimilitude"*. It stated that *"these false reports are given a certain verisimilitude by the suppression of essential facts: by the gross misstatements of certain details and by the deliberate addition of falsehoods known to be falsehoods by those who issue the reports"*.

In this context, the juxtaposition of the *"captured report"* with the so-called *"true facts"* of the ambush, we have, I would suggest, a reasonable answer to Peter Hart's question regarding forgery: a *"captured report"* accompanied by the *"true facts"* would not only damn the IRA but also convey a positive image of the British Crown Forces in their struggle against superior numbers. Moreover, British officials, both civil and military, and those sympathetic to the British war aims, began, almost immediately, to record an account of the Kilmichael Ambush that was based on the true facts of the *"official"* report. In February 1921 Major Street's *The Administration of Ireland 1920* was published in which the Flying Column at Kilmichael was described as wearing *"khaki trench-coats and steel helmets"* and the bodies of the Auxiliaries were said to be *"hacked with axes and bayoneted"*. In 1923 W. Alison Phillips, Lecky Professor of History at Trinity College, Dublin, writing as he claimed with access to secret British documents, recounted how *"a hundred Sinn Feiners disguised as British soldiers"* attacked the Auxiliaries, leaving the dead *"savagely mutilated with axes"* (Phillips, *The Revolution in Ireland, 1906-1923*, London, 1923). In 1924 General Macready, the Commander-in-Chief of the British Army in Ireland in 1920, wrote in the second volume of his *Annals of an Active Life* (London, 1924) that the wounded at Kilmichael *"were deliberately murdered on the road, being mutilated with axes"*.

It is significant, and relevant to Peter Hart's question about a forgery, that none of these accounts make reference to a surrender of any sort. If they had done so, it would have reflected badly on the integrity and bravery of the British Crown Forces. For the same reason, it would be expected that any forgery of a "captured document" relevant to the Kilmichael Ambush would also remain silent about a *"false surrender"* and that is what we find. Indeed, on a purely speculative level, the argument of Peter Hart may, quite logically, be turned on its head: the silence about a *"false surrender"* in the *"captured report"*, far from indicating that Tom Barry was its author, suggests that sources, other than Barry, were responsible for the document. To state the matter quite simply: Barry would have wanted the *"false surrender"* version in any report of his; British sources would not.

One of the first accounts, British or Irish, to mention a *"false surrender"* at Kilmichael was that of Lionel Curtis, a prominent adviser to the British Government, who visited Ireland secretly in early 1921. His version of events is of great interest because it was made after he had met Erskine Childers, then acting head of Publicity for Dail Eireann, and was influenced by Irish source material. They met in March 1921 and Curtis published his article on Ireland in the *Round Table* in the following June. Curtis reported that:

> "an account of one notorious episode, which was obtained from a trustworthy source in the district, may enable the reader to see the truth in relation to some of the stories to which it gives rise. Last autumn a party of police was ambushed at Kilmichael, near Cork. Every member of the party but one was killed, and the bodies were shamefully mutilated. It is alleged by Sinn Fein that a white flag was put up by the police, and that when the attacking party approached to accept the surrender fire was opened upon them."

While the account by Curtis does perpetuate the British story of mutilation, it also provides an early mention of Tom Barry's *"false surrender"* version of events. In this regard it should be noted that Peter Hart's claim that General Crozier, writing in *Ireland for Ever* (1932), was *"the first writer"* to recount the false surrender is, therefore, not correct. Some ten years ago, in a review article in *The Month* (September/October, 1998), I had pointed out that the *"false surrender"* account is also to be found in the life of *Michael Collins* (1926) by Piaras Beaslai but this account by Curtis is far more significant. Coming from a British source and coming within months of the Kilmichael Ambush, it undermines Hart's claim to place *"the first writer"* of the *"false surrender"* story at some considerable distance from the actual event.

One final point needs to be made in relation to Leeson's contribution to the debate. He stated in his Indymedia article that if Peter Hart has *"made mistakes, they were honest mistakes"* and concluded that some of his critics *"should be a little more circumspect in what they say about Peter Hart and his work"*. As Meda Ryan and myself were identified as critics in the preceding sentence, I presume that the remark about circumspection refers to myself. Faced by such comments, I can only respond by citing the opening sentence of my review of Peter Hart's book, as it appeared in *The Month*: *"this is a well researched book, an important book, a controversial book"*. This sentence was considered so *"circumspect"* that it was selected to appear on the back cover of subsequent editions of Peter Hart's book as a form of recommendation. The last sentence of my review, although raising some doubts, was, I would suggest, equally fair. *"Hart's findings on this important issue of sectarianism"*, I wrote, *"are open to question, but his book is to be welcomed as providing much new and indispensable information on the IRA"*.

The issue of Peter Hart's *"honest mistakes"* and the manner in which he has responded to the critiques of his book will now be addressed. Interviewed by Brian Hanley in *History Ireland* (March/April 2005), it was put to Peter Hart that *"Meda Ryan and Brian Murphy have raised quite specific criticisms. How do you respond to these?"* In regard to Meda Ryan, Hart replied that her work was marked by *"ignorance and prejudice"*, a remark that reflects more upon himself than upon Ryan, who answered his particular charges comprehensively in *History Ireland* (September/October 2005) In regard to myself, Hart replied that *"Brian Murphy has recently done some research on British propaganda but it isn't published yet so I can't really comment"*. This reply, with particular reference to propaganda, was correct. My book, already referred to, was not published until February 2006, although an appendix in that book on *'Peter Hart and the Issue of Sources'* had been published earlier in the *Irish Political Review* of July 2005. However, in my review article in *The Month* (1998) and in my letters to the *Irish Times* I had raised several questions that might have been addressed by Hart in 2005.

There is no need to rehearse here the arguments about the *"captured report"* of the Kilmichael Ambush except to stress again two of the fundamental questions that remain to be answered by Peter Hart: firstly, why persist in calling it the *"original"* report "written" for his superiors?; and, secondly, why omit from his published version of the *"captured report"* the sentences regarding the dead and the wounded that prove that Tom Barry could not have been the author? These unanswered questions are important. Equally important are the questions that I raised about sectarianism in my review article. In many ways these questions relating to religious issues and the IRA have become increasingly significant, especially after the showing last year by RTÉ of the film on the shooting of two young Protestants at Coolacrease on 30 June 1921. This film was part of their *Hidden History* series.

Peter Hart, Eoghan Harris and the RTÉ *Hidden History* film on *The Pearsons of Coolacrease*

The film was based on the book by Alan Stanley, *I Met Murder on the Way. The Story of the Pearsons of Coolacrease* (Carlow, 2005). There is a direct connection between Peter Hart's findings on sectarianism and this film: firstly, Alan Stanley, the author of the book on which the film was based, acknowledged the help that he had received from the "excellent history" of Peter Hart; secondly, he made several particular references to Peter Hart's work in the course of his narrative; and, thirdly, the back cover of the book advertises the verdict of Eoghan Harris that *"like Hart's classic, **The IRA and its Enemies**, this book opens new pages in the hidden history of southern Protestants in the period 1916-1923, and is a welcome addition to its slim historiography"*. The conclusion of Hart, to which both Stanley and Harris subscribe, may be summed up in his assertion that *"nationalism veered towards sectarianism in late 1920 and guerrilla war became, in some places, a kind of tribal war"*. In this context the reliability of Hart's findings on sectarianism are clearly all important and yet the questions that I raised about them, as long ago as 1998, have still not been answered.

The single most important issue that I raised was made in regard to Peter Hart's use of the source material that is contained in the

Record of the Rebellion in Ireland. This important document, containing the British Army's account of the Irish War, is preserved in the Imperial War Museum. Hart affirmed, citing the *Record*, that "the truth was that, as British intelligence officers recognised, *"in the south the Protestants and those who supported the Government rarely gave much information because, except by chance, they had not got it to give""*. By maintaining that Protestants did not have sufficient knowledge to act as informers, Hart heightens the suspicion that they were killed for religious motives. However, the very next sentences of the *Record*, which Hart has chosen not to re-produce, read as follows:

> "an exception to this rule was in the Bandon area where there were many Protestant farmers who gave information. Although the Intelligence Officer of this area was exceptionally experienced and although the troops were most active it proved almost impossible to protect those brave men, many of whom were murdered while almost all the remainder suffered grave material loss."

The evidence from this important source confirms, therefore, that the IRA killings in the Bandon area were motivated by military rather than sectarian considerations. Moreover, the Bandon area was not only a central focus of Hart's work but also it was for his information on that area that he was particularly thanked by Alan Stanley. Inevitably questions arise over the findings of both authors for failing to be guided by the *Record of the Rebellion*, a source which Peter Hart, himself, has described as *"the most trustworthy"*. This description by Hart was made in his introduction to a published edition of the *Record* in a book entitled *British Intelligence on Ireland, 1920-1921* (2002). In that publication the two missing sentences, in relation to Bandon, are included. However, instead of providing an explanation for, or even an acknowledgement of, their omission from his first book, there is a lengthy footnote that serves only to blur the issue. One would have hoped that an "honest mistake" would have resulted in an honest admission.

The basic question for Peter Hart, therefore, remains: why did he choose to omit from the *Record of the Rebellion*, *"the most trustworthy"* source, the two sentences that make his sectarian thesis impossible to sustain? Significantly, he chose not to address that question when interviewed by *History Ireland* in 2005. It is also worthy of note that, in the edited version of the *Record of the Rebellion*, neither Peter Hart, nor the series editor, David Fitzpatrick, saw fit to advice readers that they had omitted a section of the *Record* on *The People*. There one reads, among other things, that *"judged by English standards the Irish are a difficult and unsatisfactory people ... many were of a degenerate type and their methods of waging war were in most cases barbarous, influenced by hatred and devoid of courage"*. In the midst of these manifestly racist sentiments on the part of the British Army, when all sorts of vicious charges were made against the Irish people, there is, significantly, no allegation that Irish republicans were motivated by sectarian feelings.

Another important issue that I raised in 1998 also related to source material. Having noted that Peter Hart had made reference to the private papers of Erskine Childers and his unpublished account of *The Irish Revolution*, I asked why he had failed to advert to the contents of that account by Childers which dealt specifically with the matter of sectarianism. The words of Childers that I cited were as follows:

> "it is worth noting once more that the violence evoked in this year (1919) was slight. Nor was it indiscriminate or undisciplined. At no time, neither then nor subsequently, have civilians—Protestant Unionists living scattered and isolated in the South and West, been victimised by the republicans on account of their religion or religious opinion."

Childers was, of course, a Protestant, and his views, and, indeed, his work for Dail Eireann, present a compelling case against the thesis of sectarian strife proposed by Hart. Moreover, I added that during the summer of 1920, when the pogroms against Catholics were taking place in the north of Ireland, many Protestants wrote letters to the press stating that there was no religious persecution in the south. The words and actions of Childers and others, who assisted in the constructive work of Dail Eireann, clearly raised questions about Hart's sectarian thesis but he failed to address these questions in his *History Ireland* interview of March/April 2005. Despite this failure on the part of Peter Hart to provide any answer to these questions about sectarianism, his views have been adopted uncritically by Eoghan Harris and, through the medium of Harris, they have been widely publicised by RTÉ and the television programme on Coolacrease.

Eoghan Harris not only endorsed the original book on Coolacrease by Alan Stanley but also played a prominent part in the subsequent RTÉ film that was based on the book. His views on Peter Hart's history are, therefore, important. Writing in the *Sunday Independent* (17 December 2006), in relation to an RTÉ *Hidden History* programme on Frank Aiken, Harris made his views known. He stated that

> "contrary to some Southern assumptions, as Peter Hart has shown in his classic work, *The IRA and its Enemies*, sectarianism was not confined to Northern Ireland ... Hart's account of atrocities in the Bandon Valley reminds us that we in the Republic have no right to feel superior to Northern sectarians."

Harris concluded that:

> "Hart's book hit hard at the most basic myths of modern Irish republicans—that unlike the lowlife loyalists of the North, our noble IRA did not kill for sectarian reasons, and if perchance Protestants had been shot we could be sure they had been shot for political and not religious reasons. Hart showed all this to be a fantasy."

The article by Harris was entitled, *At the very Hart of our Sectarian History*. In the course of the article, Harris, like Hart, provided no answer either to the selective omissions from the British source on the Bandon area, or to the significant number of Protestants who supported Dail Eireann. Emotive sound-bites about sectarianism, rather than a serious study of the source material, was the message that Harris delivered to his readers. He delivered the same message to the viewers of the *Hidden History* programme on Coolacrease: *The Four Glorious Years*, the name given by Frank Gallagher to what he termed the noble struggle for Irish freedom, were tarnished, according to Harris, by sectarian killings. Following the showing of the Coolacrease film, Harris defended it in his *Sunday Independent* column (11 November 2007) by stating that it presented an historical reality that had been buried *"until Canadian historian Peter Hart published **The IRA and its Enemies**"*.

The film did exactly that: it presented the story of the Pearson family of Coolacrease through the medium of interview and re-enactment; it told how the Pearson boys engaged in armed action against the local IRA, how the IRA responded by an attack on the family home, and how two of the boys were executed in appalling circumstances; it also portrayed the clash between the Pearsons and the IRA as part of a campaign by Irish republicans to drive Protestants from the land. During the course of the film and subsequently, most recently in a contribution by Philip McConway to *History Ireland* (May/June 2008), the details of the Pearson story and general thrust of the sectarian argument have been contested. However, the overall impact of the film was accurately summed up by Eoghan Harris: it projected an historical reality that had been buried until Peter Hart's book on the IRA was published. Irish republicans could no longer claim, as Harris put it, that *"our noble IRA did not kill for sectarian reasons"*.

The contribution to the film by Harris, himself, played no small part in promoting Hart's thesis that the IRA were sectarian killers. Not only did Harris give the impression that the Pearson brothers were shot *"very deliberately in the genitals, in their sexual parts"*, (a claim that is not substantiated by documents relating to the deaths), but also he constantly repeated the sectarian line taken by Peter Hart on the killing of Protestants. In a sense this was to be expected from Harris, a self-professed member of the Reform group, which, in his own words, *"for the past ten years, have been trying to put Southern attacks against Protestants in 1921/1922 on the public agenda"* (*Sunday Independent,* 17 Dec. 2006)

Questions clearly arise as to how the director of the film, Niamh Sammon, could allow any member of an organisation with a political/ historical agenda a privileged position on her programme. There can be no question, however, as to the influence of Peter Hart's writings on the shaping of the RTÉ's *Hidden History*. Hart's influence, through the medium of Eoghan Harris, was truly immense. Like recurring links in a chain. the connections are clear to see: Peter Hart/ Eoghan Harris for the promotion of Hart's book; Alan Stanley/Peter Hart/Eoghan Harris for the promotion of Stanley's book; Alan Stanley/Peter Hart/Eoghan Harris (Reform Group) for the promotion of the RTÉ *Hidden History* programme on Coolacrease.

Any questioning of the vital link in the chain, the historical writing of Peter Hart, had to be contested and Harris has always done that: not by engaging in academic debate but by the use of powerful and polemical prose. All opposition has had to be crushed. In his *Sunday Independent* article (11 November 2007), Harris dismissed the criticisms of Peter Hart's work by the Aubane Society as *"violent verbal polemics"* (he used more extreme language on the Joe Duffy radio show), and he suggested, among other things, that a letter of mine to the *Irish Examiner* (3 November 2007) should have considered the events in the Coolacrease film from *"a Protestant perspective"*. As my letter had dealt exclusively with the views of Protestants, I replied to his criticisms in a letter to the *Sunday Independent* (9 December 2007). The purpose of the letter was to allow the voices of Protestants to enter not only the debate on the Coolacrease film but also the debate on Peter Hart's sectarian version of Irish history. It was also intended to raise questions about a statement of Dr. Terence Dooley, which was made in the course of the film, that *"the revolutionary period was essentially used as a pretext to run many of these Protestant farmers and landlords out of a local community for locals to take up their lands"*.

Protestant Voices that Reveal an Alternative Hidden History to that of RTÉ and Peter Hart

In my letter to the *Sunday Independent*, I listed several Protestant voices and asked Eoghan Harris to respond. These voices are listed below:

Firstly, the voice of Matilda Pearson, sister of the two victims of the Coolacrease killings in 1921, who asked the IRA men taking part in the attack on her home, why they were doing it and received the reply, as recorded by herself: *"Don't think we are doing this because you are Protestants. It is not being done on that account"*. Is this evidence compatible with a sectarian interpretation of the killing of her brothers?

Secondly, the voices of Robert Barton (head of Dail Eireann's Department of Agriculture), Erskine Childers and Lionel Smith Gordon, all Protestants and all appointed by Dail Eireann in December

1919 to direct the fortunes of the National Land Bank. Is it credible that Dail Eireann would have placed Protestants, such as these, in charge of land reform, if they had wished to drive Protestants from the land?

Thirdly, the voices of Sir Horace Plunkett and George Russell (AE), both Protestants, who continued to support the work of the Co-operative Society throughout the War. Is it possible that they would have co-operated with native Irish farmers, if the farmers themselves and their families had been associated in sectarian warfare?

Fourthly, the voices of the Church of Ireland Bishops of Meath and Killaloe, Dr. Kathleen Lynn, Alice Stopford Green, Alibinia Brodrick, James Douglas and several other Protestants, as well as the distinctive voice of Dr. Herzog, the Chief Rabbi, who joined with many Catholics in January 1921 to assist the work of the Irish White Cross Society. Is it credible that so many Protestants would have joined in this charitable enterprise to redress the damages of war, if that war had been sectarian?

Fifthly, the voices of the Protestant members of the first Irish Free State Senate, which ought to have some special significance for Mr. Harris, unless he is prepared to reject the heritage of the body of which he is a member. Among these voices are to be found those of Alice Stopford Green, Sir John Griffith, James Douglas (the first three persons to be elected to the Senate by the Dail in December 1922), W.B. Yeats and Douglas Hyde. Is the election of such distinguished Protestants to the Senate in any way compatible with a sectarian war against the Protestant community?

One could have presented other examples of Protestant voices: for example that of Lionel Curtis, whose views on Kilmichael were reported above, who stated in June 1921, the very month of the attack on the Pearson home, that *"to conceive the struggle as religious in character is in any case misleading. Protestants in the South do not complain of persecution on sectarian grounds. If Protestant farmers are murdered, it is not by reason of their religion, but rather because they are under suspicion as loyalists. The distinction is a fine, but a real one."* These measured words by Curtis, coming as they do from an experienced British official, fresh from the corridors of power at the Paris Peace Conference, should alone be sufficient to send Peter Hart and Terence Dooley back to the historical drawing board. And yet even more Protestant voices, speaking the same language of religious toleration and understanding, are to be heard.

For example, other distinguished Protestant voices were provided by Lord Henry Cavendish Bentinck, Basil Williams, John Annan Bryce and many others, who joined the Peace with Ireland Council, formed in England in October 1920, to campaign for an end to war in Ireland. One might also have presented some of the Protestant voices who expressed their views publicly to the American Commission on Irish Independence in late 1920 and early 1921: for example, that of the socialist, Louie Bennett, the Dublin born secretary of the Irish Branch of the Women's International League; or that of Caroline Mary Townshend, the Gaelic organiser for Bandon, county Cork (an area that was central to Peter Hart's thesis), both of whom testified that they had not experienced any sectarianism in their work or in their organisations.

One could have selected many other Protestant voices who expressed their views to the press in the summer of 1920, while pogroms were taking place in the north of Ireland and whose views, as mentioned above, have, without explanation, been ignored by Peter Hart. For example the voice of the Reverend I.C. Trotter, a Protestant rector at Ardrahan, county Galway, who wrote (*Irish Times*, 23 July 1920) that "during my experience of over thirty years in the County of Galway, I have not only never had the slightest disrespect shown to me or to those belonging to me as Protestants, but from the priests and people, gentle and simple, have received the utmost consideration and friendship". The next day, 24 July 1920, a letter from G.W. Biggs appeared in the *Irish Times* declaring that "I have been resident in Bantry for 43 years, during 33 of which I have been engaged in business, and I have received the greatest kindness, courtesy, and support from all classes and creeds in this country". When Niall Meehan reproduced this letter (*Irish Times*, 5 November 2007), during the debate on the RTÉ film on Coolacrease, he contrasted it with two leading articles in the paper by Niamh Sammon (20 October), director of the RTÉ film on Coolacrease, and

Ann Marie Hourihane (25 October), both of which had conveyed the idea of sectarian conflict during the War of Independence.

Meehan concluded that given a choice between the views of, the Protestant, Biggs, who was on the spot, "and Hourihane and Sammon, who were not, and the reporting of the *Irish Times* then, and now, I take the Protestant view". His conclusion is compelling and revealing: compelling because it presents an authentic Protestant voice of the past; revealing because it provides an interesting glimpse into the policy of the *Irish Times* in the present. Writing as one whose letter (6 November 2007) presenting Protestant voices of the period was rejected for publication, one is forced to conclude, surprisingly but significantly, that while the *Irish Times* in 1920, at the height of the war, was willing to publish Protestant voices that spoke of toleration, the *Irish Times* of to-day resists the publication of letters that tell the same story. It has firmly committed itself to the views of Niamh Sammon and to the sectarian view of the period as presented in the RTÉ *Hidden History* programme. To their credit the *Irish Examiner* and the *Sunday Independent* have given open access in their letters pages to all points of view.

The omission of these Protestant voices from the thesis of Hart and the RTÉ *Hidden History* (and one must include the pages of the *Irish Times*) has been compounded by the failure to acknowledge the many ways in which the Dublin Castle administration and the British Crown Forces, often using the martial law legislation of the Defence of the Realm Act (1914) and the Restoration of Order in Ireland Act (1920), directly attempted to prevent Catholics and Protestants from working together. For example, the arrest of Robert Barton, the most prominent Protestant member of the Dail administration, in early January 1920 and his confinement in England until the end of the war; the regular raids on those involved in administering the funds of the National Land Bank; the destruction of many Co-operative creameries; the closure of the Dail Eireann courts which were recognised by Protestants, themselves, as dealing fairly with land disputes.

Any historical narrative that neglects these actions by the British administration in Ireland and refuses to acknowledge the many examples of Protestant and Catholic accord is open to many questions.

Peter Hart has failed to produce answers to those question; Eoghan Harris has failed to produce answers to those questions. Two conclusions may be drawn: firstly, the historical writing of Peter Hart, and the championing of it by Eoghan Harris, has introduced a sectarian dimension into Irish history that is not merited either by the source material; and, secondly, the RTÉ *Hidden History* programme, by aligning itself with the Hart/Harris ideology, has failed to provide the "truthful, honest and correct" interpretation of the events at Coolacrease that was so sincerely sought by one of the surviving Pearson family. The manner of the killings was unforgivable but, in order to respond honestly to the questions of the surviving Pearson family, the film should have been set in the context of an historical narrative that reflected accurately the religious character of the war. Protestant voices of the time, be they Irish or British, do not speak of that war as sectarian.

As for the Broadcasting Complaints Commission, which I am told has upheld the impartiality of the film, one can only presume that it was unaware of the many issues that have been raised above. Was it aware that Eoghan Harris represented an organisation, the Reform Group, with a specific public agenda? Was it aware that this agenda was only made tenable by the selective use of source material by Peter Hart in his book on *The IRA and its Enemies*? Was it aware that this same source material inspired Alan Stanley to write his book on Coolacrease on which the RTÉ film was based? Was it aware that Niamh Sammon, the film's director, in selecting the story for film purposes, opted for the opinion of Eoghan Harris that the story was about an *"atrocity against a harmless dissenting Protestant family"* and rejected the contemporary evidence of Matilda Pearson, a member of that family, that the attack was not carried out because the Pearsons were Protestants? A response to these questions would be welcomed. In the meantime, with so many questions unanswered, it seems reasonable to ask the ultimate question: is the RTÉ film on Coolacrease revealing a hidden history or is it concealing a hidden agenda?

Chapter 8

Academic Evasions:

Revisionists and the War of Independence

By

Brendan Clifford

The central issue in the Coolacrease controversy is whether legitimate political authority in Ireland in 1921 was Imperial or democratic. The makers of the television programme and the professional (that is, paid) historians who contributed to it assume that legitimate political authority was Imperial. The national broadcaster, RTÉ, condoned that assumption by broadcasting the programme without broadcasting an associated discussion of the possibility that legitimate authority might have been democratic. Then, in the face of some public protest, RTÉ personality Joe Duffy, treated as a joke the suggestion that the General Election of 1918 conferred legitimate political authority on the parties that won it, and deprived the Government parties, that did not even contest it, of any legitimate right to govern.

The Irish electorate rejected Imperial authority in the General Elections of 1918 and 1921 and in the Local Elections of 1920. The assumption that the Imperial authority nevertheless remained the legitimate authority does not rest on a reasoned case. Those elections are not subjected to scrutiny and shown to have somehow been invalid. Nor has the case been made that in the world of 1919-21 democracy was not generally regarded as being the source of legitimate authority. There is simply an assumption, unsupported by reasoning, that in June 1921 legitimate authority in Ireland was Imperial.

There was a long era during which democracy was generally regarded by those in authority as an illegitimate and unviable political form which had to be knocked on the head whenever it appeared. That was the case at the time of the United Irishmen. The British Empire at that time made war on France because the French Revolution had proclaimed the legitimacy of democratic government.

Edmund Burke, the great ideologist of the war against the French Revolution, declared that a people have a right to be governed, that they cannot govern themselves, and that, if they do not voluntarily consent to being governed by those who are fit to govern them, they must be made to submit to government by the application of force.

That was the attitude adopted by the Imperial Government in Ireland to the problem of Irish democracy after the 1918 Election. But it could not be set out clearly and coherently by the Imperial ideologists after the Great War, as it had been by Burke. And still less can it be stated explicitly today by those who want to treat the War of Independence of 1919-21 as a continuation or revival of the Insurrection of 1916: one which might be put down legitimately in the same way.

It has become fashionable to condemn the 1916 Insurrection on the grounds that those who carried it out did so without an electoral mandate. The implication of that condemnation is that, if Pearse and Connolly had had an electoral mandate to form a Republic in Ireland, they would have had the moral right to do so by whatever means were necessary. That was not the position of the Government of the British Empire in 1916, but it is the position of those who, living in the Irish Republic but wishing Ireland was still part of Britain, want to condemn the developments through which an Irish Republic came about.

I cannot see that in 1916 either those who tried to set up the Republic or those who knocked it down had an electoral mandate to do what they did. All the electoral mandates deriving from the General Election of December 1910 ran out in December 1915 and no further mandate was sought. The British Government was governing without an electoral mandate in 1916, and it never had an electoral mandate to govern Ireland.

Elected government was suspended in 1915 with the tacit consent of the British electorate. Britain—as Prime Minister Blair reminded us when he was in power—is a war-fighting state. War was its primary business for centuries and there was very widespread agreement that it would be foolish to hold an election while the war was on, just because the electoral mandate had run out.

The decision to govern without an electoral mandate was taken in 1915 without a division. The British electorate was comprehensively represented not merely in Parliament but in the Government when it was decided to carry on without an election. The Unionist Party, which had brought the state to the brink of civil war in 1914 in its opposition to the Home Rule Bill, was brought into the Government in 1915. It had threatened to force a division in Parliament on the issue of suspending elections unless it was brought into Government. A Liberal/Unionist Coalition was formed in May 1915. A Bill authorising the continuation of that Government was passed. And so we had the situation in Dublin in 1916 that two unelected bodies engaged in battle.

It might be argued that the British Government of 1916, though unelected, had representative status by virtue of the party system. The British electorate, historically, was dominated by the two-party system, whose existence predated the democratisation of the electoral franchise by a couple of centuries. The electorate chose between the parties at elections. Where the parties agreed, there was nothing to choose. Both parties were committed to total war to the bitter end without electoral distractions, and so the suspension of elected government was a measure that accorded with the popular will. It was as Constitutional as anything can be under the unwritten Constitution in which the British Parliament exercises arbitrary sovereignty.

None of this applied in Ireland. The Irish electorate was not represented in the governing institutions of the state, nor was it represented in the political system on which those institutions rested.

The Home Rule Party, led by John Redmond, which monopolised the representation of nationalist Ireland until 1910, and which held 74 of the Irish seats after 1910 (having lost ten seats to the All-For-Ireland League), went to Westminster but held itself apart from the political system of the state.

Redmond supported the British war on Germany, Austria and Turkey in 1914, and raised canon fodder in Ireland for it. But he refused the invitation to join the Coalition Government that was formed in 1915 for the purpose of concentrating all the political forces of the state on the conduct of the War.

That Coalition included the Ulster Unionist leader, Edward Carson, who had been leading an armed rebellion against the authority of Parliament on the issue of Home Rule at the moment when war was declared. In September 1914 Carson agreed that the Home Rule Bill should be signed by the King and placed in the Statute Book as an Act, on the condition that the implementation of the Act should be suspended, and that it should never be implemented as it stood.

The enactment and simultaneous suspension of the Home Rule Bill was done by agreement between the Liberal Government, which had carried the Bill through Parliament, and the Unionist Opposition, which had carried resistance to the Bill to the brink of civil war. If the Liberal Government, having warded off the danger of civil war by declaring war on Germany, had won a quick victory in the European War (as was expected at the time) the establishment of a Home Rule Government in Ireland might have remained on the agenda of practical politics. The formation of the Coalition Government took it off the political agenda.

The 1915 Coalition included the Ulster Unionist leader, Edward Carson as Attorney General, and the firebrand of the 1912-14 resistance to Home Rule, F.E. Smith (later Lord Birkenhead) as Solicitor General. Smith, though particularly active on the Ulster issue, was a leading member of the (British) Unionist Party, which was created by a merger of the Tory Party and the social reform/anti-Home Rule section of the Liberal Party, led by Joseph Chamberlain.

The Unionist Party was the most vigorous element in the War Coalition. Its influence grew steadily in the course of the War. In 1916 it brought about a new Coalition and subverted the Liberal Party.

While these major changes were occurring, and undermining the credibility of Home Rule-on-the-Statute Book, Redmond carried on recruiting for the War while refusing to take part in the Government which conducted it.

A Constitutional party which refuses in principle to take part in Constitutional government is a strange thing. It was argued in Britain that the term 'Constitutional' did not properly apply to that party, and that a major change in the Constitution should, therefore, not be made at its behest.

The self-prohibition on Home Rule participation in the British Government made sense in nationalist Ireland, where Home Rule was understood to be the greatest step away from the British state that could be gained without warfare. Participating in the government of the state was incompatible with the separatist ideal underlying the Home Rule movement.

Constitutional nationalism was a kind of self-contradiction which served as a stop-gap.

The Home Rule leaders, including Redmond himself, had stated frankly that they were Home Rulers only because they could not see their way to fighting a war against the British Empire, which was the only means by which independence could be achieved. In accordance with this position, the Home Rule Party at Westminster had generally opposed the Imperial policy of the state. It had been particularly vigorous in its opposition to the war of conquest against the Boer Republics (1899-1902).

Then in August 1914 Redmond committed his Party to support for the British Empire in its declarations of war on Germany and Austria; in September he exhorted the Home Rule Volunteers to enlist in the British Army; and in November he supported the declaration of war against Turkey.

In Britain political conflict was suspended for the duration of the War, except in the inner circles at Westminster and Whitehall. In 1915 the Whitehall inner circle was extended to include all the political parties of the state, except the Irish Home Rule Party.

By refusing to join the Government, Redmond effectively removed himself from the political life of the state.

He had held the balance of power between the Liberal and Unionist Parties from 1910 to 1915, but he lost it when the Coalition was formed. By refusing to join the Coalition, though unreservedly supporting the British Empire at war, he made himself the odd man out at Westminster.

'Constitutional nationalism' then constituted itself into a mere recruiting apparatus for a war being waged by the British Empire for increasingly obscure purposes and in an increasingly hysterical and reckless state of mind.

If it was a constitutional party, why did it not join the other constitutional parties in government to guide the conduct of the War? And, if it stood on national sovereignty as a basic principle, why did it not kick up ructions when the Coalition invaded neutral Greece and set about overthrowing the Greek Government in order to compel Greece to make war on Turkey?

It seems to me that the Home Rule Party was discredited and marginalised, not only in Ireland but also in England, by Redmond's wartime antics.

Lyons's Defence of Redmond

The multi-volume *New History Of Ireland* published by Oxford University—and advertised in a publicity brochure as a "Re-Writing of Irish History"—defends Redmond's purposeless meanderings as follows:

"For the leaders of the Irish parliamentary party the formation of the coalition represented a double blow. On the one hand it led to the inclusion of Carson in the Cabinet, where obviously he would exert enormous pressure on Irish policy. And on the other it confronted Redmond and Dillon with an acute dilemma. To balance Carson's inclusion, Asquith and Birrell urged one or other of the nationalist leaders to enter the coalition as well. This, however, they could not do without compromising the principle of independent opposition that was vital to the party's existence. Obliged to acquiesce in Carson's inclusion, they stayed outside themselves and thus preserved their independence at the expense of their influence" (Vol. VI, p.209; the author is F.S.L. Lyons).

What "opposition" did Redmond engage in between May 1915, when Carson became a Cabinet Minister, and April 1916, when an insurrectionary body, consisting largely of disillusioned Home Rulers, staged the Easter Rising? None at all, as far as I have seen. He had kept the Liberal Government in power from the back-benches from 1911 to 1915, and then in 1915-16 he supported the Liberal/Unionist Government from the back-benches, having lost the balance-of-power leverage of 1911-15.

He gave unconditional and uncritical support for the War, and, after the formation of the Coalition, politics at Westminster was about nothing else. He led *"a party of independent opposition"* which opposed nothing. He reduced the Home Rule Party to a militaristic recruiting apparatus in Ireland—a party which would neither join the Government nor oppose it—therefore, a political party without politics.

Lyons must have seen this. I don't think it is possible to look directly at the 1915 situation and not see it. But Redmond was cast for the role of the hero, or sage, in the revisionist re-writing of Irish history—he was all that was available—and it was necessary to make do with him, even if it meant writing nonsense at times.

In 1916 Redmond led a back-bench party which supported the war unconditionally but refused to play a part in its direction, and which could exert no influence on the Government with its mammoth majority in Parliament. Indeed the Home Rule Party, *"the party of independent opposition"*, was itself part of that mammoth Government majority. The actual Opposition consisted of a handful MPs who wanted the War to be ended by negotiation.

It was also an unelected Party. All the other Parties were unelected too. But the unelected status of the Irish Party was different in kind from the unelected status of the others. The others were represented in the Government, and they were parts of the interconnected party system which governed the state, while the Irish Party was not represented in the Government, and was not a component of the party system of the state.

It was a reasonable and realistic assumption that what was agreed between the party leaders in the Coalition Government was agreeable to the electorate. And this was particularly the case when the chief business—in a sense the only business—on which the state was engaged was War. Britain was an active Imperialistic state whose populace was highly adapted to the waging of war.

In Ireland, however, the fact that the Home Rule Party was implementing a militaristic Imperialist policy, in support of a Government over which it had forfeited all influence by its refusal to undertake Government responsibility, was a reason why it should not be regarded as having continued to be representative after its electoral mandate ran out. Its history was anti-imperialist and anti-militarist, and its 1910 election programme had given no hint of a change of policy.

The Suspension of Elected Government

How did the Redmondites vote in the 1915 Bill to suspend elected government for the duration of the War? This is not a question that the revisionist history books answer. Indeed, the very fact that elected government was suspended for the duration of the War is scarcely mentioned in books written by British historians for British purposes, so it would be surprising if they made an issue of it in the re-writing of Irish history, which they have been organising for about thirty years.

The 1910 electoral mandate ran out at the end of 1915. A new election should have been held in January 1916 at the latest. Questions were asked in the Commons during the Summer of 1915 about the holding of an election. The Prime Minister said on June 22nd that a Bill to postpone elections for a year would be introduced "forthwith". But no Bill appeared.

Eventually on November 4th an official announcement was made:
"I would say just a word as to the attitude of the Government towards this question. We are, broadly speaking, finally convinced that a General Election ought not to take place while the war is going on, and that we should, and so far as we are concerned we shall, spare no pains to prevent any such election taking place."

The announcement was made in passing in the course of a debate about another matter. The speaker was Lord Lansdowne—the same Lansdowne who had organised the ethnic cleansing, and Protestant plantation, at Luggacurran, on one of his Irish estates.

A Bill putting off the election for a year got its Second Reading in the Commons ten days later, on December 14th. Having been agreed by the party leaders in the Coalition, it was certain to be passed, but an Amendment to reject the measure as unconstitutional and undemocratic was proposed by W.H. Cowan, a Liberal, so there was a debate.

This was the second time that Parliament decided to overrun its electorally mandated life. The first was 200 years earlier when the

Whigs, having brought in a German King who could not speak English, were persecuting the Tories who stood for the orthodox succession of the Stuart monarchy, and for that reason were called Jacobites (from James). The Whigs saw that Jacobite sentiment was strong in the country and feared defeat in a General Election. The life of Parliament then was three years. The Whigs made use of their majority to push through the Septennial Act, retrospectively increasing it to seven years, and then used their four extra years to lay the foundations of the long Whig Ascendancy.

It so happened that the Septennial Act remained in force until 1911, and it would have covered Parliament until early 1918 if it had not been abrogated by the Parliament Act of 1911 which abolished the Lords' Veto and allowed the Home Rule Bill to pass without the consent of the Lords if it was passed in three successive sessions of the Commons. But the Lords got something in return for giving way on the Parliament Bill which abolished its veto, and that was the reduction of the life of Parliament from seven years to five, starting with 1910. And the draft Bill for reducing the life of Parliament to five years was published before the December 1910 Election. Carrying on under the Septennial Act until 1917 was considered but was not thought advisable.

Cowan's argument about unconstitutionality was summarily dismissed by E.G. Hemmende: *"We are told by the hon. Member that it is an unconstitutional measure for Parliament to extend its own life. I wonder what makes him say that."*

Ronald McNeill, a Unionist, argued for the holding of the Election at the proper time, but did so on political rather than constitutional grounds. He thought an Election would be good for the War. Jeremiah McVeagh, a Home Ruler, threw a jibe at him, but did not make an argument.

John Dillon, who said he had been 35 years in the House, asked McNeill what the election would be about:

> "The real question that one must put to himself when we hear men advocating a General Election is, on what issue are you going to the country? If hon. Members had the courage to challenge the policy of the Government—I do not say there may not be many points on which you might challenge them—and then went to the country on an issue

similar to that which was put to the country in the course of the Crimean War, that would be a perfectly defensible policy, but no one throughout the whole Debate up to this hour has said a word which indicates that he has the slightest notion as to the issue which we should put before the electors of the country or any constituency in the country. The only hint I got from any speech was the reference to the election in Merthyr. In other words the idea apparently in the minds of some hon. Members is that the only issue to be put to the electors of each constituency is who is the more war-like person. This is a nice controversy to plunge into on purely personal records. 'A' would be called a pro-German, and he would be denounced on the lines on which Lord Haldane, for instance, was denounced. Would they go to their constituents on this issue, that we have an incapable Government composed of a selection of all the statesmen that England could produce from both parties, and that they have made a mess of the situation, and we want another Government? Then might not the constituents say, 'Who are your men?' Is there a single man sitting on these Benches who is prepared to mention the men whom he would put in the place of the Government? I ask: would it be fair to the country, would it be fair to this House or to the nation to go to the country and make such an issue as that in the face of the world at this terrific crisis?"

Lord Haldane was the Liberal Minister for War who, from 1908 in Asquith's Government, had prepared the British Army for war on Germany. In August 1914, as Lord Chancellor, he had put those military preparations into effect, because the state was without a War Minister at the critical moment because of the Curragh Mutiny a few months earlier. In 1915 he was dropped from the Government in the face of mounting anti-German hysteria because it became known he could read German and had read German philosophy. (Home Rule propagandists had contributed heavily to the working up of the anti-German hysteria.)

Dillon did not want an election because an election could be about nothing but the War, and all parties were in favour of the War, and all were in the Government except his party, and that was as enthusiastic about the War as all the others, even though for some obscure reason of principle it refused to join the others in Government to contribute its experience and wisdom to the directing of the War.

With all the parties of the state in the Government, and with the

Irish Party supporting the War unconditionally in a situation in which the War was all that mattered, there was no Opposition. Without an Opposition there was no alternative Government. All the best political talent of the country was already in the Government. So what sense would there be in holding an election?

But Dillon admitted that the observance of constitutional forms counted for something. His preference was that they should be observed in the form of *"an agreed election"*. He did not, in this speech, explain what that meant. I assume it was something on the lines of the Collins/De Valera Agreement seven years later, whereby an election would be called, but the seats would not be contested so that an unchanged Parliament would be the outcome. (In 1922 Churchill declared that arrangement to be undemocratic in Ireland and Collins was given an ultimatum to break it.)

Dillon's second preference was that *"the War period should not be counted under the Parliament Act: It should be a dies non, and Parliament should go on after the five years under the Parliament Act after peace is signed."*

But his basic concern was that Parliament should carry on without an election during the war, and the procedure of annual postponement was acceptable to him.

The Government decision to carry on without election meant that Redmond was not obliged to go to the country with his radically changed policy. He went along with the decision of the British parties not to go to the country. But, going along with the British decision was not warranted by circumstances. Ireland was a different country. The Irish Party, for all its militaristic imperialism at that time, did not form part of the British body politic in a way that would enable it to be borne along safely by the British body politic in a matter like this; nor did its electorate, for all its acquiescence in the militaristic imperialism of the Party, form an organic part of the electorate from which constitutional government derived.

Redmond was marginalised in the political life of the state. And he was Prime Minister-in-waiting of Home Rule-in-the-Statute Book, as the turn of events made it increasingly unlikely that Home Rule would ever take on an existence beyond the Statute Book.

He relied on an exhausted electoral mandate to see him through the

War. It did not see him through.

What it would have been prudent for him to do, in the light of the radical change of policy that he made in August-September 1914, was to begin acting as Home Rule Prime Minister by calling his own General Election in the part of Ireland that he represented. He might have done this by resigning all the Home Rule seats and fighting the by-elections on a war policy.

If he had done that, and had held all or most of the seats, and if nevertheless there had been a Republican Insurrection, it would be to the point to condemn that Insurrection, not only for lacking an electoral mandate, but for being carried out in defiance of an electoral mandate.

As it was, there was no operative electoral mandate in April 1916.

Redmond's mandate had run out of time, and it was in any case not a mandate for participation in Imperialist war.

And the parties that governed the state had long since stopped contesting elections in Ireland.

*

Ireland as part of the UK had never been governed by representative government. The Irish electorate was never represented in the Government of the state, regardless of which party won the electoral contest to govern the state. The Home Rule Party was not a participant in the political system by which the state was governed. What it expressed was acquiescence in the governing of Ireland by whichever party won the General Election in Britain. The Home Rule mandate given by the Irish electorate was to submit to British government, not to participate in it. And the reason given for submission by the Home Rule leaders was that they could not see how sufficient military power could be raised in Ireland under British rule to make the achievement of independence a practical option.

In 1916 even the electoral mandate for submission was lacking. And the Home Rule Party had never had an electoral mandate for participation in the militaristic imperialism of the British state. The Insurrection, therefore, was enacted in a situation in which there were no operative electoral mandates of any kind.

When the General Election was held two and a half years later, a comprehensively reconstructed Sinn Féin party contested it on a programme of establishing an independent Government in Ireland, and it won three-quarters of the seats. But those who condemn the Insurrection on the ground that it lacked an electoral mandate, usually take no heed of the electoral mandate of 1918. Suddenly the electoral mandate becomes a thing of no consequence, scarcely deserving a mention.

It was not mentioned by RTÉ in its Coolacrease programme.

Senator Harris on the War of Independence

The major participant in that programme was Senator Eoghan Harris. Senator Harris has not, that I know of, published a written account of developments from 1916 to 1921 explaining why the lack of an electoral mandate was all-important with regard to 1916 but the presence of an electoral mandate was of no importance at all with regard to 1918-1921.

The most extensive presentation of his case that I know of is a television programme that he made for British television some years ago (Channel 4, 1st June 1996). A transcript of the first half of that programme is given below. It is given in full so that there can be no question of anything being taken out of context. It will be noticed that the 1918 Election is dealt with by not being even mentioned. And three situations, which are essentially different from each other from a democratic viewpoint, are run together as a continuity—the 1916 Insurrection, the war consequent on the refusal of Britain to make terms with the electoral mandate of 1918, and the Northern Ireland situation half a century later. (Kevin Myers and John A. Murphy, who made supportive statements for the programme, were at the time well-known revisionists who held influential positions):

"My name is Eoghan Harris. In Britain a few people may know me as a writer of the Sharpe series for Carlton television. But back in Ireland I'm better known as a political commentator and a political activist [shown entering News International Newspapers Ltd., past titles of The Sunday Times and The Sun]. Peter Mandelson without the Party; Andrew Neil without the charm.

"In what they call a chequered political career, I've been a pamphleteer for Marxist Sinn Féin, part of Mary Robinson's kitchen cabinet for her Presidential election, and a spin doctor for the present Prime Minister, John Bruton.

"But really what I'm known for is that I'm one of a small group of revisionist commentators who don't believe in the Peace Process: don't believe in the Peace Process as conceived as a Pan-Nationalist Peace Process; believe that Sinn Féin is cynically out to subvert the state of Northern Ireland; believe that playing footsy with Sinn Féin is contaminating the Republic; and we believe that basically the only way to have peace in the North is for John Hume and David Trimble to come together and isolate the gunmen.

Kevin Myers, an *Irish Times* columnist at the time:

"There's nothing whatsoever about Sinn Féin which would indicate to me that they are prepared to settle for their minority existence within Northern Ireland. They are determined to see an end to the Northern Ireland state come what may. They've chosen the Peace option to end the Northern Ireland state but they're not prepared to remain within existence within the Northern Ireland state. I'm absolutely sure of that."

John A. Murphy, a Professor at the University of Cork at the time:

"The IRA is about war by definitions. They are an Army. They are in pursuit of the mystical Republic, and until they go out of business and say, 'Well, look, we'll leave it now to the politicians totally, then I will be happy, otherwise No.'"

Harris, In front of the Shelburne Hotel:

"Whatever their private views, the number of commentators in the Republic who are prepared to be publicly critical of the so-called Peace Process, can be counted on the fingers of one hand. And no wonder. Argue against appeasement and you can be condemned as a warmonger, as Winston Churchill was during the 1930s. Being sceptical about the Peace Process is, in the words of a famous Irish Times columnist, Myles na Gopaleen, "neither popular nor profitable".

Kevin Myers, *Irish Times*:

"Yes, I would say that I'm just about the only person in this office who has been pessimistic about the outcome of this Peace Process. No one compares with me in pessimism. And generally throughout the Irish media it has been very much a question of supporting our team, and our team would be led by John Hume."

Harris, alongside Memorial to the 1916 founders of the State:

"Kevin Myers is called a revisionist because he rejects the founding myth of the Irish Republic, the Rising of 1916, a Rising in which my grandfather and his two brothers took part. At that time Home Rule for the South with an opt out for Ulster was on the Statute Books, to be activated as soon as the Great War was over. But on Easter Monday 1916 Patrick Pearse pre-empted that Constitutional path. Ignoring the wishes of one million Protestants in the North, he led a thousand Irish Volunteers to seize the centre of Dublin and declare an all-Ireland 32 County Republic.

"The men whose names are on this wall knew what they were doing. They knew what they wanted, and they knew what the price was. By rising up in arms against the great Empire, by going down with guns blazing, by offering themselves as a blood sacrifice, they hoped at Easter to invoke the image of Christ's death and resurrection, the resurrection of a nation. They knew that this would burn powerfully into the minds of a Catholic people, and they calculated correctly. By 1921 Ireland was ablaze. By 1922 the South of Ireland was free, the Treaty of 1921 copper-fastening the new Irish Free State.

"Things might have worked out well. But Sinn Féin believed that the message of these men had to be taken at face value. And for once I agree with them. The Republic can't have it both ways. These men operated with no mandate from the people. It was a putsch, it was a coup. So, when we say to Sinn Féin: 'By what authority do you act?', Sinn Féin turns to that wall, metaphorically runs its hand across it, and says: 'We act by the authority of the men whose names are on this wall, and they acted with no authority at all.

"In 1921, by signing the Anglo-Irish Treaty, Michael Collins came down from the high horse of Patrick Pearse's 32 Country Republic and settled for what was practically possible in the real world—a 26 County Free State in the South and a grudging recognition of the new Protestant state to the North. Republicans were resentful and threatened civil war. But Collins had a popular mandate.

"What would have happened had he lived is one of the great might-have-beens of Irish history.

At Beal na Blath:

"That's a small and mean memorial to a big and generous man. This is Beal na Blath in West Cork. On the 28th of August 1922 General Michael Collins, the Commander-in-Chief of the Free State forces came here trying like many an Irish statesman after, to talk some sense into the minds of the Republican incorrigibles who held the hills up there pursuing their ghostly dream of, their delusion of, a 32 County Irish Republic, that ignored the reality of one million Irish Protestants. And late in the afternoon, as he came here in an open touring car—he was sick, he had a heavy cold, he probably had a few pints taken—he came under rifle fire from the hills up there, and he was returning the fire—Collins was not a pacifist—when he was struck by a sniper and fell here on the grass with much the same wound as Jack Kennedy. And, as his head hit the grass, and the blood and brains spattered the wild flowers, we lost more than a statesman and a soldier and a politician—we lost a largeness of spirit, that we were to miss in the years that followed, because Collins had lived and worked in London, and liked English people, liked English literature. And we lost that generosity of spirit when he died.

"In 1922 the Republicans threw down the gauntlet to the still fragile Free State Government by occupying the Four Court at the centre of Dublin. The young men of Michael Collins's Cabinet met the threat firmly. First crushing the Four Court garrison by bringing up borrowed British artillery and continuing with a campaign of ruthless repression which included internment, summary executions, and letting Republican prisoners die on hunger strike.

"By the end of the 1920s the Republicans were finished as a military force, but in 1932 they returned as a political force under Eamon de Valera, and the mad, mystical and undemocratic dream of a 32 County Republic started all over again.

"By the time I was growing up as a teenager in Cork in the 1950s, that dream was on the point of turning into a nightmare. To grow up in that time was to be dipped deeply in double-think, at home, at school, at Church, from political platforms, parents, preachers and politicians, never stopped nagging young men like me about the North. What they didn't realise was that official Ireland was only paying lip-service to Pearse's Republic, and that anyone who did anything about it would be regarded as a right idiot and locked up. But some people, like me, are slow learners, and in the 1960s I joined the Republican movement.

"In 1970 it split. The nationalist Provisional wing started the so-called armed struggle. The smaller Marxist wing, with which I stayed, called a ceasefire and went down the Constitutional road to peace. A sense of history helped me to make the right choices, particularly the influence of my Professor of History at University College, Cork."

[This is extremely elliptical. The Marxist IRA called itself the Official IRA because it gained a majority at the Sinn Fein Ard Fheis of January 1970, and the *"Provisionals"* withdrew. The *"Marxist wing"* was on long-term Ceasefire at the time, but it returned to warfare after the split with the Provisionals. It was engaged in warfare when I took part in a debate in Limerick, organised by the late Jim Kemmy. Harris denounced me as an Orange/Unionist dupe because I proposed that the Ulster Unionist community should be recognised as a distinct national community with a view to negotiating a compromise settlement. The *"Marxist wing"* returned to Ceasefire some time after that. Its war, conducted in a medium of ideological fantasy, consisted of a number of incidents which almost everyone regarded as meaningless outrages. BC]

John A. Murphy:
"I suppose I was born and brought up in the decade after Collins's death, and therefore I was brought up in an intensely nationalist period. I believed in the rightness of a United Ireland. I believed that Partition was wrong and that Ireland was entitled, as a principle as it were, to unity. The first critical self-knowledge for the people of this state came in about the mid-1970s, when atrocities and terrorism reached an unprecedented pitch. It was the reality of bloodshed, I think, which dissipated the pretence and the mists of rhetoric and lip service to Irish unity. When we realised—I suppose for the first time, the realities of Northern Ireland were open to us—that here in Cork particularly we were remote from the kind of passions, the murderous passions, the sectarian passions, which were now becoming evident, and which hadn't been experienced in the South back since the 1830s perhaps."

Harris, standing before Sean Keating's painting, 'The Men Of The South' in the Cork Art Gallery:
"Like my old Professor of History I've had to revise and reject not only the politics of my youth but the rich tapestry of song, sign and symbol which sustained them.
"In 1966 this painting had a very simple message for me. It was a heroic iconography of the revolution. Now, with the atrocities, the mini-bus massacres, the bombs in pubs, now I was beginning to see something quite nasty beneath the oil point here. And I was beginning to realise how much I and other young men are seduced by the romanticism of revolution. For example, look at the poncy hair style there. That's not a military short-back-and-sides. There's a kind of self-indulgence there, a self-awareness. And then the long, aquiline, sensitive intellectuals' features—you know, you too can be a gunman

and blow people's brains out and still be a sensitive intellectual, bit. And the dandification, the special silk cravat. You know, likening themselves—like the Provos do nowadays when we see them on the screens, wearing good suits and silk shirts and ties sometimes. This is the Chicago gangsters' hat, you know, it bespeaks your individualism, your radical Bohemianism. The kind of thing Hitler had you know. He'd like to paint a bit. He'd like to put out little volumes of Memoirs. And then sometimes he'd like to kill somebody. You know, we do different things with our lives kind of thing. All of that stuff began to disgust me.

"And down here of course I began to really look again at that gun, which had been only a symbol in the sixties. Now in 1976 that was the gun, the kind of gun, that was taken out at Whiterock and used to blow the brains off unfortunate Protestant working men coming home at the end of a long, hard day.

"And these crowd of wasters—what they were the same wasters that the Provisionals were. Fellows with no fixed job, with no responsibility to wives or children or community, swanning around the countryside with guns in their hands, killing working men in tin helmets going home at the end of the day. And they began to make me sick. And I can't look at that painting any more now without seeing the romanticism, that lethal, brutal romanticism that lies behind the Provisional IRA's murder campaign. And I no longer find any pleasure, or take any pleasure in this painting.

"Even if the Provisionals make peace, the ghostly and ghastly Republic of Patrick Pearse can return to haunt us at any time until we confront the fundamental flaw in the founding myth of the Republic: the fact that the men of 1916 acted without any mandate or democratic authority."

The Electoral Mandate

The electoral mandate to govern Ireland, which no party had in 1916, was given to Sinn Féin in December 1918. The British Government and Parliament took no account of the election result in Ireland. The only Home Rule leaders who held their seats in a contest in the 1918 Election were Joseph Devlin of West Belfast and Willie Redmond in Waterford City.

Devlin himself did not recognise the clearly expressed will of the Irish electorate as the democratic determinant of legitimacy any more than the British parties did. He did not attend the meeting of the Dáil in January 1919. He went instead to Westminster, submitting himself to the authority of the Crown in the matter of governing Ireland. He was no longer the leader of a great party, but only an individual remnant of it. But he performed the service, as the remnant of a broken party, of confronting Parliament with what had happened electorally in Ireland, and asking what it intended to do about it. He got no answer. He repeated the question a number of times over the following months, but never got an answer.

Parliament, within months of victory in the Great War for democracy and the rights of small nations, simply ignored the Irish election result. As we say nowadays, it went into denial about it.

The last purposeful action of the Home Rule Party was the publication in 1918 of a booklet called *The Grammar Of Anarchy*. It consisted entirely of statements made by leading members of the Government five years earlier when they were leaders of the Opposition and were organising a private Army to prevent the implementation of the Home Rule Bill when it became an Act.

The Grammar Of Anarchy was not banned by the military authorities in Ireland. They did not presume to condemn a book consisting of speeches by members of the Government. But it was banned by the civil authority—by the Government.

The Home Rule remnant wanted to know why they were not allowed to publish speeches by their opponents who were now important members of the Government. They got no answer.

The Home Rule Act-on-the-Statute Book, which was to have been implemented at the end of the War, was not implemented.

The reality was that it had not been promised that it would be implemented at the end of the War. That was a story for the recruiting speeches. The bipartisan agreement of September 1914 was that the Unionists consented to the Bill being put in the Statute Book because the Liberals gave an undertaking that when it had served its recruiting purpose, it would be opened up for amendment, and the dispute of July 1914 would be resumed.

Add to this the fact that the Liberal Party, on which the Home Rule Party had become dependent, had broken itself under the stress of fighting the Great War, and that its most vigorous element, led by

Lloyd George, had formed a tight alliance with the Unionists, and fought the 1918 Election against the Liberal Party, as part of an agreed slate of candidates with the Unionist Party, and the reasons for the Home Rule collapse of December 1918 should be evident.

The Home Rule fig-leaf of British representative government in Ireland was lost in December 1918. In its place there was a democratic electoral mandate for the establishment of independent government in Ireland. The Imperial Parliament neither recognised the democratic national mandate in Ireland nor gave a reason for rejecting it. The electorally mandated party in Ireland set about implementing the mandate. The Imperial Government tried to continue governing Ireland. Therefore there was a war.

RTÉ, in its Coolacrease programme, took it that the Imperial Government was the legitimate Government in Ireland in June 1921, even though by this time it had been comprehensively rejected twice by the Irish democracy. No reason was given for this. The Irish national broadcaster in 2007 simply went into denial about electoral democracy in Ireland, as the Imperial Parliament had done in response to Joe Devlin's questioning in 1919.

More than that, RTÉ represented the war that followed the election as a *"land grab"* by thuggish elements who were stealing other people's property.

Historians, Amateur and Mercenary

Defenders of this RTÉ view of the matter rely heavily on the fact that those who dispute it are only "amateur historians", and that the land grab view was authenticated by a group of "academic historians". The operative distinction here is between those who are paid by an academic institution to lecture on history and those who are not. On the ground of reason the distinction is immaterial. A statement is true or false depending on whether it comes from sound information accurately reasoned upon. Other things being equal one would expect that somebody who is paid to apply himself full-time to discovering historical facts, and organising them into a coherent account of some event or period, would be better informed and more thorough in his reasoning that somebody who makes a living by doing something else. But other things are not equal—not in Ireland since the 1970s anyway.

Pat Muldowney is a professional mathematician with an international reputation. If an amateur mathematician disputed his sums, he would not rely on his authority as a professional to deal with the question, but would deal with it on the ground of reason. The only authority in mathematics—which is the ultimate science—is reason.

By comparison with mathematics, history as an academic subject is often little more than propaganda in the service of some state policy of the moment. The more it relies on authority, the closer it is to propaganda. And the more the kind of thinking that applies in mathematics is applied to it, the closer it would come to establishing a kind of objective knowledge.

Three academic historians took part in the Coolacrease programme and lent it their authority: Richard English of Queen's University, Terence Dooley of Maynooth, and Dr. Will Murphy of Mater Dei Institute of Education. I am familiar with the writings of the first two.

English and Dooley both acknowledge a debt to Peter Hart, whose book *The IRA and its Enemies* was hailed as a "classic" by Professor Roy Foster when it was published in 1998. The centrepiece of Hart's book—the hook on which it was sold—was a sensational account of the Kilmichael Ambush claiming that surrendered British soldiers were massacred in cold blood. Hart based his account on an alleged interview which he conducted with a Republican survivor of the Ambush. Meda Ryan, who is perhaps the best informed person in the world on the subject of the Kilmichael Ambush and associated events, said that no Republican who had taken part in the Ambush was still alive on the date when Hart said he conducted the interview. The last survivor had died before the date of the alleged interview, and for some years before that he was in mental decline and could not have given an interview.

Meda Ryan's documented assertion was not disputed by anybody within the academic circles which supported Hart, and which dominated academic life. It was ignored. It could be ignored because she was an "amateur" historian, not employed by an academic institution to lecture on history.

It would have been a very serious step for any working historian, making a living within the academic system, to have taken issue with Hart, who had the backing of the academic authorities. The academic historian was an employee doing a job. Like an employee in any other occupation, he must do the job in a way that satisfied the bosses. The bosses who controlled the fortunes of aspirant historians around the turn of the millennium were, as far as I could discover as an outsider, Professor Fitzpatrick at Trinity College and Professor Foster at Oxford.

Academic authority is usually subject to the political authority of the State and does not set itself the task of subverting it. There is usually a kind of sympathy—an organic relationship—between the political life of the state and its academic reflection. That is how it was for half a century after Republican government was established in 1919. I do not know how the great change was made whereby academic history became a force directed against the historic legitimacy of the State. The change was enacted during the decades when I was in Belfast, making out a case for the Ulster Protestant resistance to nationalist Ireland—and being denounced for it as an Orange/Imperialist apologist by, amongst others, Eoghan Harris.

Whether the great change in the way that the War of Independence is presented was made at the behest of Fianna Fáil—which it would not be a great exaggeration to describe as the only real political party in the State—or occurred through its negligence, I cannot say. But the thing has happened. Irish history has been given over to Oxbridge and Trinity, who never saw Irish independence as anything but an aberration.

The best way to re-write the history of 1919-21 in the British interest would be to drop the General Elections of 1918 and 1921 and treat the War of Independence as a continuation of the Easter Rising. That is what was done by Professor Charles Townshend in his pioneering work, *The British Campaign in Ireland*. And it is how Senator Harris did it in his Channel 4 programme.

Revisionism presents itself as being essentially democratic in outlook, and as being greatly concerned with accuracy as to historical fact. It began by forgetting the historical fact of the 1918 Election. It seemed for a while as if it had succeeded in inducing general amnesia

203

on that point—and it has been outstandingly successful with professional communicators on RTÉ—people like Joe Duffy and Ryan Tubridy. But a real world still exists out there. The chatter of Duffy and Tubridy passes an idle hour, but the fact remains that an Election intervened between the Rising and the War of Independence, and gave the War of Independence a character entirely different from that of the Rising. These historians must therefore make some mention of the Election. They cannot let it lie there as a remembered fact which nothing much is made of. They must mention it in order to disparage it and suggest that it was a thing of no consequence, best not mentioned.

Richard English

The major paid historian on the Coolacrease programme was Richard English of Queen's University. English published a *History of Ireland* in 1991, in which he wrote:

"The republican faith was propelled forward, ironically, by Britain's involvement in the 1st World War. Not only did the war seem to some to offer an opportunity of striking at a distracted England, but the threatened imposition of conscription on Ireland served powerfully to alienate many people from the authorities.

"A combination of factors therefore united to stimulate nationalist Ireland into a new stage of activity—the suppression of the 1916 rising, the reorganisation of the Sinn Féin movement in 1917, the tactless handling by the British of the conscription issue. But even at the point of Sinn Féin's apparent triumph—when it thrashed the Irish Parliamentary Party in the 1918 general election—the picture was far less neat than might initially have been assumed. For one thing the election also demonstrated the strength of the unionist opposition to nationalist aspirations. And what use was it anyway to invite unionists into your proposed all-Ireland nation if they firmly rejected your offer; would you—could you—force them to accept your invitation?

"Such problems were to cause lasting and painful headaches for Irish nationalists" (p.100).

"The membership of the Dáil was composed of people who had been elected in the general election of 1918. Thus it was out of the womb of the United Kingdom electoral process that the independently-minded Irish nationalist child emerged" (p.100).

"Ambiguity surrounds the Anglo-Irish war. The exact relationship between the military and non-military forces for independence; the precise interpretation which nationalists gave their objective; the question of whether what eventually emerged from the conflict would have emerged anyway without it—these and other areas remain open to a considerable measure of debate" (p.104).

The question of whether what happened as a consequence of the Rising and the War of Independence would have happened anyway is one that can be "debated" for ever with no reasonable prospect of arriving at a solution. That is its attraction for revisionist history. But it is not a historical question. History is what happened. What happened, happened through a sequence of events. The primary business of the historian is to set out the sequence of events. If, having done that thoroughly, he goes on to speculate about what might have happened if a certain event in the sequence had not happened, he indulges in a flight of fancy. The flight of fancy might be tolerable, or even stimulating, if the representation of actual history had been done well. But, with the revisionists of Irish history, the flight of fancy takes the place of history.

The question of *"the exact relationship between the military and non-military forces for independence"* prepares the way for the flight of fancy, but it is not in itself historically meaningless, as the flight of fancy is. But it can only be answered in the context of the sequence of events which revisionist history sets aside.

It will be noticed that the action of the British Government with regard to the 1918 Election is absent from the events mentioned by English. In the case of any other situation, the response of the Government to an Election result could not be set aside by the historian as having no bearing on what followed—at least not without causing astonishment. But, after 30 years of revisionist dominance of academia, it has become the orthodoxy of Irish history.

By posing the question within the relevant sequence of events, one gets the answer that, because of the response of the British Government to the Election result, the *"non-military forces"* of the independence movement were rendered impotent, and that progress towards implementation of the independence mandate depended on the military forces.

But, in terms of personnel, there was no hard and fast distinction between the two in the majority of cases. Setting an artificial distinction between the political and military wings of Irish republicanism is all part of the revisionist game.

There was an IRA because the British Government refused to negotiate a transfer of authority to the party that won the Irish Election, and refused to allow the Irish delegates to put the matter to arbitration by the Versailles Conference of the Powers that had won the Great War for Democracy and the Rights of Small Nations.

"The republican faith was propelled forward, ironically by Britain's involvement in the 1st World War" because it offered the opportunity of striking at Britain while it was at war. Certainly the IRA decided to have a go during the War, and the 1916 Rising happened.

But what happened in 1918 was not another insurrection, but a massive vote in favour of independence, which formed nationalist Ireland into a republican body politic which survived the British terror of 1919-21 and Free State terror under the Crown that followed. And the major Irish war effort was not made during the *"opportunity of striking at a distracted England"*.

The voting of 1918, 1920 and 1921 cannot be explained on the "England's difficulty" principle. England had mastered its difficulty by December 1918, and was close to being master of the world. So it must have been something else about the War that encouraged the great change in Ireland. And the obvious thing is that Ireland was comprehensively militarised by the War, not by the Fenians but by the British Government, and that the justification of that militarism was held to be that it established Democracy and the Rights of Small Nations as foundations of the world order.

English says that Sinn Féin *"thrashed the Irish Parliamentary Party"* in the 1918 Election. It does not strike him as strange, any more than it does any other revisionist, that none of the parties that governed the State took part in the election in the Irish region of the State. (The Ulster Unionist alliance did in Ulster, and it had a connection with the Unionist Party of Great Britain, but that connection was wearing thin and three years later there was an effective disconnection. The party that took office in Northern Ireland two and a half years after the 1918 Election was not the Unionist Party of the

British State.)

The British two-party system was described by the most eminent of Constitutional commentators, Erskine Mayne, as *"the life blood of the Constitution"*. That life blood had not circulated in Ireland since the 1880s, and before that it had only circulated sluggishly.

Ireland was held politically for the British State by a Home Rule party that did not wish to be part of the British State but consented to be so because it lacked the Army necessary to the achievement of independence. It submitted to the military power of British Governments which, however representative they were of British society, were authoritarian with relation to Ireland.

The Home Rule Party expressed submission to Britain, not attachment to it.

The Imperialist Perspective

Lord Cromer, who governed Egypt as Ambassador (as the United States aspired to govern Iraq after the invasion of 2003), was the most thoughtful of the British Imperialist overlords of the generation leading up to 1914. He compared the British Empire with the Roman and noted that British Imperialism, because of its different origins, operated with an ideology of nationality that was missing from Rome. There was therefore a self-contradiction at the heart of British Imperialism. It simultaneously stimulated nationality and stifled its development. This was likely to give rise to dangerous misunderstandings, and he was concerned to dispel them:

> "Let us approach this subject with the animus manendi {will to remain – P.M.} strong within us. It will be well for England, better for India, and best of all for the course of progressive civilization in general, if it be clearly understood from the outset that, however liberal may be the concessions which have now been made, and which at any future time may be made, we have not the smallest intention of abandoning our Indian possessions, and that it is highly improbable that any such intention will be entertained by our posterity. The foundation stone of Indian reform must be the steadfast maintenance of British supremacy" *(Ancient and Modern Imperialism,* 1910, p.126).

This message needed to be made explicit for the Indians in 1910.

It was well understood by the Irish for generations, which is why Irish nationalism took the form of a Home Rule movement which accepted subordination to the Imperial will.

Fifty years earlier there had been an attempt to overthrow British rule in India. It was put down with very great slaughter. There is no official figure of the number killed. Recent estimates put it at hundreds of thousands, possibly a million. The official name of the event was the 'Indian Mutiny'. In 1910 an account of the Mutiny was published by an Indian nationalist, V.D. Savarkar. He presented it as an Indian war of national liberation and was sentenced to transportation to a British Penal Colony in the Andaman Islands for twenty-five years. His chief jailer there at one point was an Irishman who told him that he too had once been a strong nationalist, but he had matured and become an Imperialist, as he was sure Savarkar would also do when he had reflected sufficiently on his fate. (He didn't!)

In 1919 there was another British massacre in India. It was minuscule by comparison with the slaughter that followed the suppression of the 'Mutiny', but it was made sensational and disturbing because it was a deliberate, cold-blooded administrative act. An unarmed demonstration at Amritsar was fired upon by the British Army and some hundreds were killed. The head of the civil authority which legitimised that action was Sir Paul O'Dwyer of Clonmel.

The Home Rule movement was a nationalist movement which accepted the limitation on Irish national development set out by Lord Cromer, and by many others before him. That is to say, it accepted subordination to the Empire.

During the Home Rule era there was extensive participation in the administration and policing of the Empire by ambitious individuals of Irish national origin, and of continuing national sentiment, though for most of the nationalist population there was no positive commitment to the Empire.

The Great War disrupted the Home Rule consensus by drawing the population at large into active participation in the affairs of the Empire by means of an intensive propaganda, of which the leaders of the Home Rule Party made themselves an active instrument. The propaganda declared that active participation in the British war effort was an Irish national duty. It said that Britain was at war to uphold Democracy and the Rights of Small Nations against the German State which denied them. There was no mention of the severe limits on national development in the British Empire set out by Lord Cromer.

There is no Irish revisionist account of the Great War. There are only militaristic accounts of Irish participation in it.

There is no book which gives an idea of the scale of the propaganda about Democracy and the Rights of Small Nations, and how the Hun wanted to extinguish them, with which the populace was bombarded every day for four years by newspapers, books, pamphlets and posters. If there was, the shift from the passive acceptance of subordination in the form of Home Rule (which even Pearse accepted in 1914) to the popular assertion of the right of independence in 1918 would be seen to have an obvious cause.

The War blew up the contradiction in the British Imperial position described by Cromer:

> "The Englishman is in truth always striving to attain two ideals, which are apt to be mutually destructive—the ideal of good government [he takes it as self-evident that this can only be British government], and the ideal of self-government, which connotes the whole or partial abdication of his supreme position. Moreover, although he is aware that empire must rest on one of two bases—an extensive military occupation or the principle of nationality—he cannot in all cases make up his mind which of the two bases he prefers. Nevertheless, as regards Egypt, he will—or at all events, in my opinion he should—reply without hesitation that he should be very glad to shake off the Imperial burden, but that at present he does not see much prospect of doing so" (p.118).

The effect of the war propaganda on the subject populations of the Empire, combined with the weakening of the Imperial apparatus by the effort which led to the expansion of the Empire in 1918, made Cromer's ploy not sustainable in the post-war era. What Britain did then—in Ireland in the first instance—was try to hold its possessions by force, and, when this became inexpedient, make the best terms it could with the murderers it had been unable to suppress, acknowledge that the murderers were representative of a nationality, and pretend that what it had been doing all along was trying to find a way to implement the national principle.

Two new States were formed under British supervision at the Versailles Conference in 1919: Czechoslovakia and Yugoslavia. These states were formed out of the Hapsburg Empire, which was destroyed because it refused to make a separate peace with Britain in 1917. Both states were presented as nation-states—the states of nations which had suffered intolerable tyranny under the Hapsburgs. Neither of those nations had ever been heard of before, and neither of them lasted. There had been no Czechoslovak Home Rule movement monopolising political representation in the regions of the Czechs and the Slovaks. There had been no Czechoslovak insurrection against the Austrian tyranny during the Great War. There had been no Election which a Czechoslovak independence party had won before being admitted to the Versailles Conference to sort out the details of its independence. The Czechoslovak nation state was formed before there was any election. The Czechs and Slovaks were distinct nationalities. The Czechs were a minority of the population in the new state formed under their hegemony, which included large populations of Hungarians and Germans as well as Slovaks. But the Versailles authorities (essentially Britain and France, and ultimately Britain) set up a Czechoslovak "nation-state" for their own purposes. It did not last.

Yugoslavia was formed by attaching Slovenes, Croats and Bosnians to the Serbian state whose expansionist ambitions triggered the Great War. The Slovenes, Croats and Bosnians had launched no national insurrection against Austrian tyranny, but had served in the Austrian Army until the Hapsburg State was destroyed by Britain and France; and the Yugoslav State had hardly been formed when these nationalities began to look on it as a tyranny.

That is how the nationality principle was implemented by Britain in 1919. Are we expected to believe that all of this escaped the notice of the Irish at the time?

The Home Rule mentality, which was general until 1914, was broken by what Britain required the Irish to do in 1914; by what it said in order to get them to do it; by the extensive Irish participation in a War that was advertised as having one purpose but fought in the service of a very different purpose; and by the formation by Britain, for its own political aims, of nation-states in enemy territory, even though there was no adequate national basis for them, while it continued to refuse national rights to the Irish. The Irish therefore voted to establish independent government, and when Britain ignored that vote, and vetoed Irish entry to the Versailles Conference, the Irish set about setting up independent government in disregard of Imperial British authority. When the Imperial authority set about breaking up the Irish Government there was a war, and therefore an IRA.

*

In another book, *Armed Struggle* (2003) English writes of *"the intersection of nationalism and violence"*, as if "violence" was something that existed apart from politics as a thing in itself, but sometimes linked up with politics. There may be *"devotees of violence"* (a term which he uses somewhere else), but devotion to violence is unlikely to account for much in the affairs of the world. The violence which counts is the violence which arises out of politics—the violence generated by British Imperial ambition in 1914 (and many times before that); or the violence arising from the Irish will to independence which Britain sought to suppress.

Here is the scheme of things set out by English in *Armed Struggle*:

> "The 1918 conscription crisis considerably strengthened Sinn Féin's hand. Although it won under half the total vote, the party nevertheless gained 73 seats to the IPP's dismal 6 and the 26 won by unionists. A kind of rebel government was formed. It was far from being a fully functioning government. From 1918 onwards, the British response to republican subversion frequently involved punishing the wider population for IRA activities. Republican action provoked state reaction" (pp.11-17).

So a rebel democracy set up a Government that was not fully functioning. I wonder why it did not function fully?

And what was the *"republican subversion"* that the state had to suppress by striking at the wider population? Why, the Government established on the basis of the democratic vote of the wider population!

And where did the effective violence on the Irish side in this conflict come from—more sustained and purposeful violence than had been seen on the Irish side since the resistance to the Williamite conquest and terror of the 1690s? From the wider population. Where else was there for it to come from?

*

Richard English writes in another book that, after 1916—

> "The complex and changing attitudes of Irish people throughout history were squeezed into the constricting garments of physical force republican zealotry. Thus, Nora Connolly's assertion that the Young Irelanders had 'made no secret of their belief that the freedom of Ireland must be won by force of arms' attempted to stifle a far more complicated historical reality" (*Radicals and the Republic*, 1994, p.5).

I knew something about the Young Irelanders and was greatly surprised to see Nora Connolly's statement disputed, so I looked up the reference that English gives in substantiation of his refutation of her: *The Young Ireland Movement* by Richard Davis (1987). The section of the book referred to by English deals with the difference between O'Connell and the Young Irelanders regarding the use of force.

When O'Connell decided to drive the Young Irelanders out of the Repeal Association he did so by means of a resolution which made a principle of absolute pacifism. The Young Irelanders, though not advocating the use of force, refused to sign up for pacifism as a principle and left.

O'Connell was near the end of his tether when he forced through that resolution. Earlier in his career his tactic had been to mobilise force in order to intimidate the Government by displaying his might. The Government was intimidated on the issue of Catholic Emancipation. Fifteen years later he built up an immense popular force on the issue of Repeal of the Union. The attempt to carry Repeal in Parliament was hopeless. So O'Connell organised the Monster Meetings around the country, building up to a final meeting at Clontarf at which O'Connell would announce the establishment of his own Government, or Committee of 100. But this time the intimidation failed. The Government banned the meeting and deployed the cavalry on the approaches to Clontarf. And it was O'Connell who was intimidated.

Davis's conclusion is that *"the Young Irelanders persisted naively in detailing the violence the Liberator preferred to suggest obliquely"* (p.250).

The British attitude reasserted by Lord Cromer in 1910 was generally understood to be the case in the 1840s. The Young Irelanders would have needed to be very obtuse to have thought that Irish independence could be gained without the use of force. They were not obtuse.

The only question with regard to English's criticism of Nora Connolly is whether *he* is obtuse, or slipshod, or devious.

*

After the Great War for Democracy and the Rights of Small Nations, and after the Irish had voted as a democratic electorate (as compared with the mobilised masses under O'Connell), it still remained the case that Irish independence could not be gained without the use of force.

They voted for independent government, and the British State refused to negotiate it. Great numbers of those who voted for independence in 1918 had supported the British war effort four years earlier, having been told it was a war for democracy and the rights of small nations. The scale of the swing against the Home Rule Party leaves no room for doubt about that. Redmond carried the bulk of nationalist opinion with him in 1914-15. The vote for independence in 1918 was not a vote of those who had opposed the War in 1914-15. It was in large part a vote of people who came to see that they had been duped and swindled by the British war propaganda. What they voted for in 1918 was to claim a right which they thought they had fought for.

Uncontested Seats

Richard English and other revisionists point to the fact that Sinn Féin gained three-quarters of the seats with a minority of the votes cast. They do so knowing that a quarter of the seats were uncontested, and that the reason they were uncontested was that the Home Rule Party knew that its support had collapsed utterly in those areas.

A *New Ireland* brochure for a Mansion House Gathering in October 2001 begins:

"In the 1918 Election there was much intimidation. In one of the most important elections of the 20th century—out of an electorate of just under 2,000,000—31% didn't vote. Sinn Féin, with 47.4% of the votes, had swept the board".

Most revisionists also assert that extensive personation was an important factor in Sinn Fein's electoral victory.

If there was evidence that personation played an influential part in Sinn Féin victories in the contested seats, or that intimidation was the reason why many seats were uncontested, the Government of the day had the means of rectifying matters. As Richard English observed, the Sinn Féin victory came *"out of the womb of the United Kingdom electoral process"*. The election was held under British election law and policed by British authority, and Sinn Féin seats gained by malpractice might have been struck out. But few allegations of malpractice were made at the time, and as far as I know there was no attempt made to invalidate any election result by an appeal to election law—a thing which had been frequently done before 1914.

The allegation that Sinn Féin won by malpractice was, to my knowledge, first made by a British television journalist, Robert Kee, in the 1970s. It has been repeated *ad nauseam* ever since. The only evidence ever presented is a handful of personal anecdotes.

As to the 25 seats won by Sinn Féin in 1918 without a contest—this was by far the lowest number of uncontested seats since 1895. The following are the numbers of seats gained by the Home Rule Party without a contest (see Craig's *Parliamentary Election Results*):

1886	66
1892	9
1895	46
1900	58
1906	74
1910 (Jan.)	55
1910 (Dec.)	53

Nationalist votes cast plummeted from 308,972 in 1892 to 150,870 in 1895, to 89,000 in 1900, reaching their lowest level of 32,223 in 1906.

The high level of contested seats in 1892 resulted from Parnell's attempt to destroy the Home Rule Party when it would not obey him when he decided to break the alliance with Gladstone. Parnellite Loyalists (led by the future Empire Loyalist, John Redmond) stood against the Party, gaining 69,194 votes to the Party's 242,293 (*The British Voter* by Michael Kinnear).

The increase in the number of contested nationalist seats in 1910 was brought about by the rise of the All-For-Ireland League in Munster, which stood against Redmond's Party on the ground that Redmond had allowed the Home Rule issue to be subordinated to a Catholic ascendancy movement (the Ancient Order of Hibernians) which had gained effective control of the Party.

The 1918 Election was more widely contested in Ireland than any election had been for a generation. The voting was not on the Tammany Hall pattern of earlier decades. There were more opportunities to vote than ever before, and there were real issues to vote on. The electorate had been jolted out of the old rut by having been drawn into both the politics and the military action of the Great War.

What was it to do when it voted for independence, and the Government which it had supported in the Great War for Democracy and the Rights of Nations said it couldn't have it? Slink away, and accept that a deadly practical joke had been played on it?

Well it didn't. There was an edge to its response, because of all it had been through since 1914, that was completely unexpected by the British authorities, who knew from the experience of two centuries that the Irish would always fall back into their allotted place when handled with a firm hand.

Senator Harris does not see the War of Independence as the action of an outraged electorate. He sees it as militaristic play-acting by a stratum of Bohemian intellectuals in search of excitement.

The implication of his criticism is that those who contested British power by use of force, after Britain ignored the Election, should have done so with military hair-cuts and in military uniforms to make it easier for them to be rounded up.

Evidence

Richard English does not in his books present any evidence for the assertion that the War of Independence was camouflage for a land grab by groups of ambitious individuals. Nor does he assert that it was a land grab. But it does not come as a surprise, to someone familiar with his writing, to see him going along with Eoghan Harris/ Niamh Samman/RTÉ inventions. The surprise was that Terence Dooley lent his authority to it.

Dooley's detailed and useful booklets on Monaghan do not lay any basis for what he said on the programme. One of them, *Inniskeen*, published in 2004, is excellent. It shows the development of Bernard O'Rourke, a substantial Monaghan businessman and a pillar of the Home Rule movement, from a Home Rule to a Sinn Fein position in 1915-16, in response to Redmond's active support of the Great War in return for an inoperative Home Rule Act. If there were comparable histories of political developments in other counties for the 1914-18 period, there would be no room—no blank spaces—for the revisionists to insert their inventions in. There is nothing about land grabs and outrages in it.

It is true that his last book, *The Land for the People*, is a bit snooty on the subject of land ownership. Dublin 4 pretentiousness must have been seeping into him from the company he kept. There is a Dublin Opinion cartoon of rural Ireland on the cover—an ambitious rural idiot asserting his rights in the Land Commission Office. But even that book contains no evidence for the thesis which he supported on the 'Hidden History' Coolacrease programme.

Having said what he said for Niamh Sammon, it remains for Dooley to substantiate it—it would be a form of unnatural cruelty to expect an ephemeral media creature like her to do so. And I am one unreconstructed rural idiot who looks forward to his attempt to develop in print the brainwave he had before the television cameras.

Chapter 9

Exposing Propaganda

By

Pat Muldowney

Eoghan Harris published his articles on Alan Stanley's account of the Pearson executions in the Sunday Independent on 9th and 16th October 2005 (see Appendix 7).

Even after factoring out the Harrisian political embellishments, what was left looked quite nasty—innocent people killed for no good reason.

I bought Alan Stanley's book, *I Met Murder on the Way: the Story of the Pearsons of Coolacrease*. It consisted of correspondence with Australian relatives of the Pearsons, interspersed with a description of the executions and some other family history. Absence of straightforward narrative made Stanley's book a difficult read, but initial reading tended to broadly confirm what Eoghan Harris had described in his *Sunday Independent* articles.

The following week a brief letter by Paddy Heaney appeared in the *Sunday Independent*. He said Harris had not told the whole story, and recommended his own book *At the Foot of Slieve Bloom*, first published in the year 2000.

I found Paddy's number in the phone book and rang him up. Paddy sent me the typescript of the section of his book which deals with the Pearson affair. His book was published in 2000, five years before Alan Stanley's, and was in wide circulation in the Offaly area. Paddy Heaney's was the first published account of the Pearsons, their involvement in the Cadamstown community, their political and paramilitary activities, and their execution.

Paddy Heaney knew Alan Stanley, who had visited Cadamstown after the death of his father William Stanley in 1981, when he had the terrain and the history of the executions explained to him by Paddy.

Alan Stanley, it would appear, had no detailed knowledge of Coolacrease, other than the anecdotes his father William had related to him in their home in Co. Carlow. These family stories included details of the executions, such as the alleged use of dum-dum bullets. (The latter allegation has been dropped from the latest edition of Stanley's book.) But William Stanley was not a witness. He had made his escape before the executions, and lived in Northern Ireland in the aftermath. According to Alan Stanley's book, contact between the Pearson and Stanley families effectively lapsed for a generation when the Pearsons departed for Australia later in the 1920's.

Because of William Stanley's 1921 loyalist paramilitary activities in their home area (the Luggacurran Plantation, near Stradbally, Co. Laois, where the last significant attempts at ethnic cleansing and colonization in Ireland were carried out in the Lansdowne evictions in 1887), he was ordered out the area by the IRA and took refuge with his close friends and distant relatives the Pearsons in nearby Coolacrease, Co. Offaly. Another of the repercussions was that his father sold his Luggacurran farm in 1921 and moved to Wales; William later joined him from Northern Ireland where he had taken refuge for six months or so with other relatives. When William got married, his father bought him a 60-acre farm at Quinagh, outside Carlow town, where he spent the rest of his life.

The Heaneys originally came from O'Neill territory in Co. Derry, where the poet Séamus Heaney comes from. They came south to the battle of Kinsale with Hugh O'Neill's army in the winter of 1600, and, on the retreat to the north in early 1601, settled in this part of Offaly with other members of O'Neill's army.

Paddy Heaney is a stoneworker and builder by trade, and also did some small-farming. He carries on a family tradition of folklore and traditional culture, and is an expert in the history of that part of Co.'s Offaly and adjacent Laois. After Alan Stanley's book appeared in 2005, Paddy published further information on the Pearson executions in *Offaly Heritage*, the journal of the Offaly Historical and Archaeological Society; along with details of the many inaccuracies and errors in Alan Stanley's book.

In doing so he brought a sharper focus to bear on the account he had published in his 2000 book, in which the Coolacrease episode was a single, relatively minor event in a local history spanning many centuries. Renewed interest in the episode has produced fresh research and greater clarity and accuracy. Following publication of his 2000 book, Paddy Heaney was contacted by many people with more details of the War of Independence in the Cadamstown area, including the Coolacrease affair. A passion for accuracy in the historical record was manifested. The information in the first Chapter of this book consists in large measure of this accumulation of new research, following from Paddy Heaney's initial publication.

So I read Paddy Heaney's and Alan Stanley's competing versions of the Pearson executions. I also got hold of some of the relevant Bureau of Military History reports, in particular the Witness Statement of Michael Cordial, Quartermaster 3rd Battalion IRA, who was present at the executions.

The Attack on the Roadblock

The key thing seemed to me to be the IRA roadblock the week before the executions. Both sides of the story have the Pearsons approaching the roadblock and firing a shot or shots. Stanley quotes his father as saying the Pearsons fired into the air as a warning. Every other account says the Pearsons fired and wounded several men.

Which of these versions is true?

From the information I had to hand at the time, the accounts which corroborated Paddy Heaney's version could hardly have been part of some cover-up conspiracy, since they were written on dates in the twentieth and twenty first centuries which made an agreed, concocted story impossible. For instance, there was no indication that Paddy Heaney had ever met Michael Cordial. Cordial's Witness Statement was written in 1957, and Paddy Heaney's book was published in 2000, before the Bureau of Military History statements, including Cordial's, were made available to be read. Yet they agree in essentials.

On the other hand, Alan Stanley's version reveals glaring anomalies. For me the most significant one was that his father never told Alan the truth about how he came to be with the Pearsons in June 1921, rather than at home in Luggacurran. He never told Alan that he had been mixed up with the Auxiliaries in a paramilitary plot. If he was prepared to withhold this embarrassing truth from Alan throughout his life, what possible credence could be given to his "firing over their heads" line? It baffled me that Alan Stanley was unshaken in his trust in his father's version of events.

What credence could be given to William's/Alan's story that the Pearsons fired into the air at the roadblock, when several people were known to have been actually shot by them? As far as I am concerned, that is still the most convincing proof that the Pearsons deliberately and consciously, though "unofficially", engaged in actual combat on the British side in the War of Independence, so their execution was a legitimate act of war.

The RIC and Court of Inquiry evidence that I came across later are just further positive indications of what actually happened. But what William Stanley said, and what he can be shown to have covered up, are the real clinchers for me.

I re-published Paddy Heaney's account, along with an assessment of Alan Stanley's version and further discussion, first in *Church & State* magazine, and then on *Indymedia*.

A wide-ranging debate took place on *Indymedia*, an internet political discussion site, and the above critique of Alan Stanley's theory was tested. It stood the test of debate as the argument went back and forth from February to November 2006.

RTÉ Documentary

Paddy Heaney had mentioned to me during that year that he had been approached by somebody from RTÉ about a Coolacrease documentary, and he'd agreed to participate; and he had also been contacted by somebody who wanted to make a film. It would appear that these two were Niamh Sammon and Perry Ogden. But Paddy hadn't much information.

At this stage I thought that the Pearsons issue, having been, after a fashion, publicly aired (in *Church & State* magazine and *Indymedia*), was no longer an interesting challenge. But Jack Lane of the Aubane Historical Society felt that the *Indymedia* debate was interesting enough to publish, and he reproduced it in booklet form: *The Pearson Executions in Co. Offaly*. That was the end of it as far as I was concerned.

During the first half of 2007 I was out of the country. But in June I made a social telephone call to Paddy Heaney. He told me that an RTÉ documentary crew had been interviewing and filming. He had liberally shared his knowledge of the subject, and provided expert guidance to people who had arrived with zero knowledge of the area. But when it came to the on-camera interview he felt he had been ambushed by a hostile interviewer with an agenda that had been deliberately concealed from him.

Out of curiosity I poked around a bit in June, trying to find out what RTÉ documentaries were in the making, and who was making them. But I found nothing. So I called Paddy again to ask if he had any contact names or addresses. He wasn't sure of the name, but gave me a mobile telephone number.

I phoned the number, and asked about a Coolacrease documentary, saying that I had been involved in some publication on the subject. Upon which, I detected a distinct and immediate lowering of the temperature, indicating to me that I was known to the person at the other end, and that my call was unwelcome. But it was confirmed that there was a documentary, and that I was speaking to its Director, Niamh Sammon. The call was brief and tense. Ms Sammon was aware of my publication, and therefore presumably aware of the position I took on the subject, and of how I arrived at that position.

With this knowledge I tried to find out whatever I could about Niamh Sammon and her documentary, and then I wrote to her saying that there were two opposing arguments in contention, and that both should be fairly aired. I received no reply. But I made further enquiries, and came into possession of an internal RTÉ document in the name of Kevin Dawson, RTÉ Commissioning Editor for Factual Programmes, giving the title of the documentary as *Atonement: Ethnic Cleansing in the Midlands in 1922*.

Atrocity Propaganda

So at this point I thought it was more than likely that the documentary was pushing the line of Eoghan Harris's Sunday Independent article. I wrote to Niamh Sammon again, and pressed these points (including the embarrassingly prejudicial programme title of Kevin Dawson).

I conducted the correspondence in semi-public by copying in RTÉ officials and politicians—so that, in the event of controversy, none of them could claim they didn't know what it was about. As a result I was eventually invited to be interviewed on-camera for the documentary in Kinnitty Castle, near Coolacrease, on 28th July 2007.

I was in contact with Seán McGouran in London, who had been investigating the work of the British government's Irish Grants Committee, a body set up to award compensation to loyalists who had suffered injury or damage during or in consequence of the War of Independence. He had been reading the papers of the Committee in the British Public Records Office, including the papers relating to the Pearsons. He sent me a copy of these, and undertook to gather up everything he could get access to on the subject.

I went to see Paddy Heaney to find out more about his experience of the documentary. What he described to me sounded like sharp practice. He put me in touch with Philip McConway, a history research student in Trinity College Dublin, who is a specialist in the history of Offaly during the War of Independence and Civil War, and who was also involved in the documentary. Philip shared Paddy's concerns about how the documentary was shaping up, and he gave me the notes of a lecture he had given in January 2007 to the Offaly Historical and Archaeological Society. He also gave me useful press cuttings about the sale of the Pearsons' farm after the executions, and the British Public Records Office reference number for the papers of the British Military Courts of Enquiry in lieu of Inquests into the deaths of the executed men, Richard and Abraham Pearson.

Paddy Heaney gave me his own copy of a book by Leigh-Ann Coffey, called *The Planters of Luggacurran*, which was useful in explaining the attitudes and mentality of the Stanleys and Pearsons in the early twentieth century. A friend gave me a history of the Cooneyite religious movement, which provided further insight.

In preparation for the interview I re-read Alan Stanley's 2005 book *I Met Murder on the Way*, and managed with some difficulty to convert it in my mind into something like a narrative account of the events before, during and after the executions, including the information he provides on the subsequent family histories of the

Pearsons and Stanleys.

Though Stanley's book defends the Pearsons and accuses the independence movement of sectarian conduct, it inadvertently provides the strongest corroboration of Paddy Heaney's account of what actually happened around the time of the executions. Of course Alan Stanley intended, and no doubt even believed, the opposite. His story is that the Pearson brothers fired on the roadblock, but "over their heads". This is like the Bart Simpson excuse: "The dog ate my homework!"

RTÉ Interview in Kinnitty Castle

It was my intention to present this argument in the interview. I thought that for any reasonable person, this was conclusive. I could imagine myself in Alan Stanley's shoes, trying to convince some hard-nosed interviewer that, actually, the dog did it, not Bart. But Bart (the Pearson brothers) was at the scene of the crime while the dog (the RIC/Auxiliaries/Black & Tans) was in kennels/barracks in Tullamore that evening. How could the dog make it across country fifteen miles to that particular roadblock, and fifteen miles back again, without anyone noticing? I could feel myself squirming under this and similar questions, if I were Alan Stanley.

The British Court of Inquiry papers, delayed by the UK postal strikes in July, arrived courtesy of Seán McGouran a couple of days in advance of the Kinnitty Castle interview on 28th July which the Hidden History Director Niamh Sammon had arranged. This proved to be quite fortuitous. Not so much because the Court of Inquiry papers provided further corroboration of Paddy Heaney's account of the executions (which they did), but because they provided much documentary detail which cast doubt on Alan Stanley's version of events, complicating detail which I thought should be fully explored in the interview.

I travelled to Kinnitty the day before the interview and asked Paddy Heaney to take me around the various locations—the mass path where the Pearsons had engaged in sectarian confrontation, the location of the roadblock, and the execution scene.

I was particularly interested in the location of the Grove in the

223

hillside where the Pearson women were taken prior to the executions, according to their testimony to the Court of Inquiry. After previously reading the various accounts of this in the newspaper reports and in Dave Pearson's 1983 letter quoted in Alan Stanley's book, the phrasing and words used left me doubting that the women were forced to watch the executions—or even that they had inadvertently witnessed them. But the Grove was mentioned only in the Court of Inquiry, where it instantly caught my attention.

When Paddy Heaney walked me around the terrain and location of the Grove, I was fully convinced that the women could not have witnessed the executions, and certainly were not forced to be present. Could they have witnessed the executions inadvertently? The terrain made this impossible. But some of the women said they saw the executions. Therefore the evidence given by the Pearsons was contradictory. In other words, not everything they said at the time was true.

What is the point of telling a lie? The only reasonable purpose for lying is to gain some advantage. Which of the two statements (*"We were taken to the Grove"; "We saw the executions"*) would have brought advantage to the Pearsons? The second one, because it made them the victims of an atrocity, even if the executions themselves were militarily justified. So why did they admit that they were taken to the Grove? I presume because at the time of the British Military Inquiry, just two days after the executions, they were still traumatized and shocked, and had not yet decided on a line they would stick to. Anyway, when the military and police arrived on the evening of the executions they probably described their movements, including the Grove episode, so could hardly retract this in the Inquiry.

There are other ambiguities and contradictions in the British Court of Inquiry papers. Such as the RIC report which attributed the execution of the Pearsons to their attack on the roadblock. But the following sentence of the RIC report declared something else to be a rumour. All in all, there was a lot in these documents which needed to be chewed over in any serious television programme about the Coolacrease episode.

On 28th July in Kinnitty, Co. Offaly, I received messages from Hidden History Director Niamh Sammon postponing the start of the interview which had been scheduled for 10.30 a.m. Eventually it started at about 4.30 p.m. in Kinnitty Castle, a hotel which used to be the residence of various aristocrats.

Before the filming, I was presented with a 'Release Form' which assigned full rights and authority in the interview to the Director, and required to sign it before the interview could proceed. The form entailed my agreement to a number of things, notably: *"the tape may be cut or edited for the programme or publicity material associated with the programme, and may be used in association with the exploitation of same"*. It also entailed granting full copyright to the programme maker over the material and to me waiving *"any moral right that may be deemed to be in existence in relation to my contributions and participation in the programme"*. There was no time or opportunity to peruse it, but I took the precaution of discreetly placing my own papers on top of a spare copy (it is published on my *Indymedia* page). It was that kind of atmosphere!

The interview consisted of Niamh Sammon repeatedly asking the question *"What is your evidence that the Pearsons were spies or informers?"*, to which the only possible direct answer would be that there is no surviving documentary evidence that I knew of. And this would be the part of the interview which I suspected would actually be broadcast—nothing else, no matter how relevant it might be.

But instead of giving a direct answer to this question, I replied that both the Irish and British military evidence—the only surviving documentary evidence—showed that the Pearsons were executed, not for informing or spying, but for attacking the roadblock. They had become combatants on the British side of the conflict, in an unofficial capacity. They carried out a paramilitary action against the forces of the elected Government.

The interviewer frequently interrupted to leave the room, and on her return would usually ask the same question, *"What is your evidence that the Pearsons were spies or informers?"*, and I would, as before, redirect the interview to the attack on the roadblock. I had been told at the start that the interview would last about half an hour, but it continued, in a repetitious way, for about two hours, with numerous interruptions.

The interviewer's ploy for evading the issue of the attack on the roadblock was to cast doubt on whether anybody was shot by the Pearsons; that in the darkness and confusion, nobody really knew what happened. The implication being that the shooting injuries were a myth devised to justify the murder of the Pearsons a week later. Though even in Alan Stanley's book, it is accepted that several people were shot at the roadblock. (The suggestion in Stanley's book is that the Pearsons aimed their weapons high and fired in the air, and that the gunshot wounds inflicted on the other side were caused by a mysterious band of Crown Forces who happened along soon after!)

The interview confirmed what I suspected, that the programme had prejudged the issue of whether the Pearsons were innocent or guilty, murdered or executed; and whether in fact there had been a sectarian atrocity in pursuance of a land-grab, in the context of an ethnic cleansing drive against Protestants. The programme appeared to be in the business of making a piece of propaganda whose purpose was to change the viewers' conception of the Irish War of Independence.

Countering the Propaganda

I wrote up a report of the interview and sent it, along with an account of my own understanding of the Coolacrease executions, to RTÉ. I also sent copies to the Department of Communications which is responsible for the national broadcasting agency, and to the Taoiseach Bertie Ahern who was linked to the programme through his Seanad nominee Eoghan Harris.

RTÉ's publicity in advance of the programme highlighted the sectarian murder and land grab interpretations. Anticipating that the actual broadcast would be controversial, I sought publicity for my view of the programme, and on 5th and 6th October, critical accounts of the programme were published in *Phoenix* magazine and in the *Offaly Independent* newspaper.

On 8th October 2007 I published my account of the executions, and of the programme, on *Indymedia*, an independent internet political discussion forum, under the title "Hidden History or hidden agenda—the real story" where it generated vigorous discussion. On 16th October I received a telephone call from the director of the programme, Niamh Sammon, informing me that the documentary would be broadcast on 23rd October and that no part of my interview would be used. On Saturday 20th October, *The Irish Times* published an article by Niamh Sammon announcing the programme and her interpretation of the 1921 events, as probably a sectarian atrocity motivated by land-grabbing. Other newspapers published anticipatory articles hyping the programme and the atrocity allegations. On 22nd October Ms Sammon was interviewed on RTÉ Radio One by Ryan Tubridy, and the propaganda case was made even more emphatically, along with an explicit description (by Tubridy) of the events as ethnic cleansing (see the chapter by Nick Folley in this book. A full transcript of the programme is available on the website http://docs.indymedia.org/view/Main/CoolaCrease).

On the day of the broadcast (Tuesday 23rd October), after an offer of an article by me, I received the following message from Vincent Browne, editor of *Village* magazine which was due to be published on Thursday: *"I would be interested in a 800-word piece on the Hidden History programme and the Tubridy show, provided you can get it to me by 9.00am tomorrow (Wednesday) morning."*

In anticipation of what I expected the Hidden History programme to be, I prepared a preliminary draft of this article. I expected the programme to place strong emphasis on the issue of whether the Pearsons were spies or informers, an issue which, at this distance in time, could not be clearly decided; and I expected some downgrading of the documentary evidence that the Pearsons had engaged in armed combat. My draft article provided counter-arguments.

When the programme was actually broadcast that night, I thought it was quite persuasive and convincing as propaganda, making powerful use of Eoghan Harris's allegations of deliberate sexual mutilation of innocent Amish-type farmers. I thought that my draft article was somehow unsatisfactory. But after watching it a few times, it eventually dawned on me later that night—to my utter astonishment—that while the programme had included all sorts of vague, unsubstantiated speculation by academic "experts" Dooley, English and Murphy, the single biggest source of hard documentary evidence was not even mentioned in the programme. There was not even a whisper about the British Military Courts of Inquiry in Lieu of Inquests into the deaths of the two men. This was an omission so unexpected, so overwhelming, and so egregiously damning that I did not spot it until some time after the actual broadcast. Surrounded by trees, for a little while I failed to see the wood. At that point I grasped the nature of the cover-up.

So I rewrote the *Village* article in time for Vincent Browne's 9 a.m. deadline, and it duly appeared in print the following (Thursday) morning, exposing the programme's cover-up of the documentary evidence which challenged the programme's allegations of land-grabbing, sectarian murder, sexual mutilation in the presence of mother and sisters, and all the rest.

The programme made a strong impact. But there was an equally strong critical reaction prompted by the *Phoenix* article, the *Indymedia* publication, and the *Village* article. On the same day as the *Village* article appeared, Thursday 25th October, Ann Marie Hourihane published a fawning *Irish Times* article which regurgitated the propaganda in cultivated tones of moral outrage.

But the impact and propaganda effect of the programme had been seriously damaged almost from the moment of broadcast. That was clear by the weekend, when Eoghan Harris fulminated in his *Sunday Independent* (28th October) column against the Aubane Historical Society and the *"highly organized brigade of green ink bloggers"* who had muddied the waters for the programme, so that many people realized it was dishonest. This was the first of a series of attacks by Harris.

It was also the first clear indication that the programme had been successfully exposed as mere propaganda. From then on, a rearguard action was conducted by the programme's protagonists and defenders, the most notable being Joe Duffy's *Liveline* programmes on RTÉ Radio One on 5th and 6th November, in which, apparently with Duffy's full complicity, all the resources that Eoghan Harris could muster were brought out in a vain attempt to salvage the Hidden History documentary.

Eventually *The Irish Times* agreed to publish an article by me in response to a number of articles by Niamh Sammon (20th October 2007), Ann Marie Hourihane (25th October and 8th November), and David Adams (9th November). My article was published on 17th November. Niamh Sammon published a letter in reply (24th November) to which I responded (27th November). Some of this material is reproduced in Appendix 8 below.

Broadcasting Complaint

I submitted a complaint about the Hidden History programme to the Broadcasting Complaints Commission (BCC) on 20th November 2007.

This was one of seven formal complaints to the BCC about the programme. The complaints were against breaches of the Broadcasting Act 2001 (section 24 (2) (a)) on grounds of lack of fairness, objectivity and impartiality.

The complaints, and the responses to them can be read in full at http://docs.indymedia.org/view/Main/CoolaCrease

Paddy Heaney put in a complaint that the programme had knowingly and deliberately selected and edited his words in a way which conveyed the direct opposite of what he was saying. The defence put forward by the Director/Producer was that the Release Form signed by Paddy gave her the legal right and power to edit his interview in any way she chose. The BCC agreed with this, on the grounds that their remit was to consider and adjudicate on what was actually broadcast, not what was omitted, even if the omissions reversed the sense and meaning of what was actually said by the interviewee.

A significant part of the complaints was that the programme omitted crucial evidence. The BCC response was that the Producer/ Director Niamh Sammon had full editorial control and independence, and if she decided to exclude certain information, that was a matter for her judgement and the BCC had no criticism of that.

In other words, it was OK to produce propaganda, and it was OK for RTÉ to broadcast it. All that is fine by the BCC. The BCC said it could only comment on what was broadcast, not what was excluded. So when RTÉ broadcast spurious speculation, but concealed solid evidence disproving the speculation, the BCC found that what was concealed was irrelevant to its deliberations.

The BCC said, reasonably enough, that it could not make any judgement on what happened in 1921. Yet the first paragraph of the BCC response said: *"The Commission has considered the broadcast, the submissions made by the complainant, the broadcaster and the independent producer. The broadcast in question is Hidden History: The Killings at Coolacrease, which explored the **murder** of two brothers in Coolacrease during the War of Independence in 1921."* (Emphasis added.)

In other words, not only did the BCC make a judgement (murder) on the execution of enemy combatants, it **pre-judged** the issue of what happened in 1921.

Farrel Corcoran, Chairman of the RTÉ Authority from 1995 to 2000, reported in his 2004 book, *RTÉ and the Globalisation of Irish Television,* that the Authority agreed at a meeting in January 1998 that in history documentaries the Consultant Historian should not hold the additional role of participant in the documentary itself.

This implies that a Consultant Historian was then a requirement in such productions, so that, with an independent expert in charge, a degree of quality control could be ensured. In other words, a Consultant Historian could prevent the broadcasting of junk history.

One of the broadcasting complaints to the BCC noted that the programme credits listed no Consultant Historian. RTÉ's response included the statement that UCD history academic Dr. Paul Rouse was Consultant Historian. But when I asked him about this, Dr. Rouse said that his correct designation was as stated in the programme credits. In other words, he was correctly described as Researcher. His job was to provide information to the programme, but not to exercise control or influence over the quality of the programme as history.

The BCC was informed of this. Then, in a further response, the programme Director/Producer Niamh Sammon acknowledged that her programme did not have a Consultant Historian. And in its ruling, the BCC declared that the programme was under no obligation to have a Consultant Historian.

In other words, RTÉ told a straight lie. The BCC was informed of the lie, and it ruled that the historical content of programmes like this could be decided by amateurs and propagandists.

This does not bode well for RTÉ's role as the national broadcaster, the holder and producer of a significant part of the country's historical archive.

A further point in the complaints was the allegation that the Pearsons were murdered in pursuance of a land grab, and that the murderers benefited personally by being awarded portions of the Pearson farm by the Land Commission in 1923.

This produced the most brazen of RTÉ's lies. In response to the complaints RTÉ said:

"The theory that the Pearson killings were the result of a land grab was also examined by the programme makers. Documentation from the Land Registry office and the Land Commission was made available to Dr. Terence Dooley, a highly respected historian and author of 'The Land for the People'. Dr. Dooley used the contents of these files as the basis for his comments."

And the programme Producer/Director Niamh Sammon said:

"The production team was given access to these original [Land Commission] files."

But the Archivist of the Land Commission files told me in a letter that: *"I can find no record that RTÉ has had access to the former Irish Land Commission documents, stored in the Records Branch of the Department of Agriculture, Fisheries and Food, relating to the townland of Coolacrease (Pearson Farm)."*

It is apparent that RTÉ is in the business of producing junk history; and when it is challenged it bluffs, blusters and lies; and the Broadcasting Complaints Commission's role is to cover up this disgraceful, incompetent and unprofessional shambles.

The "Dublin Four" Mentality

In an *Irish Times* article of 20th October 2007, Niamh Sammon (producer/director of the RTÉ documentary *The Killings at Coolacrease*) wrote that Alan Stanley's book

"was the kind of history you don't learn about in school and, notwithstanding Ken Loach's film dramatisation of the period in The Wind that Shakes the Barley, here was proof of a much darker side to the republican fight for independence. ... It's a story [that the older generation of Cadamstown] would have heard in childhood; it would have been whispered by adults when they thought no children were listening. When we went knocking on doors in the area, however, nobody wanted to talk. ... People didn't want to talk about Coolacrease because for them this story was not about folk memory or history or sectarianism; it was about protecting the reputations of their fathers and uncles. The memory of the dead generation was at stake. That old adage 'Blood will out' had more than one meaning in Cadamstown."

The impression is given that the enlightened, modern, civilised programme maker had ventured into hill-billy Deliverance country. This is the mentality that produced RTÉ's junk history of the Pearsons. But contrary to such prejudice, rural Ireland has always

231

contained a high degree of intellect and sensibility. The people were very well attuned to ethnic and religious fracture lines and how to cope with them.

The condescension for which the term "Dublin Four" is a convenient shorthand, and which in one form or another has been around for centuries, is best regarded as something akin to adolescent arrogance and self-absorption, to be contrasted with grown-up objectivity and experience.

It is often noted that rural Ireland has provided the initiative and leadership in political, industrial, cultural, sporting and other fields. Looking back over a century or two, the extent to which this generalisation is borne out is remarkable.

(Over the past couple of millennia, towns and cities are relative newcomers in Ireland, and, in comparison with great monasteries and other rural seats of power and influence, they have contributed relatively little in the form of schools, literature and social development. The cities were, in comparison, practically dead zones—mere places of trade. Dublin was a place to visit once or twice a year to buy Christmas presents or to see a medical specialist. More important were the fairs, marts, games and fleadh's.)

"Dublin Four", or "Palesman", is a psychological phenomenon, not geographical, though it finds its purest expression in academia, and in the Irish Times and RTÉ which are physically located in Dublin. It is a widespread and chronically disabling mentality. The mentality can produce lots of shallow condescension and witty sneering but no coherent outlook, and no leadership with sufficient strength and substance to attract people away from their own values. It can subvert, but not create.

"Dublin Four" looks into its own soul and finds nothing there. So it submits with bad grace to Irish modes, while looking longingly across the water for relief from its plight.

(NOTE: Full transcripts of the RTÉ radio and television programmes referred to, of Pat Muldowney's interview by Niamh Sammon for her documentary, the texts of his correspondence with her, as well as the documentation of the Broadcasting Complaints Commission are available on http://docs.indymedia.org/view/Main/CoolaCrease)

Chapter 10

RTÉ and the Holy Grail of Revisionism

By

Nick Folley

The debate in the media which followed RTÉ's airing of *Hidden History: The Killing at Coolacrease* shed light on some of the difficulties involved in discussing this period of Irish history. The loose use of terminology and the difficulty in getting past the soundbites favoured by a media which often seems unaware of certain important basic facts make it difficult for a proper history of the War of Independence to be widely and properly understood here.

Protestant or Loyalist?

It has long been the 'Holy Grail' of the revisionist movement to find the cause celebre that will prove their thesis that the War of Independence was not a political struggle for independence but the eruption of sectarian hatreds emanating mainly from the Catholic side (they rarely if ever probe whether atrocities were committed by Protestants against Catholics). Many commentators felt such a moment had arrived when Peter Hart published *The IRA and its Enemies* in 1998. The case seemed proven in his analysis of the murder of 11 Protestants in Dunmanway in April 1922.[1]

On a technical note, this occurred outside the frame of the War of Independence and when the Free State had come about as a result of the 1921 Anglo-Irish Treaty. Nonetheless it was treated as the

---

[1] Peter Hart, 'Taking it out on the Protestants', in *The IRA and its Enemies*. Oxford University Press. Oxford: 1998.

definitive proof that the republican struggle for independence was tainted with sectarianism and indeed ethnic cleansing and relied on as such by many commentators and letter writers to the papers in the debate that followed. But it soon became apparent that the situation was not so simple.

Meda Ryan's research [2] revealed that most of the 11 victims were listed in documents left behind by evacuating British forces (in this case, K Company of the Black and Tans) as being informers and / or active supporters of the British attempt to destroy the republican movement and stymie their bid for independence. This would have made them obvious targets for the IRA. The local IRA condemned the attacks [3] and offered to mount guard on other individuals thought to be at risk. It is still not exactly clear who was responsible for the attacks but that it was an official IRA action seems quite unlikely. It is of course possible that people may have tried to take advantage of the confusion and lawlessness of the time to carry out private acts of violence. People may have tried to use the IRA to enforce their own interests and the IRA had to be vigilant on occasion in rebuffing such attempts. Mossie Hartnett of the West Limerick IRA recounted how his brigade was approached by a girl trying to get them to oblige the boy who had made her pregnant to marry her. [4] Of course he had to decline and tell her this was a matter outside their scope! Given the status of most of the 11 Dunmanway victims as named informers [5] it is far less likely their religion was a deciding factor in their killing. Catholic spies and informers generally met the same fate once their activities had been uncovered. To suggest that a person or persons

---

[2] Meda Ryan, '"The Dunmanway Find" of Informers' Dossier', in *Tom Barry IRA Freedom Fighter*. Mercier Press. Cork: 2003 (pp. 156–170).

[3] Peter Hart, *ibid.* p.283. Hart says IRA commander Tom Hales condemned the attacks and offered protection, but Hart feels this was too little, too late.

[4] Mossie Hartnett, *Victory and Woe*. University College Dublin. Dublin: 2002 (p.91-92).

[5] Two were probably cases of mistaken identity—they may have been killed in mistake for a brother in the case of one and a father in the case of the other. See: Ryan, Meda. '"The Dunmanway Find" of Informers' Dossier', in *Tom Barry IRA Freedom Fighter*. Mercier Press. Cork: 2003 (pp. 156–170).

unknown took advantage of the situation prevailing in 1922 to carry out a private act of violence is a far different matter from attempting to portray the republican movement and its struggle for independence as a sectarian conflict.

The wide debate that followed the publication of Hart's book had the happy consequence of focusing the spotlight on the sectarian issue and allowing it to be contested in the open. Cracks soon began to appear in the picture. Apart from Meda Ryan's research, revisionist commentators found themselves in the awkward position of having to explain away how the supposedly anti-Protestant republican movement contained many Protestant members, how Dáil Éireann contained some senior Protestant TDs, how Catholics who actively opposed the republican movement were targetted, why only some Protestants were targeted and there were no pogroms like those against Catholics around the same time in Belfast; and not least, the IRA campaign against the overwhelmingly Catholic RIC. The only common denominator among the victims was their active opposition—real or supposed—to the republican movement's struggle for independence from the UK.

With such a cloud of uncertainty hanging over what had seemed a clear-cut case of sectarianism, the revisionist movement continued its search for the Holy Grail. The execution of the Pearsons seemed to be the case they were looking for. The general argument of the programme was that two young inoffensive—and Protestant—boys were murdered by republicans as part of their larger drive to clear the country of Protestants and seize their land. Thus, the War of Independence was to be re-cast as an eruption of centuries-old sectarian hatreds (though once again, Catholic hatreds only) and 19th century land agitation. The Republican movement's lofty political claims of self-determination and sovereignty were to be replaced by lowly parochial motives of greed and irrational sectarian hatred. In one sense it can be seen as the modern literary equivalent of the crude 19th-century Punch cartoons where 'Paddy' is depicted as a simian, dynamite-wielding monster.

The debate also highlighted one of the recurring difficulties in discussing whether or not the War of Independence was sectarian: the frequent conflation of the terms 'protestant' and 'loyalist'. This can be seen over and over in the letters page of the national newspapers, in discussions on radio and even in casual conversation. A few examples suffice to illustrate:

Hidden History producer Niamh Sammon made her own position clear on the Tubridy Show [6] "...*faith was always an important badge of identity...the sectarian split along Protestant loyalist and Catholic nationalist lines had already been cemented in the 19th century.*"

The use made of an editorial in a Presbyterian paper *The Witness* of 17th June 1921 by 'revisionists' arguing the sectarian line, in the flurry of letters to the national daily papers that followed the November 2007 transmission of RTÉ's Hidden History on the Pearsons.[7] The editorial had stated that "*...the plight of the Protestants in the south and west is sad in the extreme. They are marked, they are watched, they are raided, and some of them have been dragged out and shot like beasts. An air of suspicion and dread is about them day and night...*"

Again, in a letter to *History Ireland* (March-April 2008) one Clive Sinclair-Poulton makes the same basic assertion "*...[there was a] sustained campaign of destruction of Ascendancy houses...the murder of the Pearsons fitted into a perception that there would be a physical undoing of the conquest...how else to explain...the Protestant population fell by a third?...*"

While all this would seem, on the face of it, to confirm the revisionists' arguments on sectarianism it soon becomes apparent that that is not the case.

Starting with Peter Hart's own thesis, while arguing there was a sectarian campaign against Protestants *because* they were Protestants, he yet throughout the chapter simultaneously refers to them also as 'unionists' or 'loyalists' and seems to accept them as such.[8]

In the case of Ms Sammon's assertion about religion and political affiliation it undermines the thrust of her *Hidden History* programme. While Ms Sammon argues that "*...the Pearsons... they were different*

---

[6] Aired on The Tubridy Show, RTÉ Radio One, Monday 22 October 2007.

[7] For example, in a letter to the *Irish Times* by Brendan Cafferty on 17th December 2007.

[8] Peter Hart, *ibid*.

again because they were Cooneyites" (a Protestant sub-sect), nonetheless she still attempts to use their religious affiliation as a primary motive for the attack on them. In doing so she seems to miss her own point—that if Catholics were mainly nationalist and Protestants were mainly loyalist, in the context of a war for independence from an occupying power, the root reason for any antagonism was political rather than religious.

The editorial from *The Witness* had been based on quotes from the Honourable H.M. Pollock, D.L., M.P., the Minister of Finance in the Northern Parliament. He explained it thus:

> "...the Sinn Feiners, of course, deny that Protestants as such are persecuted, and there is an amount of truth in their contention, for their vengeance falls upon all who hinder them without regard to creed or class. But it is easy to see that this does not invalidate Mr Pollock's assertion of the persecution of Protestants, for Protestants are loyal and law-abiding, and feel it as a duty which they owe to God and their own conscience to support the forces of the Crown in the repression of crime..."

Two basic facts emerge from this part of Mr Pollock's speech. Firstly that the 'Sinn Feiners' (a shorthand of the time for the Republican movement) targeted all those *"who hinder them without regard to creed or class"*. Politics therefore and not religion, is the motive. Secondly, that *"...Protestants are loyal...feel it a duty...to support the Crown..."* This quite clearly states that the Protestants in question are supporting British (Crown) forces in a fight against the Republican movement. Their loyalty was to the British Crown and not to Dáil Éireann. The situation of the time meant that two forces were lined up in conflict with each other: the democratically elected Dáil Éireann and the broader Republican movement which supported it. and on the other hand the Crown forces of Britain and its supporters, which continued to occupy and attempt to rule this country after Dáil Éireann had come into being. While many Protestants were loyal to the British Crown, others were not. Both the IRA and Sinn Féin numbered Protestants among their ranks. Many people choose not to openly align themselves to either side but those that did were aware they could and probably would suffer the consequences of taking such a stance in troubled times. Many (though by no means all) Protestants who supported an occupying British force in defiance of the mandate of Dáil Éireann did suffer adverse consequences such as those described in *The Witness* editorial. But it seems clear that it was their political affiliation and not their religion, which supplied the motive for such attacks as were made on them.

In his letter above Mr Sinclair-Poulton attempts to claim a form of [ethnic or sectarian] cleansing took place but fails to recognize the full implications of his own argument. The Ascendancy represented the socio-political class—mainly Protestant but with some Catholic members—who originally owed their position to, had most to gain from, and most reason to support, loyalty to the British Crown. In some instances they were responsible for implementing its will here, supplying Justices of the Peace and other important civil functionaries. Mr Sinclair-Poulton—perhaps unwittingly—drives this point home in saying *"there would be a physical undoing of the conquest"*. Once again we find political affiliation and not religion, to be the root motive.

Many more examples like those above could be given but the first problem of the debate on sectarianism should by now be apparent: the use of the term *Protestant* as a kind of sloppy shorthand for the very different terms *unionist* or *loyalist*. While many Protestants were indeed also loyalists or unionists the misuse of the term has lead to the mistaken or intentional perception that Protestants were targeted on account of their religion alone. That is not to claim that all Protestants targeted by republicans were actually loyalists. But even if they were wrongly perceived to have been loyalist the motive would still have to be regarded as political rather than religious. Yet the notion that Protestants were targeted by the IRA in the 1919-1923 period in a sectarian war of ethnic cleansing seems to be accepted uncritically in some quarters.

Is our Media Informed on our History?

A further difficulty in debating our history was underlined in the radio discussions that followed *Hidden History: The Killing at Coolacrease* in October 2007. As a vox pop forum radio (and television) obviously has its place but cannot be compared to the academic work undertaken in national universities in terms of providing a detailed understanding and analysis of our history. Nonetheless radio has a particularly important role for two reasons. Firstly much of the academic history being written about Ireland emanates from universities in the UK or elsewhere with our own national universities lagging somewhat behind. Secondly the detailed research of academia reaches a smaller portion of the general population whose main easily accessible source of information on our history may come from more digestible TV programs like the *Hidden History* series or radio talk shows. Yet the format of radio talk shows in particular with its time-pressure constraints allows little time for very detached detailed analysis, favouring soundbites and the more emotive personal touch that stirs listeners to tune in or participate.

One would nevertheless expect that the host of a radio talk show to be sufficiently acquainted with the background details and facts of the subject matter in order to ask the probing questions and challenge assertions.

Tubridy interviewed Niamh Sammon on the Coolacrease story about the time the *Hidden History* was aired.[9] In fairness to Tubridy, his main role seems to have been to allow Niamh Sammon discuss and advertise her programme: (Tubridy) *"...I want to tell you about a documentary which will be shown as part of the excellent Hidden History series on RTÉ One television"*. Yet he could have challenged Niamh Sammon on a number of points, such as the assertion that nothing was happening in Offaly until mid 1921. In fact between 21st September 1920 and 29th June 1921 no less than 6 RIC men were shot in Offaly.[10] While compared to the very active areas such as Cork and Tipperary this may seem insignificant, it does show that it's not exactly correct to describe Offaly—with its smaller area and population—as a place which was *"really, really quiet"* and only started to *"hot up in 1921"* (Niamh Sammon). Three of the above RIC

---

[9] The Tubridy Show, RTÉ Radio One, Monday 22 October 2007.

[10] Source: Richard Abbot, *Police Casualties in Ireland 1919–1922*. Mercier Press. Cork: 2000.

men had been shot in the latter half of 1920, the other three in 1921. Furthermore, when Ms Sammon corrects herself in describing the Pearsons as spies *("suspected spies, I should say")* Tubridy concurs immediately *("well, absolutely!")* without even posing the challenge of asking if there was any grounds to suggest they had been spying. Later in the programme Ms Sammon tells Tubridy that *"...The fatal shots were to the groin. And then they turned away from the fire. And they, they, they were shot in the buttocks. And they were left then to die, because none of the shots were fatal...,"* a contradiction which Tubridy doesn't even seem to notice. Tubridy concludes Ms Sammon's account of the executions by saying: *"...The interesting thing is that nobody, there is no verdict as to who or what actually happened in terms of the innocence or guilt of the Pearsons..."* But *Hidden History: The Killing at Coolacrease* is in fact one verdict and it comes down in favour of declaring the Pearsons as innocent and arguing they were killed because they were Protestant and because persons unknown wanted their land. It was only towards the end of the programme that Tubridy began to challenge the *Hidden History* account *"...maybe their family were spies and traitors?..."* but didn't press the point.

Tubridy's main purpose seems to have been simply to advertise the *Hidden History* programme by raising awareness of it in the public arena (exposition) and get Niamh Sammon to outline its content briefly, rather than enter a polemic with her. Moreover Ms Sammon was alone in the interview, a format which would be unlikely to encourage much debate. This could explain why he didn't make any real attempt to challenge the *Hidden History* version or stimulate debate. On the other hand Joe Duffy on *Liveline* took a much more proactive approach, simultaneously outlining the story while challenging the various callers on their contributions. Therefore some of his comments on aspects of the War of Independence deserve closer scrutiny.

The principal problem here is that Mr Duffy seemed uninformed about the origins of our State, a most curious state of affairs for a presenter on the national radio station. While surely aware of the basic facts—the War of Independence and civil war—he seemed unclear about other very important details, for instance when he informed Jack Lane [11] that

> "...The only, the only courts—and I know you would say unfortunately—a lot of people would say the only courts at the time [1921] were the British courts..."

This suggests that Mr. Duffy is unaware of the existence of the republican or so-called Sinn Féin courts that operated all over the country [12] and played a major role in ending British rule here by creating a parallel system to replace it. They have been described extensively in republican literature—IRA veterans' memoirs and in sources such as Dorothy McArdle's *The Irish Republic*.
Mr. Lane tried to correct this view:

> "...Yeah, well there was an Irish court system as well..."

But Mr Duffy 'stuck to his guns':

> "There was, there was, there was a Court Martial".

So, no civil republican courts then, only IRA courts martial.

More seriously he seems unaware of the existence of an Irish Government at the time, or at least doesn't recognize the validity of the First Dáil. Mr Lane explained that the IRA were the *"legitimate army of the Irish government"* but Mr Duffy rejects this view and refined it to the IRA being the

> "...legitimate army of the party that got the majority votes..."

In case anyone was in any doubt—as the party with the majority of votes normally forms the government in any democracy—Mr. Duffy further added

> "...But there wasn't a constituted government as such [in 1921]..."

Mr. Lane immediately pointed out that there was in fact an Irish Government in existence at the time. It is hardly a secret that the First

---

[11] RTÉ radio *Liveline* programme with Joe Duffy. Transmission date: 6th November 2007.

[12] According to Dorothy McArdle, Dáil Éireann had already established Arbitration Courts in June 1919 and the first Law Court was held in Ballinrobe in Co.Mayo on May 17th 1920. Dorothy McArdle, *The Irish Republic*. Wolfhound Press. Dublin: 1999 (p.348).

Dáil met in Mansion House on January 21st 1919 and set about implementing its mandate of seeking political separation and independence from the UK. Its first act was to ratify the republic [13] which had been declared in 1916: *"and whereas the Irish Republic was proclaimed in Dublin on Easter Monday in 1916...we...ratify the establishment of the Irish Republic and pledge ourselves and our people to make this declaration effective by every means possible."* It appointed Ministers and a President (i.e. Prime Minister) and sent a delegation to the Versailles Peace Conference the same year (which was only rebuffed on account of pressure from Britain, despite Woodrow Wilson's 14-point plan and the supposed aims for which the First World War had been fought). County Councils in large areas of Ireland stopped sending the minutes of their meetings to Dublin castle and instead sent them to the Dáil in recognition of that body. The Irish Volunteers began to change their name from the time of the First Dáil onwards and become known as the Irish Republican Army, or IRA. They swore their allegiance to Dáil Éireann and the Irish Republic.

This begs one obvious question: if Mr Duffy doesn't recognize the legitimacy of the First Dáil, which Dáil does he think is currently (2008) in session—the 30th or the 29th?

To add to the confusion Mr. Duffy then stated that

"...But let's be clear about this, whether you like it or not: in 1918 the Government of Ireland was the British Government..."

The Pearsons' story occurred in 1921 by which time there certainly was a constituted Irish government. But even in 1918 there is a case to be made that the British Government was not the legitimate government of Ireland. Firstly, it was a government that had come into being through conquest and force rather then by consent. By early 1917 there was open disenchantment with the British presence.[14]

---

[13] See p.15-16, Dail Éireann. *Miontuairisc an Chead Dala (minutes of proceedings) 1919-1921*. Pub. Dublin: The Stationery Office.

[14] Cpl.Robert William Iley of the King's Royal Rifle Corps, posted to the regimental depot in Southern Tipperary in 1917, noted how he "found the southern Irish very bitter against British troops" Recounted in Jon E.Lewis (Ed). *True World War I Stories*. Robinson. London: 1999 (p.195).

People did not had an alternative separatist government for which they could vote but Sinn Fein was to provide such a platform by 1917 and 1918. By the end of the 1918 elections Sinn Féin's landslide victory had provided them with the mandate they needed to pursue a separatist programme . Effectively Ireland now had a de-facto separatist republican government mandated by the people. While the British administration remained, it did so as an occupier-by-force and was quickly replaced by a parallel Republican administration which operated very effectively despite the state of siege under which it carried out its duties. Joe Duffy continued—

"…But you can't say that the IRA, in 1918 were, were, the army of Ireland—they weren't, whether you like it or not… The British army were in Ireland".

Why Mr. Duffy was now focusing on 1918 rather than the period in question (1921) was unclear. Technically he had a point since in 1918 the IRA—under that name -didn't exist. And while Sinn Féin had the mandate by late 1918, the First Dáil had yet to convene and the IRA to be formally inaugurated as the army of the Irish Republic. But the Irish Volunteers—the forerunner of the IRA—had already been in existence since 1913 and Jack Lane is certainly correct also in saying

"…[The British Army] represented Ireland? They, they represented the electorate who voted for independence? Did they?..."

At this point Joe Duffy moved back to the Coolacrease incident but seemed far from convinced by Mr Lane's explanations. Pat Muldowney had tried to impress the same points on Joe Duffy the previous day[15] with the same lack of success:

Joc Duffy:

"…No but I know (indistinct) there wasn't, there was a British Government running the country, there wasn't an Irish Government, but you say there was a Courts Martial?..."

Pat Muldowney:

---

[15] RTÉ radio 1, *Liveline* programme, presented by Joe Duffy. Transmission date: 5 November 2007.

"...There was an elected Government Joe, you see, that's the whole point, the elected—the legitimate—authority there was held by the, by the, Irish, by the elected Government ..."

And further, when Mr Muldowney explained that Thomas Burke, an IRA officer was responsible to the Irish Government, Joe Duffy added –

"...Insofar as we had an Irish Government..."

It shouldn't be difficult at this point to see one of the serious difficulties in conducting debate in the national media on this period of history. When a radio presenter with the national broadcaster seems unclear about the mechanisms of the founding of the state in which he lives and does not really accept their legitimacy, what hope is there for honest and accurate debate? Nor is Mr Duffy's view unique but rather strangely seems to typify the view held by much of the State media personnel. It is in such circumstances that a programme like *Hidden History: The Killing at Coolacrease* comes to be made.

The Conduct of Debate on the National Airwaves

Finally, it was worth taking a brief look at how such matters are discussed and debated on our airwaves. Many people might suppose it is simply a case of 'may the best, and honest, argument win'.

Firstly there is the role of the presenter. While any radio (or TV) presenter may be interested in helping to inform a wider audience of the topic, s/he is also mindful of how the discussion will help ratings. After all, unpopular shows are axed! Vigorous debate and emotive issues make for ideal radio, and Coolacrease certainly provided all that. The first difficulty though for any presenter is the obscurity of the incident. Two people were shot at a time when people were being shot every week, a minor though tragic sideshow in a bigger scene which occurred over 86 years ago. Prior to the Hidden History programme many people would probably have been quite unaware of what had occurred there. The initial callers to the radio were all people well-acquainted with the events and the problem would be to stop the discussion from becoming so arcane that the average listener simply tuned out. Joe Duffy's approach on *Liveline* [16] was fairly straightforward: try to get the callers being interviewed to explain the events and the controversy surrounding them in their own words for the benefit off the less-informed listener.

However this approach proved problematic from the outset with Joe Duffy unsuccessfully trying to elicit from Paddy Heaney the exact reasons why he felt the Hidden History programme was biased

> Joe Duffy: "And what is your problem with the Hidden History programme?"
> Paddy Heaney: "It is biased."
> JD: "In what way?"
> PH: "It wasn't balanced. Eh, well, any of us who live around here and who know the history of the whole episode, know clearly that the, the documentary showed those two boys taken out of the field, they showed them being executed."

'Biased' and 'not balanced' are effectively synonyms so Joe was obliged to resort to trying to supply the exposition himself:

> PH: "They showed, they showed they were being executed twice. But they did not do a documentary on the Mass [party / path] incident, or they did not do a documentary on the shooting of the two IRA men at the roadblock."
> JD: "So, what was the motive given in the TV programme for the killings?"
> PH: "On the TV? Well, they... as you said, as I'm telling you now, the TV documentary was very biased, was completely biased."
> JD: "In that you said the background wasn't included."

Paddy Heaney, a historian from the area and well-familiar with the events surrounding Coolacrease, seemed unaware that Joe Duffy wanted him to explain all this for the benefit of the listener. This led to Mr Duffy trying to supply the missing words *"in that you said the background wasn't included."* We see something similar happening when he interviewed Claire Guerin:

> Joe Duffy: "And what were those reasons which the programme proffered?"

---

[16] Ditto.

> Claire Guerin: "Well, well, I'm not saying that the programme didn't try to give both sides but, but some historians have the view that, that people were targeted unfairly for sectarian reasons."
> JD: "Because they were Protestants and to get their land."
> CG: "Exactly."

His palpable frustration over the vagueness concerning the key issue insofar as the radio show was concerned—why there is an ongoing row regarding the *Hidden History* programme—became evident when he decided to make a fresh start after Brendan Cafferty called midway through the programme—

> Joe Duffy: "Now Brendan, can you—I'm going to stop you and try and start again. I'll tell you why. Because…there's an ongoing row about this programme."
> Brendan Cafferty: "Yeah"
> JD: "… and I'm asking Paddy Heaney, I'm asking you now, tell me, having watched the programme, what do you think the row is about?"

It is also evident from his requests to callers during the programme to explain aspects of the story (e.g when he asks Paddy Heaney to explain what Cooneyites were, or why the Pearson boys were shot), while he is apparently already aware of the details, as he explains to Niall Ginty:

> Niall Ginty: "Based on the doctor's evidence—I don't know if you are, are you familiar with the story yourself?"
> Joe Duffy: "Yes, I am, yeah—I read up on it this morning."

There is of course, nothing particularly sinister about any of this. Rather it is simply that callers to radio often seem unaware that they are being steered to phrase things in a certain way for the benefit of exposition—in order to fill in details of the plot for less-well acquainted listeners.

Likewise the presenter often has to feign a kind of ignorance for much the same reason. This is very evident when Niall Ginty calls *Liveline* and opens with a salvo against the Aubane Historical Society, trying to discredit them as troublemakers and so, by association, rubbish their line of argument. He says:

> Niall Ginty: " …Because there's been, there's been, there's a crowd from North Cork, they're, they, they, they've been roaming the country,

it's been going round the country stirring up trouble anywhere, where such an, any event as it happens. I don't know, have you heard of the Aubane Society?"

Joe Duffy: "No, I haven't no."

NG: "Well anyway, they're, they're, they're ..."

And a split second later Joe Duffy is able to prompt him

JD: "They're a historical society?"

NG: "Yeah, they're a historical society, yeah, correct. But there are people who are going around and particularly now with this story ..."

Now it may have been that someone in the studio had just handed Joe Duffy a piece of paper with an explanation of who the Aubane Society were, but the speed of Mr Duffy's reaction seems to preclude this.

Secondly, the interaction between the various 'camps' engaged in the debate is of interest. The following is a synopsis and commentary on some of the main points made by callers to both RTÉ Radio 1 *Liveline* shows hosted by Joe Duffy on the 5th and 6th of November and an interview with Niamh Sammon on the RTÉ radio 1 *Tubridy Show* of 22nd October 2007.

The first key point on *Liveline* (5th November) was made by Paddy Heaney who argued the *Hidden History* programme was biased because it did not give the full facts about the two Pearson boys, namely that they were working for the Crown forces. Niamh Sammon countered this by stating that everything had been included in the programme. She added that if she had wanted an unbalanced, biased programme, she wouldn't have included Paddy Heaney's contribution. This is something of a false logic though, as if she had not included contributions such as Paddy Heaney's the programme would indeed have been biased but very evidently so. It would be possible to have included Heaney's contribution *and* still have made a biased programme through careful editing or framing of the contribution. This was what Paddy Heaney himself seemed to have thought, and said so. Indeed, it would have been the more effective for having a veneer of objectivity and fairness.

Regarding her choice of interviewees she says

"...It was absolutely essential to interview the people of the community, which we did—five local people were interviewed in the programme..."

Interestingly, on Tubridy she had spoken about the reluctance of local people to speak about Coolacrease—

"...Everybody knew about this story. Everybody had an opinion about this story. For every person who said the Pearsons got what they deserved, other people would say it was absolutely dreadful, and really this was a land-grab and it shouldn't have happened. But a lot of the people who would say things like that, they just simply wouldn't go on camera, as they said we have to live in this area. We couldn't live in this area if we said these things ...."

While she gave part of the reason as being sympathy for the republican cause and for the reputations of the men involved her last phrase above seems intended to give the unmistakable impression that the people of Offaly live under a cloud of fear, fear of republican intimidation. Yet this was supposed to have been one of the quietest areas' in the country during the war of independence, with "the Keystone cops of the IRA"—as Tubridy described them—in residence. And with all that, what was there to be afraid of 86 years later? It also leaves us with a second problem. She leaves us with the impression that lots of anonymous people would have backed up her contention that the Pearsons were murdered in a sectarian land-grab, but they can't be interviewed on account of their fear. So while there's no way to check this assertion Niamh Sammon can still benefit from making it. The use of anonymous sources is not something new in revisionism and was echoed towards the end of the *Liveline* programme when a caller who gave his name simply as 'Luke' from Kilkenny was able to make assertions about his grand-uncle being shot for no other motive than a sectarian one. His grand-uncle wouldn't hurt a fly, he assured us. And since we don't know his identity, we can never check this assertion. And since Luke *"didn't want to stay on the line too long as [he] didn't feel comfy about being here at all"* (again, the spectre of republican intimidation?) it would have been difficult for either Joe Duffy or any of the other callers to challenge him further. There may (or may not) be history attached to his grand-uncle that Luke himself is not aware of, but without knowing the man's identity there's no way of conducting the research necessary to determine if this was truly a case of sectarian murder. Not only was Luke able to assure us that this was the case with his grandfather, but in a sweeping assertion included all low-church Protestants such as the Pearsons—

> "...And these people, believe you me, they wouldn't have been colluding or co-operating with anybody..."

Niall Ginty was the next caller after Niamh Sammon, and he had read a *Sunday Times* article that made much of the fact that the Pearsons had been shot *"in the genitals"*. This genital business was to become one of the *"big stories"* of the Coolacrease incident. Quasi-Freudian analysis was added by Eoghan Harris—

> "...they were shot in the groin or genitals as I recall it because I thought there was a deliberately sexual kind of, form of contempt to shoot them like that..."

Niamh Sammon also took this view, speaking on Tubridy—

> "...But it does seem that a lot of [the shots] ended up in the groin area. So some people say it was deliberate. It was symbolic. I mean these were Protestants. They were Outsiders..."

The image of the 'outsider' in the War of Independence can first be found in Peter Hart's 1998 book *The IRA and its Enemies*. Sammon says that some people say it was deliberate without telling us who these people are. Eoghan Harris obviously, but then he wasn't in Coolacrease 86 years ago, so that doesn't help our inquiry much. The doctor's report on the Pearsons indicated they had been shot a number of times in various parts of the body—for instance, the back, the thigh and so on, and that many of the wounds were superficial. It never mentioned anything about being *"shot in the genitals."* But according to Niall Ginty being shot in the groin *"...is as near to the genitals as you can possibly get..."* True, apart from actually being shot in the genitals, of course. It's a bit like having a bullet clip the ear or strike the shoulder and saying that the person was shot in the head. The end effect would be different of course.

Niall Ginty then went on to accuse the Aubane Society of trying to blame the people of Offaly for what happened but didn't elaborate on what he meant by this or provide any evidence to back up his assertion. Actually it was Eoghan Harris who was trying to blame the people of Offaly, insisting they apologize for what had happened 86 years ago—

> "...It would be far better if the people of Offaly just accepted that a bad thing happened and just allowed the ordinary people of Offaly to deal with it by apologising..."

This is despite the fact that it was an IRA group from outside the area, under Thomas Burke, that was responsible for the executions /killings. Paddy Heaney ably responded to this suggestion by putting it in a wider context—

> "...Well, nobody apologizes for anything. If we were to start apologizing we go back to when the Normans came in here, 1169 and start apologizing up through the centuries..."

The exchange between Brendan Cafferty (the next caller after Niall Ginty) and Paddy Heaney was as enjoyable as a good tennis match at Wimbledon, with all the back-and-forth action of serve and counter-serve. Brendan, perhaps unaware of Meda Ryan's research, began by comparing Coolacrease to Peter Hart's account of the 1922 Dunmanway killing of 11 Protestants. His assertion was basic—they were shot because they were Protestants. Paddy Heaney responded by pointing out there were many other Protestant families in the area who had been left untouched. Mr Cafferty quickly asked if they had big farms. The motive for this question was clear—if these other Protestants had had small farms (Niamh Sammon had painted a picture of the huge Pearson farm as being surrounded by much smaller farms) then they wouldn't have been worth bothering with. The Pearsons farm would have been the 'best pickings'. Unfortunately for Cafferty's thesis Heaney affirmed many of these Protestants did indeed have big farms—some of them much bigger than the Pearsons'. Cafferty was momentarily derailed by this unexpected piece of information and struggled to retain control of the ball by switching the topic to the theme of 'labelling' people as spies and informers

> "...Yes, you know, well, you know, this, this, this thing of labelling them you know, those people cannot speak for themselves..."

And recovering his composure shifted the goal posts even further by returning to a question he had posed earlier and that is often resorted to in this topic

> "...And, and, and my question is who gave, who gave anybody the right to do that to them, you know? I mean can you please answer that? To mutilate, leave them die in agony without medical assistance for hours, you know..."

Sensing that he has his quarry in his sights, Cafferty insists again on an answer to this very detailed and complex question

> "...Paddy Heaney—Could I answer you again?
> Brendan Cafferty: "Can you please justify that?"
> PH: "You ..."
> BC: "I'd like to hear your justification for that..."

Kevin Myers has posed the same question many times in relation to 1916, the War of Independence and individual killings during that time in his *Irishman's Diary* column in *The Irish Times*.[17] In an absolute moral sense any and all killing is wrong (the 5th Commandment). But in any war, this absolute moral standard has already been abandoned and so cannot be appealed to any longer. There remains only degrees of difference in civil, secular justifications. If the Pearsons had consciously engaged in acts of war—such as assisting the British Crown forces in some way or by shooting up an IRA road-blocking party—against the republican government and its forces, who, as we saw earlier, were the legitimate government of the time, then the republican Government and its forces would have a legitimate right to take counter-action. From an emotive 'soundbite' point of view it's a very effective question to pose in a debate like this as it leaves the recipient in the unenviable position of having to justify killing and helps to make them look inhumane. As well as placing Heaney on the defensive in trying to answer two questions at once—whether or not the Pearsons were spies and justifying their

---

[17] See Nick Folley, *Irish Political Review* May 2007, Vol.22 No.5 p.16-18 for a more extensive answer to Myers' question and rebuttal of his suggestion that no authority existed for executions and killings carried out by republicans during the period from 1916 – 1923.

killing—it also had the happy consequence of moving the debate away from an area where Cafferty had received a setback (the 'big farms 'issue). But Caffery was again to be thwarted as Heaney returned to the land question. Cafferty tried to move to another topic by referring to the note left on the plough as described in *Hidden History* warning the Pearsons not to try and re-occupy their farm. This story comes from David Pearsons's 1983 letter to Hilary Stanley, as quoted by Alan Stanley in his book. Heaney dismissed this as propaganda. This exchange moved the debate away from facts that could be verified or arguments that could be worked through theoretically and into the realm of 'whose word do you take?'

A caller named Patricia Howard spoke of how Protestants felt they 'were not wanted' in the Ireland brought about by the War of Independence. Presumably she meant not wanted by the Catholic majority population. She added that Protestants were not wanted in politics in the Republic. Again, presumably she is talking of the Free State period, since there were prominent Protestant members of Dáil Éireann and other important bodies such as the Land Bank. Protestants withdrew defensively into their own little groups as Ms Howard described it. It is conceivable in a country where much of the social life revolved around the church that minority religions such as Protestants might feel excluded here from that in the same way up to recently Catholics in Britain felt excluded from much of the social life there: not attending or networking via church-related social functions of the Church of England. But it would be difficult to argue Protestants here were discriminated against in the manner northern Catholics were. Ms Howard said that Protestants in the south were denied 'their civil rights' for most of the last eighty years, but it's not clear what she means. Protestants were free to practise their religion, hold their own social functions and assemblies, engage in politics and so on. Such restrictions in areas such as 'sexual-morality issues' (divorce, abortion etc.,) affected Catholics equally and similar rules also applied to Protestants in the north.[18]

---

[18] We have been informed that the Howards were business people in Co. Wexford who had a "No Catholics need apply" employment policy up to mid 20th century—*Editor's note.*

But by far the most extraordinary part of the *Liveline* show was Eoghan Harris' outburst regarding the Aubane Society. Niall Ginty was the first caller to try and rubbish the Aubane Society, saying—

"…there's a crowd from North Cork, they're, they, they, they've been roaming the country, it's been going round the country stirring up trouble anywhere, where such an, any event as it happens. I don't know, have you heard of the Aubane Society…"

Apparently while Mr Ginty sees no problem in presenting an obscure and almost forgotten incident from the War of Independence as a petty sectarian murder he regards any challenge to this thesis as *"stirring up trouble"*. Perhaps there's some truth in this allegation, as it creates some 'trouble' for dedicated revisionists as they struggle to explain the cracks in the thesis. There's only one version of events to be allowed—that of sectarian murder—and anything else is just *muddying the waters* as Mr Ginty puts it. This line was taken up at much greater length by Eoghan Harris later in the programme when he likened them to 'holocaust deniers'—not just once, but twice:

"…a group of people, of which Paddy Muldowney is one, who seem to make an itinerant travelling circus of—they're like holocaust deniers—flood the letters, bombard RTÉ with letters, proving that it really didn't happen at all…"

and later

"…there's a lot of this rubbish being pushed out by Muldowney and his friends like Niall Meehan, and the Aubane group that were mentioned in the programme, they're like a professional crowd of holocaust deniers. They run around the place bombarding, and trying to tell lies about simple facts…"

Once again, we are left with the feeling that Harris—like Niall Ginty—believes the world would be a better place if there was no one to challenge his version of events, that he objects to them *"proving that it didn't really happen at all."* Such was the intemperate nature of his outburst that Joe Duffy felt obliged to interject, saying *"all right, hang on…"* and state soon after

"…by the way I just want to point out that it was mentioned earlier by Eoghan about different people on Live; now I know it was a general [sop?] about revisionism, history and all that carry-on, but the people that are mentioned, Niall Meehan for example, is a respected lecturer in Dublin and there's no allegation of untruth there, I just want to clarify that…" (my emphasis)

Though ironically it was Joe Duffy himself who on *Liveline* the following day (6th November) came close to suggesting Jack Lane was being dishonest during a discussion on who got the Pearson's land afterwards –

"Yeah, but they were, now let's go through this again, let's not be too economical with it, and I'm not suggest- you, I'm not suggesting— but there's other people got land as well, the first three people" (my emphasis).

Harris explained his motivation as

"…I have been going round for years trying to dig up some of that buried history because, the last taboo in Ireland. And I've been doing it because if we don't dig up that history and tell the truth about that period, what chance have the people of Fermanagh, or the Northern Catholics, what kind of chance have we of any kind of peace on the island, of any kind of truce?…"

But the issue at stake here is whether or not these events do represent the truth. And if Harris is not willing to even tolerate any discussion or dissent on this, one is forced to conclude the truth may be further down the list of priorities than he states. If sectarian murders were a fact of the War of Independence, then Harris would be correct in saying we need to acknowledge this, even simply for the sake of open truth and historical accuracy. But if sectarian murders were not a typical aspect of the Irish struggle for independence, it's hard to see how fabricating such accounts could be helpful to peace and unity on this island and Harris fails to develop this point further. Harris seemed genuinely irked that every time he publishes something claiming that Protestants were targeted in a dirty sectarian war by the IRA some people dare to challenge this view. When Pat Muldowney tried to challenge Harris by referring to documents he had researched, Harris' basic technique was to heckle, interrupt and shout him down. This reached a crescendo when Pat Muldowney was speaking about the medical report of the shootings

Pat Muldowney: "…[Harris interrupts again, shouting] But I, I look, you, [indistinct, Harris shouting over Muldowney: 'look, I've got, got forty pages…you're famous for sending enormous boring letters to people, you did the same, you did the same thing…']…"

Joe Duffy had to intervene at this point to enable the discussion to continue. Harris went on to accuse the Aubane Society and its associates of

"…doing the people of Offaly no service to drag this out like that mystifying and mud-raking and trying to pretend it was IRA Court Martials…"

Presumably Harris thinks it serves the people of Offaly better to humbly view themselves as parochial sectarian murderers rather than as participants in this country's struggle for independence. Paddy Heaney—who *is* from Offaly—referred to Harris' article on the same and said that people 'were raging about it'.

At this point there was a surprise development as one Roger Pearson came on line. Roger was a direct descendant of the Pearson family of Coolacrease. From Australia, he had gone to live in Dublin. Roger came across as a genuinely nice fellow. He was aware of the events but didn't seem to harbour any bad feelings

"…But, em you know em, they were dirty days and you know I, we don't, like you know, hold, [harbour?] any grudges or anything you know, what happened happened and you know…"

This did not seem to suit the purpose of Eoghan Harris at all and he asked Joe Duffy:

"…Can I ask a question of Roger through you? Did Roger get any personal reaction, did anyone say anything to him? Because there was other relatives, there was one relative reported as saying that she wondered if there'd be reprisals. I just wonder if Roger feels totally free to say what's in his mind in all this?…"

Roger Pearson didn't feel under any threat unlike the unknown relative mentioned by Harris. He had received some 'slagging' from workmates but that was the extent of it. He just wanted to move on. Duffy then asked Harris if this wasn't a fair point—did digging up these stories hinder more than help? Harris was still convinced despite Roger Pearson's assertion to the contrary, that he, along with all other Protestants, were not free to speak their minds.

"...I don't think you see, if you're a tiny Protestant community living in a place like Offaly or West Cork I don't think you're free actually to speak out and say what you really think about what happened to your relatives..."

Not even if you have lived most of your life in Australia, it seems. Despite what Roger Pearson was telling him, Harris still wanted to ascribe other motives to him—

"...I mean for example, Roger—he's been very good there and he's trying to sort of put the best face on it but I doubt very much like, if it's as simple as..."

It was becoming absurd. Harris was acting like 'the policeman at the front door' who realizes a kidnapping is going on in the house and tells the owner 'you could make some sign to indicate if you were being kidnapped' He was still fishing—

"...I, I would ask [Roger] straight out did any workmates say anything about, did the word 'informer' cross anyone's lips?...was the word Cooneyite used to you?"

As though the word 'Cooneyite' was some form of pejorative in common usage!

Roger affirmed they had, but indicated that he took it as some slagging.

"...Oh well, you know, I just sort of like, took it with a pinch of salt really, because I sort of knew, you know, it was only my work mates really, and they were just like, messing really—well, I think they were! [laughter from Roger's workmates in the background]"

Roger Pearson didn't fit into the profile favoured by Harris: Protestant victim, afraid to speak out, championed by Harris. So he returned to his theme in a more general way:

"...He's just got a bit of slagging but there's different ways of keeping social control, like that.

And despite trying to put words in Pearson's mouth and telling him "[you're] being very good there" (in other words '*I* know what you *really* want to say') he accuses Paddy Heaney of being patronizing—

> "...I think that sometimes Paddy Heaney's voice, when you heard the sort of patronising sounds he made to Patricia Howard—you see the way a certain kind of person with Sinn Féin sympathies can keep a grip on, on quite a timid Protestant community..."

One gets the feeling that Paddy Heaney, for his part, would be quite surprised to learn that he has any 'grip' which he keeps on 'a timid Protestant community'.

Niall Meehan entered the debate at this point, referring to the statement made by Protestants at a convention on 11th May 1922 at the Dublin Mansion House to the effect that sectarian attacks were not a feature of the War of Independence period. Joe Duffy challenged him on this, referring to Harris' view that Protestants don't feel free to speak their minds. To which Meehan replied

> "...Well, it'd be the first time in human history when a group en masse said that, denied they were being attacked, and said that they were in fact being protected. There's no, no evidence of that ever occurring in human history..." [19]

---

[19] Editor's Note: The transcripts of the radio programmes examined in this article are available on the website http://docs.indymedia.org/view/Main/CoolaCrease. Nick Folley is the grandson of Vol. Herbert Mitchell, one of a Protestant Offaly family who were active in the IRA. Herbert left Offaly for Cork after the 1916 Rising to evade the attentions of the RIC and, known as Seán Mitchell, fought there with an IRA Flying Column in the War of Independence.

Chapter 11

Defending Their Own
The Broadcasting Commission

By

John Martin

Complaints against 'Hidden History':
The Killings at Coolacrease

The broadcast of the "Killings at Coolacrease" has ramifications that go far beyond the details of what happened in a field in Offaly in 1921. The controversy surrounding this documentary raises questions as to what the role of the national broadcaster should be. Should it be independent of the political parties? Indeed should it be independent of the society? If a citizen of the Republic is unhappy with what is broadcast what recourse does he have? Should the onus be placed on an individual or group of private individuals to ensure that the National Broadcaster reflects the republican values of the State?

RTÉ like other media is constrained by the laws of libel. It also is required not to breach standards of decency or good taste. And it must give the appearance of being fair and objective. It sees its role as representing different points of view within the society including minority viewpoints. There is no requirement to promote or preserve the values of the State. Neither is there a requirement to represent the State's interests. Although it is largely financed by the State, through licence fees, it is not—as former Taoiseach Sean Lemass once envisaged—an organ of the State.

There may be many readers who will think that this relatively passive and open-ended role of RTÉ is the proper function of a national broadcaster. But how does this work in practice? In my view the absence of a clearly defined role for RTÉ allows individual programme makers to advance their own political agenda. Providing that these programme makers conform to some very loosely defined guidelines there is nothing that anyone can do about it. Political interference is anathema. And ordinary citizens—even highly motivated citizens—are largely impotent. That has been my experience in attempting to counteract what I perceived as the biased political agenda being pursued by the makers of "The Killings at Coolacrease".

As has been shown elsewhere in this book the broadcast of this documentary was not a thing in itself, but a strategic point in a long political campaign which began before the broadcast and continued after it. Although like most people I was subjected to the barrage of propaganda in the *Sunday Independent* and *The Irish Times*, I was fortunate in having an opportunity to read an alternative view in the pages of two small circulation magazines *Church & State* and the *Irish Political Review*. So by the day of the broadcast I was well prepared to examine the programme critically.

My Complaint

As expected the programme gave a completely biased account of the killings, but in the immediate aftermath it was unclear as to what I or anyone else could do about it. Nobody had been libelled or slandered because the events portrayed related to people who had long since passed away. Therefore there was no remedy available in a court of law. Apart from writing a letter to RTÉ the only other option was to submit a complaint to the Broadcasting Complaints Commission (BCC) which claims to be an independent statutory authority empowered to adjudicate on such complaints.

It was unclear that my belief that the programme was politically biased could be adjudicated on by the BCC. There was a description of previous complaints on the BCC web site, but they were very different from the complaint, which I wished to make. Some of them related to taste and decency. Others related to insensitivity regarding handicapped people or unbalanced handling of a political topic.

However, there was one complaint by an Inge Clissman, which seemed to be relevant. This complaint also related to the Hidden

History series, which was the category that the Coolacrease documentary was included under. And one of her complaints relating to the portrayal of her father during the Second World War was upheld. Although the BCC did not find that the documentary had broadcast any factual errors about her father, the fact that he was included in a part of the documentary with war criminals gave the false impression that he himself was a war criminal. The BCC upheld Clissman's complaint.

This seemed to indicate that it was within the remit of the BCC to adjudicate on history programmes. I also felt that if I could demonstrate that there were factual errors in the programme designed to reinforce a biased political viewpoint, my case would be all the more convincing.

The most dramatic part of the documentary, in my view, was comments made by Eoghan Harris relating to the shooting of the Pearsons. Harris said that the Pearsons were shot:

> "…very deliberately in the genitals, in their sexual parts, in their sexual organs".

This was presented as a statement of fact. It is either true or false. If it is true, both Pearsons, not just one, would have to be shown to have been shot in the *"genitals, in their sexual parts, in their sexual organs"*.

In the next sentence Harris draws the following political conclusion from his statement of "fact":

> "What it really says is you are the other. You are an outsider. We hate you. Go away and die".

The "fact" of being shot in the genitals is proof that the killings had nothing to do with a war of liberation but were motivated by hatred because the Pearsons were different from their killers. In case anyone was uncertain of what that meant David Adams in his *Irish Times* column spelt it out. In his opinion it was a comment on *"Protestant procreation"*. In other articles the phrase "ethnic cleansing" was used.

In the documentary itself the statement of "fact" was reinforced by an opinion expressed by Alan Stanley that the executioners aimed at the "groin and buttocks area". Stanley's opinion would be credible if Harris's statement of "fact" were true. But Harris's statement is false.

The medical evidence at a British Military Court of Inquiry lists the wounds incurred by the Pearsons and there are no wounds to the *"genitals or sexual organs"*.

The wounds to Richard Pearson were:

> "...superficial wound in the left shoulder, a deep wound in the right groin and right buttock, the entrance of the latter being in front. In addition there were wounds in the left lower leg of a superficial nature and about six in the back which were glancing wounds."

The groin is the depression or fold between the upper thigh and abdomen. It is farther from the genitals than the ear lobe is from the brain.

The wounds to Abraham Pearson were:

> "...left cheek, left shoulder, left thigh and lower third of left leg. In addition there was a wound through the abdomen. The latter wound had an entrance at the front and appeared to have its exit at the lower part of the back, fracturing the lower part of the spinal column."

In my submission to the BCC I stated that Harris's statement was a *"complete fabrication"*. But this was a polite way of saying that it was a complete "lie" perpetrated by the programme makers since they were aware of the evidence.

When I submitted my complaint it seemed to me that Harris's allegation, which was the most dramatic part of the documentary was also its point of greatest weakness... or so I thought.

Peter Feeney on behalf of RTÉ attempted to lump my complaint in with other complaints. The only reference to my complaint was the following:

> "The medical evidence to the Court of Inquiry states that the fatal shot to Richard Pearson was to the groin. Furthermore the medical evidence is that many of the shots to both Pearson brothers were to the groin/abdomen/buttock areas.
>
> "The programme presented two views on this. Senator Eoghan Harris expressed the opinion that the shooting of the Pearsons in the genitals was a symbolic act. John Joe Dillon expressed the contrary

view that the shootings were botched because the local IRA members were poor marksmen, simply too inexperienced to conduct the executions in a humane manner."

In my response to Feeney I was tempted to dissect Feeney's devious mode of reasoning. First of all Feeney implies that Harris said *"many of the shots to both Pearsons were to the groin/abdomen area"*. He then pretends that the issue was whether the shooting was *"a symbolic act"* or not while slipping in the false statement that they were shot in the genitals.

I could have parsed and analysed each clause but decided that it would have been a waste of time. So I contented myself with restating my case. In my reply I wrote:

> "Mr Feeney has not disputed my allegation that RTÉ broadcast a false statement from Mr Eoghan Harris in order to present a biased view of the killings at Coolacrease.
>
> "The Pearsons were not "deliberately shot in the genitals" as Mr Harris stated. They were not shot in "their sexual parts" and they were not shot "in their sexual organs".
>
> "If only one of the Pearsons was shot in the genitals. Harris's statement would have been inaccurate. But Richard Pearson was not shot in the genitals. And Abraham Pearson was not shot in the genitals.
>
> "RTÉ is entitled to broadcast different opinions about historical events, but it is not entitled to broadcast factual inaccuracies in support of a particular historical view.
>
> "Mr Feeney says John Joe Dillon said the executions were botched (it was in fact Phillip McConway). But by no stretch of the imagination could it be said that McConway or anyone else corrected Eoghan Harris's false statement in the documentary. Stating that the executions were "botched" is not a rebuttal of Eoghan Harris's false statement.
>
> "Mr Feeney says that the medical evidence stated that the fatal shot was to the groin in the case of Richard Pearson. But the groin is not a sexual part or a sexual organ. Richard Pearson also received shots on the left shoulder, left lower leg, six glancing wounds in the back as well as a wound to the right buttock. Abraham Pearson did not receive a wound to either the groin or the buttock. His wounds were to the left cheek, left shoulder, left thigh, lower third of the left leg and abdomen."

At that stage I thought the matter rested and all that remained was for the BCC to adjudicate. However at a late stage in the proceedings the producer of the programme Niamh Sammon decided to make an intervention. Perhaps she was not happy with RTÉ's response? But if she was unhappy she didn't add much to the case for the defence. In her submission relating to my complaint she employed an almost identical mode of reasoning to RTÉ. Like RTÉ she begins by pretending that Harris said that the Pearsons were shot in the *"groin/abdomen"* area. Again like RTÉ she pretends that the complaint is about something other than what it is. In her case she pretends that the issue is about whether the shooting was "deliberate" or not (RTÉ pretended that it was whether it was a *"symbolic act"* or not). And again like RTÉ she slips in towards the end of her submission Harris's false assertion that the Pearsons were shot in the genitals in such a way as to give the impression that this was not the point of dispute. Here is Sammon's concluding paragraph:

> "Crucially, the programme did not take a view as to whether the shooting of the Pearsons in the groin area was an accident, or a deliberate act. There were two points of view on this. Both opinions were clearly presented in the programme. Eoghan Harris's statement that the Pearsons were shot deliberately in the genitals did not go uncontested, as Mr Martin claims. John Joe Dillon's contribution, which follows the Harris contribution, says: 'A lot of those people, they weren't really trained to kill. They were overawed, frightened, they were victims as well in a different kind of way. Probably haunted by it maybe for the rest of their lives.'. Both statements balance each other. This section of the programme was at all times impartial and objective."

I can only assume that Feeney and Sammon were using the same lawyer or they went to the same course on how to defend the indefensible. I replied in the following terms:

> "In her reply Niamh Sammon claims:
> *'The medical evidence supports the view that many of the shots fired at the Pearson brothers were to the groin/abdomen/upper leg area'.*
> "But Eoghan Harris didn't say that many of the shots were fired to the *"groin/abdomen/upper leg area"*. He said that the Pearsons were shot in "the genitals, in their sexual parts, in their sexual organs".

"As I said in my reply to Peter Feeney: RTÉ is entitled to broadcast different opinions, but it is not entitled to broadcast factual inaccuracies in support of a particular historical view.

"Ms Sammon in her response reproduces the medical evidence on Richard Pearson. This evidence was not presented in the programme that was broadcast. Neither was the medical evidence on Abraham Pearson presented in the programme. And Ms Sammon does not reproduce the latter in her response even though Harris claimed that both Pearson brothers were shot in the genitals.

"In the final paragraph of her response to my complaint Ms Sammon reveals the modus operandi of the programme. The programme sets up a false premise—in this case that both of the Pearsons were shot in the genitals. It then has a "discussion" about this false premise.

"But the question of whether the Pearsons were "deliberately" shot in the genitals does not arise because neither of them were shot in the genitals in the first place.

"In no sense can John Joe Dillon's contribution be considered to have countered Eoghan Harris's false statement. Indeed it could be interpreted as an admission of guilt at the sexual mutilation of the Pearsons, which never took place."

The Commission in its submission gave a reasonable summary of my complaint and the responses of RTÉ and Niamh Sammon. However, it appears that it is not the policy to publish the complainant's response to the broadcaster or Producer of the programme.

Almost from the outset the Commission showed that it was incapable of adjudicating on my complaint. The second sentence in its decision read as follows:

"The broadcast in question is Hidden History: The Killings at Coolacrease, which explored the murder of two brothers in Coolacrease during the War of Independence."

By describing the killings as *"murder"* the Commission was indicating that it was incapable of dealing with my complaint in an objective manner. The documentary itself did not even make this explicit claim even though, in my opinion this was the message that it wished to convey. My complaint wasn't the only one submitted. And in each of the other complaints the Commission described the killings as *"murder"*.

Although the Commission felt that it was capable of deciding that the programme was *"fair and balanced"*, it stated:

"It was not within the remit of the Commission to assess the veracity, or otherwise, of the claims being made in this broadcast. Nor could one expect the Commission to do so."

But all I was asking the Commission to do was adjudicate on Mr. Harris's claims against the clear and unambiguous medical evidence, which in my opinion indicated the contrary. Neither the broadcaster nor the producer disputed the veracity of the evidence. Indeed they quoted selectively from it. And yet the Commission could not adjudicate on this.

In RTÉ's submission Feeney suggested that the BCC was not qualified to adjudicate on programmes on historical subjects. The Commission, in effect, accepted this. Its decision on the Inge Clissman complaint was an aberration (possibly because the complainant had a direct personal interest in the decision because the portrayal of her father was at issue).

We shall see from the other complaints that programme makers are at liberty to pursue their own political agenda with impunity. All that they are required to do is present "two sides" to the story. But the side that doesn't accord with the programme makers can be presented in a weak or distorted form. We have already seen that programme makers are free to invent "facts" to advance their agenda. They can suppress evidence which doesn't support their views. The most outrageous assertion can be made on the flimsiest of evidence. RTÉ is not obliged to have any quality control from a professional historian. And as we have seen the BCC cannot adjudicate on the accuracy of history programmes. In short, as regards history programmes, programme makers can do what they want. And all the citizen can do is switch off the television and continue to pay the licence fee.

Paddy Heaney's Complaint

The manner in which Paddy Heaney's complaint was dealt with was even more outrageous. Heaney was a participant in the programme. In his complaint he said that Niamh Sammon subjected him to a gruelling and hostile one hour interview on camera, which took him by surprise because it was the reverse of her attitude throughout their previous acquaintance. A substantial part of the interview was on the subject of how the Pearsons' land was distributed after it was sold to the Land Commission. This was a key issue for the programme maker since one of the themes of the documentary was that the motivation for the executions was *"land hunger"*.

It is Paddy Heaney's firm view that the first people to obtain access to the Pearsons' land were ex British soldiers. And it was only later that on a subsequent divide out that ex IRA men received some land. He also said that the Land Commission consulted with Father Houlahan, a local priest who was fiercely anti-Republican in his political views. But the only statement that was broadcast from Mr Heaney was the following:

> "When the land was divided by the Irish land commission, I think two, maybe three, whose people were involved in the IRA received parcels of land there."

The clear impression was created that IRA men were the sole beneficiaries of the Pearsons' land at knock down prices (the land was in fact transferred to the new owners at greater than the market price). And that impression was given by misrepresenting Paddy Heaney's own views of the matter by taking his words out of context.

Incredibly, Niamh Sammon did not deny that she misrepresented Heaney. Here is what she said:

> "Mr Heaney's broadcast comment ('When the land was divided by the Irish Land Commission, I think two, maybe three whose people were involved in the IRA received parcels of land there') is a true reflection of the information which the programme team uncovered in the Land Commission files. To include Mr Heaney's original statement—stating that British army soldiers received land in a 'first division', and it is only then that former IRA men got land—would have been a distortion of the truth."

Apparently, in this case unlike with the comments of Eoghan Harris, there is only one *"truth"* and that *"truth"* must be revealed even if in doing so one of the participants is misrepresented in the process. It is interesting that earlier in her submission Sammon admits that two of the people who received part of the Pearsons' land were ex British Army. But this *"truth"* didn't emerge in the documentary.

She concludes with the following legalistic justification for her behaviour:

> "This section of the programme, on the division of the Pearson's land, relied solely on fact, not opinion. Mr Heaney signed a release form granting the production the right to select material, which they did so in a fair and balanced way. At all times the production team behaved in a professional and fair manner towards Mr Heaney."

Elsewhere in this book there is a detailed examination of what the Land Commission records reveal. In my opinion they do not support in any way the thesis of the programme that the killings were motivated by "land hunger".

Paddy Heaney was understandably incensed by Sammon's reply. In his response he repeated the original grounds for his complaint:

> "My complaint is that my contribution to the documentary was edited to give it the opposite meaning, thereby misrepresenting my widely known and publicised views on the Coolacrease land issue, to the detriment of my reputation and social standing in my community.
>
> "Ms Sammon admits that she misrepresented my views, but not only does she not apologise for this she justifies it on the grounds that she knows better. I find her conduct unethical and her arrogance breathtaking.
>
> "My view is straightforward. The fact that the first three people to be allocated farms were ex-British soldiers disproves the land grab theory of her documentary. Her theory is further disproved by the fact that two or three ex-IRA men were able to receive land only after it had been rejected or given up by other people.
>
> "Ms Sammon agrees that the first part of this is correct. Yet she edited my contribution in a way which caused the second part to advance her theory and contradict mine.
>
> "She did this even though she claims that she can prove her theory

by means of documentation which she did not disclose."

Paddy Heaney's complaint and Niamh Sammon's response were short and succinct, but the Commission managed to produce a long rambling decision in support of Sammon. The following sentences from the Commission's decision summarise its position:

> "The statement about the allocation of the land by the Land Commission must be taken in context. The statement included in the programme was made by Mr. Heaney. The Producer believed the statement to be accurate and therefore, included it in the broadcast. In doing so, the Commission was of the view that it was used to reflect fact and in no way indicated that Mr. Heaney supported that part of the motive of the killings was land."

So although the Commission was unable to adjudicate on the factual accuracy or otherwise of Eoghan Harris's statement with the medical evidence laid out before it, it was able to pronounce on the factual accuracy of Sammon's statement about the Land Commission without seeing any of the Land Commission documents. As far as the Commission was concerned Sammon's assertion of factual accuracy entitled her to misrepresent Paddy Heaney's views on this question.

Pat Muldowney's Complaint

In general most complaints to the BCC tend to relate to a specific aspect of a programme. But Pat Muldowney obviously felt that the overall thrust of the programme was unfair and biased. And therefore complaints about specific aspects of the programme would not adequately highlight what he believed to be the true nature of the programme.

Pat Muldowney believed that the documentary wished to portray the motive for the killings as being a combination of land hunger and sectarian hatred. The suggestion was made by Eoghan Harris that the killings were an incident in a campaign of ethnic cleansing. Although the phrase "ethnic cleansing" was not actually used in the documentary, it was inferred by commentators on the programme (e.g. *Sunday Independent*, 21.10.07 and on the Ryan Tubridy radio show, 22.10.07).

Muldowney in his complaint claimed that the makers of the documentary used the following methods to advance their biased point of view:

a) Evidence was suppressed, which would lead the viewer to a contrary view to that which was intended (e.g. see my complaint above)
b) The views of contributors were misrepresented (e.g. see Paddy Heaney's complaint)
c) Assertions were made with no factual basis.
d) In cases where contrary evidence was submitted there were instant rebuttals, while assertions supporting the documentary's themes were not contradicted.
e) The political context of the time was not explained.
f) Participants with a contrary view were dismissed as being "in denial" or having some unworthy motive for their opinions.
g) The Cooneyite religion was incorrectly described as pacifist (comparing it to the Amish religion).
h) False or secondary reasons were posited for the killings and then dismissed as having no basis in reality in order to prove that the real reasons were a sectarian land grab.

On the theme of land hunger being a motive for the killings Richard English, an academic, says that the purchase of the land by the Pearsons was seen as an *"alien incursion"*. But no evidence was presented to support this assertion.

The same academic refers to a shooting incident in the following terms:

"The Pearsons are merely doing what any law abiding citizen should do and legally they are within their rights to defend their land".

But as we shall see later the incident above had nothing to do with defending their land since their land was not under attack.

Part 2 of the documentary begins with some groundless speculation from Alan Stanley whose father was a friend of the Pearsons.

"It's very hard to wonder if somebody who knew that the truce was imminent did not decide: well look, lads, there's some nice pickings here, let's go for it. I know it's very dangerous to say that. But the land, of course, the land of Ireland for the people of Ireland."

This statement is followed by a statement from J.J. Dillon (son of an Offaly I.R.A. man in the War of Independence) who says:

"In conflict those things occur. Like hatred comes into it, revenge comes into it."

The impression given is that Dillon is confirming Stanley's speculation. But nowhere in Dillon's statement is the land issue mentioned. Indeed, although there are a number of quotations from Dillon in the documentary, nowhere is there any suggestion in the actual statements themselves that the killings had anything to do with the land. Could this be another example of misrepresentation?
Later Richard English says:

"It's quite comforting if you do target people, afterwards, to build up as much justifications as possible. I think the real justification is the fact that the IRA and their authority in the area had been challenged in an unacceptable way and in order to show who is boss in the area they had to teach the Pearsons a lesson. You can exert your authority and in the long run you maximise access to land."

That is a very curious statement. He begins by suggesting that the authority of the IRA was being challenged by the Pearsons and then tags on at the end the bit about maximising access to land. The part about maximising access to the land has no connection with the first part of the statement, but accords with one of the main themes of the documentary. The part about challenging the authority of the IRA would make sense if the political context were explained. But the documentary did not once refer to the 1918 Election, which gave the Sinn Fein Government an overwhelming democratic mandate to run the country. The government of the 1919 Dail is considered to be the first democratic government of this State. As such the current Dail is officially designated the 30th Dail. This Irish Government had 900 local Courts during the war of independence, which were accepted by both Catholics and Protestants.

But the documentary portrayed the IRA as some kind of criminal conspiracy against the lawful authority of the British Government. This interpretation is completely at variance with the official history of the State.

Later on in the documentary the impression given is that after the killings of their two sons the Pearsons had to flee their land and sell it at below its real value. Dr. Dooley says:

> "What he [William Pearson—JM] intended to do was cut his losses by selling the land to the land commission for around 5,000 pounds."

But as discussed elsewhere in the book the Pearsons bought the land for 2,000 pounds in 1911. So how could they have been *"cutting their losses"*. Land prices were at a low ebb in the 1920s.

Throughout the documentary there was an attempt to suggest that as well as land there was a sectarian motive for the killings. For example Dr. Dooley says:

> "There were often Protestant farmers who owned substantially larger farms than their surrounding Catholic nationalist neighbours. The revolutionary period was used as a pretext to run many of these Protestant farmers and landlords out of the community, for locals to take up their land."

But, apart from the alleged case of the Pearsons, no examples of this were given in this part of Offaly. Other Protestants with substantial land holdings were left completely unmolested. Dooley goes on to say:

> "There is the added tinge of sectarianism, in the sense that Protestant land remains in Protestant hands."

After indicating that the Pearsons initially (1911 to Autumn 1918) got on very well with their neighbours (in seeming contradiction to the opinions of Dooley and English) the narrator states:

> "But the atmosphere was changing. By 1919 Ireland was heading for a bloody break from Britain. Like most Protestant families, the Pearsons were strongly loyal to the Crown forces."

This implies that the War of Independence itself had a sectarian character. But the facts show otherwise. In this part of Offaly the wealthy and respected local Protestant Biddulph and Drought families armed the Cadamstown IRA unit, and one of the local Protestant Mitchell family was a prominent and well-known Offaly IRA man, Another member of the same family served in the Cork IRA, having left Offaly to evade the RIC after the 1916 Rising. So in this part of Offaly the narrator's comment seems to be unfounded.

The documentary then gives examples of deterioration in relations between the Pearsons and the local community. The local historians as well as J.J. Dillon suggest that the Pearsons, in particular Richard Pearson, began to take an aggressive attitude to the rest of the community. They were particularly hostile to the IRA.

But as so often with this documentary the last word is given to someone who believed there was a base motive for the killings. In this case Jenny Turnidge (a grand daughter of the Pearsons) stated the following:

> "I believe that there's a lot of stories going around to make people feel better about their part in the actions. They really don't want to have another reason to make themselves feel better. They don't want to face the truth of the past."

As with the theme of a Land Grab, the suggestion is that not only are the people who don't agree with this theory wrong, but their reasons for doubting the theory are suspect.

The documentary spent an inordinate amount of time discussing either spurious or secondary motives for the killings. In Muldowney's opinion the reason for this was to set up weak theories for the killings in order to knock them down and reinforce the idea that the real motives were to do with land hunger and religious sectarianism.

The allegation that the Pearsons were fraternising with the Crown forces was explained by a relationship that one of the Pearson daughters had with an RIC man. But this was not given as a reason by any of the local historians for the killing of the Pearson brothers.

Nevertheless, Eoghan Harris is given the opportunity to debunk a reason for the killings, which was never suggested:

> "The Pearson girls were supposed to be going out with British

soldiers or went out with British soldiers. What else would they do!? Would they make dancing partners for local IRA officers do you think…!! …I doubt very much that the Cooneyite girls went out with British soldiers. But if they did, so what!"

There were other trivial examples of fraternising with the enemy, such as stray cattle being reported to the British authorities and the Pearsons helping British army personnel who had run out of petrol. But since these were not reasons given by the IRA for the killing of the Pearsons it is difficult to see the point of this other than to muddy the waters.

Spying along with the suspicion that the Pearsons were involved with loyalist paramilitaries were given as reasons for the killings. These were given as reasons by the IRA for the killings so although, they were only secondary reasons, the documentary was justified in exploring them. The spying allegation, by its nature, is difficult to prove. The local historians were given an opportunity to discuss the allegation but admitted that the evidence was largely anecdotal.

The evidence for involvement with loyalist paramilitaries was only touched on. There was a brief reference to a person who stayed with the Pearsons called William Stanley. But the documentary only mentioned that he was in "trouble with the IRA". There was no mention of the nature of that "trouble".

An interview with William Stanley's son Alan suggested that it merely amounted to fraternising with the enemy, but in Alan Stanley's own book (*I Met Murder on the Way*) there is a description of the loyalist paramilitarism that his father was involved with.

Evidence that they were actively engaged in loyalist politics is either suppressed altogether or dismissed in the documentary. William Murphy briefly refers to William Pearson's declaration to the Irish Grants Committee that he was an *"ardent loyalist"*, but then instantly dismisses the statement by saying he was merely ingratiating himself to the British who ran this committee for the purposes of giving compensation to loyalists during the war of independence. Murphy doesn't mention at all the following more active statement of Pearson:

"I helped the Crown forces on every occasion."

It is very arguable that Pearson needed to make the above statement to receive compensation. But if this evidence is suspect why does Dr. Dooley accept as gospel evidence at the same hearing that the valuation of the Pearsons' property was £10,000 to support his theory that the Pearsons were the victims of a land grab?

But as was typical of this documentary the final word on this subject was left to Professor English who rejected the allegation. Again it was alleged that not only were the supporters of the allegation wrong, but their motivations for making the allegation were suspect:

> "I've seen no evidence that would persuade me that the Pearsons were running an underground militia from the farm, or passing on information about the local IRA. I think it's a convenient claim, because if you can present them as being effectively a militia force, then taking violent action against the Pearson brothers would seem to be more an act of legitimate war between combatant groups."

The key episode leading up to the killings at Coolacrease was the shooting by the Pearsons of IRA men on active service. This was the primary reason given by the IRA for the killing of the Pearson brothers. It casts serious doubt on the Pearsons' pacifist credentials and gives them the status of armed combatants in a war.

In an objective documentary on the killings this incident would have been examined on its merits and formed a key part in explaining the killings. But the discussion of this episode took place in the context of the land grab theory. It has already been mentioned that Richard English refers to this episode as evidence of a land grab. Another academic, William Murphy, says about the episode that it:

> "...allowed the local IRA to express the fears they had about the Pearsons. It justified their paranoia. It justified their social resentment at their landholding. And now they had a reason."

Again, no evidence is produced to substantiate this allegation. The IRA were cutting down a Tree to cause a roadblock at 11.30 pm on a June night. Three of the Pearson brothers saw them and opened fire. According to both a British Military Enquiry report and an IRA report the Pearsons hit two IRA men. According to the IRA report one of the men was *"somewhat seriously injured"*. This IRA man, Mick Heaney, who was related to Paddy Heaney, died five years later. The Heaney family believe that this shooting incident was a determining factor in his premature demise.

The British Military Enquiry report was quoting from an RIC report. The RIC was in a position to know the Pearsons' version since they had the Pearsons themselves in their custody. Also, one of their own retired members, Bert Hogg, had also been shot by the Pearsons at the roadblock.

And yet incredibly the documentary casts doubt on whether the Pearsons actually hit any IRA man. Alan Stanley claims that the Pearsons merely fired a warning shot in the air. And Eoghan Harris also questions whether the Pearsons hit anyone. Here is Harris's opinion:

> "I don't know if they hit anybody or not. Paddy Heaney says they did. I don't know. When Paddy Heaney tells me things like that I want documentary corroboration in evidence."

But there are two items of documentary evidence. One is the British Military enquiry report which was not mentioned at all in the documentary. The other is an IRA report which was only mentioned in the context of the theory that the motivation for the killings of the Pearsons was a land grab.

Both of these documents were brought to the attention of Niamh Sammon, the producer and director of the documentary. Pat Muldowney was also interviewed about them, but the interview was not included in the documentary.

The handling of this key incident in the story of the killing of the Pearson brothers demonstrates the Orwellian scope of the documentary. The shooting by the Pearsons of Mick Heaney and Bert Hogg has been long accepted as a fact by their respective families and by the local community. It never occurred to anyone to doubt that this was what happened until Niamh Sammon and her crew decided to make a documentary about the killing of the Pearson brothers. The carefully constructed message which the programme makers wished to convey collapses like a house of cards when this incident is examined and therefore it must be explained away. The community's memory of this incident must be denied because it doesn't accord with the documentary makers' preconceptions.

Pat Muldowney concluded his submission as follows:

> "Finally, I note the highly significant fact that there was no Consultant Historian listed in the credits of the programme. Therefore there was no professional historian charged with overall responsibility for the historical accuracy of the programme. My understanding is that this is a serious breach of RTÉ guidelines."

In RTÉ's submission Peter Feeney claimed that Paul Rouse was the programme's "researcher and historical consultant". However, when Mr/ Rouse was contacted, he denied that he was a historical consultant and said that the credits in the programme accurately described him as a researcher.

So Feeney's statement was deliberately misleading. Niamh Sammon in her submission admitted that there was no historical consultant, but claimed that there was no obligation to have one. It might be thought that the BCC would give Feeney at least a gentle slap on the wrists for his "faux pas", particularly since Feeney showed no hesitation in lecturing the BCC on what its proper role should be. But far from noting Feeney's indiscretion, it left out all reference to it in its published summary of Feeney's submission. It appears that the BCC knows its true place in the scheme of things and it is not there to scrutinise RTÉ's "historical" programmes.

Sammon in her submission claimed that there was evidence that *"land"* was a motive for the killings. She based this on the submissions by the Pearsons and their supporters to the Irish Grants Committee. But other evidence from this Committee which showed that the Pearsons were active loyalists was dismissed by Dr. William Murphy in the documentary on the grounds that the Pearsons were allegedly trying to ingratiate themselves with the committee to maximise the level of compensation. But this begs the question that if the Pearsons could allegedly mislead the committee on their political allegiances would there not be an even greater incentive to mislead on the value of land, which would directly determine the level of compensation.

Curiously, Sammon denies that the programme ever used the phrase *"land grab"*. This may be true, but even RTÉ in its submission conceded:

> "the theory that the Pearson killings were the result of a land grab was also examined by the programme makers."

However, the BCC found in favour of RTÉ and Niamh Sammon and rejected Pat Muldowney's complaint. It found that the *"broadcaster/producer has editorial independence and can decide what material to include in the programming"*. The decision not to refer to the 1918 election was an editorial decision, which could not *"determine the bias of the broadcast"*.

Interestingly, the Commission claimed that the programme examined two themes:

> "1. the motive for the killings was sectarian and ultimately for land; and 2. The Pearsons were supporters of, and informers for, the Crown and therefore the shootings were inevitable in the context of the War of Independence."

That may be what the documentary explored, but it was precisely this that Pat Muldowney objected to. It did not or at least inadequately explored the overwhelming evidence that the Pearsons were armed combatants. Even RTÉ in its submission conceded that this was an issue. In my view this is another example of the BCC facilitating the Broadcaster/Producer.

The Commission went on to say:

> "The complainant also asserts that those who believe the 'sectarian' motive are always given the last word. This cannot, whether accurate or otherwise, determine the bias of a programme."

Furthermore:

> "The complainant further takes issue with the fact that there was no consultant historian assigned to the programme. It is not within the remit of the Commission to comment on who participated in the making of the programme."

It is difficult to know how a *"historical"* programme could possibly be unfair and biased using the BCC's criteria.

Conclusion

The experience of complaining to the BCC about "The Killings at Coolacrease" indicates that programmes on historical matters are largely exempt from the BCC's scrutiny. The makers of historical documentaries are free to pursue whatever political agenda they wish with impunity.

As a result we are left with the bizarre situation that the State broadcasting service is being used to undermine the historical basis for this Independent State. The statutory (i.e. State) authority set up to adjudicate on programmes declares that the killings at Coolacrease, which were authorised by the emerging State, were *"murders"* or, in effect, a criminal conspiracy against the British State in Ireland.

We are also left with the bizarre situation that the only people prepared to defend the legitimacy of the State are a few local historians and a small, if energetic, historical society.

This state of affairs cannot be allowed to continue.

Documentation

Annotated by Philip O'Connor

***

Appendix 1

Photographs

Photo sources:

1-3 Paddy Heaney; 4 Offaly Historical & Archaeological Society (OHAS); 5-8 OHAS; 9-10 Paddy Heaney; 12-18 Paddy Heaney; 19 OHAS; 20-21 Paddy Heaney; 23 OHAS; 24-28 From photographs in the 'Tullamore Tribune' (with special thanks to Alan Stanley for not objecting to our use of them); 29-33 Paddy Heaney; 34-35 Sinn Féin; 36 Bureau of Military History; 37-39 Contemporary newspaper releases; 40-42 National Archive; 43 Drawing by Timothy Lane from a contemporary photograph; 44 Imperial War Museum; 45 Philip O'Connor; 46 Contemporary postcard; 47-48 Paddy Heaney; 49 RTÉ. 50 Irish Government

1. Cadamstown School 1910. Mick Heaney and Jimmy Delahunty (back row, 3rd and 5th left) were later founding members (with Tom Donnelly) of Cadamstown IRA. Mick Heaney was badly wounded in the Pearson attack on the IRA roadblock. Far right is Mrs Carroll, an inspirational teacher in the Fenian tradition. Some of the Pearsons attended this school, one playing for the hurling team.

2. Offaly County hurling team 1900. No less than eight of the men are from Cadamstown, which boasted one of the first GAA clubs in the county.

3. Cadamstown men after several months' imprisonment in the Curragh, 1921, all except John Carroll IRA volunteers. *Back row, L-R:* Tom Donnelly, Tom Horan, John Joe Horan, John McRedmond. *Front L-R:* John Carroll, Jimmy Delahunty, John Dillon, Joe Carroll. Taken prisoner in June and July and interned until late 1921, they include elected local politicians, farmers and workmen. Colonel Kemp's official history of the Royal Scots Fusiliers later described the Offaly IRA as an effective resistance movement which greatly limited British military mobility and intelligence operations in the county.

4. Michael Cordial and Peter Lyons, later officers of Offaly No. 2 Brigade IRA, here with Offaly Junior Hurlers, 1915 Leinster title winners.

5. *(Above)* Thomas Burke, O/C Offaly No. 2 Brigade IRA, presided at the Court of Enquiry that ordered the execution of the Pearson brothers for the attack on the roadblock and passing information to the enemy. Not from Offaly, he later farmed in his native Portumna.
6. *(Above right)* Michael McCormack, O/C 3rd Southern Division IRA (Offaly, Leix, North Tipp.) which included Offaly No. 2 Brigade.
7. *(Below left)* Michael Cordial later in Free State uniform. As an officer of 3rd Battalion (Kilcormac) in 1921, he was involved in the Pearson execution. His Witness Statement is given in Appendix 3.
8. *(Below right)* Joe Connolly (as an Irish Army officer in later years) commanded the IRA flying column which carried out the execution.

9. *(Right)* Tom Donnelly, a leading figure in Cadamstown IRA. Interned after being wounded in the roadblock attack, he was held at the Curragh until November. Mick Heaney, another leading figure, was also 'out of action' for several months, recovering from the severe stomach wounds he received (from which he died a few years later). The Pearsons wounded four men in the roadblock attack.

10. *(Below left)* Jimmy Delahunty, founding member and quartermaster of Cadamstown IRA, responsible for supplies. Following the roadblock attack, he was interned throughout the second half of 1921 and again during the Civil War. He was a labourer and later the district postman, and one of only three IRA volunteers to be allocated land from the Pearson farm in 1923 (a small 18-acre piece of mostly poor land)after it was turned down by two others, Jack Fehery and John Walsh. The high cost of the land meant that it later reverted to the Land Commission.

11. *(Below right)* Peter Lyons, Intelligence Officer, Drumcullen Company, helped procure weapons for the Kilcormac Battalion.

12. *Above, top left:* J.J. Horan, who had a 100-acre farm adjoining the Pearsons, was a leading local Republican and elected Sinn Féin councillor for Kinnity. He tried to collect guns from the Pearson house and was interned after the Mass path incident in early June 1921.

13. *Above, bottom left:* John Dillon, also a substantial farmer and leading local Republican, was arrested with J.J. Horan and is seen here after being badly mistreated by the British military in Tullamore Jail.

14. *(Above right)* John Dillon in later years with sisters Mary Ellen and Anne, and niece Johanna.

15. Jim McCormack, local blacksmith, in later years. Though supporting the republicans, he was not politically involved, and in 1923 received a small allocation of Pearson land (18 acres) from the Land Commission.

284

16. Bill Glenn, local IRA volunteer, with brother Pat, a British Army soldier. Bill, a republican, was interned in the Civil War. He was allocated 30 acres at Coolacrease on his return in late 1923.

17-18. Bill's Scottish father William *(below left)* had also been a soldier. When stationed with a Scottish regiment at Crinkle Barracks, Birr *(below right),* he met and married Mary Egan, a local girl. The Scottish soldiers were liked and some of them were present both as stewards and spectators at the first All Ireland Hurling Final in Birr in 1888. William was killed in WWI. His wife, now a 'Somme widow', lived with Bill in the coach house at Coolacrease.

19. *(Above)* Walter Mitchell of Rahan, a Protestant volunteer with Offaly IRA. His brother Herbert (Seán) fought with a flying column in Cork. A relative, Tom Mitchell of Roscomroe, provided a safe house and military training for the Cadamstown IRA

20. *(Above left)* Brian Heaney returned from New York in late 1921 where he had lived since 1900 and been an active fundraiser for Sinn Féin. He received some land at Coolacrease. **21.***(Below)* Invitation to anniversary celebrations for *The Sinn Féiner,* New York, June 1921.

FIRST ANNIVERSARY CELEBRATION
of the founding of
THE SINN FEINER
AT LEXINGTON OPERA HOUSE
Lexington Avenue and 51st Street

Sunday Evening, June 12th, 1921, at 8 o'clock
under the auspices of 350 stockholders
THE HOLDER OF THIS TICKET IS INVITED TO BE PRESENT
Speakers:
Rt. Rev. Monsignor James W. Power   Rev. Francis J. Sexton   Professor Hardy
Rev. John H. Dooley   Jeremiah A. O'Leary   Catherine Gilmore
Charles R. Delmage, Chairman

22. Edward Cooney. Much is made in the 'Hidden History' programme of the fact that the Pearsons were "Cooneyites" (see Chapter 5), who Eoghan Harris described as *"pastoral" "Amish-type"* people given to *"quiet evenings spent in meditation and reflection."* But the Pearsons ran a modern mechanised farm and the sons attended local dances. Cooney's own attitude to other Christian faiths – including Anglicanism (*"this dirty devilish poison"*) - was one of denunciation. In the *"Condemnation of Fermanagh"* he declared their adherents doomed to hell. Cooneyism in the early 20th century had more in common with Anabaptists, who regarded the bible, on which much score is set in mainstream Protestantism, as the *"paper pope."* While the Pearsons' faith may have played some role in their cool relationship with their Protestant neighbours, it played no part in their relations with local Catholics (who regarded them simply as Protestants). The Pearsons mingled locally and attended Cadamstown Catholic school where the boys played hurling. The Harris mythology on the Pearsons' Cooneyism was adopted uncritically in the RTÉ 2008 announcement for the 'Hidden History' programme, 'The Killings at Coollacrease' (see Doc. 59).

23. *(Above)* Coolacrease house before the tragedy. It was built by the Odlums, a family with roots in the area since Cromwellian times.
24. *(Below left)* Richard Pearson, executed on the orders of the senior IRA command following the armed attack on the IRA roadblock.
25. *(Below right)* William Stanley, Sidney and Abraham Pearson, summer 1921. Stanley, a relative of the Pearsons, was on the run from Luggacurren for loyalist paramilitary activity and in hiding with the Pearsons as workman "Jimmy Bradley". Abraham was the other brother to be executed. Sidney, absent from Coolacrease on the day of the execution, survived and lodged the first claim to the "Irish Grants Committee" for special compensation in 1926 (which was rejected).

26. *(Above)* The Pearsons before their burned out house, July 1921. *Left to right:* Emily, mother Matilda, father William, David and Ethel.
27. *(Below left)* William Pearson: lodged the successful compensation claim to the Irish Grants Committee in 1927.
28. *(Below right)* William Stanley in 1926. He fled to Northern Ireland and then to Britain, returning in 1927 to farm in Co. Carlow.

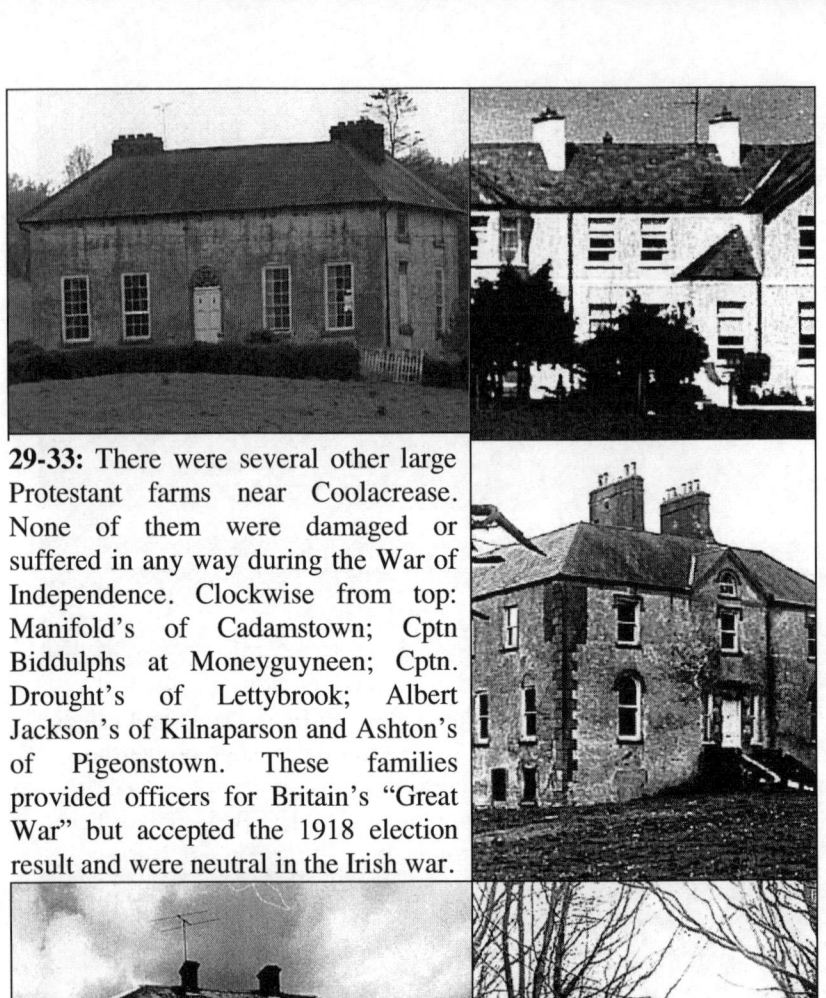

29-33: There were several other large Protestant farms near Coolacrease. None of them were damaged or suffered in any way during the War of Independence. Clockwise from top: Manifold's of Cadamstown; Cptn Biddulphs at Moneyguyneen; Cptn. Drought's of Lettybrook; Albert Jackson's of Kilnaparson and Ashton's of Pigeonstown. These families provided officers for Britain's "Great War" but accepted the 1918 election result and were neutral in the Irish war.

34-35. The British War included a policy of *"official"* and *"unofficial"* reprisals such as the burning of Cork after the Kilmichael ambush *(above left)* and of Templemore *(above right)*.

36. *(Below left)* The elected authority had to operate underground: arrest of TDs D. J. O'Donovan, Sean O'Mahoney and Dick McKee. McKee, who led the resistance in Dublin, was tortured and murdered in Dublin Castle along with two comrades, *"shot while trying to escape."*

37. *(Below right)* The RIC was boosted by the "Auxiliary Division" of 2,000 veteran officers created on Churchill's proposal. Their own commander, Crozier, described as *"fascist"* the British *"war on the Irish democracy."* The Luggacurran paramilitary group in which William Stanley was involved worked closely with the Auxiliaries.

38-39. The Military Court of Inquiry into the Pearson deaths included Cptn. Beak, a war hero who won the Victoria Cross in France. In WW2 as a General he commanded the British Army in Malta. *(Above right):* Beak shortly before joining the Royal Scots Fusiliers in Offaly in February 1921. After the "Great War for Democracy", it was back to business as usual for the Royal Scots: one battalion went to fight the Revolution in Russia, the other to suppress the democracy in Ireland.

40-41. *Below:* The report of the Court of Inquiry circulated at the highest levels in Dublin Castle. *From left:* Under Secretary Sir John Anderson, Asst. Under Sec. Mark Sturgis, and G.N. Crutchley, leading figures in the new regime installed at the Castle in 1920. Sturgis – a supporter of military dictatorship – and Crutchley were connected with propaganda work at the Castle at the time of the Pearson execution, and in 1923-26 made up two of the four-man "Irish Grants Committee" to which the Pearsons later appealed for compensation.

42. Cptn W. Darling of the Royal Scots Fusiliers. Their official history, describing the war of *"reprisals,"* says *"Fortunately the Scots Fusiliers were not involved in this repugnant role."* But Darling was involved in the "dirty" war, editing the infamous RIC *Weekly Summary* which goaded the police and military to terrorist reprisals.
43. Auxiliary Division commander, General Crozier, who resigned in February 1921 in protest at the counter-productive effect of British terror tactics, also had a Fusiliers connection. His father, a Royal Scots officer, had been stationed at Birr in the 1880s to "assist" the R.I.C. in "upholding order" during the Land War.
44. *(Below left)* Men of the Leinster Regiment, France 1917. A depot unit of the Leinsters was the other British Army force in South Offaly. Unenthusiastic at *"rebellion quelling"*, the Leinsters were regarded as friendly by the men of the Republican army.
45. *(Right)* Crinkle Barracks today, former base of the Leinsters.

46. Main Street Kilcormac (Frankford), early 20th century.
47. Brian Heaney, a great piper in the Slieve Bloom tradition, in later life. In 1922, on his return from New York, he played at the Belfast Pipers Club. The region is rich in music and heritage.
48. Paddy Heaney, Brian's son and author of *At the foot of Slieve Bloom*. Published in 2000 this history contained the first account of the events at Coolacrease in 1921.

Factual Programmes

Commissioning Editor: Kevin Dawson

Clontarf Castle Open Day

May 30 2007

History: new commissions

- **Churchill v de Valera** – face-off over 4 decades
- **Collins & The Castle** – espionage and secret deals
- **The Catalpa Rescue** - Drama-Doc co-pro
- **Fenian Fire** – a plot to kill Queen Victoria
- **William Martin Murphy**: hate figure of the 1913 Lockout
- **Atonement:** ethnic cleansing in the midlands in 1922
- **Historians:** Who Writes our History?

RTÉ Television

49. RTÉ sets the tone: This slide announcing its autumn 2007 TV schedule gives the lie to later denials. Note the working title *'Atonement: Ethnic Cleansing in the Midlands 1922'* for the film – finally called 'The Killings at Coolacrease' – that portrayed the execution of the Pearson brothers as a sectarian murder by the local IRA in pursuance of a land grab. The producer also inferred the complicity of Land Commission officials in this. (From the slide show by Kevin Dawson of RTÉ at Clontarf Castle, 30th May 2007).

> **POBLACHT NA H EIREANN.**
> **THE PROVISIONAL GOVERNMENT**
> OF THE
> **IRISH REPUBLIC**
> **TO THE PEOPLE OF IRELAND.**
>
> IRISHMEN AND IRISHWOMEN: In the name of God and of the dead generations from which she receives her old tradition of nationhood, Ireland, through us, summons her children to her flag and strikes for her freedom.
>
> Having organised and trained her manhood through her secret revolutionary organisation, the Irish Republican Brotherhood, and through her open military organisations, the Irish Volunteers and the Irish Citizen Army, having patiently perfected her discipline, having resolutely waited for the right moment to reveal itself, she now seizes that moment, and, supported by her exiled children in America and by gallant allies in Europe, but relying in the first on her own strength, she strikes in full confidence of victory.
>
> We declare the right of the people of Ireland to the ownership of Ireland, and to the unfettered control of Irish destinies, to be sovereign and indefeasible. The long usurpation of that right by a foreign people and government has not extinguished the right, nor can it ever be extinguished except by the destruction of the Irish people. In every generation the Irish people have asserted their right to national freedom and sovereignty: six times during the past three hundred years they have asserted it in arms. Standing on that fundamental right and again asserting it in arms in the face of the world, we hereby proclaim the Irish Republic as a Sovereign Independent State, and we pledge our lives and the lives of our comrades-in-arms to the cause of its freedom, of its welfare, and of its exaltation among the nations.
>
> The Irish Republic is entitled to, and hereby claims, the allegiance of every Irishman and Irishwoman. The Republic guarantees religious and civil liberty, equal rights and equal opportunities to all its citizens, and declares its resolve to pursue the happiness and prosperity of the whole nation and of all its parts, cherishing all the children of the nation equally, and oblivious of the differences carefully fostered by an alien government, which have divided a minority from the majority in the past.
>
> Until our arms have brought the opportune moment for the establishment of a permanent National Government, representative of the whole people of Ireland and elected by the suffrages of all her men and women, the Provisional Government, hereby constituted, will administer the civil and military affairs of the Republic in trust for the people.
>
> We place the cause of the Irish Republic under the protection of the Most High God, Whose blessing we invoke upon our arms, and we pray that no one who serves that cause will dishonour it by cowardice, inhumanity, or rapine. In this supreme hour the Irish nation must, by its valour and discipline and by the readiness of its children to sacrifice themselves for the common good, prove itself worthy of the august destiny to which it is called.
>
> Signed on Behalf of the Provisional Government,
> THOMAS J. CLARKE,
> SEAN Mac DIARMADA, THOMAS MacDONAGH,
> P. H. PEARSE, EAMONN CEANNT,
> JAMES CONNOLLY, JOSEPH PLUNKETT.

50. What it was all about: the *1916 Proclamation*, endorsed by the people in the 1918 General Election. The 'War of Independence' was in fact the popular resistance to the war launched against Irish democracy by the British State. This copy hangs in Seanad Éireann, presented by former President of Ireland, Seán T Ó Ceallaigh.

Appendix 2

Irish Army Reports on the Pearson Executions

1. Reprisals: G.H.Q. Order, 22nd June 1921

Source: Dorothy MacArdle, *The Irish Republic*, 1951, pp. 935-6

Irish Republican Army
General Headquarters
Dublin

22nd June 1921

1. Brigade Commandants are authorised to answer reprisals against property on the part of the Enemy in the following way:

2. On every occasion on which the Enemy destroys house property, or house contents, whether alleging military necessity or not, the following counter-reprisals may be taken:
   a. A similar number of houses belonging to the most active enemies of Ireland may be destroyed in the Battalion area in which the original destruction took place.
   b. An equal number of houses belonging to the most active enemies of Ireland, may, in addition, be destroyed at that point in the Brigade area concerned which may be considered as the centre most strongly occupied by such enemies.
   c. The case should be reported to G.G.Q. with a covering statement of what has been done; and with a view to possible further action.
   d. Where the Enemy persists in taking counter-reprisals, they may be answered in the same way; stopping only when the district concerned has been entirely cleared of active enemies of Ireland.

3. Formal notice shall be served on any person whose house is so destroyed, stating clearly that it is a reprisal because of similar destruction carried out by the military forces; and specifying the particular property for whose destruction it is a reprisal.

4. In any particular case, or in any particular area in which, in addition to such reprisals, it would seem desirable that:
   a. The members of any particular family concerned should be ordered out of the country; or
   b. Have their lands confiscated;

   a special report should be submitted.

5. For the purposes of such reprisals no persons shall be regarded as enemies of Ireland, whether they may be described locally as Unionists, Orangemen, etc., unless they are actively anti-Irish in their actions.

6. No house shall be selected for destruction or destroyed without the personal approval and permission of the Brigade Commandant.

By Order

Adjutant General

[Garóid O'Sullivan]

[This order was issued in response to the stepped up British campaign of *"official reprisals"* launched in early 1921. The War of Independence reached its most intense in spring and early summer 1921. Note particularly sections 3, 5 and 6, procedures followed at Coolacrease in the burning of the Pearson house – Ed.]

2. Report by Thomas Burke, O/C Offaly No. 2 Brigade, on the execution of the Pearson brothers

Source: *Béaslaí Papers, National Library of Ireland* Ms. 33,913 (4)

'Reports re. execution of spies' [on folder]

Executions of Michael Reilly, ex-soldier, Cloghan, Thomas Cunningham, ex-soldier and carpenter, Cloghan, Sgt King, RIC, Castlerea, and the Pearson brothers, Kinnity; and remarks on the execution of spies in Offaly. 15 items, 1921.

1.
Remarks on Execution of ~~Spys~~ Spies [handwritten, n.d.]

The enclosed reports of execution of ~~Spys~~ Spies is forwarded by Bde Adjutant who was present with me at Court of Enquiry into the charges against these men.

It was definitely established at the court that these men were continuously communicating with the Enemy and helping to point out houses in which Officers of the Battn were staying. Warning in such cases is useless. It [The] only result in a few cases here in which suspected spys were warned was that these men joined the Black & Tans.

There have been numerous and continuous arrests of our men in this district and spying is rampant. It is to be hoped that the executions will have a saluatary [sic] effect.

        O/C
        Offaly 2
To
1. DI
2. Ed (?) Óglach

2.
Preliminary Report of execution of the two brothers Pearson of Cadamstown, Kinnity. *[Taken from typed copy - there is an almost identical handwritten one.]*

C. Coy. (Kinnity) 3rd Battalion reported to me on 26/6/21 that some of their men have been fired on a few nights previously, whilst engaged in a road blockade operation, by three men armed with shotguns. As a result one of their men was somewhat seriously wounded.

The men who fired were recognised by the men present to be three brothers named Pearson. These Pearsons were sons of a Protestant farmer in the district. They had always displayed open hostility towards I.R.A. and had been active in promoting the Ulster Volunteers movement in their district in which there are a number of "Planters".

Having satisfied myself by enquiries from Coy. Capt. Kinnity, and Officers present at Battalion Council, that there was no doubt about the identity of the men who fired, I ordered that these men be executed and their houses destroyed. Destruction of their premises was essential /and also to remove other members of the family from the district to safeguard our forces. The enemy is kept well informed of the actions and personnel of our force in the district and arrests have been frequent. There is good ground for suspecting this family of transmitting information.

Two of these men - Pearsons - were duly executed on 1/7/21 and their house destroyed by fire. I understand that the other brother was absent but have not yet received a proper report of the execution from the Battalion yet.

      Signed:- O/C Offaly.

3. Witness Statement of Michael Cordial, Formerly Quartermaster, 3rd Battalion, Offaly No. 2 Brigade

Source: Statement by Witness, Document No. W.S. 1712, *Bureau of Military History,* Cathal Brugha Barracks, Dublin.

Witness: Michael Cordial, Kinnitty, Co. Offaly.
Identity: Q/M, 3rd Battalion, Offaly No. 2 Brigade.
Subject: "C" (Kinnitty) Coy., 3rd Battalion, Offaly No. 2 Bgde., I.R.A.

Conditions, if any, stipulated by Witness: Nil
File No. S.3024

STATEMENT BY MR. MICHAEL CORDIAL, Kinnitty, Co. Offaly. Formerly Quartermaster, 3rd Battalion, Offaly No. 2 Brigade.

EXTRACT FROM WITNESS STATEMENT:

The attack on Pearson's.
====================

The Pearsons were a family who lived on an extensive farm or estate about one mile from Cadamstown and about three miles from Kinnitty. They were – particularly so, the male members of the family, father and three sons – violently opposed to the National Movement and they looked with contempt on local Volunteers or I.R.A. men.

Things reached a climax some time before the Truce when they fired with shotguns on a small party of Volunteers who were blocking a road. One Volunteer, a man named Heaney, was seriously wounded. A full report on the matter was made to the Brigade staff who after serious deliberation ordered that the four male members of the Pearson family should be executed and their house burned down.

On 30th June, 1921, a party of about thirty men were mobilised to implement the order. The house was surrounded and all women folk were removed from the scene. Fortunately for themselves, the father and one son were away from home that day. The other two sons, Richard and Abraham, were captured in a hay field. They were brought into the yard and informed of the order. A firing party was appointed and the executions were there and then duly carried out. Next, the house and out-offices were set on fire. Heavy explosions were heard while the house was burning which indicated that a large amount of ammunition was stored in it.

The remaining members of the Pearson family left the district and did not return. Years later, the Irish Land Commission acquired their estate and divided it up amongst the local people.

SIGNED: Michael Cordial
DATE: 13th December 1957
WITNESS: J. Grace

[Note: Michael Cordial's statement in 1957 is a remarkably accurate recollection of the event. He does not refer to the other three men who were lightly wounded by the Pearsons' gunfire. Also, the outhouses were not destroyed. – Ed.]

4. Extract: Report of 3rd Battalion (Kilcormac), Offaly No. 2 Brigade IRA on activities in June 1921

Source: Bureau of Military History. Provided by Philip McConway

On the Evening of 30th [June 1921] Two hostile Unionists executed for levying War on members of this [Kinnity] Coy when operating on road blockade a week previous. Also the House and its contents were destroyed.

301

Appendix 3

Location maps of the events at Coolacrease

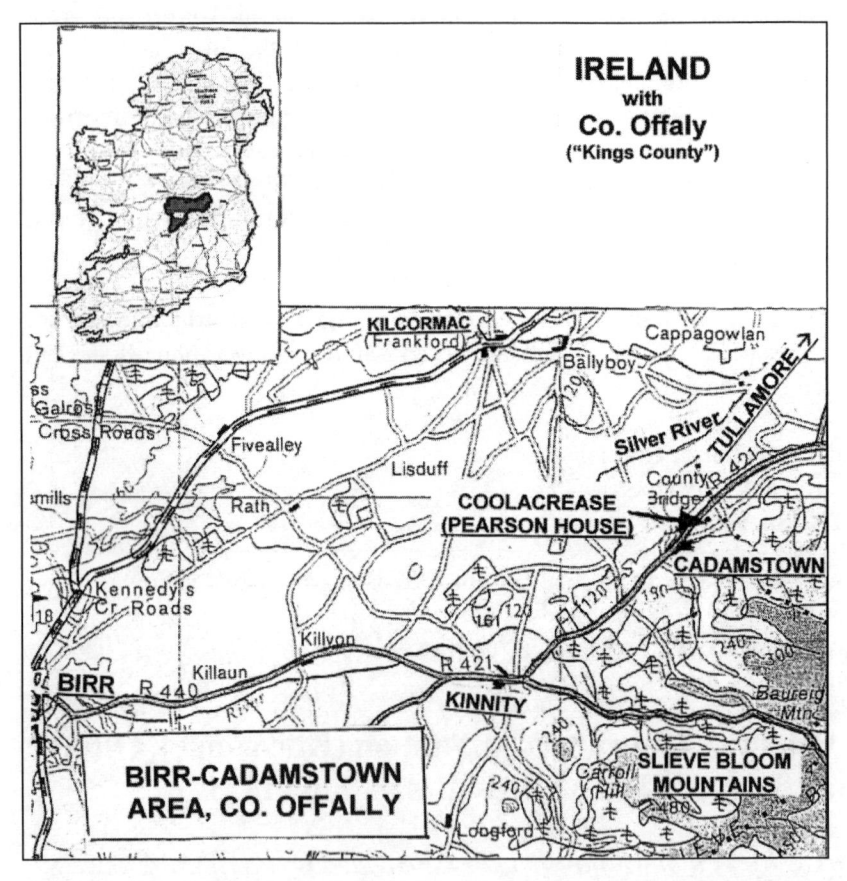

5. Cadamstown and Coolacrease, at the foot of Slieve Bloom on the strategic Birr-Tullamore road in Co. Offaly (then King's County). The IRA roadblock at Coolacrease was part of a county wide IRA operation to bring British military mobility to a standstill.

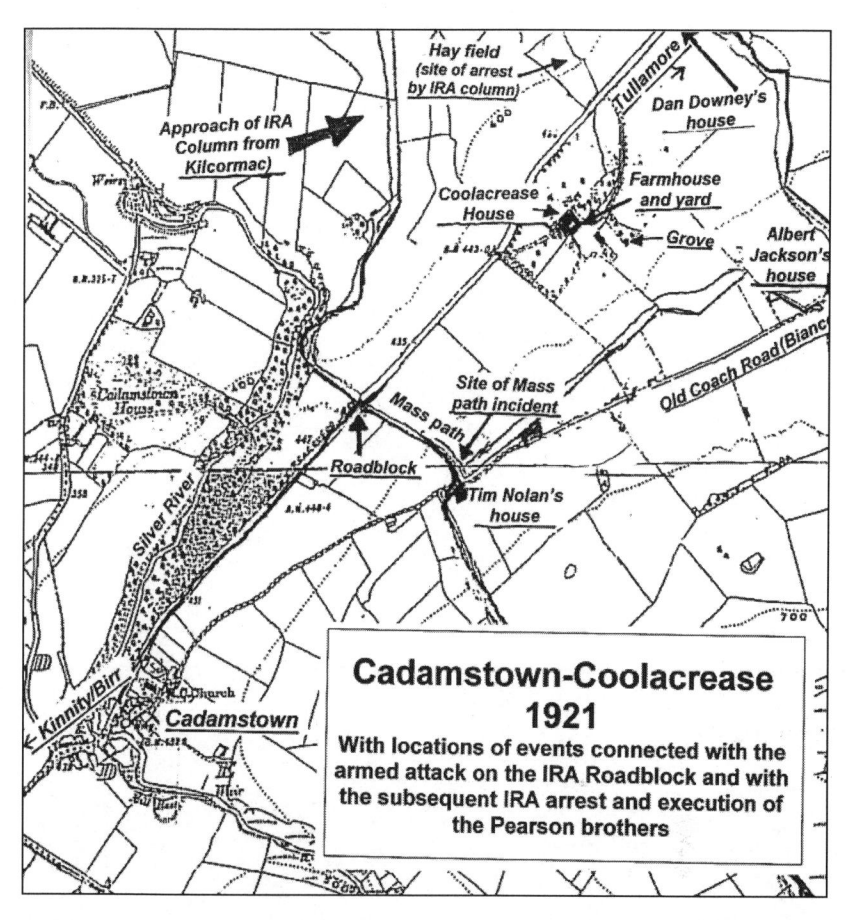

Cadamstown-Coolacrease 1921
With locations of events connected with the armed attack on the IRA Roadblock and with the subsequent IRA arrest and execution of the Pearson brothers

6. Coolacrease with locations associated with the attack on the IRA roadblock on ca. 24th June 1921 (mass path, roadblock, etc.) in which three volunteers and an RIC man held by the roadblock party were wounded by the Pearsons. Also shown are locations associated with the execution of the two Pearson brothers and the burning of Coolacrease House on 30th June 1921 (approach of the IRA flying column, hay field where the Pearson brothers were arrested, farmyard where the execution took place and the grove where the family was held). Marked also are the Downey, Nolan and Jackson houses and the Old Coach Road, at one time the Bianconi highway to Cork.

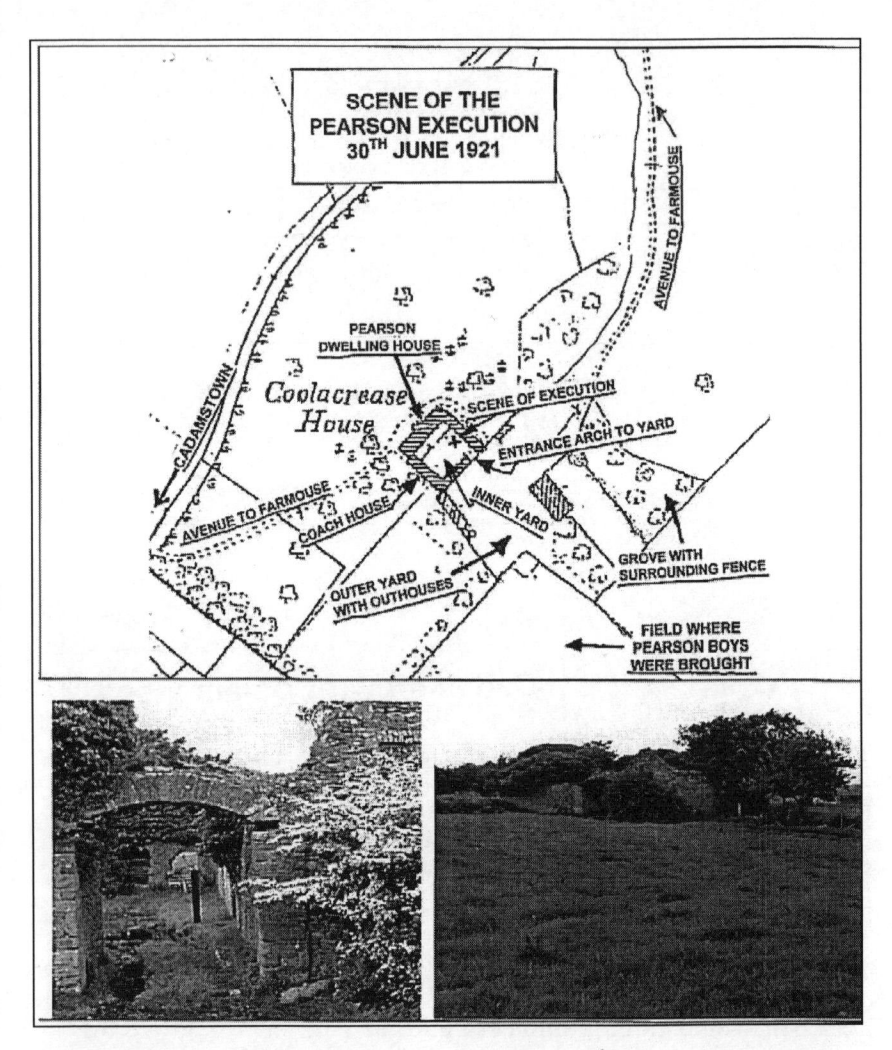

7: *Top:* Scene of the Pearson Execution 30th June 1921. *Photo bottom left:* The brothers were executed against the right wall inside the walled yard. *Photo bottom right:* View of the farmyard entrance from the grove area where the family was held. The executions could not be witnessed from the grove., where Matilda Pearson recalled being told: *"Don't think we are doing this because you are Protestants. It is not being done on that account."*

304

Appendix 4

Proceedings of the British Military Court of Inquiry, July 1921

8. Courts of Inquiry in lieu of Inquests into the deaths of Richard and Abraham Pearson

Source: UK National Archive, Kew (London)

COVER NOTE:
Civilians Richard H Pearson & Abraham P Pearson, Cadamstown, Kings Co.
7.7.21

PROCEEDINGS of a Court of Inquiry held in lieu of inquest at CRINKLE Barracks BIRR on the 2nd July 1921 by order of Lt. Col. T.A. Andrus C.M.G. …. For the purpose of investigating and reporting upon the circumstances in which Richard Henry Pearson civilian came by his death.
President: Major G.W. Browne I/R. Sc.Fus.
Members: Capt. D.M.W. Beake V.C.,D.S.O.,M.C. I/R. Sc.Fus.
Lieut. J.J. Kingston DEPOT The Leinster Regt.
In Attendance:

The Court having assembled pursuant to order, proceed to view the body and take evidence.

<u>1st Witness:</u> Frederick William Woods civilian medical Practitioner of Kinnity Kings County having been duly sworn in states:-

At Kinnitty on the 30th June 1921 I was leaving the dispensary in the village at about 18.55 hours. A civilian informed me that he was sent in to ask me to go out to attend to two of the PEARSON boys who had been shot. I at once proceeded to COOLACREASE house where the PEARSONS live, arriving there about 1930 hours and found RICHARD H PEARSON lying on a mattress in a field at the back of the house. I examined him and found a superficial wound in the left shoulder, a deep wound in the right groin and right buttock, the entrance (?) of the latter being in front. In addition there were wounds in the left lower leg of a superficial nature and about six in the back which were glancing (?) wounds. In my opinion these wounds were all caused by either revolver or rifle bullets, and were fired at close quarters. I dressed the wounds antiseptically and after attending to his brother ABRAHAM PEARSON I returned to KINNITTY at about 20.45 hours. At about 22.40 hours the Police came to my house and asked me to come to COOLACREASE House I found RICHARD H PEARSON dead. In my opinion the cause of death was shock and sudden haemorrhage as a result of gunshot wounds. The fatal wound in my opinion was that on the groin.

Cross-examining by the Court

Q No. 1 Do you not consider a groin wound to be a serious one?
A 1 I do if such a wound implicates the blood vessels.
Q2 Did the groin wound of the deceased implicate the principal blood vessels?
A2 It did not
Q3 Did any of the other wounds implicate any of the principal blood vessels?
A3 None that I saw.
Q4 When you first saw the deceased was he losing much blood?
A4 He had apparently lost a considerable amount of blood.
Q5 In view of this loss of blood was the deceased's condition precarious?
A5 It was.
Q6 On being called by the Police to examine the deceased for the second time did you find any wounds which you had not previously discovered?
A6 I did find one.
Q7 Was this wound a dangerous one?
A7 It was.

Fredk Wm Woods LRCP+SI

2nd witness:- ETHEL MAY PEARSON having been duly sworn states:-
I am the sister of the deceased. About 4 p.m. on the 30th June 1921 I came into the hall at COOLACREASE house and found it full of armed men, some of them in masks. My mother, my two sisters and my two girl cousins were with me in the hall and we were all ordered into the dining room. My mother fainted and we asked for water but we were not given any for twenty minutes and then we were given dirty water. During this time some of the raiders were searching the house, and I heard them breaking things up, while others were bringing in petrol and hay. We were

then ordered outside and went out by the back door where I saw my two brothers surrounded by the raiders. The deceased was one of the two. I saw the flames burst out. I heard a raider say to another, "Am I much burnt". My mother who was in a fainting condition was carried by my two brothers into a little wood we call the Grove and we all went with her by the order of the raiders. Six of the raiders, two or three of whom were masked, ordered my brothers down into the yard. I saw the raiders search my brothers and place them against the wall of the barn and shoot them. There were about six or eight who shot and they used rifles and shotguns. At this moment there were ~~about~~ 35 raiders in the yard. Within two or three minutes after the shooting the raiders all disappeared. I got on a horse and proceeded to CADAMSTOWN to fetch a Doctor. On the way I saw the raiders proceeding over the bog land towards FRANKFORD. I have seen the deceased in the Military Barracks Mortuary at CRINKLE and I identify the body as that of my brother Richard. He was 24 years old last birthday. He was not a member of any political organisation. I could identify the man who appeared to be the leader, and some of the others. (Signed)

3rd witness Susan Matilda Pearson, having been duly sworn in states:-
I am the sister of the deceased. At about 4 p.m. on the 30.6.21 I was lying on the sofa in the kitchen at Coolacrease Ho. when armed and masked men came to our house. Some had service rifles, others shotguns and revolvers. They pointed rifles at us and ordered us into the dining room where we were kept for about an hour. During this time the raiders searched the house and took away five bicycles, my brothers' suits and the girls' clothes. Then they scattered hay about the house and sprinkled petrol over it, ordering us out of the house before setting fire to it. They placed my brothers, shortly afterwards, against the wall of the barn and shot them. When they fell they shot them again. The raiders almost immediately started off in the direction of FRANKFORD. I could identify some of the raiders as I have seen them in KINNITTY. I identify the body which I have seen in the Mortuary of the Barracks at CRINKLE as that of the deceased. Susan M. Pearson.

FINDING:
The Court finds that the deceased RICHARD HENRY PEARSON, male 24 years of age farmer of COOLACREASE House Kings County died on 30.6.1921 of shock and haemorrhage as a result of gunshot wounds

inflicted at COOLACREASE House by armed persons unknown and that these persons are guilty of wilful murder.
Given under our hand this 2nd day of July at BIRR, Kings County.
 (Signatures) ...President ... Beak...Kingston members

I am of the opinion that deceased was murdered by Members, unknown, of the I.R.A.
Curragh 16.7.21
(S.d) P.C.E. SKINNER Colonel Commandant, Commanding 14th Infantry Brigade, C.M.A.
For the remarks by the G.O.C.
Curragh

****

PROCEEDINGS of a Court of Inquiry held in lieu of inquest at CRINKLE Barracks BIRR on the 2nd July 1921 by order of Lt. Col. T.A. Andrus C.M.G. .... For the purpose of investigating and reporting upon the circumstances in which Abraham Pratt Pearson civilian came by his death.

President: Major G.W. Browne I/R. Sc.Fus.
Members: Capt. D.M.W. Beake V.C.,D.S.O.,M.C. I/R. Sc.Fus.
Lieut. J.J. Kingston DEPOT The Leinster Regt.
In Attendance:

The Court having assembled pursuant to order, proceed to view the body and take evidence.

1st Witness. Lt. Colonel C.R. Woods R.A.M.C. (retired) in medical charge of CRINKLE BARRACKS, BIRR, having been duly sworn states:-
At 0200 hrs on 1 July 1921 I was called to the MILTARY HOSPITAL, BIRR. I found the deceased lying there suffering from gunshot wounds. His wounds were dressed by me. I examined his wounds and found extensive wounds on left cheek, left shoulder, left thigh and lower third of left leg. In addition there was a wound through the abdomen. The latter wound had an entrance at the front and appeared to have its exit at the lower part of the back, fracturing the lower part of the spinal column. In my opinion death resulted from shock due to gunshot wounds.
(Signed) C.R.Woods Lt. Col. RAMC Retired.

2nd witness:- ETHEL MAY PEARSON having been duly sworn states:-
I am the sister of the deceased. About 4 p.m. on the 30th June 1921 I came into the hall at COOLACREASE house and found it full of armed men, some of them in masks. My mother, my two sisters and my two girl cousins were with me in the hall and we were all ordered into the dining room. My mother fainted and we asked for water but we were not given any for twenty minutes and then we were given dirty water. During this time some of the raiders were searching the house, and I heard them breaking things up, while others were bringing in petrol and hay. We were then ordered outside and went out by the back door where I saw my two brothers surrounded by the raiders. The deceased was one of the two. I saw the flames burst out. I heard a raider say to another, "Am I much burnt". My mother who was in a fainting condition was carried by my two brothers into a little wood we call the Grove and we all went with her by the order of the raiders. Six of the raiders, two or three of whom were masked, ordered my brothers down into the yard. I saw the raiders search my brothers and place them against the wall of the barn and shoot them. There were about six or eight who shot and they used rifles and shotguns. At this moment there were ~~about~~ 35 raiders in the yard. Within two or three minutes after the shooting the raiders all disappeared. I got on a horse and proceeded to CADAMSTOWN to fetch a Doctor. On the way I saw the raiders proceeding over the bog land towards FRANKFORD. I have seen the deceased in the Military Barracks Mortuary at CRINKLE and I identify the body as that of my brother Abraham. He was nineteen years old last birthday. He was not a member of any political organisation. I could identify the man who appeared to be the leader, and some of the others. (Signed)

3rd witness Susan Matilda Pearson, having been duly sworn in states:-
I am the sister of the deceased. At about 4 p.m. on the 30.6.21 I was lying on the sofa in the kitchen at Coolacrease Ho. when armed and masked men came to our house. Some had service rifles, others shotguns and revolvers. They pointed rifles at us and ordered us into the dining room where we were kept for about an hour. During this time the raiders searched the house and took away five bicycles, my brothers' suits and the girls' clothes. Then they scattered hay about the house and sprinkled petrol over it, ordering us out of the house before setting fire to it. They placed my brothers, shortly afterwards, against the wall of the barn and shot them. When they fell they shot them again. The raiders almost immediately started off in the direction of FRANKFORD. I could identify some of the raiders as I have seen them in

309

KINNITTY. I identify the body which I have seen in the Mortuary of the Barracks at CRINKLE as that of the deceased. Susan M. Pearson.

FINDING:
The Court finds that the deceased ABRAHAM PRATT PEARSON, male 19 years of age farmer civilian of COOLACREASE House Kings County died on 1.7.1921 of shock, the a result of gunshot wounds inflicted at COOLACREASE House by armed persons unknown and that these persons are guilty of wilful murder.
Given under our hand this 2nd day of July at BIRR, Kings County.
(Signatures) …President … Beak…Kingston members

I am of the opinion that deceased was murdered by Members, unknown, of the I.R.A.
 (S.d) P.C.E. SKINNER Colonel Commandant, Commanding 14th Infantry Brigade, C.M.A.
Curragh 16.7.21

****

> Army Form A. 2.
>
> PROCEEDINGS of a **Court of Inquiry**
>
> assembled at **Crinkle Barracks, Birr**
>
> on the **2nd July 1921**
> **Lt. T. Andrus CMG**
> by order of **Competent Military Authority**
> **Cog. 14th of Bde. GOC**
> **King's County**
>
> for the purpose of investigating and reporting upon the circumstances in which **Abraham Pratt Pearson, civilian,** came by his death.
>
> PRESIDENT.
> **Major G. W. Browne 1/R. Sc. Fus.**
>
> MEMBERS.
> **Capt D. M. W. Beak V.C., D.S.O., M.P.**
> **1/R. Sc. Fus**
> **Lieut J.J. Kingston, Depot The Leinster Regt.**
>
> IN ATTENDANCE.
>
> The **Court** having assembled pursuant to order, proceed to view the body and take evidence.
> 1st Witness, **Lt Colonel C.R. Woods R.A.M.C. (retired)** a medical Charge of Crinkle Barracks, Birr, having been duly sworn states:—

9. Original proceedings of the Court of Inquiry in lieu of Inquest into the death of Abraham Pearson, Crinkle Barracks, Birr, 2nd July 1921. The Court consisted of three officers: Captain Beak and Maj. Browne of the Royal Scots Fusiliers and Lt. J.J. Kingston of the Leinster Regiment. Beak was a war hero (Victoria Cross) and Browne commanded 3rd Coy, 1st Btl. stationed at Crinkle from January 1921. Lt. Kingston was a staff officer with the Depot unit of the Leinsters, which played a secondary role.

311

Evidence of Lt.Col. Wood RAMC (1st witness) and Ethell Pearson (2nd witness). Richard's wounds were to the cheek, shoulder, leg and abdomen, while Abraham's were to the shoulders, leg, back, arms and groin areas. Senator Harris's claims that the brothers were purposely shot *"in the genitals"* is an outrageous (but deliberate) distortion of the facts.

> was carried by his two brothers into a little wood, we
> called the priest and we all went with her by the
> order of the raiders. Six of the raiders two or three of
> whom were masked, ordered my brothers down
> into the road. I saw the raiders search my
> brothers and place them against the wall of the
> barn and shot them. There were about six or
> eight who shot and they used rifles and shot
> guns. At this moment there were 35 raiders in the
> yard. Within two or three minutes after the
> shooting the raiders all disappeared. I got on a
> horse and proceeded to Croghanstown to fetch a doctor.
> On the way I saw the raiders proceeding over the
> bogland towards Frankford. I have seen the
> deceased in the hutting, Rk Mortuary, at Crinkill
> and I identify the body as that of my brother
> Abraham. He was nineteen years old last birthday.
> He was not a member of any Political organisation.
> I could identify the man who appeared to be the leader
> and some of the others.

3rd Witness: Susan Matilda Pearson, having been duly sworn
states:-

> I am the sister of the deceased. At about 10 P.M. on the
> 30.6.21 I was lying on the sofa in the kitchen at
> Coolacrease Ho. when armed and masked men came to
> our house. Some had service rifles others shot guns and
> revolvers. They pointed rifles at us and ordered us
> into the dining room where we were kept for about an
> hour. During this time the raiders searched the
> house and took away few bicycles, my brothers suits
> and the girls clothes. They then scattered hay about
> the house and sprinkled petrol over it and...
> of the house before setting fire to it. They placed by

Ethel and Matilda Pearson (3rd witness). Ethel says the family was held in the grove while the execution was carried out. Matilda says she might recognise some of the men involved, having seen them in Kinnity in the past. At a line up of local Republicans the following day she failed to identify any.

> *[handwritten:]* Inclusion.
> brothers shortly afterwards, against the wall of the barn and shot them. When they fell they shot them again... The raiders almost immediately cleared off in the direction of FRANKFORD. I could identify some of the raiders as I have seen them in Kinnitty. I identify the body which I have seen in the Mortuary of the Barracks at Crinkle as that of the deceased, Susan M. Pearson.

End of Susan Pearson's signed evidence. None of the later extravagant claims by the family are mentioned, such as the shooting of one of the girls, the family being forced to watch the execution, various acts of discourtesy and brutality by the raiding force and even the playing of musical instruments by IRA men. The story first became embellished in the contemporary *Kings County Chronicle* report of the events (a reporter of this newspaper was present at Crinkle Barracks). This is reprinted in Alan Stanley's book, *I met murder on the way* (2005). But the most outrageous claims were raised only five years' later, in the Pearson case to the British compensation body, the "Irish Grants Committee." It is these later fully unsubstantiated and fanciful claims that formed the basis for the Harris-Sammon "documentary".

The Court finds that Abraham died of *"shock and haemorrhage as a result of gunshot wounds inflicted ... by armed persons unknown"* and that these persons are *"guilty of wilful murder."* The commander of 14th Infantry Brigade adds: *"I am of the opinion that deceased was murdered by Members, unknown, of the I.R.A."* We do not reproduce the originals of the Inquiry into the death of Richard Pearson as the copies from the PRO are of very poor quality. The witness statements are similar and the findings identical. See transcript above.

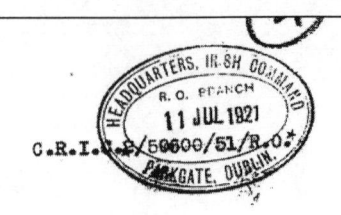

```
                                                    [stamp: HEADQUARTERS, IRISH COMMAND
                                                     R.O. BRANCH
                                                     11 JUL 1921
        Under Secretary,              C.R.I. /59600/51/R.O.
                                                     PARKGATE, DUBLIN]
            Dublin Castle.
        _____


                    Richard H. Pearson & Abraham P. Pearson.
        _____

                    With reference to this office minute
        of even number dated 9/7/21, forwarding a copy
        of the proceedings of the Court of Inquiry held
        in lieu of Inquest in the case of the above named.

                    The Certificates of Finding of the
        Court in relation to this case are forwarded here-
        with.

                                    [signature]  Staff Captain.
                                    for Deputy Adjutant General.
        G.H.Q. Ireland,
        Parkgate.
        11th July '21.
        H.G.M.
```

10. Distribution of the proceedings of the "Courts of Inquiry in lieu of Inquest" went up the British chain of command, here from British Army Headquarters (G.H.Q.) in Parkgate Street, Dublin, to the Under Secretary in Dublin Castle. The proceedings led to the propaganda report circulated to various agencies by Dublin Castle (given in transcript below).

On the development of the propaganda unit at Dublin Castle see Dr. Brian P. Murphy OSB. *The Origins and Organisation of British Propaganda in Ireland 1920* (Aubane, 2006).

11. Dublin Castle Statement on the Pearson executions, 9th July 1921

[Date-stamp: 9 JUL1921, Code 1029]

Report on the Sinn Fein Outrage at COOLACREASE HO.
Nr. CADAMSTOWN

COOLACREASE HO. is owned by a farmer named Pearson, a Protestant and a Loyalist.

For some time past the family has received warnings from SinnFeiners. The family consists of PEARSON, his wife, 4 sons, 3 daughters, and, in addition, there were two cousins living in the house.

At about 16.30 on 30.6.21, a party of between 30 and 40 armed men arrived, some of them masked, bringing with them the two elder sons of PEARSON, whom they had found in a hayfield. They locked the whole family in a room and then proceeded to loot the house and the outbuildings. Whilst this was going on, Mrs. PEARSON fainted. When the daughter asked for water to bring her round, it was refused. Later, the Sinn Feiners brought some muddy water for her. Plenty of clean water was obtainable.

The house was then fired and the family allowed out. They were placed on a little hill just outside the back of the house. The two eldest sons were then taken, and in full view of the rest of the family were put up against a wall and shot, meanwhile the Sinn Feiners played ragtime music, on the piano and one of the sons' violins.

The shooting was carried out so that both men should die in agony, both being hit in the stomach and thighs. As soon as the shooting was finished, the SinnFeiners beat a hasty retreat, leaving behind them a blazing house, and a group of broken-hearted women looking after two dying men. One of them died in about four hours.

The other lived for 12 hours and died in the hospital at BIRR barracks. The women were not even allowed to keep any spare clothing at all, all of it being burned in the house.

One of the daughters succeeded in getting the news to BIRR, and troops and police from BIRR and TULLAMORE arrived on the scene with all possible speed.

The father and one son were away in MOUNTMELLICK at the time, and steps have been taken to warn and protect them.

One of the cousins, a man, was chased by the raiders and fired at but it is not yet known whether he escaped or not.

The rest of the family was transported to BIRR, where the D.I. is making arrangements for their housing and safety.

The matter was left in the hands of BIRR detachment 1st R.S.F., and the BIRR Police, who are doing all in their power to trace the perpetrators of the crime.

[Editor's note: Dublin Castle propagandists typically embellished the story with lurid claims of sadism, looting and brutality. This characterised their reports on all IRA actions which official policy declared had to be treated as criminal activity. The abbreviations "D.I." and "RSF" refer to R.I.C. District Inspector and Royal Scots Fusiliers respectively.
These reports remain on record but were not treated seriously by the contemporary press. The *Irish Independent* (12th July 1921) reported the incident soberly under the heading "Two Farmers Sons Killed" while *The Irish Times* (2nd July 1921) – characteristically – headed its report "Two Sons Murdered"]

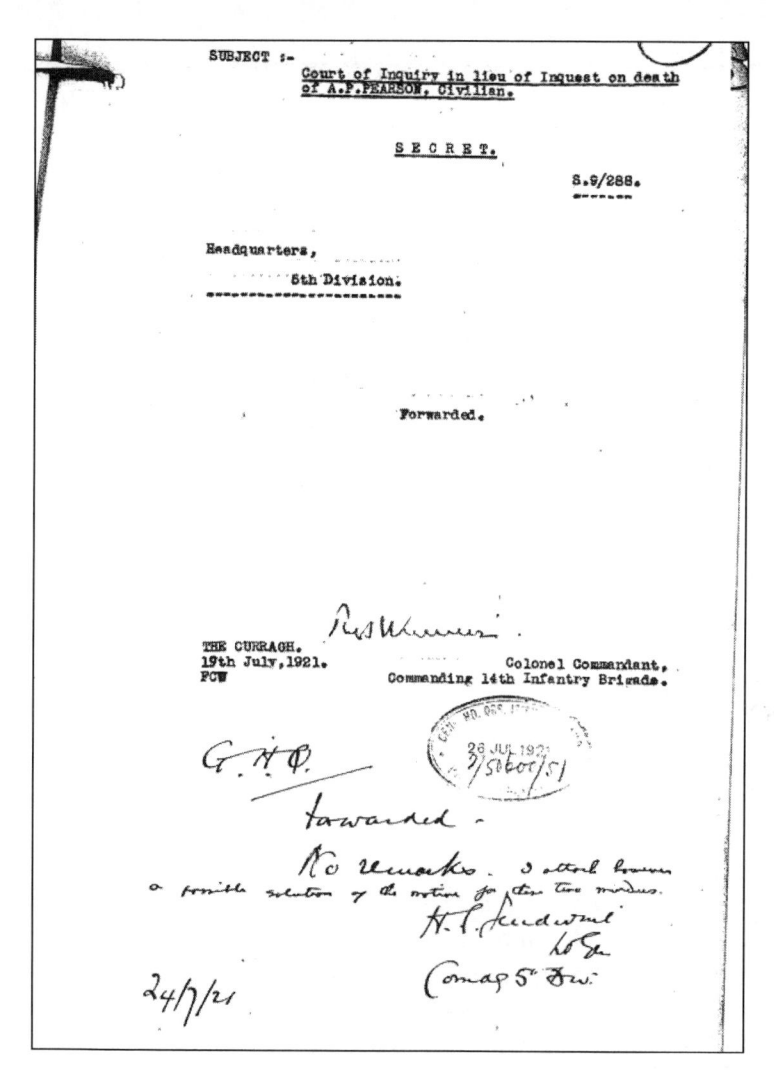

> SUBJECT :-
> Court of Inquiry in lieu of Inquest on death of A.F.PEARSON, Civilian.
>
> SECRET.
>
> S.9/288.
>
> Headquarters,
> 5th Division.
>
> Forwarded.
>
> THE CURRAGH.
> 19th July, 1921.
> FCW
>
> Colonel Commandant,
> Commanding 14th Infantry Brigade.

12. Note on Possible Motives: On 19th July, two weeks after the Inquiry, a further note on the case was forwarded by Colonel Skinner, 14th Infantry Brigade (parent unit of Royal Scots Fusiliers) to 5th Div. headquarters. It was sent on by the divisional commander to GHQ on 24th July with a note: *"Forwarded. No remarks. I attach herewith a possible solution of the motive for these two murders."* This was no mere local enquiry but dealt with by senior British military officials.

319

> The COOLACREASE Murders – 30.6.21.
>
> **Possible motives.-**
>
> 1.   The acquisition of Pearson's land which is very rich. In support of this, Pearson was driving through KINNITY in a Police lorry on the morning after his sons murder when Father Houlahan, a local Priest, asked him what he was going to do with the farm now.
>
> 2.   Revenge by Sinn Fein. It is said by the C.I. Queens County that the two Pearson boys a few days previously had seen two men felling a tree on their land adjoining the road. Had told the men concerned to go away, and when they refused had fetched two guns and fired and wounded two Sinn Feiners, one of whom it is believed died. It is further rumoured when the Farm house was burning, two guns fell out of the roof.
>
> Para. 1 above is the substance of a story told by Miss Pearson the daughter to Major Browne, Royal Scots Fus. stationed at BIRR.

The note *"The Coolacrease Murders – 30.6.21. Possible motives"* includes the first claim by a Pearson of land envy, and also the alternative assessment by the RIC of a reprisal for an armed attack by the Pearsons on an IRA roadblock (*"fired and wounded two Sinn Feiners, one of whom it is believed died."*). William and Sidney Pearson themselves are the most likely source of this evidence: on the evening of the executions they were picked up by the RIC in Mountmellick, Co. Laois, and the evidence is from the County Inspector for Laois (Queen's County), not Offaly, where Coolacrease is located. In fact four men were wounded: Mick Heaney, Tom Donnelly, Jack Brophy and Bert Hogg, an RIC man apprehended by the IRA roadblock party on his way from the Pearson house.

320

```
                                              27 JUL 1921
                                         O.R.I. 2/50800/51/R.O.


     Under Secretary,
          Dublin Castle.
     _____


                    Richard H. Pearson,  }
                    Abraham P. Pearson.  }  Cadmanstown, King's County.
     _____


                    With reference to my office letters of even
          number dated 9/7/21 and 11/7/21 forwarding copy of proceedings of
          Court of Inquiry in lieu of Inquest and Certificate of Finding of
          the Court respectively, in the case of the above named.
                    A copy of correspondence as to possible motives
          for these murders is forwarded herewith.


                                                    Staff Captain.
                                           for Deputy Adjutant General.
     G.H.Q. Ireland,
     Parkgate, Dublin.
     27-7-1921.
     H.G.M.
```

13. British Army GHQ forwarded the note *"Possible Motives"* to the Under Secretary in Dublin Castle on 27th July. The letter refers to the proceedings of the Inquiry and Certificates of Finding already forwarded on 9th and 11th July.

The Court of Inquiry documentation was available to the 'Hidden History' team, but the evidence it contains of the Pearson attack on the roadblock, details of the execution and the clear nature of the wounds suffered was suppressed, as it would be the undoing of the central theses of the TV show. Suppression of this information only makes sense where the intention was to produce propaganda rather than history

Appendix 5
Selected Land Documents

14. Land Registry Folio 1863. Sale of the 341 acre farm through the Land Commission to the sitting tenants, the elderly Benwell sisters, for £2,490 on 2nd June 1909. The Benwells had lived on the farm since the mid-19th century and were a well regarded family locally. All holdings on the L'Estrange Malone estate were transferred to its tenant occupiers in 1909.

Land Registry Folio 1863 (contd.). In February 1911 ownership is restructured to include relations in England for inheritance purposes. A few months later (29th June 1911) the farm is sold to William Pearson *"of Derrylea, Monasterevan, Co. Kildare"* (not his actual residence - see above pp. 106-8) for £2,000 *("owner in fee simple")*. A bank loan of £900 to part-finance the purchase is recorded as a charge on the farm.

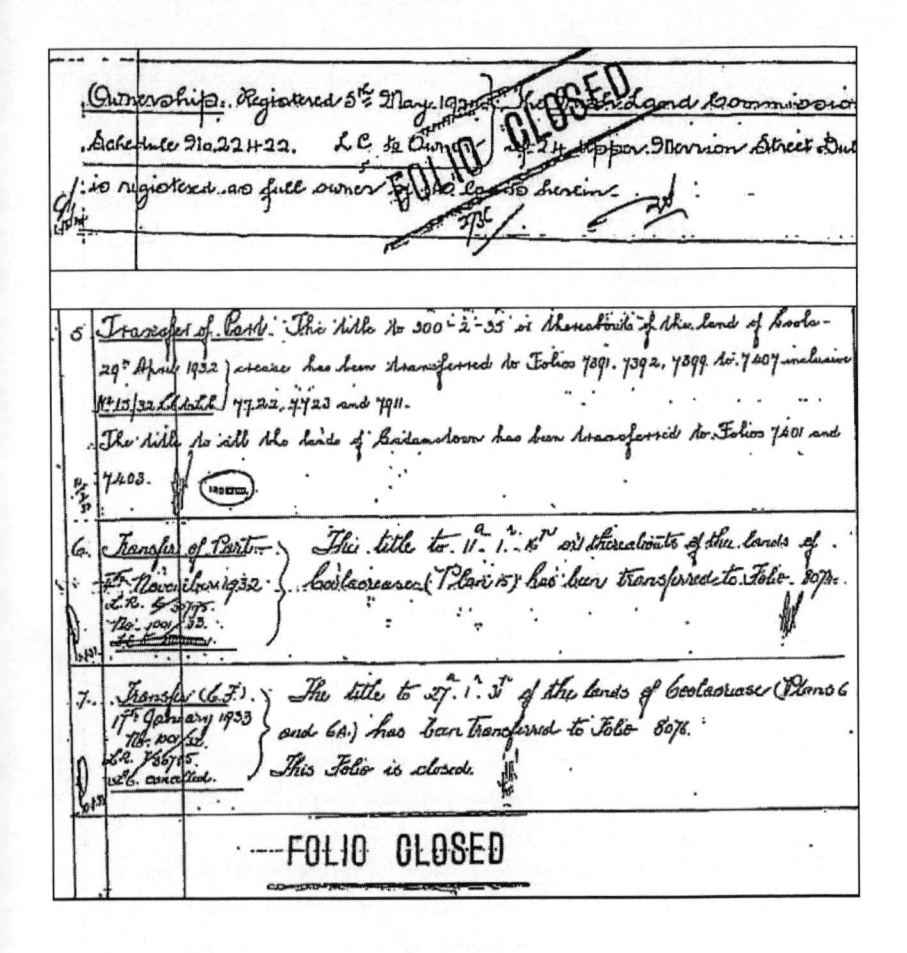

Land Registry Folio 1863 (contd.). *Top:* on 5th May 1924 *"all lands herein"* were registered to the Irish Land Commission as *"full owner."* The purchase had occurred on 2nd August 1923. The Folio is then closed, with subsequent entries in 1932-33 recording transfers of various parcels of the estate, and consolidation with outside parcels, to other title folders.

THE DEPARTMENT OF
AGRICULTURE & FOOD
AN ROINN TALMHAÍOCHTA AGUS BÍA

13 March 2008

Dr Pat Muldowney
Magee College
University of Ulster
Derry
BT48 7RR

Dear Dr Muldowney,

I refer to your application to view former Irish Land Commission documents relating to the townland of Coolacrease (Pearson Farm).

The former Irish Land Commission documents/maps are held at this Office, a section of the Department of Agriculture, Fisheries and Food. These documents, even though they are stored in the National Archives Building in Bishop Street, have not been handed over to the Archives under the National Archives Act 1986 and remain under the control of the Department of Agriculture, Fisheries and Food as successor to the former Commission. The title documents form part of the root of title of those allotted land on the Estate and are not available to the general public for research etc, unlike other State documents in the custody of the National Archives. The other files in this Office are files on private individuals who sold land to the former Commission and those who applied for and were allotted land by the former Commission.

The Irish Land Commission was dissolved by the commencement in 1999 of the Irish Land Commission (Dissolution) Act 1992. This Act also provided that all records, deeds and documents lodged with the Commission should be transferred to the Minister for Agriculture and Food at that time. In this regard this Department now has responsibilities under the Freedom of Information and Data Protection Acts in relation to these documents.

These files contain private and personal information on the individuals concerned and are not generally available for public inspection. This Department considers them to be day to day working documents that are often consulted in land ownership matters. Owners and purchasers and/or their personal/ legal representatives are allowed access to relevant documents/maps by prior consultation with this Office.

I am the recently appointed Keeper of Records and I can find no record that RTE has had access to the former Irish Land Commission documents, stored in the Records Branch of the Department of Agriculture, Fisheries and Food, relating to the townland of Coolacrease (Pearson Farm). It is not possible to say if access to the documents was granted to Dr Dooley at some stage by the former Commission. In the circumstances I regret that I am unable to grant you general access to these documents.

Records Branch, Land Services Division,
Bishop Street, Dublin 8, Ireland

15. Letter from Melanie Hall, Keeper of Records, 13th March 2008: Land Commission title records are not publicly available and RTÉ did not access the records of the Pearson Estate. After broadcast of the 'Hidden History' film, its producer claimed *"confidential"* Land Commission records proved her claims of a sectarian land grab.

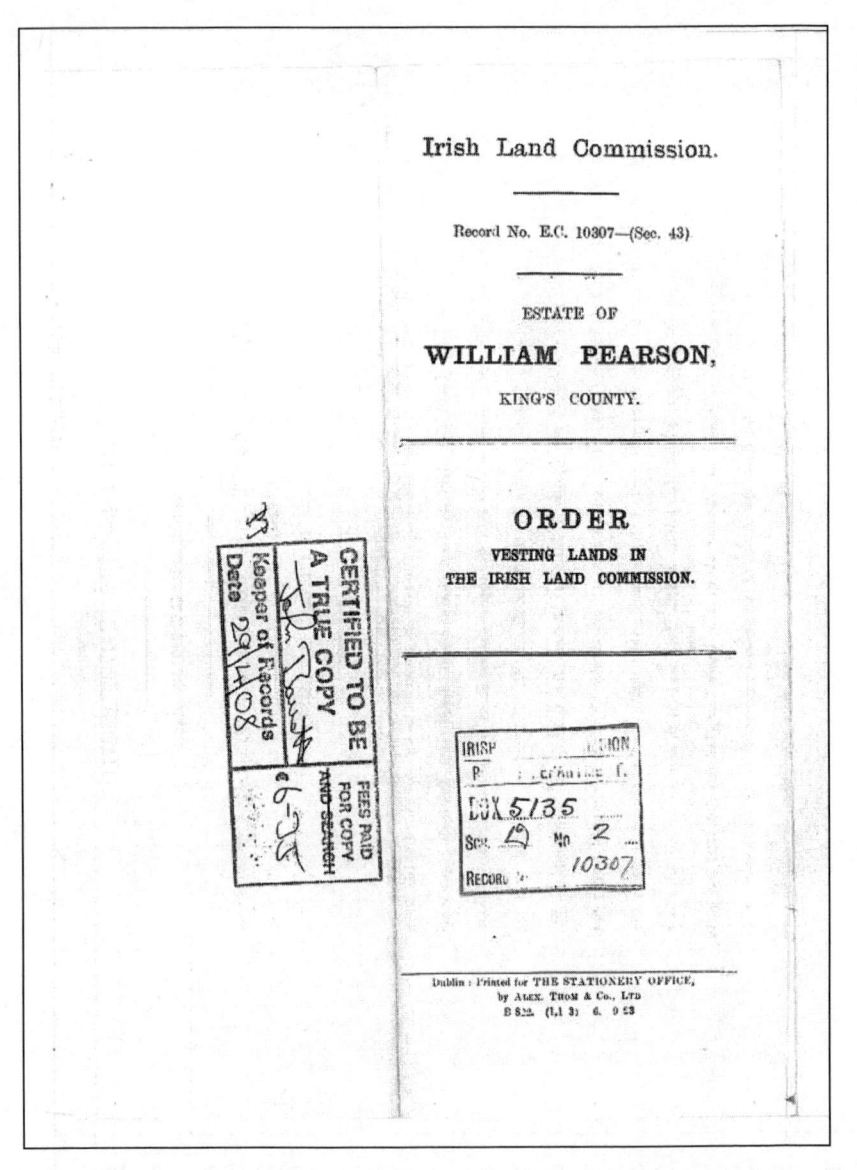

16. Order vesting the Pearson Farm in the Land Commission, 2nd August 1923 (File 10307). Contrary to Niamh Sammon's claim of a *"forced sale"*, it was a voluntary transaction. The purchase price agreed after protracted negotiations was £4,817.

REGISTERED LAND.

IRISH LAND COMMISSION.

Record Number E.C. 10307 (Sec. 43).

Tuesday the second day of August One Thousand Nine Hundred and Twenty-three.

Estate of WILLIAM PEARSON,

KING'S COUNTY.

IT IS ORDERED by the Irish Land Commission pursuant to the powers vested in them by the Irish Land Acts 1903 and 1909 that the lands described in the second and third columns of the Schedule hereto with the appurtenances Excepting and Reserving thereout the concurrent sporting rights to the Rev. Saville R. W. L'Estrange Malone and his son Lieut. Edmond G. Saville L'Estrange Malone for their joint lives and the life of the survivor DO VEST and the same are hereby VESTED in the said Irish Land Commission in fee-simple subject (a) to any public rights affecting the lands (b) to any maintenance charge under the Public Works Acts and (c) to any easements rights and appurtenances mentioned in Section 34 of the Land Law (Ireland) Act 1896 but save as aforesaid discharged from the claims of all persons interested in the lands whether in respect of superior or intervening interests or incumbrances or otherwise.

Signed and Sealed in presence of

Commissioner.

SCHEDULE REFERRED TO IN THE FOREGOING ORDER.

1	2		3
Number on Map.	Townland.	Barony.	County.	Area.
				A. R. P.
Lands edged red	Coolacrease	Ballybritt	King's	339 2 2
Same	Cadamstown	Same	Same	1 2 35

Examined,

Commissioner.

Order vesting the estate in the Irish Land Commission, 2nd August 1923 (contd.).

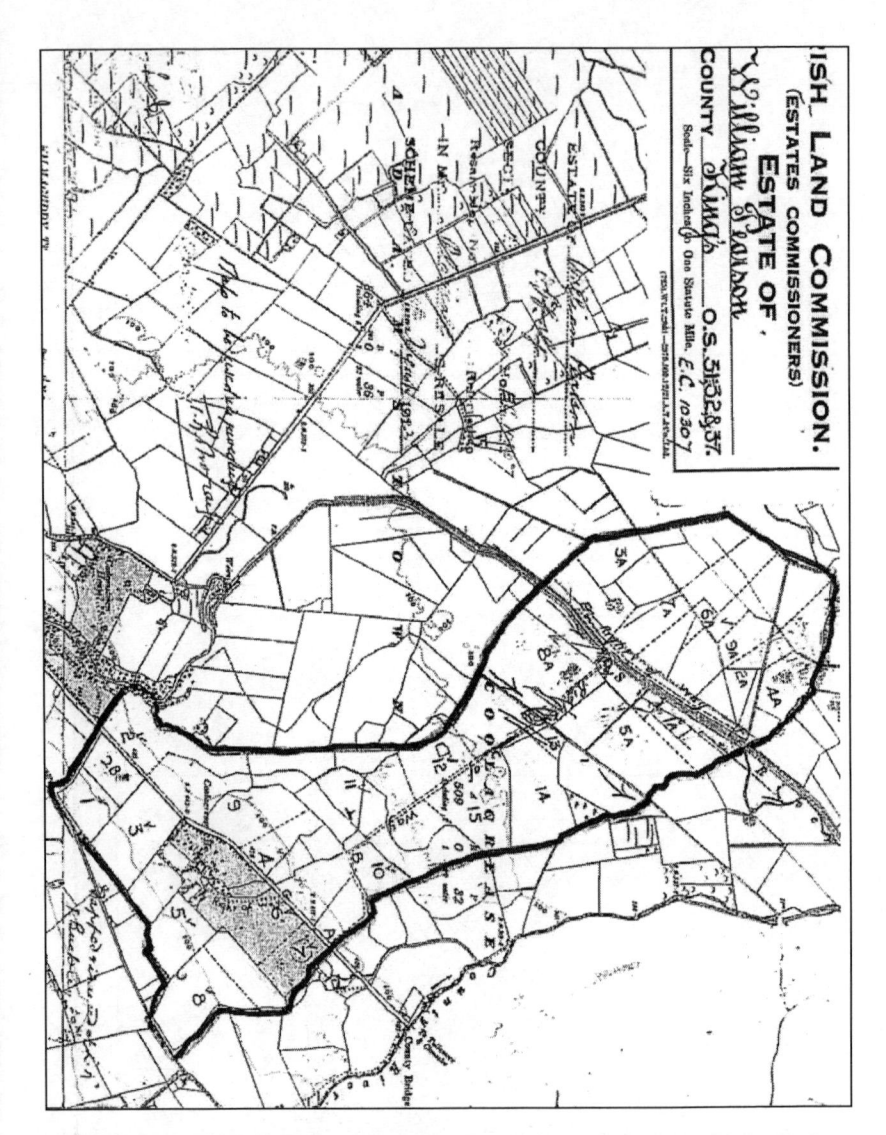

17. *Land Commission, Doc. E.C. 10307*. Sub-division of the Pearson Farm. Note numbered land parcels. The farmhouse is in the shaded area bottom left (Parcels 6-7). The parcels of poor land (with addition "A") are clustered mostly around the Silver River. The sub-division into parcels was made on 11th August 1923 and thus pre-dated allocation to individuals.

328

Schedule of Areas.

ESTATE OF W. Pearson RECORD No. _____ COUNTY OF Kings

Reference Numbers on Map.	TENANTS' NAMES	Area Statute Measure A. R. P.	TENURE AND OTHER REMARKS.
	TOWNLAND OF Coolcrease.		
1		5 1 16	
1A		11 0 12	
2		16 2 33	
2A		12 2 32	
3		10 2 34	
3A		22 2 7½	
4		21 3 10	
4A		8 2 26	
5		12 1 2	
5A		17 3 19	
6		15 3 24	
6A		11 2 2	
7		10 2 12	
7A		17 2 28	
8		11 0 2	
8H		19 0 33	
9		14 0 9	
9A		13 2 35	
10		18 1 27	
11		19 2 33	
12		6 2 18	
13		16 3 2	
14		13 2 2	
15		11 1 16	
		339 2 5½	
	Cadamstown	1 2 3⅜	
	Total	341 0 34	

18. *Land Commission. 'Schedule of Area':* size of each parcel (acres/roods/perches) (1 acre = 0.4 hectare). Note: *"compiled by Mapping Depart"* initialled T. H. B. [= Insp. T.H. Blackall] is dated 11th August 1923. Sub-division was scrupulously in line with established procedure. There was no *"land grab"*.

Reference No. on Re-sale Map (See Direction No. 10) (1)	ORDNANCE SURVEY Names of Townlands. (2)	Area (S. M.) (3)	Name and Address of Proposed Purchaser (4)	[Act col.] (5)	Area S.M. (6)	P. L. Val. (7)	Purchase Money (if applicable) (8)	Estate (9)
	Brought forward							
1, 1A	Coolacreade	16 1 28	Michael Carroll, Deerpark, Cadamstown	a		6		Malone
2	"	11 1 2	Bernard Henry	a				
~~2, 2A~~	"	~~29 1 25~~	~~John Fehery, Larkin, Cadamstown~~	~~b~~				
2A 2B 3, 3A	" "	18 0 22¼ 33 0 39	Jas Delahunt, Cadamstown Martin Egan, Glenlicky, Cadamstown	d d				
4, 4A 1	" Cadamstown	30 1 36 3 17	John F. Redmond, Corragh, Cadamstown	d				a
5, 5A	Coolacreade	30 0 21	William Glenn, Cadamstown	d				
6, 6A	"	27 1 31	John Grogan, Cadamstown	a		Ex-service man, R.?.A. …		¼
7, 7A 2	" Cadamstown	28 1 0 3 18	Daniel Downey, Coolacreade, Cadamstown	a		Herd		

19. Land Commission. Record 10307. "Schedule giving Particulars of Division." Columns (l-r): map ref., townland, acreage, recipient, basis under Land Acts, valuation/other, distance from existing holding ("1 mile", "adjoin.", "¼ mile"). A column on the right [omitted] gives information on personal means and circumstances. Notes to Fehery (2) and Grogan (6) refer to British Army service records. See above pp. 126-9.

"*Schedule giving Particulars...*" (contd.). Figures on right record outright purchase and *"French"* refers to adjoining holdings on the French Estate. Bernard Heaney (13) had an adjacent farm and his allocation of Pearson land was mostly bogland. The note to 14 - *"R.O. in Bank"* - is "Receivable Order" for payment lodged. The note to Multany (9, 9A) reads *"Ex-serviceman: 3 ½ years in France."* The note on the 1928 transfer of the O'Brien parcel (8, 8A) to Rowe is illegible. Details of each allocation are given above, pp. 126-9.

331

20. Typical Land Commission re-allocation: Recommendation of 18th Sept. 1923 (i.e. six weeks after purchase of the Pearson land) from LC inspector T. H. Blackall to Commissioner Hogan that the allocation turned down by John Fehery be re-allocated: small plots 2A and 2B (12 and 5 acres) to John Walsh of Spink, who occupied a labourer's cottage and plot, and Plot 2 to Bernard Heaney of Cadamstown. Walsh did not take up the allocation due to the price and does not feature on the Commission lists. This parcel was later allocated to Jim Delahunty. Note that the Pearson farm is still referred to as the Malone estate after the original landlord, Rev. Saville L'Estrange Malone, who retained hunting and fishing rights.

21. Resolving typical disputes in a Land Commission allocation: letter from Bernard (Brian) Heaney, Cadamstown, to the Commission (28th September 1923) pointing out that in the sub-division a second allocation to another Bernard Heaney (Glenlitter) was an error, as *"my name was down for a portion of it as I am a small holder"* (this is confirmed by the Blackall letter on the previous page). If the matter was not resolved, writes Heaney, a Republican, *"I will lay the matter before my member of parliament."* Hardly the Republican intimidation/land grab claimed by Sammon! The dispute was resolved when Brian Heaney bought the land from Bernard.

333

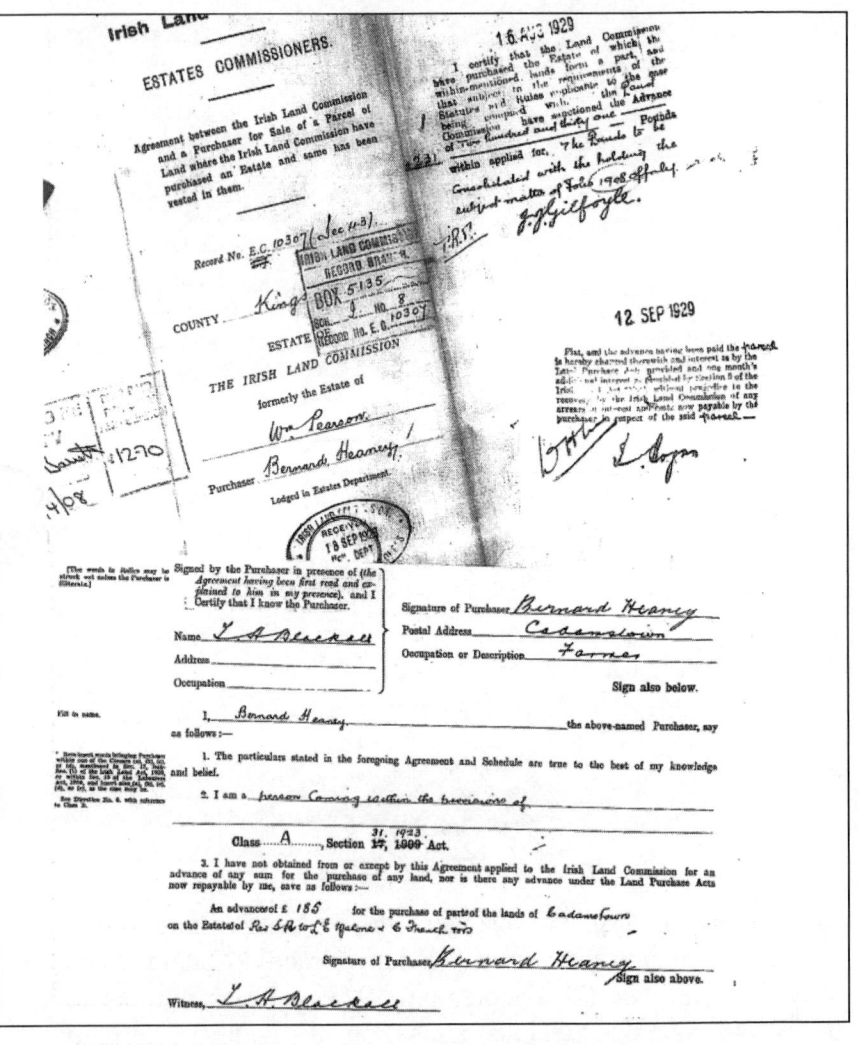

22. From a purchase agreement of 12th September 1923 for the allocation to Bernard (Brian) Heaney, detailing conditions of sale, liabilities, applicable sections of the Land Acts, purchase price etc. It is signed by Inspector T.H. Blackall, and a later consolidation with other land is confirmed by Inspector J. J. Gilfoyle and Commissioner Hogan in 1929. Sub-division of the estate was in strict conformity with process and procedure.

23. By 1929 one parcel of land had changed hands three times and, as in this recommendation by Inspector Gilfoyle, the Commission now encouraged consolidation of small holdings. Land Commission officials acted at all times in strict adherence with procedure, and the unprecedented inferences by Niamh Sammon and Eoghan Harris - allegedly corroborated by Dr. Dooley - of their complicity in a sectarian land grab is yet another reputation the RTÉ film sought to drag in the mud. This book demolishes that malicious claim.

335

County of ___

Barony of Ballybritt   Parish of Letterluna

Reference to Map.	NAMES.		Description of Te
	Townlands and Occupiers.	Immediate Lessors.	
OS.32.37	Coolacrease		
1	~~John~~ Bridget Horan	Rev. Saville L'E. Malone	Ho. offs. & land
2	Patrick Deegan	"	Ho. & land
3	~~Mary Hannah Benwell~~ George T. Benwell ~~& Rhoda Benwell~~	"	Ho. offs. & land
4	Winifred Downey ~~James Dunne~~ ~~Guardians of the Poor~~	Rural Dist Co. Dis. Not Guardians of the Poor fee	~~Land~~ Ho. offs & land
			Total

24. *Valuation Office: Valuation Birr 1 1857-1934 Book A,* p.14: Acreage and rateable valuations for land in the Townland of Coolacrease, 1909 (see Chapter 4). All are listed as tenancies of Rev. Saville L'Estrange-Malone. *Columns l-r:* Map ref., Townland/Occupier, Immediate Lessors, Description, Area (acres/roods/perches), Rateable Val.: Land/Buildings, Total. The

Kings
Parsonstown   Electoral Division of *Lotten*

Area Statute Measure.			Rateable Annual Valuation.							
			Land.			Buildings.			Total.		
A.	R.	P.	£	s.	d.	£	s.	d.	£	s.	d.
130	2	38	84	5	0	1	15	0	86	0	0
37	0	37	32	10	0	2	10	0	35	0	0
339	3	35	232	0	0	7	0	0	239	0	0
1	0	6	1	0	0	1	0	0	2	0	0
508	3	36	349	15	0	12	5	0	362	0	0

Benwell farm (later Pearson's) is at No. 3, with a valuation of £232, i.e.13 shillings per acre. The other farms range from 11 to 18 shillings p.a. A good farm, it was far from *"one of the first farms in Ireland,"* as stated in the later Pearson compensation claims to the "Irish Grants Committee."

(A.)	COUNTY OF King's		OFFALY

Townland of Coolacrease   O.S. 32. 37   Rural District

Reference to Map	NAMES.		Description of Tenement
	Occupiers.	Immediate Lessors.	
4853	1 Bridget Horan	Revd Saville L'E. Malone In fee L.A.P.	Ho. off & Land
4854	2 ~~Patrick~~ Denis Deegan	" L.A.P.	Ho. & Land
3 A Ba	John J. McRedmond	"	Offices & Land
4855	3 Mary Hannah ~~Benwell~~ Pearson & Rhoda ~~Benwell~~	" L.A.P.	~~Ho off & Land~~
4.5	Daniel Downey	In fee LAP	Land
4856 28 44	~~Winifred~~ Daniel Downey	Rural District Council of Birr No 1	Ho. off & Land

Townland Continued on page 35

Total

25. *Valuation Office: Valuation Birr 1 1857-1934 Book D*, p.17, valuation for 1912-23 (No. 3 is the Pearson farm). Following Land Commission purchase of the L'Estrange Malone Estate in 1911, the landlord has been replaced by freehold occupiers. The note (at left) *"Townland continued on page 35"*, refers to the list of new occupiers following the sub-division.

In 1923 the entry "Wm Pearson" (above "Hannah Benwell") is crossed out, and the buildings re-valued from £7 to £3 (margin note *"house burned"*). The first of the new owners – J. J. McRedmond (Parcels 3A, B, including the ruined house) - is listed above the Pearson entry.

339

Book D (contd.), p.35 (extracts): Valuation for 1923-25 of the holdings created from the Pearson farm. This is the rateable valuation and not the sale value, but allows for relative land values to be determined. The rateable valuation served as a basis for rent and later for annuity payments. The entry for John Multany (19-20) includes a valuation for a house provided under the British Army veterans housing scheme. The entry for William Glenn (13-14) includes outhouses. After 1923 he lived with his mother, a Somme widow, in the former coach-house (also subject to annuities). The range in valuations for the various holdings is examined above pp. 109-112.

Book D (contd.), p.36 (extract): Entry 14 is the 16 acres of poor land allotted to Bernard Heaney who had an adjoining farm in Glenlitter. He was father of Mick Heaney, the volunteer badly wounded at the roadblock, who emigrated to Australia with other local Republicans after his release from internment in 1923, and died of his wounds a few years later.

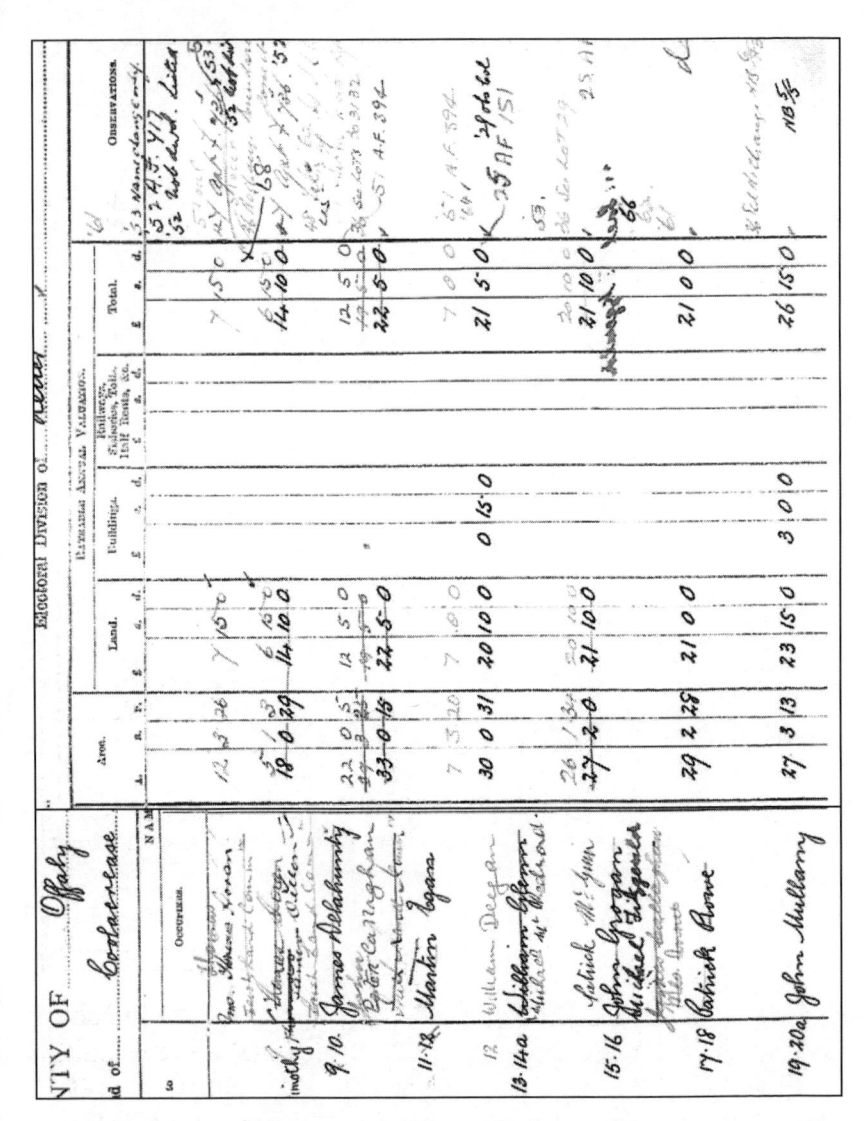

26. *Valuation Office, Valuation Birr I 1934-69, Book No. 23, Co. Offaly, R.D. Birr No. 1,* p.23: Some of the smaller holdings were uneconomic and changed hands several times over the following twenty years. The land was expensive and several holdings reverted to the Land Commission.

27. Land Registry Folio 7911 (Extract). Land allocated to John Multany. As a former British soldier, he also had a house built by the British Government under the veteran's scheme. Parcels 9, 9A (27 acres). Purchase cost £657, i.e. £24 per acre. A valuer (Telford of Birr) reckoned the best of the Pearson land was worth £10 per acre in 1921 and Dr. Dooley himself gives the average Irish per acre price up to 1940 as £10. Multany's annuity was £23, revised under the De Valera relief scheme to £14.6. The land was finally redeemed in 1972, i.e. 50 years later.

28. Land Registry Folio 7399 (Extract). Land allocated to Jim Delahunty, a Volunteer interned after the roadblock attack. 18 acres, Parcels 2A, 2B, cost £375 (= £21 per acre). This was a small holding of poor land. Delahunty did not have other land, and worked from 1923 as district postman. The annuity of £13.3 p.a. was revised under De Valera to £8. In 1950 the land reverted to the Land Commission. This plot was originally allotted to John Fehery, a former British Army soldier, but he declined it because of the price, as did John Walsh, a labourer.

29. Land Registry Folio 7400 (Extract). Land allocated to Martin Egan. Parcels 3, 3A: 33 acres, cost £586 (£25.5 p.a.). Annuity £20.5. Following his death in 1930, it passed to his widow, Kathleen. Annuity reduced under De Valera to £11. In 1947 the land reverted to the Land Commission and the annuity transferred to a new owner.

30. *Land Registry Folio 7405* (Extract). Land allocated to Jim McCormack, the village blacksmith. Parcel 10, 18 acres. Cost £345 (i.e. £19 p.a.). Annuity of £12, i.e. 13s per acre per annum. Purchase from Land Commission finally redeemed in 1975.

Note on currency: 20 shillings = £1

Appendix 6
The Pearson Case before the 'Irish Grants Committee'

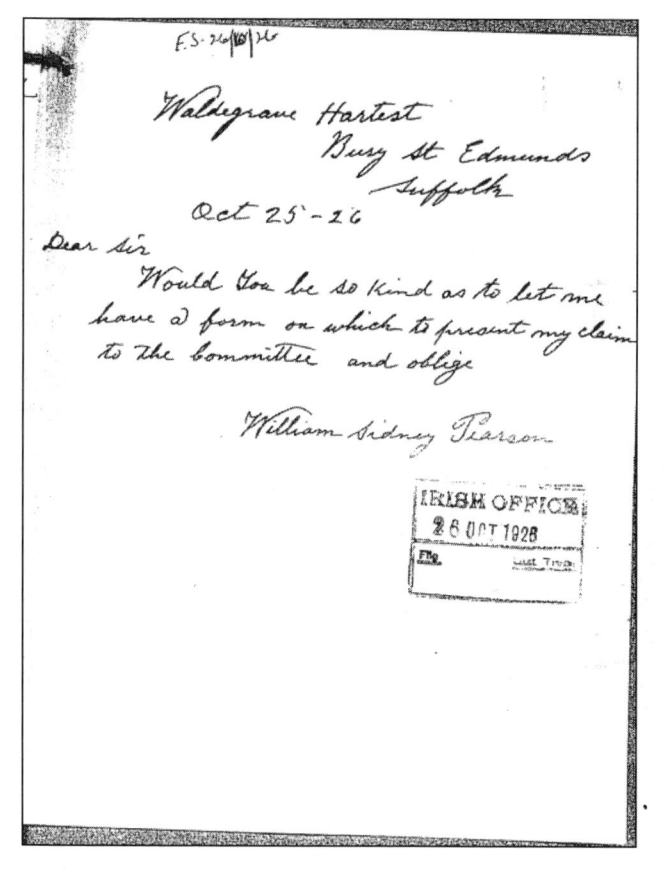

> F.S. 26/10/26
>
> Waldegrave Hartest
> Bury St Edmunds
> Suffolk
>
> Oct 25 - 26
>
> Dear Sir
>
> Would You be so Kind as to let me have a form on which to present my claim to the Committee and oblige
>
> William Sidney Pearson
>
> IRISH OFFICE
> 26 OCT 1926

31. On 25th October 1926, Sidney Pearson sought to lodge a claim to the "Irish Grants Committee," just ten days after it was announced that the re-formed Committee would accept claims for *"additional hardship"* suffered *"on account of their support for His Majesty's Government"* prior to July 1921, including from people who were not "refugees" and who had already been paid compensation by Irish or British authorities.

347

IRISH GRANTS COMMITTEE.

INFORMATION GIVEN ON THIS FORM WILL BE TREATED AS CONFIDENTIAL, BUT INQUIRIES WILL IN ALL PROBABILITY BE MADE FROM THE REFERENCES GIVEN).

1. Name (in full, and in block letters) WILLIAM Sidney PEARSON
2. Age Twenty five
3. Address (for correspondence) Waldegrave. Hartest Bury St Edmunds Suffolk

4. State here the nature of the loss in respect of which application is made, giving material dates. Detailed particulars need not be furnished at this stage.

My Fathers Farm known as Coolacrease Farm situated at Cadamstown. Birr Kings County Ireland was burned down by the I.R.A. in 1921 through Severe Boycotting. Terrorism he was compelled to sell it to the Irish Land Commission in 1922 for about ¼ its value. This farm should have been mine after a few years but my two Brothers being shot down by the I.R.A. My own life being threatened, I was forced to leave the country & come over to England for safety, leave all at the mercy of the Rifle men, who overpowered my father in such a way. He having neither help nor protection was compelled to accept what they offered, as no other farmer would be allowed to buy the value of the farm before the burning would be £17,000 with live and dead stock over £3,000

32. Pearson claims his father *"through severe boycotting + terrorism"* was *"compelled to sell* [the farm] t*o the Irish Land Commission"* for *"about ¼ its value." "Rifle men… overpowered"* him and he *"was compelled to accept what they offered."* The *"value of the farm before the burning would be £17,000"* with *"live and dead stock over £3,000."*

348

5. Do you claim that the loss or injury described was occasioned in respect or on account of your allegiance to the Government of the United Kingdom? If so, give particulars on which you base this claim. *We were accused by the I.R.A. of giving information to government officials of their movements*

6. Can you define the actual financial loss directly attributable to the injuries described above? If so, give particulars. *House and furniture clothing jewelry cash about £10000 then in land about the same 10000 consequential*

7. The amount for which you now make application. *Twenty thousand Pounds*

8. Was application for compensation made to any Court, Commission or Committee in respect of the injuries described? If so, give particulars and state with what result. *In October 6th county court at Birr Judge Fleming awarded My father 1300 £ compensation for his two sons 300 for farm buildings and farm produce 1000 for furniture clothing 5000 for house burning out of which the Irish Government stopped 4000 because he did not rebuild, which he could not as he had the farm sold before they passed This rebuilding act*

9. Give particulars of any moneys recovered by way of compensation, insurance or ex gratia grant in respect of the injuries or loss described. *I received none. My father got 3800 out of 7800 awarded by the county court judge.*

10. Give names and addresses of two responsible persons to whom, if necessary, reference may be made (e.g. Bank Managers, Solicitors, Ministers of Religion).

*Rev R. E Weir
The Rectory
Mountrath
Queens County
Ireland*

*Mr Rolleston
Solicitor
Maryborough
Queens County
Ireland* [and overleaf.

He claims the execution by the IRA was due to *"giving information to government officials of their movements"*, explains the compensation received from the Irish courts, names two referees and boldly claims £20,000 from the Committee.

> 11. State briefly your present financial position. *I have a small agricultural farm here of 163 acres but no cash to work it*
>
> I certify that the foregoing particulars are correct.
>
> *October 28 - 1926*   Signed *William Sidney Pearson*

Neither of the witnesses named lived in Offaly, where Pearson had lived for 10 years. According to R.B. McDowell, Rev. Robert E. Weir – one of the referees – was a member of the Advisory Committee of the Southern Irish Loyalists Relief Association, and had been an evangelical firebrand active *"in a very disturbed part of Queen's County"*. The application ends stating that he (Pearson) had *"a small agricultural farm here* [= Suffolk] *of 163 acres but no cash to work with."* The Committee later established that William Pearson had £6,000 in the bank.

> **THE IRISH LAND FINANCE COMPANY, LIMITED.**
>
> Registered Offices: THE RECTORY, MOUNTRATH, QUEEN'S CO.
>
> SECRETARY: REV. R. E. WEIR.
>
> 324.
> 1st December 1926.
>
> re Wm. S. Pearson,
> Coolacrease Farm,
> Cadamstown,
> Birr.
>
> IRISH OFFICE
> 4 DEC 1926
> File
>
> Dear Sir,
> Illness prevented me from answering your letter sooner.
> Mr Pearson was treated in a fiendish manner by the Republicans in the King's Co. I doubt very much if the wrongs which he suffered could be equalled by the horrors of the Black Hole of Calcutta. His sons were murdered and his home burnt. After that Mr Pearson went to England. It would be impossible for me to estimate Mr Pearson's monetary loss altho I have discussed it with him on several occasions. He had one of the best farms in King's Co. I believe that he is perfectly trustworthy, not liable to overestimate his losses and it was wholly and solely due to his loyalty that he lost his home and children. Yours faithfully
> The Secy. I.G. Committee
> Robert E. Weir.

33. The record indicates that only one referee, Rev. Weir of Mountrath, Co. Kildare, a fellow militant loyalist (see previous page) and friend of William Pearson, supplied a reference (1st December 1926): *"the wrongs he suffered could be equalled by the horrors of the Black Hole of Calcutta."*

16th December 1926.

Dear Sir,

I have to acknowledge the receipt of your form of claim to the Irish Grants Committee.

As far as I can ascertain from the statement which you submitted with your claim your father was obliged to dispose of his property in Ireland at a figure below his estimated valuation and that you have thereby been deprived of his prospect of inheritance. Please state if this is so.

In your reply will you please state if your father is still alive.

Yours faithfully
(signature) A.J.S. [= Alan Reid Jamieson}
Secretary, Irish Grants Committee]

Waldegrave Hartest
Suffolk
Dec 28 – [19]26

Gentlemen

In answer to your letter of the 18 Dec I beg to say You have the correct meaning of my letter or claim I saw by the papers that the Government was holding out a helping hand to the third party or those who lost indirectly through being victimized and intimidated by the Irish Republican that is the reason I made my claim if it is not the case of course You need not mind any further My Father is still alive and will be presenting his claim later on

Faithfully Yours
W. S. Pearson

34. Correspondence on Sidney Pearson's claim (transcript). Even the sympathetic Irish Grants Committee was suspicious of the ludicrously exaggerated Pearson claim, especially the value he claimed for the farm and for property damaged or destroyed, and sought clarification. Sidney Pearson in his answer of 28th December avoids the questions raised.

> Chairman
>
> This claim is not unamusing of 18/12/26. Please see my letter to claimant & his reply of 28/12/26.
>
> ? it unnecessary to circl. to Cmttee & may be rejected forthwith
>
> certainly A.W.R. 3.1.27
>
> ARJ 3/1/2

> .32 1 5.1.27
>
> Sir,
>
> I am directed to inform you that your claim has been submitted to and considered by the Irish Grants Committee. The Committee regret that after careful consideration of all the facts before them they are unable to make any recommendation in your case and are accordingly reporting to the Government in this sense.
>
> I am,
> Sir,
> Your obedient Servant,

Following Pearson's evasive response, Committee secretary ARJ (= Alan Reid Jamieson) recommends to the Chairman that *"the claim is not unamusing,"* is *"unnecessary to circl. the Committee & may be rejected forthwith"*. Chairman (A.W.R. = Sir Alexander Wood Renton) agrees *("certainly")* and Jamieson then wrote to Sidney Pearson (5th January 1927) stating that the Committee was unable to recommend compensation.

SOUTHERN IRISH LOYALISTS RELIEF ASSOCIATION

VICTORIA 6699.

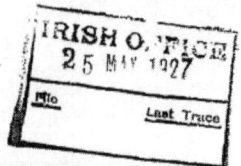

IRISH OFFICE
25 MAY 1927
No.   Last Trace

12 PALMER STREET,
WESTMINSTER, S.W.1
(OPPOSITE WEST ENTRANCE)
(ST. JAMES' PARK STATION)

24th May, 1927.

Major A. Reid Jamieson,
Irish Grants Committee,
38, Old Queen Street, S.W.1.

Dear Major Jamieson,

    I am asked by my Committee to forward you the enclosed application from Mr. William Pearson. As you will see the case is somewhat complicated, and upon our advice Mr. Pearson desires to employ Counsel, and my Committee desire me to apply to your Committee for permission for Mr. Pearson to be so represented.

    I am to say that Mr. L.R. Lipsett, K.C., has consented to act for Mr. Pearson subject to the approval of your Committee, and I would be glad if you could inform me whether Mr. Pearson's application for Mr. Lipsett to appear on his behalf is approved of by your Committee.

Yours sincerely,

---

35. On 24th May 1927 Sidney's father, William Pearson, lodged a new and more sophisticated claim with the Grants Committee, this time managed by the Southern Irish Loyalists Relief Association and seeking approval for employing counsel, Mr L. R. Lipsett K.C., as *"the case is somewhat complicated."* Lipsett had been involved with the previous Compensation Claims Commission also chaired by Renton.

Presented by Southern Irish Loyalists Relief Association.

IRISH GRANTS COMMITTEE.

(THE INFORMATION GIVEN ON THIS FORM WILL BE TREATED AS CONFIDENTIAL, BUT INQUIRIES WILL IN ALL PROBABILITY BE MADE FROM THE REFERENCES GIVEN).

1. Name (in full, and in block letters) .... WILLIAM PEARSON

2. Age 61

3. Address (for correspondence) .... WALDERGRAVE FARM,

HARTEST,

BURY-ST-EDMUNDS, SUFFOLK.

4. State here the nature of the loss in respect of which application is made, giving material dates. Detailed particulars need not be furnished at this stage.

I lived at and farmed on a large scale, some 341 acres at Coolacreass, King's County. I was very well to do farmer. Under the Tillage Order of 1918 I tilled all the land I could, and leased a large field from Captain Drought in order to grow more corn. The local Sinn Fein people were enraged at this and said I had done it to help the British Government; they accordingly when the corn was ripe trampled the entire down rendering it of very little value.
In the end of June 1921 after constant threatening, I had a private warning that a band of murderers were going to attack my house: This was on June 30, 1921. I accordingly set out with one of my boys on bicycles to get assistance from the British Forces, but I failed to get immediate help but was promised some protection. We returned home to find the house completely burnt out, two of my sons lying dead in the yard having been murdered in the presence of my wife and other children. These sons were grown up and worked on my land. There were about 500 men engaged in the outrage and the boys were put up against a wall, compelled to watch their home being burnt, and were then riddled with bullets by a squad of 10 men. One of their sisters tried to save them and a volley was fired at her and the hair was cut away from her scalp by bullets: My wife nearly died of fright and has never been and never will be normal.
For the murder of my sons I claimed £3000 and received £1500. For the burning of my home Judge Fleming awarded me £5000, and intimated that if I had given an undertaking to rebuild he would have made a larger award. but I would not rebuild with the country in the state it was, and my own life in danger. For the burning of my haggard, yard, stable, storehouses, forge, wool, hay, straw, haylifters, machinery, turf, tractor, tools, etc., valued at £1000; I received £300. For the destruction of furniture, clothing, bedding, and the entire contents of the house, valued at £2000, I received £1000, and for the contents of the Dairy with its machinery, etc. £40.
After the house was burnt I sold the land to the Land Commission before the Act was passed dealing with the rebuilding of house burnt out.

to sell the land - one of the best farms in Ireland - for a quarter of the value to the Land Commission. Subsequently my award of £5000 was cut down to £1000.
After the murder of my sons we took refuge in Birr Barracks, and the Military came out and looked after the live stock on the farm. The value of my crops this year was £600, and as I had no one to look after things

[and overleaf.]

> **4.** State here the nature of the loss in respect of which application is made, giving material dates. Detailed particulars need not be furnished at this stage.
>
> I lived at and farmed on a large scale, some 341 acres at Coolacrease, King's County. I was very well to do farmer. Under the Tillage Order of 1918 I tilled all the land I could, and leased a large field from Captain Drought in order to grow more corn. The local Sinn Fein people were enraged at this and said I had done it to help the British Government; they accordingly when the corn was ripe trampled the entire down rendering it of very little value.
>
> In the end of June 1921 after constant threatening, I had a private warning that a band of murderers were going to attack my house: This was on June 30, 1921. I accordingly set out with one of my boys on bicycles to get assistance from the British Forces, but I failed to get immediate help but was promised some protection. We returned home to find the house completely burnt out, two of my sons lying dead in the yard having been murdered in the presence of my wife and other children. These sons were grown up and worked on my land. There were about 500 men engaged in the outrage and the boys were put up against a wall, compelled to watch their home being burnt, and were then riddled with bullets by a squad of 10 men. One of their sisters tried to save them and a volley was fired at her and the hair was cut away from her scalp by bullets; My wife nearly died of fright and has never been and never will be normal.
>
> For the murder of my sons I claimed £3000 and received £1500. For the burning of my home Judge Fleming awarded me £5000, and intimated that if I had given an undertaking to rebuild he would have made a larger award, but I would not rebuild with the country in the state it was, and my own life in danger. For the burning of my haggard, yard, stable, storehouses, forge, wool, hay, straw, haylifters, machinery, turf, tractor, tools, etc., valued at £1000: I received £300. For the destruction of furniture, clothing, bedding, and the entire contents of the house, valued at £2000, I received £1000, and for the contents of the Dairy with its machinery, etc. £40.
>
> After the house was burnt I sold the land to the Land Commission before the Act was passed dealing with the rebuilding of house burnt out. As a result of subsequent persecution and destruction of property I had to sell the land - one of the best farms in Ireland - for a quarter of the value to the Land Commission. Subsequently my award of £5000 was cut down to £1000.
>
> After the murder of my sons we took refuge in Birr Barracks, and the Military came out and looked after the live stock on the farm. The value of my crops this year was £600, and as I had no one to look after things
>
> *[and overleaf]*

36. Original of William Pearson's claim (full transcript below). This is the story repeated almost verbatim by the RTÉ programme. The more outlandish claims now include the house attacked by *"about 500 men,"* the family forced to witness the execution, one daughter being fired on and wounded: *"the hair was cut away from the scalp by bullets."* He claims that, following a tip-off, he was away on the day of the executions seeking assistance from British forces: in fact he was at a religious convention at Carrick House near Mountmellick (Co. Laois).

but myself I lost heavily. I had to send my wife and children over to England for safety and keep them there two years which cost me £600. I came over to England seven or eight times to look for farms and these journeys cost me £100. I continued to farm my land alone so far as I was able. In October 1921 I had 40 fat cattle. I managed to get 20 of them off the land secretly at night and sold them for £32 per head. After that I was well watched by the Republicans, and whenever I took them to a fair pickets were put round them and no one dared ask the price, so I had to sell them in the end privately for £20 each which was a loss to me of £240.

In 1922 & 1923, my land was used by anyone who cared to drive their cattle upon it. In the Spring of 1922 & 1923 I fenced certain land for the purpose of meadowing, the fences were torn down in my presence and the cattle driven in on the land, and I was dared to take any action. The Republicans were determined to drive me out and get possession or what was always known as one of the first farms in Ireland.

I estimate my loss in 1922 for not being able to use my land and for having no one to help me owing to the boycott at £750 - This was net profit of a normal year and not a war time profit.

I tried to sell the farm but no auction was allowed, and one man wanted to buy it and would have given me £10,000. He applied to the local Priest for permission to buy and permission was refused. This offer was made after I had been burnt out. In normal times I could have sold the farm at £15,000. In the end I was forced to sell it to the Land Commission as it was utterly impossible to carry on, as not only was I severely boycotted but my land was a commonage and my life was constantly in danger. After selling to the Land Commission the net sum left to me was £4,189. I had to redeem the Annuity on the land and pay all the costs of sale, the total of these being £1,749. I therefore received £4,189 for land for which I was privately offered £10,000 without a house and few farm buildings, and the offer included the taking over of the purchase of all charges on the land. I was therefore at a loss of £5,811. on a sale which was illegally forbidden, not to mention what my loss might have been if I had offered the farm for sale in normal times as a going concern.

During 1922 & 1923 my horses and cattle were frequently driven off the land. ~~into a bog and being unable to get out died~~ One horse was driven into a bog and being unable to get out died, another driven into a wire fence and broke its leg and had to be destroyed, and one had its eye maliciously injured, and I sold it for £15. All these horses were bred as hunters and were valued at £80 each. Loss on these was £225.

In December 1921 there was a heavy flood in the river. The Republicans at the height of the flood dug an outlet in the bank and the water ~~covered about~~ carried away about 100 yards of the bank and flooded over 100 acres of my land. The Drainage Board refused to repair the River Bank. In 1922 & 1923 there were again floods and great damage was done to my meadow lands estimated at £200. In 1923 I spent £50 on trying to repair the damage but the next flood carried away all the repairs. I refused to pay the Drainage Board the Annuity due by me for the upkeep of the River Bank and they sued me in a Republican Court and I had to pay £33 including costs.

During 1921, 1922 & 1923 among minor losses I suffered were the following:-
Iron gates taken away, wooden gates smashed, fencing taken away £30.
Three sets of harness stolen. 15.
Raleigh car smashed to matchwood, the horse bolting by reason of being hit on the head with stones thrown by bystanders. £15.
New machinery bought in attempt to carry on, and had to sell at a loss when I had to leave the country - Tractor cars £100.
" " " " Grinding Mill 40.
" " " " Binder 25.
                                                                £165.

I never got one penny of compensation except that I have stated. I attach a Schedule showing all my losses and the amount I received as compensation for Pre Truce damage.

Attempts to sell stock were picketed by *"Republicans"* and boycotted; there was malicious flooding and damage and cattle put on his land; he couldn't sell the farm (worth £15,000) as the priest refused the (Protestant) purchaser permission to buy etc.

357

5. Do you claim that the loss or injury described was occasioned in respect or on account of your allegiance to the Government of the United Kingdom? If so, give particulars on which you base this claim.

   Yes. I was always known as a staunch Loyalist and upholder of the Crown. I assisted the Crown Forces on every occasion, and I helped those who were persecuted around me at all times.

6. Can you define the actual financial loss <u>directly</u> attributable to the injuries described above? If so, give particulars.

   See separate sheet.

7. The amount for which you now make application.

   £11,469. 0. 0

8. Was application for compensation made to any Court, Commission or Committee in respect of the injuries described? If so, give particulars and state with what result.

   Yes, for pre Truce losses. I was advised that by post Truce losses came within no Compensation Act, except the malicious injury to my house, and at the time I was warned not to apply for any compensation; My life at the time was hardly worth a day's purchase.

9. Give particulars of any moneys recovered by way of compensation, insurance or ex gratia grant in respect of the injuries or loss described.

   For pre Truce damage I claimed £14,100, and received £3,840.
   For post Truce damage nothing received.

10. Give names and addresses of two responsible persons to whom, if necessary, reference may be made (e.g. Bank Managers, Solicitors, Ministers of Religion).

    Eyre C. Falkiner, Esq., Castle Cuffe, Clonaslee, Queen's County.
    A. Jackson, Esq., Kilnaparson, Cadamstown, Birr, King's County.

"I was always known as a staunch Loyalist and upholder of the Crown. I assisted the Crown Forces on every occasion, and I helped those who were persecuted around me at all times." Full claim: £11,469.

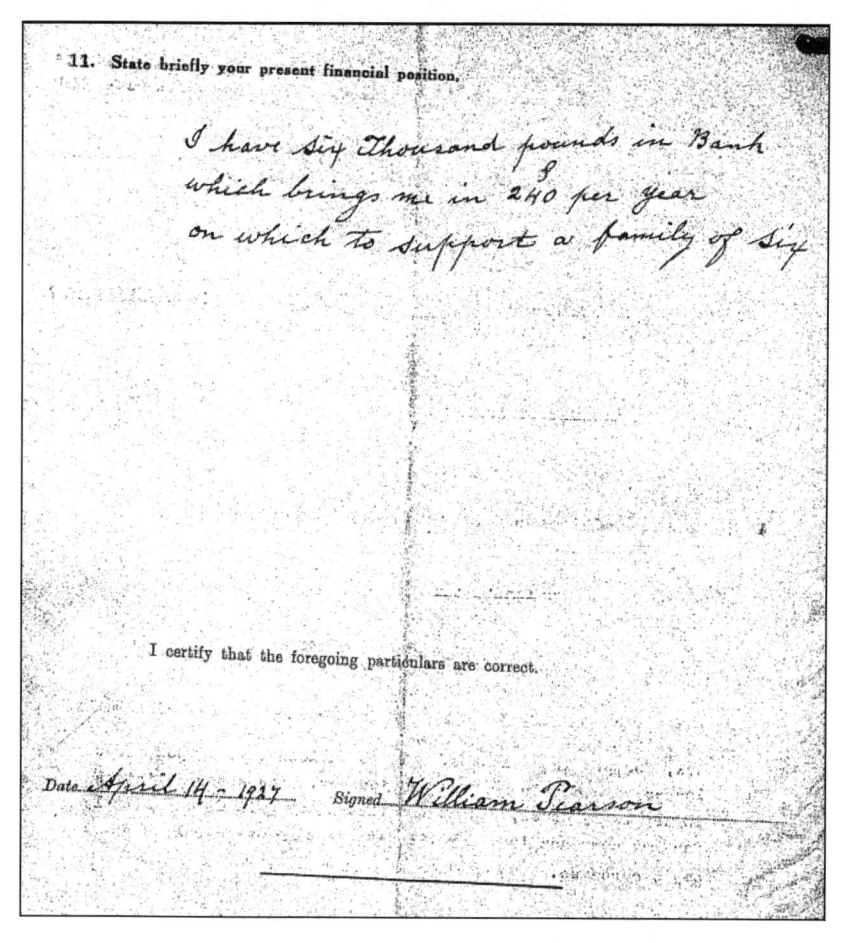

> **11.** State briefly your present financial position.
>
> *I have Six Thousand pounds in Bank which brings me in 240 per year on which to support a family of Six*
>
> I certify that the foregoing particulars are correct.
>
> Date *April 14 - 1927* Signed *William Pearson*

"I have Six Thousand pounds in Bank which brings me in £240 per year on which to support a family of six." He does not mention the 163-acre farm in Suffolk.

A full transcript of the claim is given on the following pages.

37. Transcript of William Pearson's claim to the Irish Grants Committee
(entries by William Pearson are given in italic)

Presented by Southern Irish Loyalists Relief Association.

Irish Grants Committee

(Information given on this form will be treated as Confidential, but inquiries will in all probability be made from the references given).

1. **Name (in full, and in block letters)** *William Pearson*

2. **Age** *61*

3. **Address (for correspondence)** *Waldergrave Hartest, Bury-St-Edmunds. Suffolk.*

4. **State here the nature of the loss in respect of which application is made, giving material dates. Detailed particulars need not be furnished at this stage.**

I lived at and farmed on a large scale, some 341 acres at Coolacrease, King's County. I was very well to do farmer. Under the Tillage Order of 1918 I tilled all the land I could, and leased a large field from Captain Drought in order to grow more corn. The local Sinn Fein people were enraged at this and said I had done it to help the British Government; they accordingly when the corn was ripe trampled the entire down rendering it of very little value.

In the end of June 1921 after constant threatening, I had a private warning that a band of murderers was going to attack my house: This was on June 30, 1921. I accordingly set out with one of my boys on bicycles to get assistance from the British Forces, but I failed to get immediate help but was promised some protection. We returned home to find the house completely burnt out, two of my sons lying dead in the yard having been murdered in the presence of my wife and other children. These sons were grown up and worked on my land. There were about 500 men engaged in the outrage and the boys were put up against a wall, compelled to watch their home being burnt, and were then riddled with bullets by a squad of 10 men. One of their sisters tried to save them and a volley was fired at her and the hair was cut away from her scalp by bullets: My wife nearly died of fright and has never been and never will be normal.

For the murder of my sons I claimed £3000 and received £1500. For the burning of my home Judge Fleming awarded me £5000, and intimated that if I had given an undertaking to rebuild he would have made a larger award, but I would not rebuild with the country in the state it was, and my own life in danger. For the burning of my haggard, yard, stable, storehouses, forge, wool, hay, straw, haylifters, machinery, turf, tractor, tools, etc., valued at £1000: I received £300. For the destruction of furniture, clothing, bedding, and the entire contents of the house, valued at £2000, I received £1000, and for the contents of the Dairy with its machinery, etc. £40.

After the house was burnt I sold the land to the Land Commission before the Act was passed dealing with the rebuilding of house burnt out. As a result of subsequent persecutions and destruction of property I had to sell the land – one of the best farms in Ireland – for a quarter of the value to the Land Commission. Subsequently my award of £5000 was cut down to £1000.

After the murder of my sons we took refuge in Birr Barracks, and the Military came out and looked after the live stock on the farm. The value of my crops this year was £600, and as I had no one to look after things but myself I lost heavily. I had to send my wife and children over to England for safety and keep them there two years which cost me £600. I came over to England seven or eight times to look for farms and these journeys cost me £100. I continued to farm my land alone as far as I was able. In October 1921 I had 40 fat cattle. I managed to get 20 of them off the land secretly at night and sold them for £32 per head. After that I was well watched by the Republicans, and whenever I took them to a fair pickets were put round them and no one dared ask the price, so I had to sell them in the end privately for £20 each which was a loss to me of £240.

In 1922 & 1923, my land was used by anyone who cared to drive their cattle upon it. In the Spring of 1922 & 1923 I fenced certain land for the purpose of meadowing, the fences were torn down in my presence and the cattle driven in on the land, and I was dared to take any action. The Republicans were determined to drive me out and get possession of what was always known as one of the best farms in Ireland.

I tried to sell the farm but no auction was allowed, and one man wanted to buy it and would have given me £10,000. He applied to the local Priest for permission to buy and permission was refused. This offer was made after I had been burnt out. In normal times I could have sold the farm at £15,000. In the end I was forced to sell it to the Land Commission as it was utterly impossible to carry on, as not only was I severely boycotted but my land was a commonage and my life was constantly in danger. After selling to the Land Commission the net sum left to me was £4,189. I had to redeem the Annuity on the land and pay all the costs of sale, the total of these being £1,749. I therefore received £4,189 for land [HANDWRITTEN ANNOTATION: no] for which I was privately offered £10,000 without a house and few farm buildings, and the offer included the taking over of the purchase of all charges on the land. I was therefore at a loss of £5,811. on a sale which was illegally forbidden, not to mention what my loss might have been if I had offered the farm for sale in normal times as a going concern.

During 1922 & 1923 my horses and cattle were frequently driven off the land. One horse was driven into a bog and being unable to get out died, another driven into a wire fence and broke its leg and had to be destroyed, and one had its eye maliciously injured, and I sold it for £15. All these horses were bred as hunters and were valued at £80 each. Loss on these was £225.

In December 1921 there was a heavy flood on the river. The republicans at the height of the flood dug an outlet in the bank and the water carried away about 100 yards of the bank and flooded over 100 acres of my land. The Drainage Board refused to repair the River Bank. In 1923 & 1923 there were again floods and great damage was done to my meadow lands estimated at £200. In 1923 I spent £50 on trying to repair the damage but the next flood carried away all the repairs. I refused to pay the Drainage Board the Annuity due by me for the upkeep of the River Bank and they sued me in a Republican Court and I had to pay £33 including costs.
During 1921, 1922 & 1923 among minor losses I suffered were the following:-

Iron gates taken away, wooden gates smashed, fencing taken away £30. Three sets of harness stolen 15.

Raleigh car smashed to matchwood, the horse bolting by reason of being hit on the head with stones thrown by bystanders. £15.

New machinery bought in attempt to carry on, and had to sell at a loss when I had to leave the country – Tractor cars £100. Grinding Mill 40. Binder 25.

I never got one penny of compensation except that I have stated. I attach a Schedule showing all my losses and the amount I received as compensation for Pre Truce damage.

5. Do you claim that the loss or injury described was occasioned in respect or on account of your allegiance to the Government of the United Kingdom? If so, give particulars on which you base this claim.
Yes. I was always known as a staunch Loyalist and upholder of the Crown. I assisted the Crown Forces on every occasion, and I helped those who were persecuted around me at all times.

6. Can you define the actual financial loss directly attributable to the injuries described above? If so, give particulars.
See separate sheet.

7. The amount for which you now make application.
£11,469.00

8. Was application for compensation made to any Court, Commission or Committee in respect of the injuries described? If so, give particulars and state with what result.
Yes, for pre Truce losses. I was advised that by post Truce losses came within no Compensation Act, except the malicious injury to my house, and at the time I was warned not to apply for any compensation: My life at the time was hardly worth a day's purchase.

9. Give particulars of any moneys recovered by way of compensation or ex gratis grant in respect of the injuries or loss described.
For pre Truce damage I claimed £14,100, and received £3,840. For post truce damage nothing received.

10. Give names and addresses of two responsible persons, to whom, if necessary, reference may be made (e.g. Bank Managers, Solicitors, Ministers of religion).
Eyre C. Falkiner, Esq., Castle Cuffe, Clonaslee, Queen's County.
A. Jackson, Esq., Kilnaparson, Cadamstown, Birr, King's County.

11. State briefly your present financial position.
I have Six Thousand pounds in Bank which brings me in £240 per year on which to support a family of six.

I certify that the foregoing particulars are correct.
Date April 14 – 1927   Signed William Pearson

SCHEDULE SHOWING VALUE OF LOSSES
AND
COMPENSATION CLAIMED AND RECEIVED.

Dates	SCHEDULE "A".	Value of Losses.	Compensation Claimed.	Compensation Received.
1919. August.	Corn crop trampled into ground because I was growing extra corn by Government Order	£ 200.	Was advised I had no claim	-
1921. June 30	House burnt (originally awarded £5,000, subsequently reduced to £1,000.	£8,000.	£8,000.	£1,000.
"	Contents of house, personal belongings, etc.	£2,000.	£2,000.	£1,000.
"	Haggard, yard, stables, forge, wool, turf in sheds, machinery, tools, hay barn, etc.	£1.000.	£1.000.	£ 300
"	Dairy and contents, bacon curing, machinery in dairy, etc. ...	£ 100.	£ 100.	£ 40
"	Two sons murdered.	£3,000.	£3,000.	£1,500.
		£14,300	£14,100	£3,840.

38. **"Schedule A: Schedule Showing Value of Losses and Compensation Claimed and Received."** The court at Birr had awarded standard war compensation of £1,500 for the sons killed, £2,000 for house and contents, and £340 for other items, total: £3,840. Note his claim of £8,000 for the house! He could not claim compensation to rebuild the house as the farm was already sold. Propaganda from Dublin Castle (12th July 1921) alleged numerous stock and equipment stolen. But the RIC County Inspector recorded just 3 pigs, a gate and a harness taken, which a Dáil Court ordered returned.

365

SCHEDULE "B"   Value of Losses.

1921
July 13   (1) 3 fat pigs stolen, valued at £15 ea.
              (In May 1921 a similar pig was sold
              for £19.10.0) ...   £45. 0. 0

Oct.   (2) One cow and calf stolen ...   30. 0. 0

          (3) 40 acres of meadow lost: no one was
              allowed to work for me, val. at £10
              per acre ...   400. 0. 0

          (4) 12 acres of oats lost for same reason
              as in (3), valued at £15 per acres..   180. 0. 0

          (5) 2 acres of potatoes lost ...   40. 0. 0

          (6) 1½ acres of mangolds lost ...   22. 0. 0

          (7) 7 acres of swedes lost ...   90. 0. 0

          (8) 100 acres of pasture wilfully flooded
              and rendered useless, Aug. 1921 ...   100. 0. 0

          (9) Expenses of moving family to England
              and keeping them there for 2 years,
              and my own expenses in visiting
              England looking for a farm ...   600. 0. 0

         (10) Half year's loss of dairy & poultry
              business. Kept on an average 12 cows
              in milk, and 100 head of poultry -
              average profit weekly £7.0.0. ...   180. 0. 0

         (11) Loss on sale of 20 head of cattle
              (fat) by reason of being boycotted by
              pickets of armed men - £12 per head   240. 0. 0

1922   (12) Pasture land ruined by public trespass.
              I had 150 acres of such land, and in a
              normal season grazed and fattened 150
              head of cattle which I would buy at the
              average price of £12 per head and sell
              at an average of £24 per head. Loss
              would be between £1800 & £1900 ...   1,850. 0. 0

         (13) Loss of 3 valuable horses maliciously
              injured, valued at £80 each - less £15
              received for sale of only surviving one   225. 0. 0

         (14) Loss of pasture land maliciously
              flooded ...   100. 0. 0

                              Carried fwd:-   £4,102. 0. 0

39. "Schedule B: Losses for which no Compensation was Paid." Most of the thefts and damage alleged in July and October 1921 are disproved by RIC and newspaper records. While the Committee was to accept claims for lost earnings (though regarded the amounts sought as *"excessive,"* e.g. it reduced item 12 from £1,250 to £240), it rejected as unfounded the claims of malicious trespass and flooding (8, 14, 15).

SCHEDULE "B" Continued.	Value of Losses.
Brought forward	£4,102. 0. 0
(15) Loss incurred by trying unsuccessfully to repair River Bank when Drainage Board refused to do so.	50. 0. 0
(16) Fine and costs inflicted in Republican Court when I refused to pay annuity to Drainage Board	33. 0. 0
(17) Iron Gates taken away, wooden gates smashed, and fencing repeatedly broken	30. 0. 0
(18) Three sets of harness taken	15. 0. 0
(19) Loss of 22 acres of meadow ready for cutting, by having cattle driven in at night - value of crop (say) £10 per acre (In 1917 I sold one acre of meadow for £27.	220. 0. 0
(20) Loss for being unable to sow any crops: I was threatened and could not get anyone to work for me. I had about the same tillage yearly, as set out in losses for year 1921	330. 0. 0
(21) Loss of profit from Dairy & Poultry business @ £7 per week	364. 0. 0
(22) Trespass on 150 acres of pasture land unable to use it. 150 head of cattle up to end of June (when I left the country) partly fattened	900. 0. 0
(23) Loss on sale of machinery which I had bought after all mine had been burnt (see answer 4)	165. 0. 0
(24) Loss on sale of 25 store cattle sold and taken away secretly by night owing to boycott	37. 0. 0
(25) Loss on sale of farm to Land Commission through inability to carry on from persecution. Was offered after burning £10,000 but sale was prohibited by local gunmen. Offer £10,000 @ received from Land Commission £4,817 (net sum)	5,183. 0. 0
(26) Two years supply of turf cut and dried, stolen.	40. 0. 0
Total Value of Losses	£11,469. 0. 0

Besides minor claims for lost earnings and alleged thefts, he also says he was unable to sow crops in 1922 as he was *"threatened and could not get anyone to work for me"* (20). He claims *"trespass"* on 150 acres in 1923 (22) and the resulting forced sale of stock and machinery below value (23, 24). The Committee found the stock and machinery had been auctioned and *"fair prices achieved."* The largest claim, £5,183 (Item 25), is the difference between the Land Commission price for the farm (£4,817) and the alleged offer for it (£10,000). The assessment of each claim by the Committee is given later below.

1st June 1927.

Dear Major White,

I have received your letter of the 24th of May in reference to the application of Mr. W. Pearson.

In the circumstances the Committee would certainly be prepared to hear Counsel in regard to this case, but as it was not received in this Office until the 25th of May it will be, I am afraid, some time before it can be considered, as, as far as possible, the Committee are taking cases in the order in which they have been received.

In an important case of this character it will be necessary for the claimant to submit some time prior to the final consideration of the claim such evidence as may be available in support of each item. I would suggest, to avoid subsequent delay, he should proceed to obtain such evidence forthwith. The prices claimed under most heads appear on a preliminary survey to be very high. In most of the

40. In its initial reply to Pearson's application, the Irish Grants Committee accepts Major White's request that Pearson employ council (Mr. L.R. Lipsett K.C.) but also stresses that *"In an important case of this character"* individual claims will need supporting evidence. *"The prices claimed under most heads appear on a preliminary survey to be very high."*

> **SOUTHERN IRISH LOYALISTS RELIEF ASSOCIATION**
> 12 PALMER STREET,
> WESTMINSTER, S.W.1
> (OPPOSITE WEST ENTRANCE)
> (ST. JAMES' PARK STATION)
>
> *[Stamp: IRISH OFFICE 13 JUN 1927]*
>
> 11th June, 1927.
>
> Major A. Reid Jamieson,
> Irish Grants Committee,
> 36, Old Queen Street, S.W.1.
>
> Dear Major Jamieson,
>
> Thank you for your letter - ref. No. 2376 - of the 1st inst. re the claim of Mr. J. Pearson.
>
> I note what you say that I have not followed my usual custom in submitting a certificate or general statement in support of the application. I think there must be some mistake as I am confident that I sent 2 or 3 letters generally supporting and confirming Mr. Pearson's statement. The reason I am so confident on this point is, that there was considerable delay in obtaining these certificates as the people concerned did not reply to my letter for some time, and the forwarding of the application was held up until I received these letters.
>
> I note what you say as to a general statement being advisable, and also that evidence would be required in support of each item. This will be a matter of some difficulty, as nearly all the people who were intimately acquainted with Mr. Pearson have either been forced to leave the country or have left as life had become impossible.
>
> I may say that I understand that Mr. Pearson's farm though divided up by the Land Commission is now for the most part derelict, the people who were placed on it having been unable to carry on.
>
> With regard to prices quoted. I would ask you to bear in mind that Mr. Pearson's farm was one of the best farms in Ireland, and Mr. Pearson was a skilled farmer and obtained higher and better yield from his land than most farmers did.
>
> Yours sincerely,
>
> *[signature]*

41. White responds (11th June): *"2 or 3"* letters *"generally supporting or confirming Mr Pearson's statement"* had been submitted (there is no evidence of these on file – Ed.); collecting evidence was difficult *"as nearly all the people who were intimately acquainted with Mr. Pearson have either been forced to leave the country or have left as life had become impossible"*. The farm *"was one of the best farms in Ireland"* and since its sub-division by the Land Commission, was *"derelict, the people who were placed on it having been unable to carry on."* This comes close to a classic tissue of lies.

> **SOUTHERN IRISH LOYALISTS RELIEF ASSOCIATION**
>
> VICTORIA 6699.
> 12, PALMER STREET,
> WESTMINSTER, S.W.1
> (OPPOSITE WEST ENTRANCE
> ST. JAMES' PARK STATION)
>
> [IRISH OFFICE — 8 JUL 1927]
>
> Reference 2376.
>
> July 27th., 1927.
>
> MAJOR REID JAMIESON,
>   Irish Grants Committee,
>   38, Old Queen Street,
>   S.W.1.
>
> Dear Major Jamieson,
>
>   Re the case of William Pearson.
>
>   I have your letter of the 26th. inst. dealing with this case. Last week I was present at a long interview which Mr. Lipett had with Mr. Pearson relative to his claim. I propose in due course to submit to you with a view of explaining and expanding as it was sent in to you with a few amendments to his claim certain points which that claim contains. Steps have already been taken to obtain more evidence in support of those items of the claim which can be supported by evidence. The farm was eventually sold to the Land Commission in 1923, but Mr. Pearson did not obtain payment until 1925. Mr. Pearson's family and himself were removed by the British authorities, subsequent to the truce, to Birr Barracks. Mrs. Pearson and family were then sent over to England and Mr. Pearson returned to the farm and lived in an out-house till 1923. During the period from August 1921 to July 1923 Mr. Pearson endeavoured to carry on his farm, but as you will observe from the statements he made, owing to the extreme boycott and persecution which he experienced, it was impossible for him to carry on normal farming, therefore he was obliged to sell.
>
>   I note your point about a competent valuer and I will communicate with Mr. Franks and convey your suggestion to him.
>
>   I shall be shortly forwarding to you a medical certificate of Mr. Pearson's present medical adviser which will set forth that that gentleman considers Mr. Pearson should leave this country and should live in a climate more suitable to his complaint - bronchitis. It is Mr. Pearson's intention as soon as his case has been heard by your Committee to leave England and proceed to Australia. I take it that your Committee will not be in a position to hear this case much before the latter end of September?
>
>   Yours sincerely,

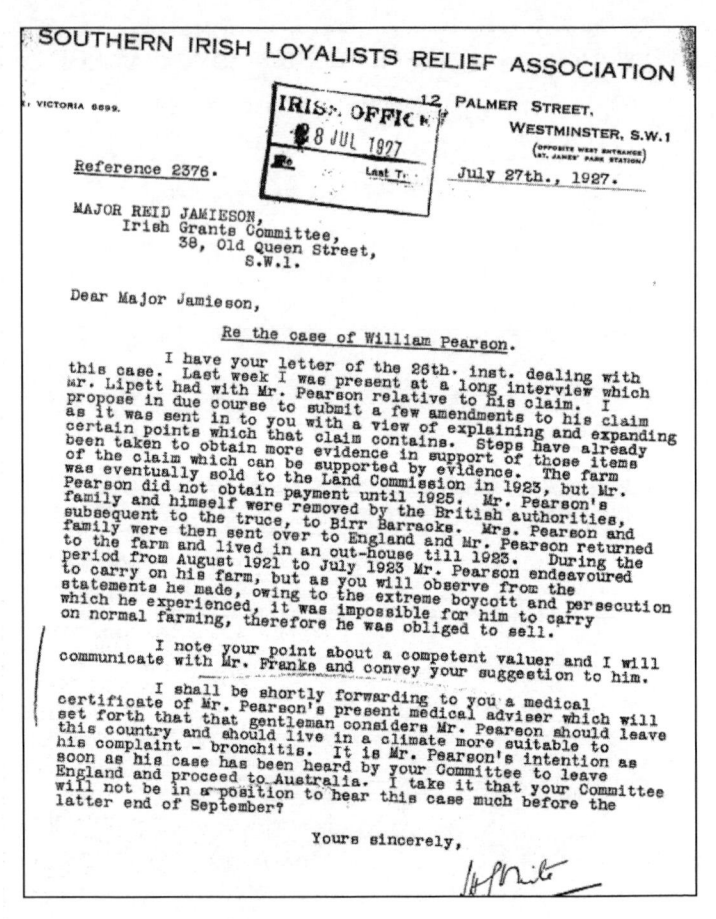

42. The correspondence betrays the scepticism of the Committee. On 14th June, Jamieson sought a meeting with White and Lipsett and, after the meeting he again wrote (26th July) seeking evidence and a valuer's assessment for the claims. He also asked if Pearson had stayed on the farm until it was sold. White replied *(above)* that after the Truce Pearson sent his family to England while he *"endeavoured to carry on his farm"*, living in an *"out-house"* from August 1921 to July 1923, but due to *"boycott and persecution"* this became impossible and *"he was obliged to sell."* He accepted the appointment of a valuer (Harry Franks).

> **SOUTHERN IRISH LOYALISTS RELIEF ASSOCIATION**
>
> 12 PALMER STREET,
> WESTMINSTER. S.W.1
> (OPPOSITE WEST ENTRANCE)
> (ST. JAMES' PARK STATION)
>
> PHONE: VICTORIA 6899.
>
> 25th January, 1928.
>
> Major A. Reid Jamieson,
> Irish Grants Committee.
>
> Dear Major Jamieson,
>
> re William Pearson. - Ref. No. 2376.
>
> This case which is to be heard on February 2nd has been the subject of correspondence between us. I now send you the following documents which have a direct bearing on Mr. Pearson's application:-
>
> "A". Original receipt from Land Commission for the payment of £1674. 0. 0.
>
> "B". Correspondence re sale of Mr. Pearsons farm.
>
> "C". Original letters re the offer received for his farm.
>
> "D". Medical Certificate concerning Mr. Pearson's health.
>
> The other information which you asked for some months ago, viz:- re the valuation of the farm, and re the approximate value of crops grown thereon has been given you by Mr. Franks.
> Will you please let me have back the original receipt from the Land Commission.
> I have instructed Mr. Pearson to be present on Feb. 2nd at 2-30 p.m., and with the permission of your Committee I propose to be present also.
> I understood from you a few days ago that you have informed Mr. Lipsett as to the date of hearing.
>
> May I call your attention to the state of Mr. Pearson's health. He has never got over the murder of his two sons, and the destruction of his home. Physically he is aged greatly and is in bad health; mentally he is not able to think quickly, and I would ask that due consideration be made by your Committee if he is called upon to answer questions.
>
> Yours sincerely,

43. On 25th January 1928 White finally submitted the additional documentation, and agreed that the report by Franks on the value of the farm and crops be sent directly to the Committee. The comments on Pearson's health in the last paragraph are special pleading. William Pearson, now aged 61, was of slight build. He suffered from asthma and emphysema and in fact had never undertaken the heavy physical work on the farm himself.

> **TELFORD & SONS,**
> Auctioneers and Valuers,
> Estate and Insurance Agents,
>
> *John's Mall,*
> *Birr,*
>
> 6th. Oct. 1927.
>
> Having an intimate knowledge of the lands of Coolacrease formerly in the occupation of Mr. William Pearson in my opinion the Meadows on said lands in the years 1921 and 1922 were worth £ 10. per acre and the interest in the holding previous to the burning of the residence was value for £ 17,000. or thereabouts.
>
> *M. L. Telford*

44. The documentation supplied by White included this note from Telford, a unionist auctioneer in Birr, claiming the *"meadows on said land"* (i.e. the best of it) was worth £10 per acre in 1921-22 (which would give a total value of max. £3,400) but with the *"interest in the holding"* the total value of the farm would be £17,000! Niamh Sammon used this note as "evidence" of the true value of the farm in the dispute before the Broadcasting Complaints Tribunal in 2008. The figure is nonsense. The farm had been purchased in 1911 for £2,000.

White also submitted a Medical Certificate signed by JS Lyons M.R.C.S. dated 29th Sept 1927: *"This is to certify that Mr. Pearson residing at Wallegrave Farm, Hartest is suffering from Asthma and Emphysema and is at present unable to follow occupation. Advised to leave England."*

> Regarding the sale of Coolacrease after the burning
> The Price I offered was £10,000 & I might have gone higher only the people would not allow any outsider to purchase the Lands I was not allowed to close the bargain
>
> William Percy
> Williamsfort
> Frankford
> Kings CO.

45. *Piéce de résistance:* White's letter of 25th January was accompanied by this (undated) note from William Percy of Frankford (Kilcormac) claiming that he had offered £10,000 for the Pearson farm and *"might have gone higher"* except for a local boycott. Pearson in his claim stated that the sale could not proceed because the priest would not permit Percy to purchase! It is a bogus claim. This price represents £29.3 an acre, a price not achieved for farms in Offaly until the 1950s. The note features prominently in the 'Hidden History' film and is quoted by Dr Doolay as *"evidence"* of both the real value of the farm and of an alleged boycott of its sale, claims refuted in this book.

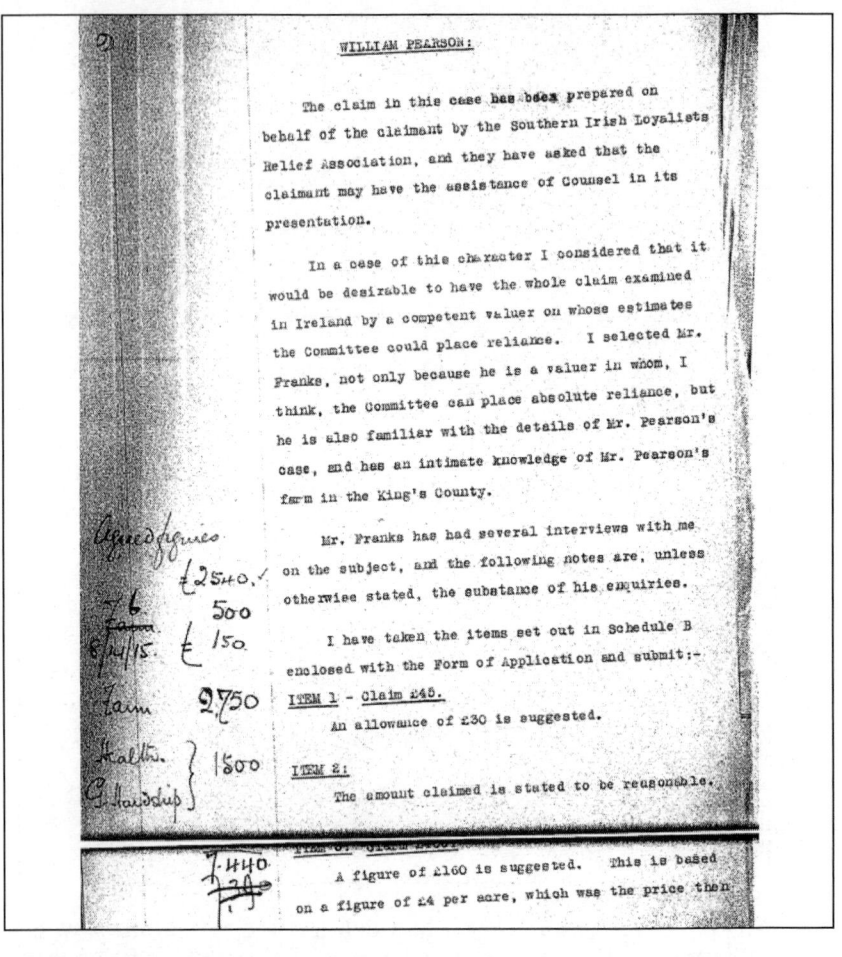

> WILLIAM PEARSON:
>
> The claim in this case has been prepared on behalf of the claimant by the Southern Irish Loyalists Relief Association, and they have asked that the claimant may have the assistance of Counsel in its presentation.
>
> In a case of this character I considered that it would be desirable to have the whole claim examined in Ireland by a competent valuer on whose estimates the Committee could place reliance. I selected Mr. Franks, not only because he is a valuer in whom, I think, the Committee can place absolute reliance, but he is also familiar with the details of Mr. Pearson's case, and has an intimate knowledge of Mr. Pearson's farm in the King's County.
>
> Mr. Franks has had several interviews with me on the subject, and the following notes are, unless otherwise stated, the substance of his enquiries.
>
> I have taken the items set out in Schedule B enclosed with the Form of Application and submit:-
>
> ITEM 1 - Claim £45.
> An allowance of £30 is suggested.
>
> ITEM 2:
> The amount claimed is stated to be reasonable.
>
> A figure of £160 is suggested. This is based on a figure of £4 per acre, which was the price then

46. Harry Franks of the Dublin-based 'Advisory Committee' for claims brought by the Southern Irish Loyalists Relief Association, was appointed to assess the Pearson claims. Jamieson compiled this report on the basis of Franks' assessment. Throughout the process, Franks wrote from the address of Rev. Weir in Mountrath – his colleague on the 'Advisory Committee' and the *"evangelical firebrand"* who previously supplied a reference for Sidney's claim (see Docs. 34-35). The *"Item"* numbers refer to corresponding *'Items'* in Schedule B of Pearson's claim, Doc. 41 above.

ruling in this District for meadows of this class.

ITEM 4 - Claim £180:

The figure of £118.10.0 is suggested. This figure is arrived at on an estimate that the grain would produce a profit of £66, and the straw if lost £52.10.0, and it is on the calculation that one acre of oats produced 10 barrels. Against this suggested figure, however, the claimant could perhaps have used the crop for the feeding of his own stock.

ITEMS 5, 6 & 7:

The amount claimed is considered reasonable, and indeed an undervaluation.

ITEM 8 - Claim £100:

It is suggested that this claim should be disallowed. The fields in question had been flooded every year since about 1885. There was no malicious damage as far as can be ascertained.

ITEM 9 - Claim £600:

The claim which is really one for increased cost of living and alternative accommodation appears excessive, but it is left for the Committee's consideration.

ITEMS 10 & 11:

From enquiries which have been made Mr. Franks is satisfied that these are fair claims.

Committee Secretary Jamieson – himself a southern Unionist who had worked with the Irish Office and Dublin Castle during the War in Ireland – endorses Franks' rejection of malicious flood damage and flattening of crops (8, 14,15) and finds many other claims excessive. Much reduced amounts are suggested for the claims accepted - mainly lost earnings from the farm not being worked at its previous intensity.

> ITEM 12 - Claim £1,850:
> An allowance of £240 is suggested. From Mr. Franks' knowledge of the land he considers that the maximum which the 150 acres would carry would be 80 head. Making allowance for produce and feeding of the cattle and £6 per head on the average, it is considered that a net profit on 150 acres would be reasonable at £240.
>
> ITEM 13 £225:
> The figure of £90 is suggested.
>
> ITEM 14 - Claim of £100:
> It is suggested that this item should be disallowed, and I refer to the remarks under Item 8.
>
> ITEM 15 - Claim £50:
> It is suggested that this item should be disallowed. There was no malicious damage to the river bank, and flooding has always taken place during wet seasons in this District.
>
> ITEM 16 - £33:
> This amount was in fact paid by the claimant.
>
> ITEM 17 - £30:
> An allowance of £10 is suggested.
>
> ITEM 18 - Claim £15:
> This claim is considered reasonable.
>
> ITEM 19 - Claim £220:
> It is considered that £5 per acre would be a *similar* allowance in view of Mr. Franks' knowledge of *smaller*

£1,850 (Claim 12) for profit cattle would have produced on 150 acres allegedly *"ruined by public trespass"* in 1922 is marked down to £240. Even this *"trespass"* claim is in fact demoted to loss of potential earnings. Many claims deemed *"reasonable"* are for small sums. A claim for a drainage fine (16) is rejected as Pearson had paid the fine to a Republican Court.

376

>   meadows, and the price was previously obtained
>   for this particular district. An allowance
>   of £110 is therefore suggested.
>
>   ITEMS 20 & 21:
>   The amounts claimed are considered reasonable.
>   Item 21 is based on the profit from 50 cows.
>
>   ITEM 22 - Claim of £900:
>   An allowance of £250 is suggested. The stock in question was sold by auction, and it is considered that on the whole fair prices were obtained.
>
>   ITEM 23 - Claim £165:
>   An allowance of £100 is suggested. The machinery was sold by auction and fair prices were obtained.
>
>   ITEM 24 - £37:
>   This claim is considered reasonable.
>
>   ITEM 25:
>   Evidence is produced that the claimant did have the offer of £10,000. Having been driven from the country the lands were acquired by the Irish Land Commission at a price of £4,817, and a loss through depreciation through being driven from Ireland of £5,183 is therefore claimed.

Prices achieved at auction in 1923 for livestock and machinery are considered *"fair prices"* and Pearson's claims rejected (22, 23). This refutes the story of local boycott. But the major claim (25) – that, as *"evidence produced"* showed the farm could achieve £10,000 at sale, the balance of £5,183 after deducting the Land Commission payment should be met – is not commented upon. This sum, about which the Committee is neutral, in fact forms the major financial element of the claim.

(1)	... ...	£30.
(2)	... ...	Fair.
(3)	... ...	£160.
(4)	Grain ... £66. 0. 0.)	
(5)	Straw if lost 52.10. 0.)	£118. 10. 0.
(6)	... ...	Fair.
(7)	... ...	Fair.
(8)	... ...	Fair.
(9)	... ...	Disallow.
(10)	... ...	No information.
(11)	... ...	Fair.
(12)	... ...	Fair.
(13)	... ...	£240. ✓
(14)	... ...	£90.
(15)	... ...	Disallow.
(16)	... ...	Disallow.
(17)	... ...	Fair.
(18)	... ...	£10.
(19)	... ...	Fair.
(20)	... ...	£110.
(21)	... ...	Fair.
(22)	... ...	Fair.
(23)	... ...	£250.
(24)	... ...	£100.
(25)	... ...	Fair.
(26)	... ...	No information.
		Fair.

Summary of the 26 claims: Twelve (all minor) were upheld by the Committee as *"fair"* and the others were summarily disallowed or accepted at much reduced values. But, as regards the largest claim – £5,183 for the balance on the alleged value of the farm – it adopted the "don't know" attitude of Franks and simply noted: *"No Information."* Yet this was to form the major element of the compensation.

> These observations refer to the detailed claim presented only, but this is a case to which considerable history attaches. It is undoubtedly a case of quite exceptional hardship, and the claimant since 1920 has suffered terrible persecution and annoyance, his property being burnt and destroyed, and his two sons murdered. After an examination of the detailed items the Committee may wish to consider this general question of hardship, more especially as no claim is included in the detailed items in respect of loss of the potential profits since the claimant was driven from Ireland.
>
> It does not, however, appear that the claimant is suffering any acute financial hardship. He has a good farm in this country, and in addition has an income from a sum of £6000 which he holds in the Bank
>
> This is a type of case on which certain general considerations apply, and these can no doubt best be discussed when the case has been presented.

Hand-written margin note: "As the result of the numerous outrages applic's wife is now almost an imbecile. The claimant himself is suffering from a complete breakdown & must leave England."

Pearson's claim could not be met on the basis of claimed losses, as these lacked credibility (his farm in Suffolk and £6,000 in the bank are also noted). Instead, because of the *"exceptional hardship"* and *"persecution"* endured, certain *"general considerations"* should apply. Jamieson doesn't specify these but writes *"these can no doubt best be discussed when the case has been presented."* Pearson was to be compensated not for losses but for "hardships" endured as a result of his active loyalty, the basis, after all, for claims to the Committee since it was reformed in October 1926.

Hand-written addition: *"As the result of the numerous outrages applic's wife is now almost imbecile. The claimant himself is suffering from a complete breakdown and must leave England."* Mrs Pearson lived throughout this period in England, and Pearson and his wife left in 1929 for Australia where they lived successfully. He died aged 72 in 1938 and she aged 74 in 1947.

47. Jameson records the Committee decision:

"The Committee heard the case on 2.2.28 when Mr Lipsett KC was acc[ompanied] *by claimant, Mr Franks and Major White. Committee consider that this is a case of exceptional hardship & should be noted as such. Case to be brought up later for sp*[ecia]*l consider*[ation]*. A recommendation of £7,500 [...illegible...]. This sum includes £60 costs & expenses £30 of which is to be for Mr. H Franks."*

The Dominions Office agreed and awarded £7,440 to Pearson, of which £4,864 was payable under its terms of reference (first £1,000 in full, and 60% on remaining sums above £1,000). A payment order for this amount was issued on 3rd March and a few days later the Grants Committee wrote that a further payment might be made.

The Committee reached its decision on the basis of *"exceptional hardship"* explained – presumably – at the (unrecorded) meeting with the claimant and not on the basis of the material claims made (most of which were rejected).

48. Drayson of the Dominions Office proposes acceptance of the Committee's recommendation, based on the story presented by Pearson: *"This is one of the most terrible cases of many bad ones which have come before the Dept. No summary would do justice to it. <u>The case is fully presented on the application form.</u> Applicant had for Ireland a large farm and claims that it was one of the best. Some compensation was received for pre-truce damage but nothing for his post-Truce sufferings and experiences. The Committee regard it as a case of exceptional hardship and recommends £7,500 which includes £60 for costs and expenses..."* [emphasis added – Ed.]. He suggests the remaining sum (£2,557) be paid. On the bottom of the document, a note signed by Under Secretary H. Batterbee agrees to the re-assessment.

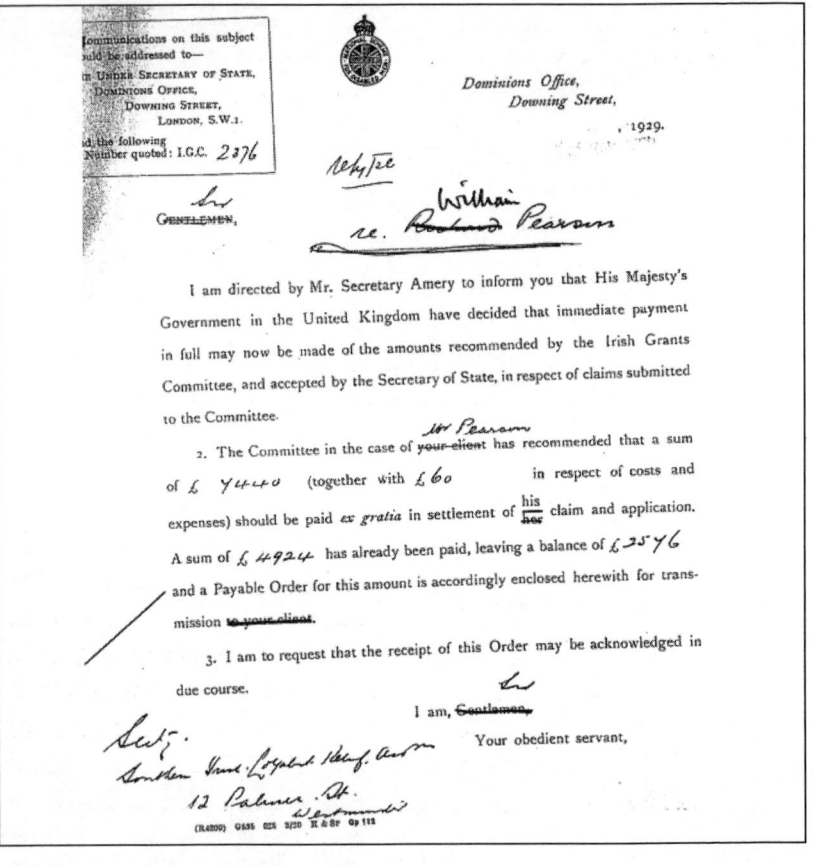

> Communications on this subject
> should be addressed to:—
> The UNDER SECRETARY OF STATE,
> DOMINIONS OFFICE,
> DOWNING STREET,
> LONDON, S.W.1.
> and the following
> Number quoted: I.G.C. 2376
>
> Dominions Office,
> Downing Street,
> , 1929.
>
> Reply/re
>
> GENTLEMEN, re. William Pearson
>
> I am directed by Mr. Secretary Amery to inform you that His Majesty's Government in the United Kingdom have decided that immediate payment in full may now be made of the amounts recommended by the Irish Grants Committee, and accepted by the Secretary of State, in respect of claims submitted to the Committee.
>
> 2. The Committee in the case of ~~your client~~ Mr Pearson has recommended that a sum of £ 7440 (together with £ 60 in respect of costs and expenses) should be paid *ex gratia* in settlement of ~~her~~ his claim and application. A sum of £ 4924 has already been paid, leaving a balance of £ 2576 and a Payable Order for this amount is accordingly enclosed herewith for transmission ~~to your client~~.
>
> 3. I am to request that the receipt of this Order may be acknowledged in due course.
>
> I am, ~~Gentlemen,~~
>
> Your obedient servant,

49. A change of policy was announced in the Lords on 1st March 1929 allowing 100% pay-out of awards (see above pp. 157-8) and the next day Under Secretary Batterbee directed the Pearson payment to be brought up to the full award (£7,440).

Later a member of the "Irish Situation Committee", Sir Harry Batterbee was a key figure confronting the De Valera government in the conflict which led to the Anglo-Irish Agreement of 1938 that finally established Irish sovereignty. His own former chief, J.H. Thomas, Amery's successor as Dominions Secretary, described Batterbee to the Irish diplomat John Dulanty as a *"reactionary"* on Ireland (*Documents on Irish Foreign Policy*, Dublin, RIA, 2006, Vol. 5, p. 315)

Appendix 7

On executions by popular resistance movements: Extract from *The Gadfly* by E.L. Voynich

Introduction

The most awful but fundamental aspect of war is killing, the killing of people. This is the basic business of soldiers, which no amount of dashing uniforms or glittering medals can hide, however much that is their purpose.

The basic fact of the Irish War of Independence is that it was a war launched *against* that independence. In the first election in British history held on the basis of a general franchise of the adult population in 1918, the Sinn Féin movement in Ireland presented itself to the electorate on a platform of abstaining from taking their seats at Westminister, constituting themselves, if elected, as a parliament in Ireland (Dáil Éireann) on the basis of the Republic of the 1916 Proclamation, and seeking international recognition for this Republic at the Peace Conference in Paris.

Sinn Féin won an overwhelming majority of the seats in that election and when the Dáil assembled in Dublin in January 1919 it implemented the mandate entrusted to it by the electorate. The British State responded by rejecting the outcome of the election and sending a massive armed force to Ireland to suppress the Dáil and its institutions. The Dáil called on the Irish Volunteers to defend the Republic against this military onslaught, and called on the people to rally to it. A mass resistance movement rapidly came into being, pledged by oath to defend the institutions of the Republic as determined by the democratic Dáil. The Volunteers – Óglaigh na hÉireann and Cumann na mBan – soon became known as the Irish Republican Army (IRA). Yet volunteers is what they were; armed citizens challenging the professional military might of the British Empire sent to crush the parliament elected by the people.

In the British war on the Irish democracy, the British forces were composed of the Royal Irish Constabulary re-organised as a paramilitary gendarmerie and massively reinforced by regular and irregular units of an army hardened in Britain's "Great War." Against this force was ranged the Irish resistance movement so disparaged by Niamh Sammon in her shameful "documentary" and by the chorus of journalists and commentators from *The Irish Times* and other journals and of chat show hosts from RTÉ who rallied to her cause.

The vast majority of Volunteers who rallied to defend the Republic established on the basis of the mandate of the 1918 election had never before held a gun in anger, let alone been hardened by the experience of a "Great War" of catastrophic proportions, or of the long history that preceded it of empire building and the policing of native populations. But they did it, no matter how unpleasant they feared the business of killing would be. There are numerous stories of men sickening at the moment of pulling a trigger at another man, either in combat or in the terrible up front experience of participating in a firing squad. Inexperienced volunteers will often fire to miss or wound – no-one wants to be the one who lands the fatal shot. In addition, most unnerving – as seems to have been the case in the Pearson execution - is the pride and defiance of the prisoners, at once both defenceless and proud, bravely facing their fate.

Just what it was like for volunteers of a popular resistance movement facing this predicament in a war against the forces of a great and militaristic empire was well captured in a 19th century novel – *The Gadfly* by E.L. Voynich. This was brought to our attention by a contributor to the *Indymedia* debate on the 'Hidden History' programme, a blogger who went by the pseudonym "Limerickman", in a contribution posted on 27th November 2007.

50. THE GADFLY, by E.L. Voynich

He stood and faced them, smiling, and the carbines shook in their hands. "I am quite ready," he said. The lieutenant stepped forward, trembling a little with excitement. He had never given the word of command for an execution before.

"Ready--present--fire!"

The Gadfly staggered a little and recovered his balance. One unsteady shot had grazed his cheek, and a little blood fell on to the white cravat. Another ball had struck him above the knee. When the smoke cleared away the soldiers looked and saw him smiling still and wiping the blood from his cheek with the mutilated hand

"A bad shot, men!" he said; and his voice cut in, clear and articulate, upon the dazed stupor of the wretched soldiers. "Have another try."

A general groan and shudder passed through the row of carabineers. Each man had aimed aside, with a secret hope that the death-shot would come from his neighbour's hand, not his; and there the Gadfly stood and smiled at them; they had only turned the execution into a butchery, and the whole ghastly business was to do again. They were seized with sudden terror, and, lowering their

carbines, listened hopelessly to the furious curses and reproaches of the officers, staring in dull horror at the man whom they had killed and who somehow was not dead. The Governor shook his fist in their faces, savagely shouting to them to stand in position, to present arms, to make haste and get the thing over. He had become as thoroughly demoralized as they were, and dared not look at the terrible figure that stood, and stood, and would not fall. When the Gadfly spoke to him he started and shuddered at the sound of the mocking voice.

"You have brought out the awkward squad this morning, colonel! Let me see if I can manage them better. Now, men! Hold your tool higher there, you to the left. Bless your heart, man, it's a carbine you've got in your hand, not a frying-pan! Are you all straight? Now then! Ready--present----"

385

"Fire!" the colonel interrupted, starting forward.

It was intolerable that this man should give the command for his own death. There was another confused, disorganized volley, and the line broke up into a knot of shivering figures, staring before them with wild eyes. One of the soldiers had not even discharged his carbine; he had flung it away, and crouched down, moaning under his breath: "I can't--I can't!" The smoke cleared slowly away, floating up into the glimmer of the early sunlight; and they saw that the Gadfly had fallen; and saw, too, that he was still not dead. For the first moment soldiers and officials stood as if they had been turned to stone, and watched the ghastly thing that writhed and struggled on the ground; then both doctor and colonel rushed forward with a cry, for he had dragged himself up on one knee and was still facing the soldiers, and still laughing.

"Another miss! Try--again, lads--see--if you can't----"
He suddenly swayed and fell over sideways on the grass.

"Is he dead?" the colonel asked under his breath; and the doctor, kneeling down, with a hand on the bloody shirt, answered softly:

"I think so--God be praised!"

"God be praised!" the colonel repeated. "At last!"
His nephew was touching him on the arm.

"Uncle! It's the Cardinal! He's at the gate and wants to come in."

"What? He can't come in--I won't have it! What are the guards about? Your Eminence----"

The gate had opened and shut, and Montanelli was standing in the courtyard, looking before him with still and awful eyes.

"Your Eminence! I must beg of you--this is not a fit sight for you! The execution is only just over; the body is not yet----"

"I have come to look at him," Montanelli said. Even at the moment it struck the Governor that his voice and bearing were those of a sleep-walker.

"Oh, my God!" one of the soldiers cried out suddenly; and the Governor glanced hastily back. Surely------ The blood-stained heap on the grass had once more begun to struggle and moan. The

doctor flung himself down and lifted the head upon his knee. "Make haste!" he cried in desperation. "You savages, make haste! Get it over, for God's sake! There's no bearing this!"
Great jets of blood poured over his hands, and the convulsions of the figure that he held in his arms shook him, too, from head to foot. As he looked frantically round for help, the priest bent over his shoulder and put a crucifix to the lips of the dying man.

"In the name of the Father and of the Son----"
The Gadfly raised himself against the doctor's knee, and, with wide-open eyes, looked straight upon the crucifix. Slowly, amid hushed and frozen stillness, he lifted the broken right hand and pushed away the image. There was a red smear across its face. "Padre--is your--God--satisfied?" His head fell back on the doctor's arm.. . . . . "Your Eminence!"

As the Cardinal did not awake from his stupor, Colonel Ferrari repeated, louder:

"Your Eminence!"
Montanelli looked up.

"He is dead."

"Quite dead, your Eminence. Will you not come away? This is a horrible sight."

"He is dead," Montanelli repeated, and looked down again at the face. "I touched him; and he is dead."

"What does he expect a man to be with half a dozen bullets in him?" the lieutenant whispered.

Appendix 8
A Note on the Debate in the Press

A debate on Coolacrease took place in the national and local press. The debate began with a piece by Eoghan Harris, 'This tree has rotten roots and bitter fruit', in the *Sunday Independent* of 23rd October 2005, accompanied by an article in the newspaper's magazine supplement by Alan Staney, 'I met murder on the way'. Various responses were published to this. The preparation of the Niamh Sammon "documentary" in the RTÉ 'Hidden History' series was first announced by Kevin Dawson at a slide show in Clontarf Castle on 30th May 2007 unambiguously as 'Atonement: Ethnic Cleansing in the Midlands.' The actual transmission of the programme as 'The Killings at Coolacrease' on 23rd October 2007 was accompanied by a series of tendentious articles in *The Irish Times* and *Sunday Independent* immediately before and after the programme, including by Niamh Sammon herself, Eoghan Harris, Ann Marie Hourihane, David Adams and Sarah Caden (the latter entitled 'Speak it in a whisper: Irish ethnic cleansing'). There followed heated exchanges in the press in succeeding weeks and below is a list of many of the contributions which appeared (full texts of all of this material are available at http://docs.indymedia.org/view/Main/CoolaCrease). We reproduce a few samples (indicated below with an asterisk *) from *The Irish Times*, the *Sunday Independent, Indymedia, History Ireland* and the RTÉ schedule announcements. By the time of the re-broadcast of the programme in on 15th May 2008, RTÉ in its description of the programme had adopted in full the sectarian language of the Harris-Sammon propaganda.

* Eoghan Harris, 'This tree has rotten roots and bitter fruit', *Sunday Independent*, 9/10/2005
   Alan Stanley, 'I met murder on the way', *Sunday Independent Life Magazine*, 9/10/2005

Paddy Heaney, letter, *Sunday Independent*, 23rd October 2005

Paddy Heaney, 'Coolacrease: A Place with a Tragic History', *Offaly Heritage Journal*, Vol. 4 (2006), pp. 220-225

Pat Muldowney, *The Pearson Executions in Co. Offaly: a debate on alleged sectarianism during the War of Independence*, Aubane Historical Society, 2007

Philip McConway, *Spies, Informers and Militant Loyalists: The Intelligence War in Offaly 1920-21,* Public Lecture organised by the Offaly Historical & Archaeological Society at Bury Quay, Tullamore on 15/1/2007.

* RTÉ: Autumn 2007 Schedules (with slide show of 30th May 2007)

Correspondence, Jack Lane, Aubane Historical Society, and Niamh Sammon, July 2007

Pat Muldowney, 'RTÉ's Hidden History Documentary on the Pearson Executions - Atonement: Ethnic Cleansing in the Midlands', *Irish Political Review,* August 2007

'RTÉ to expose Old IRA', *Phoenix Magazine,* 5/10/2007

* Niamh Sammon, 'A true history of violence', *The Irish Times,* 20/10/07

Pierce Martin, Celbridge, Co Kildare, 'Time for honesty about our past', letter, *Sunday Independent,*18/11/07

Sarah Caden, 'Speak it in a whisper: Irish ethnic cleansing', *Sunday Independent,* 21/10/07

Ann Marie Hourihane, 'We are still hiding from our history', *The Irish Times,* 25/10/07

Pat Muldowney, 'The Killings at Coolacrease', *Village Magazine,* 26/10/07

Emmanuel Kehoe, 'When History and hearsay collide', *Sunday Business Post,* 28/10/07

Eoghan Harris, 'Having a ball -- having two balls in the Senate', *Sunday Independent,* October 28 2007

D. Kelly, 'The Killings at Coolacrease', Letters, *The Irish Times,* 31/10/07

'The Killings at Coolacrease', Letters from Daithí Ó hAilbhe and Niall Ginty, Dublin, *The Irish Times,* 2/11/07

Jan Battles, 'RTÉ in the firing line over IRA execution film', *Sunday Times,* 4/11/07

'The Killings at Coolacrease', Letters from Gerard Hayden, Tullamore (formerly of Coolacrease), Noel Flannery, Limerick, and Niall Meehan, Dublin, *The Irish Times,* 5/11/07

Ann Marie Hourihane, 'Sensitive strands of our history', *The Irish Times,* 8/11/07

* David Adams, 'Diehards reveal true colours', *The Irish Times,* 9/11/07

Eoghan Harris, 'Why bodies buried deep in the green bog must be raised', *Sunday Independent,* 11/11/07

* John Martin, 'Disarray', article posted on *Indymedi,* 11/11/07

Philip McConway, 'The Pearsons of Coolacrease', *Tullamore Tribune,* 7 & 14/11/07

Eoghan Harris, 'Denials do more damage than the original crime', *Sunday Independent,* 18/11/07

Philip McConway, 'The Killings at Coolacrease', letters, *Western People,* 14/11/07

'Muddying the waters on deaths', letters from Pierce Martin, Pat Muldowney, Philip McConway, *Sunday Independent,* 18/11/07

'The killings at Coolacrease', Niamh Sammon, letters, *The Irish Times,* 14/11/07

'Unfounded claims about killings - RTÉ doing us a great service', Niamh Sammon, Brendan Cafferty, letters, *Sunday Independent,* 25/11/07

'The killings at Coolacrease', Pat Muldowney, letter, *The Irish Times,* 27/11/07

* Pat Muldowney, 'Evidence excluded from Pearsons programme: The Pearson brothers sided with the British and forfeited their civilian status', *The Irish Times,* 27/11/07

'Limerickman', 'Preview of a letter to Ms Sammon', with text of 'The Gadfly' by E.L.Voynich, *Indymedia,* 27/11/07

'Pearsons of Coolacrease' – letters from Brendan Cafferty, Paddy Heaney, Pat Muldowney, Sean Lyons, *Tullamore Tribune,* 28/11/07

'Protestants whose actions give the lie to the "sectarian war" theory', Dr Brian P Murphy osb, Glenstal Abbey, Murroe, Co Limerick, letter, *Irish Examiner,* 3/12/07

'Airing Protestant voices', Dr Brian P Murphy osb, Glenastal Abbey, Murroe, Co Limerick, letter, *Sunday Independent,* 9/12/07

'Pearson brothers killed a week after siblings attacked an IRA roadblock', Paddy Heaney, *Midlands Tribune,* ../12/07

* Tommy Graham. Editorial – 'Let's hear him deny it', *History Ireland,* vol. 16, no. 1, Jan-Feb 2008

* Brian Hanley, 'Platform', *History Ireland,* vol. 16, no. 1, Jan-Feb 2008

Book Review: Brendan Ó Cathaoir on *Rising Out: Seán Connolly of Longford* by Ernie O'Malley, *The Irish Times,* Dr Martin Mansergh TD, 'Hidden History debate casts light into some dark corners', *Irish Examiner,* 7/01/08

Jack Lane, 'Coolacrease – Mistaken Identity?', *Indymedia,* 9/01/08

'The Ultimate Taboo: War or Democracy', Pat Muldowney, letters, *Irish Examiner,* 21/01/08

'Sectarian or not? Presbyterian view of IRA actions in War of Independence', Brendan Cafferty, Jack Lane, letters, *Irish Examiner,* 21/01/08

* RTÉ Website Announcement: Summer 2008 Schedules, February 2008

51. Eoghan Harris, 'This tree has rotten roots and bitter fruit' *Sunday Independent,* 9/10/2005

THE story Alan Stanley tells in Life magazine today touches a raw nerve in the Irish Republic. Based on his self-published book, *I Met Murder on the Way,* he tells how in June 1921, shortly before the Truce, an IRA gang descended on a defenceless Protestant farm family, the Pearsons of Coolacrease, Co Offaly, and carried out an appalling atrocity. Alan's account asks awkward questions, not just of Roman Catholic nationalists, but of those who call themselves Protestant republicans. But first let me say why the story affected me so deeply at a personal level. The Pearsons of Coolacrease belonged to a small Protestant sect called the Cooneyites, whom Alan Stanly aptly compares to the Amish of Pennsylvania. Many years ago in Cork I knew such a Cooneyite family.

Back in the fifties, as a boy, I worked for my father in his small wholesale grocery business in James St. This was before the days of cash and carry and there were few personal callers to break the monotony. So I well remember the rainy day when I was packing tea and looked up to see I was not alone. Standing patiently inside the draughty door, waiting for me to finish my task, were a small family of what I would have called country people. But these figures seemed from a far-off time: a tall angular man with a short beard in a plain black coat, a tall handsome woman in a brown bonnet and a long brown coat that almost touched the ground, a young girl, my age, with blue woollen gloves, blue coat, and plain black buttoned shoes, whose modest gaze could not disguise her delight at the rare treat of being up in town. Later my father told me they were called Cooneyites. I have never forgotten their aura of invincible innocence. It was the start of my life-long respect for low-church Protestants. Tildy Pearson would have looked like the girl with the gloves whom I saw in my father's store so many years ago, and who thanked me with a sweetness which still breathes its benediction after almost 50 years.

To attack a family like that calls to high heaven for atonement. Alan Stanley's book helps make historical amends, not only to the Pearsons, but to the 50,000 Protestants who were bullied, frightened and burned out of their modest farms, both before and after the Truce, and whose story has been suppressed by nationalists. And thereby hangs a complex tale.

First a few facts. Between 1911 and 1925 the number of Protestants in the South fell by a massive 34 per cent with a sharp peak between 1920-24 when about 10,000 Protestants left Ireland. In his forthcoming book, with the appropriate working title Buried Lives, Robin Bury has factored in the deaths of World War One and those who left with the British garrison. That still leaves 50,000 Irish Protestants, modest artisans, small farmers and shopkeepers, run out of the country. This may have encouraged the emigration of some 10,000 Protestant artisans from Dublin. Among those who left were Pearsons of Coolacrease.

Naturally you will have no trouble figuring out why Southern nationalists might not want to hear about these tribal intimidations by the IRA. These stories subvert our smug assumption that the only sectarians are Loyalist sectarians. But the Pearson atrocity was not an isolated incident but part of a persistent pattern of persecution, intimidation and murder - what might charitably be called "erratic ethnic cleansing". Increasingly, in my experience, Roman Catholic nationalists can cope with these truths. Admittedly a minority of mad nationalists, still believe that admitting these atrocities gives 'ammunition' to Paisley & Co. Actually the opposite is true. Northern unionists are always relieved when Southerners admit to such atrocities. It means that we have no hidden agendas.

But what is truly amazing is the sort of well-heeled Southern Protestant who will claim to be speaking in the name of ecumenism or the peace process or whatever they believe will go down well with people in certain circles. Actually most Dublin Protestants don't know anything about the atrocities against their rural co-religionists in places like Cork, Carlow and Longford. And most don't want these tragedies dragged up because it is socially inconvenient. But their cowardly desires do not close the case. As Yeats says, buried men thrust their way back into the public mind. Besides, many rural Roman Catholics well remember secrets whispered at home. The Pearsons suffered in silence. So did thousands of Protestants in modest circumstances. And I have a hunch that the persistent self-suppression of this dark history and the policy of keeping the head down must have done some damage to the Southern Protestant psyche.

Martin Mansergh has some title to being the top Southern Protestant in denial. And it has left its mark. Last week, in his *Irish Times* column, he said something which pins down the peculiar psychology of many Southern republican Protestants. "The grounds of my family home in Tipperary, let when my father was young, was the scene of the murder in 1931 of Garda Supt Curtin, who had allegedly threatened some local volunteers with the law. This led to the introduction of draconian legislation in the final months of the Cosgrave administration in 1931 and to a split in the Labour Party. A faded cross on the wall by the gate marks the spot. Close by, I have planted a beech tree, given to me five years agoby Gerry Adams, as a 'Tree of Peace'." This makes me sick for three reasons. First, the bad politics of the phrase about the "draconian legislation" of the Cosgrave government. Second, the repugnant spectacle of a republican Protestant planting a tree given him by Gerry

Adams. Third, because it provides a rotten role model for any young Protestant Irishman.

Let me, from my Roman Catholic nationalist background, put the matter simply. The Pearsons family did not deserve what was done to them, and neither did the 50,000 artisans and farmers who were driven out of their homes and across the world. Facing our tribal past helps us understand the fears of Northern Protestants - and is good for our souls. That is why I reject the right of posh Protestants to plant some green plastic Tree of Liberty with Gerry Adams. Any such tree is rotten to the roots and will bear only bitter fruit. Peace starts with a prayer for the Pearson boys.

52. RTÉ Announcement, Autumn 2007 Schedules

> **Factual** Programmes
>
> Commissioning Editor: Kevin Dawson
>
> Clontarf Castle Open Day
>
> May 30 2007
>
> **History:** new commissions
>
> - **Churchill v de Valera** – face-off over 4 decades
> - **Collins & The Castle** – espionage and secret deals
> - **The Catalpa Rescue** - Drama-Doc co-pro
> - **Fenian Fire** – a plot to kill Queen Victoria
> - **William Martin Murphy:** hate figure of the 1913 Lockout
> - **Atonement:** ethnic cleansing in the midlands in 1922
> - **Historians:** Who Writes our History?
>
> **RTÉ Television**

'*Atonement: Ethnic Cleansing in the Midlands*': from the slide presentation by Kevin Dawson, RTÉ 'Head of Factual Programmes', announcing the Coolacrease "documentary," Clontarf Castle, 30th May 2007

RTÉ Website Announcement, Autumn 2007 Schedules:
http://tvsales.rte.ie/autumn/content/factual/hidden-history.html

The Coolacrease Killings

The bloody tale of a bitter land dispute, involving a family of Protestant farmers in County Offally, which comes to a deadly conclusion during the War of Independence. Featuring interviews with descendants of the men who carried out the killings, this portrait of a forgotten atrocity features substantial newspaper archive research, IRA witness statements and military documents from the period.

HIDDEN HISTORY Guns and Neighbours | The Killings at Coolacrease RTÉ One The bloody tale of a bitter land dispute, involving a family of Protestant farmers in County Offaly, which comes to a deadly conclusion during the War of Independence. Featuring interviews with descendants of the men who carried out the killings, this portrait of a forgotten atrocity features substantial newspaper archive research, IRA witness statements and military documents from the period.

Broadcast October 23 2007

53. Niamh Sammon, 'A true history of violence' *The Irish Times*, 20/10/07

A brutal crime just before the end of the War of Independence hints at the darker side of the conflict, writes Niamh Sammon

No doubt June 30th, 1921, began like any other for the Pearson family of Coolacrease, Co Offaly. Life on that day would have revolved around the usual farm chores, but today, there was an extra task at hand. With the sun in the sky, two sons of the family, Richard (24) and Abraham (19), and a friend of theirs, William Stanley, were saving the hay, determined to make the most of the good weather.

Late in the afternoon, Stanley looked up from his work to see a gang of armed IRA men converging on the hayfield from all sides. He knew something terrible was coming, and yelled to Richard and Abraham to run for their lives. He then ran himself, a stumbling desperate bid for survival, but looking back over his shoulder, he saw the Pearson boys rooted to the spot.

Within the hour, the Pearson women were driven from their home, which in turn was burned to the ground. As the house blazed, they saw Richard and Abraham lined up and shot - their father William and another brother Sidney, would have met with the same fate, had they not been away that day. Mrs Pearson and her daughters nursed Richard and Abraham for many hours as they slowly bled to death.

All of this happened just seven days before the truce ended all hostilities in the War of Independence. The fighting stopped, but a question remained: what had this family done to deserve such a dreadful retribution? The Pearsons were members of a peaceable, non- political, dissenting Protestant sect known as the Cooneyites, and their attackers were drawn from the local Catholic community. These were their friends and neighbours; people they must have greeted on the roads around Cadamstown, lads who'd sat with them at school. What forces had changed these friends into the enemies who came to their home, burned it to the ground, and shot them in a brutal manner as their helpless mother and sisters looked on?

These are the questions that leaped out at me just over a year ago when a friend gave me a book by Alan Stanley, the son of William Stanley who'd escaped with his life that day. Alan had written a powerful account of the single most defining event in his family's history. He told how, after the killings at Coolacrease House, the Pearsons fled to Australia, and of his own search to trace their descendants. In this slim volume, Stanley published his correspondence with the Australian Pearsons, who were desperate to try and understand how the country of their forebears had turned so violently against them.

The story he had unravelled was the starting point of the journey toward making a television documentary about the truly hidden history of what happened at Coolacrease. It seemed that this was the kind of history you don't learn about in school and, notwithstanding Ken Loach's film dramatisation of the period in The Wind that Shakes the Barley, here was proof of a much darker side to the republican fight for independence. They say that the victor writes the history, but was that as true in Ireland as elsewhere?

COOLACREASE IS THE townland, in the foothills of the Slieve Bloom mountains, where the Pearsons had lived and farmed the land. Even today, it's a place apart. Travel through the Slieve Bloom mountains and you won't meet a soul.

It's just outside the commuter belt, and despite its pastoral beauty, definitely off the tourist trail. Nothing remains now of the Pearson's presence apart from the ivy-choked ruin of their former home. Yet for the older generation in Cadamstown, ruined walls are unnecessary to remind them of the events of June 1921. It's a story they would have heard in childhood; it would have been whispered by adults when they thought no children were listening.

When we went knocking on doors in the area, however, nobody wanted to talk. This event took place 86 years ago, before telephones and 24-7 perma-communication, yet, even now in our confessional era of blogs and memoirs, a veil of silence continues to shroud that summer's day long ago. It was hard to understand. Older members of my own family, though, could venture a compelling explanation. People didn't want to talk about Coolacrease because for them this story was not about folk memory or history or sectarianism; it was about protecting the reputations of their fathers and uncles. The memory of the dead generation was at stake. That old adage "Blood will out" had more than one meaning in Cadamstown.

Eventually, some people agreed to talk, but only on the understanding that their identities would not be revealed. More than one person said that they wouldn't be able to live in the area if it was known they had co-operated with the documentary. During a previous life as a TV news producer, I'd heard such words plenty of times, in Belfast,
in Derry - it was amazing to hear those same caveats aired in the south of Ireland in 2007. And it was more surprising still when an old man made it his business to let our camera crew know "You could get shot for asking those kind of questions."

But in the end, some people did talk on camera. What emerged quite strongly was the stark division within the community of Cadamstown over the events of that day in June 1921. Some believe the Pearsons were innocent victims targeted purely for their land. The two boys had been killed at a time of great land hunger and that hunger was
keenly felt in Offaly, where good farmland was hard to come by. The attack on the family was, some argue, merely a land grab, perpetrated by men desperate to get their strike in before the war came to an end. Others dispute this, claiming the Pearsons were "spies and informers" who collaborated with the Black and Tans, and who ultimately got what they deserved.

Just two months after the events of June 1921, an advertisement for the auction of Coolacrease appeared in The Irish Times. It described a farm "of excellent quality, sound and healthy for all kinds of stock, and well known in the locality for its dairy and fattening qualities".

Tellingly, and because Coolacrease House was now no more than a scorched ruin, the ad delicately states that "the site for the residence is situated on a well timbered lawn, and is approached by an avenue". Like the Pearsons, many Protestant families at this time were torn from their roots and forced out.

Many scattered to the new world to escape the old, and their stories have silently mouldered among hundreds of files at the British National Archives in Kew. But the files are there - preserved, indelible - and they reveal some uncomfortable truths long forgotten in the victor's version of the past.

54. David Adams, 'Diehards reveal true colours' *The Irish Times* 9/11/07

Programme reflected maturity of a State able to deal honestly with its own past

The amateur historian in Ireland is often little more than a propagandist masquerading as an expert. Such was the case with RTÉ's *Hidden History – The Killings at Coolacrease* (broadcast on October 23rd) about the brutal murder by the IRA of two young Protestant brothers, Richard (24) and Abraham Pearson (19), at their farm in Co. Offaly in 1921. This meticulously researched and studiously even-handed documentary benefited enormously, if inadvertently, from the contributions of a couple of local historians determined to lend post-dated justification to what was clearly a sectarian, land-grabbing atrocity.

Ludicrous claims delivered in blank-faced fashion, complete with pseudo-military jargon, juxtaposed perfectly with dignified contributions by descendants of the deceased to give a vivid illustration of fanaticism and people's ability to fool themselves into believing almost anything. In a magnificent display of the power of wishful thinking, one of the apologists claimed it was "impossible" for any member of the Offaly IRA to have been an informer.

The other has claimed that his research has been deliberately played down by the programme makers. Perhaps, for reasons obvious to everyone but himself, RTÉ thought it best to rely upon professional historians and their own impartial research team. The only thing worse in the historical field than an enthusiastic amateur with an axe to grind, is a collection of them pursuing a common agenda.

By screening *The Killings at Coolacrease*, both RTÉ and the producer, Niamh Sammon, reflected perfectly the maturity of a State now prepared to deal openly and honestly with its past. Despite this, or maybe because of it, since the screening of the programme, there has been an orchestrated campaign of complaint directed at politicians, RTÉ, individual journalists, newspapers and various other media outlets. Many of those involved appear to have connections with the Aubane Historical Society and/or the *Irish Political Review*.

These groups previously gained some prominence when, at different times, they declared Elizabeth Bowen not to be an Irish author, instigated a vicious little spat with (then senator) Martin Mansergh TD, and suggested that this newspaper was a tool of the British government. Their complaints accusations then, as now, stand up to no examination.

Were the Pearson brothers shot in the groin or genitals? What does it matter? The real question is, if it wasn't deliberate, how did so many gunmen (about 30) manage to shoot the men only in their lower abdomens? This can only be interpreted as a brutal comment on Protestant procreation, and a deliberate attempt to cause an agonising death. They succeeded in the latter; Richard Pearson took six hours to die, and his brother Abraham 14.

Were the Pearson women forced to watch the murders or, ever so chivalrously, taken to the rear of the farmhouse? Ethel Pearson, one of the sisters, claimed only days after the atrocity that she, her mother and sisters were made to watch the shootings. Against this, an IRA man claimed they were taken behind the house. Given the perverse brutality on display that day, it isn't hard to decide which version is more believable.

Did an RIC investigation conclude that the double murder was revenge for the shooting of two IRA men who had previously been found felling a tree on Pearson land? Most emphatically, it did not. There was no RIC investigation, merely a written report from the police to a Court of Enquiry, which outlined rumours circulating after the murders.

The report mentioned land acquisition and revenge by Sinn Féin as rumoured motives. Indeed, there is still a belief locally that preceding the murders an IRA man was accidentally killed by one of his own comrades.

Were the Pearsons ever proved to be British agents? No, in fact the evidence points in the opposite direction. A surviving brother, Sidney

399

Pearson, was turned down for compensation for the loss of the family farm precisely because he could not prove his allegiance to the Crown. Later, on advice from the Southern Irish Relief association, and with nothing left to lose as his family was fleeing Ireland anyway, William Pearson (the father) grossly exaggerated his loyalty in order to achieve a paltry £7,500 in compensation for his 340-acre farm.

What reasonable person could not imagine themselves doing precisely the same thing in those circumstances? The Aubane Historical Society, their friends and fellow-travellers must surely realise all of the above. Their campaign seems designed merely to sow doubt, create confusion and muddy the waters around the Coolacrease murders. If they are lucky, it might have the effect of ensuring that no other such programmes are made.

Journalists might well decide that forensic examination of countless similar atrocities isn't worth the trouble. Such capitulation would be a huge mistake. History deniers should never be pandered to.

55. John Martin (*Irish Political Review*), 'Disarray' *Indymedia* , 11/11/2007

If anyone doubts the disarray of the defenders of the Coolacrease documentary, they only need to read Eoghan Harris's diary in today's Sunday Independent. It seems his whole week has been dominated by the Coolacrease documentary, but he is incapable of dealing with any of the issues raised.

He talks about Pat Muldowney, the Aubane Historical Society, Athol Books, the Irish Political Review, a conversation with David Norris re: Phillip McConway, extensive quotes from David Adams's article in The Irish Times, the killings in Bandon, Peter Hart etc etc. But no engagement with the issues raised by the Coolacrease documentary.

This follows his hysterical rant ("holocaust deniers", "liars" etc) on Monday's Live Line.

He has failed to produce any evidence supporting his allegations that the killings were about ethnic cleansing, a land grab or sectarianism.

He and for that matter David Adams are at their most embarrassing when they accuse the IRA volunteers of shooting at the Pearsons' genitals.

How is it that even the propaganda department in Dublin Castle didn't spot this? Were they "keeping their heads down" as well? How is it that no contemporary source in 1921 can be found to support Harris/Adams's lurid allegation that the IRA volunteers deliberately shot the Pearsons in the genitals (and missed) so as to send a message re: Protestant reproduction per David Adams.

But David Adams in The Irish Times plunged to the very depths when he suggested that locals believe that the IRA shot themselves.

We now have a situation where the loyalist apologist Alan Stanley accepts that the Pearsons' fired a shot. He says that the shot was fired in the air. David Adams, on the other hand, implies that the Pearson's didn't fire a shot at all but accepts that an IRA man was injured.

It would be nice if the defenders of the Hidden History documentary could get their stories straight!

56. Pat Muldowney, 'Evidence excluded from Pearsons programme', *The Irish Times,* 27/11/2007

The principal problem with RTÉ's controversial Hidden History documentary broadcast on October 23rd was its failure to mention the British Military Court of Enquiry in Lieu of Inquest into the deaths of the Pearson brothers, Richard and Abraham.

This inquiry is the best single source of hard evidence about what actually happened and why it happened. But nobody who watched the programme was given the slightest inkling of such an inquiry.

The British inquiry was held in Crinkle Military Barracks, Birr, Co Offaly, on July 2nd, 1921, the second day after the men's deaths.

It took sworn evidence from doctors and eye-witnesses and the papers include a high-level police report stating the result of the RIC investigation of the episode: "It is said by the C I [county inspector] Queen's County that the two Pearson boys a few days previously had seen two men felling a tree on their land adjoining the road. Had told the men concerned to go away and when they refused had fetched two guns and fired and wounded two Sinn Féiners, one of whom it is believed died."

Compare this with the Irish military report sent to GHQ by the responsible officer Thomas Burke: "C Coy (Kinnity) 3rd Battalion reported to me on 26/6/21 that some of their men have been fired on a few nights previously, whilst engaged in a road blockade operation, by three men armed with shotguns. As a result one of their men was somewhat seriously wounded. The men who fired were recognised by the men present to be three brothers named Pearson.

"Having satisfied myself by inquiries from Coy Capt, Kinnity, and officers present at battalion council, that there was no doubt about the identity of the men who fired, I ordered that these men be executed and their houses destroyed."

This could hardly be clearer. Authoritative investigations on behalf of both the elected Irish government and the British military government reported that the Pearsons had, in effect, forfeited civilian status in becoming armed combatants on the side of the unelected imperial power.

This does not lessen the tragedy for the Pearson family who had no personal responsibility for starting this war, no more than any other person in Ireland, of whatever persuasion; a great many of whom suffered dreadfully. But it puts into perspective the statement in the Hidden History programme: "There was no official investigation into what actually happened that night."

And it puts into perspective the mass of flimsy, dubious and unsupported speculation in the documentary about motives of sectarianism, land-grabbing and possible punishment for the lesser offence of spying. Informing by non-combatants assists combatants to attack and attempt to kill combatants of the other side.

Combatants put their lives on the line. The Pearsons had become combatants. Both the Irish and British authorities were agreed on this.

The British military court of inquiry evidence puts paid to inflammatory assertions made by Eoghan Harris in the programme that the brothers were shot deliberately in the genitals, in an act of sectarian hatred. There were no injuries to the genitals.

Dr FW Woods examined Richard Pearson and found a superficial wound in the left shoulder; a deep but not life-threatening wound in the right groin (which is farther from the genitals than an ear lobe is from the brain); another in the right buttock; superficial wounds in the left lower leg; and about six glancing wounds in the back.

Lt Col CR Woods RAMC (an army doctor) examined Abraham Pearson and found extensive wounds on left cheek, left shoulder, left thigh and lower third of left leg. In addition there was a wound through the abdomen.

As to the second atrocity allegation, that the men's mother and sisters were forced to watch the men being shot, here is what Ethel Pearson told the court: "My mother who was in a fainting condition was carried by my two brothers into a little wood we call the grove and we all went with her by the order of the raiders.

"Six of the raiders, two or three of whom were masked, ordered my brothers down into the yard."

The grove has been grubbed out, but is clearly marked in the Ordnance Survey maps, which also prove that it is not physically possible for anyone located inside the grove to see into the enclosed, walled courtyard where the two brothers were shot.

The Pearson execution was no war crime, no act of ethnic cleansing, and no land grab. It was an incident in the war forced on the Irish electorate by the imperial government's determination to suppress the democratic government formed on foot of the 1918 general election and confirmed in office by further elections in 1920 and 1921.

57. Tommy Graham, Editorial, 'Let's hear him deny it', *History Ireland,* vol. 16, no. 1, Jan-Feb 2008

RTÉ is to be congratulated for its recent Hidden History series. In general these were a model of how to present sometimes complex (and controversial) subjects to a wider public. Thus, William Martin Murphy, while not quite shaking off his well-deserved image as the 'villain' of the 1913 Dublin Lockout, was also presented as the remarkable international entrepreneur that he was (See 'TV Eye', pp. 50-1, in this issue). Readers of Owen McGee's two 'sources' articles in the last two issues (*HI* 15.5, Sept./Oct. 2007, pp. 44-9; *HI* 15.6, Nov./Dec. 2007, pp. 36-41) on recently released British secret service papers will have profited greatly from the programme on the alleged Fenian plot to assassinate Queen Victoria, one of several labyrinthine *provocateur* plots hatched by elements within the British secret service itself.

He concluding documentary in particular, 'Making History', which summed up the debate over the past generation on 'revisionism' and developments in Irish historiography, did great public service. While many in the profession, and possibly some long-standing readers of History Ireland (we have tracked this debate closely over the years), may have found the programme 'old hat', there is no doubting its appeal for the wider viewing public.

Inevitably, where the programmes were commissioned from independent production companies, there was a certain unevenness. The one on the *Catalpa* managed to make an inherently exciting topic (the rescue of Fenian prisoners from Freemantle, Western Australia, in 1876) seem a bit dull (in stark contrast, for example, to Donal O'Kelly's amazing one-man theatrical treatment of the incident, first staged in 1995). Such a criticism, however, may simply be a matter of personal taste.

'The Killings at Coolacrease' is a different matter entirely. (See 'Platform' opposite). On the face of it this was an excellent topic, a truly 'hidden history'. What we got instead was a textbook (and brilliant) exercise in media spin, where the 'line' of the programme – that this was an incidence of ethnic cleansing carried out for sectarian and/or land-grabbing motives in a deliberately sadistic manner involving sexual mutilation – was taken up by other branches of the media and a predictably ill-informed and emotive 'debate' ensued. This is like the apocryphal story of the politician who, when asked to comment on an allegation that he had made against an opponent, agreed that it was untrue but added: 'Let's hear him deny it'. Such was the nature of the limited opportunities afforded to those critical of the documentary's general line. The programme-makers can congratulate themselves on conjuring up a media will-o'-the-wisp but it is doubtful whether they have made any long-term contribution to scholarship on this sensitive issue.

58. Brian Hanley, 'Platform', *History Ireland,* vol. 16, no. 1, Jan-Feb 2008

November's Hidden History documentary on the killing of the Pearson brothers, Richard and Abraham, at Coolacrease, Co. Offaly, in June 1921 struck a raw nerve. The subsequent comment in the press, radio and on the web generated more heat than light and highlighted the extent to which comment about the War of Independence period is still driven by present-day ideological concerns. The fact that the Pearsons were Protestant 'strong farmers' and members of the Cooneyite sect added extra weight to charges that the killings were carried out for sectarian and/or land-grabbing motives, and this was inferred throughout the documentary. The evidence, however, suggests that the Pearsons were killed because they had previously fired on IRA volunteers (seriously wounding one) who were cutting down trees on Pearson land for the purpose of mounting a roadblock. Should we be surprised that the IRA responded to an attack on its volunteers by punishing those responsible (as it did elsewhere)? Nor do the medical records support the programme's contention that there was sexual mutilation involved (i.e. that the Pearsons were deliberately shot in the genitals and the buttocks) but rather that this was a botched execution carried out by inexperienced volunteers. The orders to shoot the Pearsons came directly from IRA headquarters; while local animosities may have existed, the decision was not made locally.

59. RTÉ Announcement, Summer 2008 Schedules:
http://www.rte.ie/tv/hiddenhistory/coolacrease.html

The Killings at Coolacrease

On June 30, 1921, a violent event that still resonates to this day occurred at Coolacrease House, County Offaly.

30 IRA men raided the farmhouse of the Protestant Pearson family, dragged two of the sons, Richard (24) and Abraham (19), out into the yard, and in front of their mother and sisters, shot them by firing squad. None of the shots were fatal, so it took 14 hours before the brothers eventually bled to death.

In the aftermath of the killings the surviving members of the Pearson family left Ireland and lived out their lives in Australia.

For years, few outside the tiny Offaly village of Cadamstown ever heard this story because few there ever spoke of it.

In 'The Killings at Coolacrease' some members of the local community speak publicly for the first time about their belief that the Pearsons were 'spies and informers' who deserved what they got that day in June. Others reveal an uneasy suspicion that men who fought for the nation may have committed an atrocity against an innocent family.

'The Killings at Coolacrease' recounts in vivid detail the lead-up to this chilling event. It tells the story of how the Pearsons, members of a small Amish-type sect called the Cooneyites - came to buy a large farm in Offaly at a time of great land hunger.

Despite their religious differences, the Pearsons had integrated into the community. Interviewees recall how they were regarded as 'great neighbours', how the sons played hurling and all seven children attended the local Catholic school.

However, new information in the documentary reveals that land may have played a more central role in the fate of the Pearsons than previously thought. They were a family of Protestant outsiders who had bought 340 acres, which some thought should rightfully have been in local hands.

When the War of Independence broke out in 1919, it is alleged that some within the community may have seen their chance.

The documentary also examines local claims that the Pearsons themselves contributed to the tragedy that befell them. It is claimed that a shootout on the Pearson's land involving two of the Pearson sons and members of the IRA may have played a key part in the ensuing events.

However, a story handed down by the Pearson family, and aired here for the first time, questions if this was the pivotal event that sealed their fate or if a cruel series of misapprehensions conspired to cast them in the role of 'spies and informers'.

The direct descendants of the family, interviewed in Australia, recall the terrible toll it took on their parents' lives. Never recovering from the tragedy, the sisters and mother lived in fear of attack.

The great grand-daughter of William and Susan Pearson, the parents of the two boys who were killed, recalls: 'You've lost your family, you've lost your country, you've lost your identity and the part of Ireland that you are passionate about doesn't want to know you because you don't exist. This isn't the Ireland that they wanted to create. You've got an atrocity committed, and no-one cared.'

Coolacrease House - PHOTO

Repeat broadcast: May 13 2008

Appendix 9

THE KILLINGS AT COOLACREASE

A "Reel Story Production"

FOR RTE

Hidden History Series

As broadcast on Tuesday 23rd of October 2007
but.........

[with script by Malachi Lawless
commentary/annotations by Pat Muldowney]

Produced/Directed by: **Niamh Sammon**

Narrator: **Orla Brady**
Script consultant: **Pat Sammon**

Research: **Paul Rouse**
Philip Mc Conway

Introduction

[Interview/V/Oice over]

JJ Dillon (Son of Offaly IRA Volunteer 1920-21):
The silence... that people didn't want to talk about it. I never wanted to talk about it and I never did!

Olive Boothman (Grandniece of Susan Pearson):
There were no words that fitted. The legacy would be one of great fear. It was never spoken of except only in whispers.

Voiceover/Senator Eoghan Harris:
Of all the stories I've heard the story of the Pearsons is easily the saddest one I have heard.

Voiceover/Paddy Heaney (local Historian):
When they got their orders it had to be carried out, they had no choice. No, indeed, no

Voiceover/Prof. Richard English (Historian):
One of the depressing things about conflict is the speed with which neighbours and friends can become killers and enemies.

Voiceover/Philip McConway (Local IRA Historian):
In the context of the times it was a necessary military action to protect and safeguard local Republicans.

####### COMMENT 1:[Pat Muldowney]

The tragedy is presented from one side only. But if the Pearsons were guilty of the activities for which they were charged and two of them executed, then their own tragedy was something they brought on themselves. And we then have to factor in the tragedy of Mick Heaney – blasted in the stomach by shotgun – and the other men they shot. And the tragedy and loss of lives wrecked and loved ones imprisoned in the harsh conditions of Tullamore Jail and Rath Internment Camp because of the Pearsons, if they were guilty.

The Republican side is portrayed as harsh, unfeeling and militaristic. But on the side of the Pearsons, Alan Stanley's book, for instance, talks of putting down "the Rebels" with full military force. Innocent or guilty, it is impossible to deny that the Pearsons were reckless, gun-toting and trigger-happy.

There is also not moral equivalence between the two sides. The citizen V/Olunteer forces of the democratically elected Irish Dáil were conducting a gallant resistance to the

[Picture/soundtrack]

Wide Shot: ....Cornfields/trees/flowers
Close up:...........Dillon
(Mood Music)
Wide shot: .....More trees, corn field/two young men pitching hay on sunny day
Close up:.... ...Pearson woman
Close up: ....IRA men at meeting/fields
Close up:...... IRA men at meeting
Close up:....... Heaney
Close up:...... Men in Hay field/men running
Close up: ......IRA men coming over ridge of hill
Close up:........Frightened faces

Close up:......... Philip Mc Conway

[Pat Muldowney...comment:]
Now suppose that the Pearsons were innocent. In that case we are dealing with, perhaps, a miscarriage of justice or mistake by a popular resistance movemnt, or at worst a rogue element which perpetrated a crime under cover of an otherwise heroic and honourable struggle.

On the other hand, if the Pearsons were guilty, the military contest they joined of their own volition was not a morally neutral one. They attacked the popular resistance on behalf of the aggression of a powerful, terrorist, imperial force which sought to suppress the elected government. From that standpoint the IRA are a popular resistance movement waging a People's War, with sheer solidarity, courage and determination, against vastly superior armed forces.

	imperial forces.
Main Title (White against black)	[Picture/soundtrack]
## THE KILLINGS AT COOLACREASE	Wide shot: ....Slieve Bloom Mts/....sky..../landscapes
[Interview/Voiceover]	[gothic mood music]
Voiceover/narrator: Buried in the land around the Slieve Bloom Mountains is a dark and violent story. Hidden there during the fight for independence is a story that was supposed to have died with time. It was a bloody episode that caused a family to leave the land of their birth for distant exile.	Wideshot:...... Fields/skies Close up:...... Turnidge
Voiceover/Jenny Turnidge (Great-granddaughter of William & Susan Pearson): You've lost your family, country, identity, and the part of Ireland that you are passionate about doesn't want to know you because you don't exist; this isn't the Ireland that we'd wanted to create.	Close up: ....Archive photo of house.[Coolacrease] CU: ....Ruins
Voiceover/narrator: At four pm on the 30th of June 1921 the episode unfolded at Coolacrease House Co. Offaly. Few dispute the central facts of this event but, nearly a century on, this one story continues to divide itself into two...two sides... two sympathies... two truths.	CU: ....Harris
Interview/ Senator E. Harris: I think the fact that that took place in broad day light... It was carried out by thirty men, em, it was so traumatic for the community... that it has to go into denial.	CU : ....Heaney
Interview/Paddy Heaney (Local Historian): I heard it first hand from all the fellows who were involved. At the time there was a War of Independence going on. There was information there that the Pearsons were active. They had to be dealt with.	Archive:........ British Auxilary raid Wideshots:...... Cornfields Farm House : Landscape : Sheep
V/O Narrator: The story of the Pearsons begins over a century ago in Ballygeehan, Co. Laois. The family had farmed the land for three generations. In 1894 William Pearson and his wife Susan inherited a holding of over 200 acres. They and their seven children shared a farmhouse with the family of a cousin.	CU:............. Vernon

V/O Vernon Pearson (Grandson Wm. Pearson): There was a number of kids from both families. At dinner-time they used to go to where the best smell was, and that's where they all went for dinner.	Archive Pictures: ....Susan Pearson
Interview/Ruth Kelly (Granddaughter William/Susan Pearson): Grandma had been busy with the children in the family all the time when, y' know, they were little. There were seven of them... She was a very caring person too. She was all right. There was nothing wrong with Nanna.	(Sound track/........Big House Choral Church music)
	CU....Family shots
Voiceover/Edna Black (Gr/daughter/Wm./Susan Pearson): She was a quiet softly spoken lady, genteel, kindly... very... well, shy, in exposing herself to the world.	Close up: ......Flowers
	Close up:.... William Pearson
VO/Ruth Kelly: Grandpa ... I loved him... I thought he was gorgeous... ha, ha, ha. Always had time to stop and play with ye, y'know, sort of thing, and when ye lived in the country ye didn't have many people to play with.	
	Close up: .....House ruins Fields
VO/Vernon Pearson: My Grandfather would be fairly strict on them, not to the extent that he treated them roughly but they would not know a lot of bad vices there.	Close up.... Vernon
	Close up:......... Pearson family photos.
VO/Ruth Kelly: Grandma decided that each girl should learn something different. My mother, she used to do sewing and she used to play the piano too. She made all her own clothes and everything. Uncle Abraham, well, I know he played the melodeon. He was her favourite brother. She talked a lot about him y'know, Abe did this, Abe did that, y'know. They were very close.	
	Close up:..... men pitching hay in fields.
	church choral music
VO/Narrator: The Pearsons stood out from their neighbours in one significant respect. They were members of a small Protestant sect known sometimes as Cooneyites after a leading preacher, Edward Cooney	
	Close up: .....Ed Cooney and the Cooneyites.
Interview/Dr. Raymond Gillespie (Dept. History Maynooth): The most characteristic feature of this group is they didn't believe in any sort of church organisation as we would understand it. They had no form of churches. They had meetings in houses for bible study. There are some similarities with the Amishes. There are some ideas that underly both groups. They conserve simplicity, they try to live out the word of the bible as they read it.	Close up:...... Gillespie
	(Music: Big House Choral music continues) Close up:... hands turn bible page
	Close up:.... two men come over hill with scythe on shoulders (choral music).
VO: Ruth Kelly: The women...they don't wear makeup. They don't cut their hair, and they don't have wirelesses. They only do good, helping people. They didn't expect payment for what they did. It was the life they led, y'know.	Close up: ......Cooneyite groups (black/white photos)

VO: Sen. E.Harris: My father ran a small grocery wholesale business in the 1950's. And the Cooneyites used to come into him. **I/V..Sen E. Harris:** They were terribly quiet. Very, very gentle, decent people. They were pretty much withdrawn from the world as a whole. I would say they found the whole world outside confusing. They were really a husbandry people, y'know,…the land…quiet evenings spent in meditation…reflection. These were the kind of people they were.	Archive shots:……… Groups of Cooneyites in old photos Close Up:…..Sen. Harris.. CU's…. : Hands playing piano….women sitting,sowing,reading, C.U,s….girl looks pensively out of window…piano plays reflectively …
******* COMMENT 2: [Pat Muldowney] A highly debatable view of early twentieth century Cooneyism is presented. Professor English's description is factually wrong. More importantly, a compassionate and attractive picture of the human qualities of the Pearsons is presented. A balanced account, in which the guilt of the Pearsons was not ruled out, would require similar presentation of the people and community against whom the Pearsons set themselves when the political Troubles were at their most intense. This balance is omitted.	C.U.,s…men in field pitching hay on sunny day [mood music] C.U,… woman at window watching men… C.U…shots.. of big house Burnt out…
Narrator [VO]: In the coming years the Pearsons' lives were to change dramatically. In 1909 William Pearson decided to sell Ballygeehan and buy land elsewhere, at a time of huge rural unrest.	[piano music] Archive photos… of poor peasants.hats in hand… shots… fields of hay shots… of big house in ruins
Dr. Terence Dooley [Author: *The Land for the People*]: Land hunger was endemic in Irish rural society at this time. There were often Protestant farmers who owned substantially larger farms than their surrounding Catholic nationalist neighbours. The Revolutionary period was used essentially as a pretext to run many of these Protestant farmers and landlords out of the local community, for locals to take up their land.	[piano music]
******* COMMENT 3:[Pat Muldowney] Dr Dooley contradicts himself on the general issue. In his book, *The Land for the People,* he demonstrates how both the First Dáil and the Free State authorities intervened to prevent seizures of land and restored land to its owners in such cases. As regards Offaly, no evidence of any kind is produced that any of this is true in regard to the area and community of Cadamstown. If there were any such evidence, e.g. in the form of newspaper or RIC reports, then it would have been presented in the programme. None was presented. So it is reasonable to conclude that there is no such evidence.	archive: footage…documents… names of estates and cost of same CU…shots of big house Protestant houses…..[burnt] CU…[archive b&w photo….poor peasants …caps in hand….]
Narrator…[VO]: To solve the growing crisis, Land Acts were	

introduced to break up large estates and divide them amongst local tenants.

> ******* COMMENT 4:[PM]
> The first Land Act was 1885, the last one was 1909. The subject of the programme belongs to a later period in which new issues, other than Land Tenure, had come to the fore.

Cu...fields of hay...
CU....big house...

[piano music].
Shots... of map of farm, #{339 acres}

Dr. Terence Dooley [VO]: It certainly was successful in terms of a revolutionary transfer of ownership of land from landlord to tenants. But the majority of these holdings could be termed uneconomic and unviable.

[piano music
C.U. ..name of Wm. Pearson on document showing purchase price of Coolacrease in 1911, £2000.

> ******* COMMENT 5:[Pat Muldowney]
> Before the Land Acts, most people scratched a living as insecure tenants. After the Land Acts they farmed the same holdings as secure owner-occupiers confident enough to make personal investments in a fledgling food-processing industry (creamery co-ops), and in the vast network of commerce and light industry which, in conjunction with the initiatives (semi-state etc.) of the Irish government – first with Dominion/Free State status and later with Independence – laid down the basic economic warp and woof on which present-day Irish industry is founded. So the Land Acts enabled a vast economic and personal improvement which was perceived and experienced as such by those involved. Dr Dooley is anachronistically projecting modern criteria onto the situation. Modern criteria projected back onto shopkeepers, labourers or history professors would produce similar anomalies. Would Dooley be prepared now to accept a salary which would not pay for a centrally heated house, a horseless carriage, foreign holidays and trips to history conferences?

C.U...map of farms..

C.U. Dr. Dooley....

Narrator [VO]: In Co. Offaly, one estate of 4,000 acres was divided into almost 100 holdings. One farm at Coolacrease was substantially bigger, and was bought by the sitting tenants, a Protestant family called the Benwells. Just two years after buying the land they sold up.

Cu...various names of estates in the area....
CU....map of farm....339 acres..

Dr. Dooley.[.VO]: William Pearson purchased the farm at Coolacrease in 1911. So, he moves into an area, he takes up a 340 acre farm that is surrounded by a multitude of small uneconomic holdings, where the local people - and they tend to be Catholic and Nationalist farmers - are looking for access to this land themselves. There is the added tinge of sectarianism, ah, in the sense that Protestant land remains in Protestant hands.

CU...name of Wm Pearson on Land Commission Doc.
C.U...slow pan down from yellow confield to red poppies...
CU....Dr.Dooley

***COMMENT:[Pat Muldowney]
Here is the list of farms surrounding Pearsons: JJ Horan, 105 acres; Din Deegan; 80 acres; Brian Donnelly

******* COMMENT 6:[PM]
No evidence is presented that Catholic, nationalist farmers coveted this land, or whether they sought such access by illegal or improper means, or whether they viewed the matter in a sectarian way. Mere speculation.

330 acres; Tom Donnelly 80 acres; John and Mick McRedmond 140 acres; Joe Carroll 80 acres; Albert Jackson 900 acres. So the Pearsons' farm was surrounded by large farms, not "small, uneconomic holdings".
(This unfounded speculation of Dr Dooley is typical of the programme. In the Tubridy Show on 23rd October, Niamh Sammon made the same false statement.) Tom Horan farmed
27 acres in Deerpark and in addition had 4 acres which adjoined Pearsons – the ONLY adjoining small farm.*

C. U…Prof. English..
CU….slow pan down from yellow cornfields to red poppies
CU…[archive b&w photo]…man on huge tractor…

Prof. Richard English [Author. *Irish Freedom*]: So in that sense it was seen as an alien incursion. It was small scale, it was only the family, but in the sense that they were seen as aliens, people that didn't genuinely belong, weren't genuinely integrated into the community, and indeed were taking land from the rightful possession of the community, as locals would have seen it.

[dramatic trill of piano music]

******* COMMENT 7.[Pat Muldowney]
More unsupported speculation. If there were evidence it would have been presented in the programme. The Pearsons came from the Aghaboe area, a mere twenty miles or so distant. A well-respected, wealthy Protestant family called Drought lived near Cadamstown. The Pearsons were not alien, not strangers, and the programme went on to show that the Pearsons quickly integrated into the community and were on amicable terms with their neighbours. English does not present a shred of evidence that the locals saw the Pearsons as taking land from them. There is no such evidence.

[music…]

[music interlude…3 secs…dramatic piano]

C.U..Paddy Heaney

Paddy Heaney…[I/V]: They were very good neighbours in the beginning, and old Mr. Pearson was himself very helpful when local farmers were in trouble, or that, and actually the family went to the local school here in Cadamstown.

archive footage:..photos..
…children with horse and hay bogey…hay being drawn in..

Vernon Philips….Grandson….[VO]: My father, he would have gone to a Catholic school and the whole family would have mixed in a Catholic school.

CU…photo…Pearson family…sons..
[mood music]
CU…Dillon..
staged footage….làds playing hurling as per "Wind that shakes the Barley", in 1920's costume…

J.J. Dillon [Son of Offaly IRA V/Olunteer,1919/21[.I/V]: One time one of them actually played hurling with the local club. They were part of the community.

Jenny Turnidge, [granddaughter...Pearsons]...[I/V] Knowing them having a lot of brothers and sisters.. quite a lot of young people and boys there....I can imagine them having a lot of friends into the house and it being a social house really.	[mood music] CU....... Turnidge Shots ...lads playing hurley... [mood music] CU... Paddy Byrne
Paddy Byrne..[Cadamstown resident]... They were good neighbours. My grandfather said they were great neighbours. According to what I heard they would do anything for ye.	Shots......lads play hurling... CU: Vernon
Vernon Pearson...[VO].. I think they had life very easy, those kids, I really do. And if you don't want to do anything then I don't think you can think anything is going to happen to you. It's just natural, isn't it?	CU...more hurling shots... ...CU....hurling shots..with piano music ...
******* COMMENT 8:[Pat Muldowney] The above sequence is intended to demonstrate what decent, neighbourly people the Pearsons were (and would appear to be perfectly valid until, for political reasons, the Pearsons set their face against the democracy), thus setting the stage for the awfulness of the alleged crime against them. But these acknowledged facts of good neighbourliness are not intended to counter and contradict the earlier, unfounded speculation of Dr Dooley and Prof. English about sectarian land envy and hostility against an alien intrusion. The exchange above is about the merits of the Pearsons. In fact it cuts both ways, reflecting also the tolerance and welcoming nature of the community they had moved in to, though the programme is blind to the fact. The exchange refutes Dooley and English, demonstrating that the community was open and welcoming towards the Pearsons.	[piano music] Archive shots....War of Independence.....Irish Volunteers march....Union Jack...auxies...
Narrator...[VO]... But the atmosphere was changing. By 1919 Ireland was heading for a bloody break from Britain. Like most Protestant families, the Pearsons were strongly loyal to the Crown. As Cooneyites, they stayed out of politics.	[piano music]
******* COMMENT 9:[Pat Muldowney] The second sentence in this fails to recognise that Ireland elected an independent government, to which Britain responded by imposing military government and war. Compare this with: "*By 1919, Britain had instigated a bloody campaign of suppression of Irish democracy.*" The third sentence contradicts the argument made by Dr. Murphy later that William Pearson was lying when he said he was a "*staunch loyalist.*" The fourth sentence prejudges the very issue on which the whole programme hinges – whether the Pearsons involved themselves as combatants in the war.	
Prof. Richard English...[VO].. There was a shift as Ireland moved into the Revolutionary period, where neighbours who	

moved into the Revolutionary period, where neighbours who had gotten on, or integrated across religious or political boundaries before the troubles, found it more difficult to do so against the background of the violence from 1919, 1920 onwards.

CU......Prof. English

...[piano music] shots ....of war of independence...

Archive photos....IRA men in Cadamstown

Paddy Heaney...[VO]... There was a local battalion formed in Cadamstown, part of the Offaly Brigade, and I think about 22 or 23 local fellows joined the local company. I think at that particular time then, the Pearsons began to withdraw from the local people. They began to resent I think the fellows and girls they went to school with. When they'd meet them on the road they wouldn't speak to them.

WS....two men, one with scythe on shoulder, walking peacefully along country road...
CU....Paddy Heany

******* COMMENT 10: The peaceful Pearsons are contrasted visually, and prejudicially, with the militaristic locals.

Paddy Dermody [son of Commandant of Cumann Na mBan]... My mother told me they treated locals with contempt. On a summers evening they'd walk down to the village. The whole family, they'd link arms, and any locals that were on the road, if they wanted to pass, they'd have to get up onto the ditch.

CU...Dermody

Shots... of two men on road with scythe...
CU........feet on road...

Philip McConway..[local IRA historian..1919/1922].. Richard Pearson, in particular, was particularly aggressive towards local Volunteers who he viewed with contempt.

Mood music..

CU...P. McConway...

WS...two men on road with scythe...

J.J. Dillon..[VO].... A cousin who was in school used to tell me about it, Pearson stamping his feet and saying, y'know, the IRA are a lot of ruffians, good for nothing.

...[mood music...]
WS ....men on road...

Jenny Turnidge...[VO]... I believe that there's a lot of stories going around to make people feel better about their part in the actions. They really want to have another reason to make themselves feel better. They don't want to face the truth of the past.

CU.....Turnidge

> ******* COMMENT 11:[PM]
> Opportunity for rebuttal given to a Pearson protagonist. No reciprocal opportunity granted. There is also a flip side to the argument put forward by Turnidge. A denial syndrome gripped the Pearson family who never discussed the pivotal roadblock incident when the eldest brothers attacked local Volunteers. The truth was too unpalatable. Solace was sought in myth. The reality that the Pearsons were armed protagonists was transformed into the comforting myth of innocent victims of a dastardly outrage. Local people were acutely aware that the tragedy which befell the Pearsons was

WS....cornfield...
CU......yellow corn

[No music]....

self-inflicted. In the words of local Protestants: *'They brought it on themselves.'*

Narrator...[VO].. But there may have been another reason for the rift between the Pearsons and their neighbours. During the First World War, William Pearson had supported a Government Tillage Order to grow more crops. He also decided to rent more land to help the War effort.

Dr Dooley...[author]...[VO].. Some years later Pearson claimed that his troubles began with the rise of Sinn Féin and the Compulsory Tillage Order. And when he took that field, he said, *"the local Sinn Féin people were enraged at this and said I had done it to help the British Government. They accordingly, when the corn was ripe, trampled the entire down."* They were resentful of the fact that he was taking land that they felt they should have access to themselves.

>******* COMMENT 12:[pat Muldowney]
>The quote is from William Pearson's 1927 application for compensation from the British Government's Irish Grants Committee. Dr Dooley quotes it as a statement of fact. However, this application is riddled with lies (500 raiders attacked his house, his daughter was shot, he was prevented from selling his land on the open market (in fact he held an auction but, according to the local press (August 1921), refused all bids), his land (bought for £2,000 in 1911) was variously worth £10,000, or £15,000, or £17,000, and many more such fabrications. No uncritical credence can be given to anything in this application.

>******* COMMENT 13:[PM]
>There is no comment, criticism, questioning or rebuttal to this highly dubious statement by Dr Dooley about the cornfield. He provides no evidence for the final sentence of his statement.

[Pause for mood music interlude]

Narrator...[VO]... But in 1919 the Pearsons thought they had little to fear from their rebel neighbours. Offaly at the time was heavily garrisoned with troops stationed in Birr and Tullamore. Meanwhile, the local IRA was regarded by Chief of Staff, Richard Mulcahy, as one of the least competent Brigades in the country

>******* COMMENT 14[PM]:
>The word "rebel" is pejorative. The opposing view of the Pearsons is that they were rebels against the democratically elected government. Richard Mulcahy berated Seán Mahon,

---

WS...fields of corn....no music...
CU...Dooley

WS...Pearson House...

The cornfield:[PM]
This field was rented by the Pearsons from the Droughts. The Droughts and other local Protestant landowners appear to have been on excellent terms with the local community as a whole, and if they had land to let, would undoubtedly have made it available to anyone who was interested. The idea that there were people around who objected on principle to cashing in on the money to be made from the Great War is laughable.

In the heavy, wet soil of this part of Offaly, ripe corn crops tend to "lodge" - that is, flatten to the ground because of wind or rain.

[vocal choral music..]

...Various shots of
...Birr/Tullamore...
...zoom in on archive letter from Richard Mulcahy re. Local IRA...

the then O/C South Offaly No. 2 Brigade, as incompetent, *NOT* the local IRA. The RTÉ inspired ridicule of local Republicans also came to the fore when Ryan Tubridy derided them as 'Keystone cops.'

These comments are based on a misreading of the documentary evidence. The Offaly and Leix units were described, in fact, as *'even and average, none being outstanding'* and Offaly No. 2 was praised for its diligent engineering work. The 3rd Southern Division O/C noted the poor sniping abilities of Offaly No. 2 - with no more than 40 rifles within the entire Offaly IRA, and with limited training, this was hardly surprising.

B& W archive ...IRA men on horse and cart....men cutting down tree...

CU....English

Cu.... Murphy...

Dr. Will Murphy, Dept. of Irish Studies, Mater Dei Institute of Education [VO].. The War Of Independence In Co. Offaly was a pretty quiet affair.

CU Dillon
Cu..flag being raised
...letter

Prof. R. English[I/V]. It tended to be a low level activity. It was road blocking, marching, drilling.

Cu...Murphy

********COMMENT:
The remarks in this sequence are about the volunteer defence forces of the democracy, expressing criticism of their military effectiveness, but from a standpoint of opposition to their political objectives (or, at best, critical neutrality).

Dr W. Murphy...[I/V]... One of the IRA's boasts to headquarters was that in Offaly they had spread glass on the road to puncture the bicycles of R.I.C patrols.

J.J. Dillon [VO].. They'd hoist the flag In Cadamstown. The British would be out and they'd have to take it down.

Cu..Cadamstown IRA...looking shifty..
CU...Dillon...

Dr. W. Murphy ...[I/V]: There had been attempts to derail a train which had failed miserably and G.H.Q would be very angry about the incident.

CU...British Auxies in Ireland....

J.J. Dillon...[VO]: A raggle taggle group of peasants, thinking they're soldiers, that they're going to take on an Empire, an Empire that was just after winning a war.

WS....IRA prisoners being rounded up

********COMMENT:[PM]
Dr Murphy trots out the time-worn description of a quiescent resistance in Offaly. On a comparative level there were few politically related fatalities in Co. Offaly, but this alone is not an adequate yardstick to determine activity. While not sensational, sabotage, blocking and trenching roads, raiding mails, organising Republican Courts, and sniping were all activities which tied down Crown forces. Based on data

compiled from the local press, up to 220 people in Offaly were imprisoned and interned for politically related activity. This hardly tallies with Dr Murphy's assessment that it was a *'pretty quiet affair.'* In addition, both the RIC and the British Army regarded the Offaly IRA as an effective resistance, tying down Crown forces and greatly restricting military mobility.

The attempted railway derailment occurred at Clara in March 1921. It was Mulcahy, not GHQ, who was incensed. It was this incident which sparked Mulcahy's scathing criticism of the No.2 Brigade O/C. An internal investigation was ordered to uncover why the operation failed. The presence of an aeroplane conducting aerial surveillance of the railway line was cited as the reason. Part of the rail was removed in what the RIC described as *'the most serious crime attempted during the month.'*

JJ Dillon expressed pacifism throughout the programme, but this stance was directed editorially, in a derogatory, mocking, one-sided way, against the forces which defended the democracy against the imperial aggression.

Narrator..[V/O]... By 1920 however, this picture was about to change dramatically. The War of Independence stepped into a higher gear, and IRA suspects and their families began to come under more pressure from the authorities.

Ws...more prisoners ..

Paddy Heaney...[V/O].. They got it so hard during that period. A lot of them suffered. Their houses were raided. People were on the run. They were in jail. They were harassed.

Ws..civilians being searched

Murphy...[V/O] Once escalation happened, the IRA look around their area, who's selling them out, who's shopping them. And they eventually reach out for local targets, often typically, Protestants. There were a number of incidents that suggested to the IRA that the Pearsons may not only be quietly Loyalists, but may be active in their support for the British.

CU...Murphy

******* COMMENT 15:[PM]
This implies that informers were typically Protestant and/or that Protestants were typically the targets of IRA punishment for informing. No proof or evidence is provided for this, and it is not actually true. Several executions of people for informing occurred in South Offaly in 1921, all, apart from the Pearsons, Catholic.
Here Murphy accepts that the Pearsons were loyalist while later in the programme he presented an argument that William Pearson was lying when he declared himself a

'staunch loyalist' in his Grants Committee application

Sen. Eoghan Harris...[I/V]: To understand it, you have to cast your mind back. It's the summer of 1921. It was a halcyon summer. It was a golden summer.

CU..Harris

Ws ..Cornfields...
[piano mood music]...

Ruth Kelly...[granddaughter of William and Susan Pearson]: She was beautiful. She was a very strong woman, y'know. If she wanted to do something, she did it.

CU Ruth kelly

******* COMMENT 16:[PM]
The stage is being set here for proposing various hard-to-prove reasons – some of them complete red herrings – for the execution of the Pearsons, reasons deliberately set up for facile debunking in the programme. While the actual and real reason for the executions (the attack on the roadblock) is downgraded to one of numerous bogus allegations.

CU...actress... as Tilly Pearson. ...Lots of mood music]...Walks out with British soldier...

Narrator [V/O]: By the early summer of 1921 the actions of the Pearson family were beginning to be interpreted in two very different ways. For some, allegations of a relationship between the Pearsons eldest daughter, Tilly, and an officer of the Crown were evidence of treason.

CU....."Tilly" and soldier walk along road....

******* COMMENT 17:[Pat Muldowney]
None of the contributors on the other side of the argument made any such allegations. And neither has this ever been cited by Republicans or any others from the period. The allegation has the appearance of being inserted editorially, perhaps to give Eoghan Harris the opportunity to indulge in his righteous indignation (below) about an issue that neither the Pearson relatives nor the locals appear to have actually raised. The wording of Ruth Kelly's comment (below) indicates, not that she raised this issue herself, but that she was responding to some suggestion, put to her by an interviewer, which she had never heard of before. The editorial insertion *"For some"* is misdirection. None of the contributors on the other side of the argument made any such allegations. For the allegation to have any meaning or force, it would have to come from the Pearsons' accusers, not their defenders. This is a red herring.

P. Heaney [local historian]...[V/O].. Local people were aware at all times that the military were visiting the house, and the local police from Birr used to come out there. The IRA had their own intelligence there. And they had people watching the house.

CU....Heaney...

CU....."Tilly" and Soldier

******* COMMENT 18:[PM]

This is a completely different issue, a very valid one in a war context, and absolutely nothing to do with Matilda Pearson's courtship.

Sen. Harris....[I/V]... The Pearson girls were supposed to be going out with British soldiers, or went out with British soldiers. What else would they do..!?...Would they make dancing partners for local IRA officers, d'ye think..!!... D'ye think the local IRA wanted to dance with the Cooneyites out there..!?...I doubt very much that the Cooneyite girls went out with British soldiers. But if they did, so what!

CU.....Harris...

******* COMMENT 19:[PM]
Harris seems to be challenging and debunking Paddy Heaney's reasonable statement (which is about something else entirely) – note that no reciprocal challenge to Harris is permitted! Harris's self-indulgent rant is on a completely different topic to the one raised by Heaney.

Narrator...[V/O]... At this time Tilly Pearson may in fact have been seeing her future husband.

Archive...B&W photo of Tilly Pearson

[piano music]...

Ruth Kelly...[V/O] My father was born in Offaly and he joined the R.I.C. and he served in Belfast. They knew each other quite a while. It's possible that Mum would have been in contact with Dad at that time. They were courting, so it wouldn't have been anything untoward. It would have been just dad chasing mum.

CU ....R.I.C. man..

Shots of Ruth Kelly's parents...archive...

Cu...Ruth Kelly..

******* COMMENT 20:[PM]
Further irrelevant misdirection against Paddy Heaney's argument – except that Paddy Heaney argued something quite different which is NOT refuted.

Narrator...[V/O].. There were other incidents, however, cited as evidence that the Pearsons were enemy collaborators at a time of war.

Cu... house

WS....cows cross avenue..

Alan Stanley...[Son of William Stanley..]...[V/O] My father said a British army officer came pushing a motorcycle in the avenue, one day, and asked if they had petrol. He'd run out of petrol and the Pearsons said, certainly, yes, we have some. And they filled up his tank and off he went.

CU Stanley...fields/avenue

******* COMMENT 21:[PM]
More irrelevancies. This incident was never "cited" (see preceding comment by Narrator) by anybody except Alan Stanley. He gives it in his book, and I've never seen or heard

it anywhere else. It was certainly not put forward by anybody else in the programme. Incidentally, Kenneth Strong, a British Army Intelligence Officer with the Royal Scots Fusiliers travelled on a motor cycle throughout the south Offaly area. Uniformed officers travelled in protected transport. It is conceivable that the British officer referred to by Stanley was Strong. Stationed in Hunston House in Moystown, Strong also frequently donned various disguises for his intelligence gathering activities. Peter Lyons, an IRA Intelligence Officer with Drumcullen 'D' Company recalled how British Army personal were spotted at Coolacrease on a regular basis. This evidence is simply never examined.

	WS.....fields of corn...poppies....
Prof. Richard English...[V/O]..	
Looked at from the IRA's point of view, a family that was outside their own community, that had taken land that the IRA's community would have seen as rightfully theirs', that was fraternising with what they would have seen as the enemy. All of that would have been added together and seen as the Pearsons not only being outside the community, but as potentially targets that were legitimate.	CU....English...
******* COMMENT 22:[PM] Prof. English is simply repeating the same spurious points he made earlier (see COMMENT 7). The Pearsons were far from the social pariahs insinuated by English. The Pearson children played hurling and attended the local Catholic national school in Cadamstown. William Pearson was elected an officer on the Kinnity branch of the King's County Farmers' Association and was a representative on the County Executive in 1919. He was also part of a group of men involved in a house-to-house canvass to rally support for the farmers' cause. Another member of this group came from a prominent GAA and Republican family in the area, the Cordials. From 1920 onwards the Pearsons gradually withdrew from their community due to their obdurate Loyalism. This was exacerbated by the arrival of William Stanley.	CU.... of three lads [actors]...pitching hay on a summers day...as...Wm. Stanley.....Richard and Abraham Pearson..... [piano music]
Narrator...[V/O]... But it was the presence of William Stanley at Coolacrease House that would raise the temperature even further. Stanley, a relative of the Pearsons, was living there under the alias Jimmy Bradley, after running into trouble with the IRA in his homeplace in Co.Laois.	CU...archive .Wm. Stanley
Alan Stanley..[V/O]... The problem arose when one of the Protestant ladies of the parish invited people from the Church back for Sunday lunch. Now these were Police people, not quite the Black and Tans. They were officer material. The	WS.....haymaking..

problem was my father and the other young lads were seen to be fraternising with the enemy. When the local IRA people became aware they sent him a note and they were ordered out, and that's how he came to go to the Pearsons.

CU...[actor].....Wm. Stanley...making hay

******* COMMENT 23:[Pat Muldowney]
In other words, some rather posh British officers encountered in church were making polite conversation with Alan's father, and the Co. Laois IRA didn't like it and expelled him. But the *"officer material/police people"* referred to by Stanley is a euphemism for the notorious Auxiliaries. Of all units of the Crown forces in Co. Laois the Auxiliaries had the worst record. Two innocent civilians were killed by the Auxiliaries there. This adds a disturbing and a darkly menacing side to Stanley's collaborating activities. Stanley's militant loyalist group was plotting with the Auxiliaries to 'lift' a young Republican in the area.

In his book, Alan Stanley says:

"*Frank Stanley* [Alan's father's cousin] *said that my father used to keep company with a number of young men of the area* [Luggacurran, Co. Laois, scene of mass evictions, attempted ethnic cleansing and plantation by Lord Lansdowne in 1887]. *Like him, they were all sons of "planters"* [Protestants from the local area and it seems also from Ulster (where William Pearson spent six months after the executions, according to his son) and Scotland, brought in to replace evicted Catholic tenants]. ... *All were in possession of a pistol of one kind or other. ... At Sunday Matins* [the mother of the leader of this armed group] *espied two handsome young Englishmen, auxiliary Police Cadets, and invited them home for lunch. ... it seems there was more than a social element to their visits ...Frank's sister, who later married* [the leader of this armed group] *told me she overheard plans to "lift" a young man of the area who was an active IRA member* [... *and] went to warn* [him]. ... *If the local brigade (IRA) had tolerated "playing at soldiers", "fraternizing with the enemy" was a different matter altogether, one that in many cases exacted the extreme penalty. It was not long until this "pack of whelps", as Frank described them, got notice to leave. ... Frank believed it was the decency of the Luggacurran people that enabled them to get off so lightly.*"

It was the 'decency' and restraining influence of the Laois Brigade IRA leadership which resulted in the expulsion of the militant loyalists from the area rather than their execution. The local IRA company wanted to shoot them as informers. For this to happen it required the sanction of the Brigade O/C which was not forthcoming. In other words, the death penalty could have been expected for the loyalist paramilitary plot that was nipped in the bud in Luggacurran. But in Coolacrease, a loyalist armed attack against the democracy was successfully accomplished, a much more serious matter than the Luggacurran affair which saw the Stanley family selling up and leaving the country in 1921.

Paddy Heaney..[V/O].. I wouldn't class him as a spy, but he was there to glean information, I suppose, at the houses and the house dances that he went to, the people that he met and knew in his rambles in the area.

CU...Heaney...

Narrator...[V/O].. New information has recently come to light. It suggests that another incident convinced some in the community that the Pearsons were spies.

Cyril Pearson...[relative of Pearsons].. Cecil Pearson, who was around at the time, was related to the Pearsons of Coolacrease. He told me that at that time it was common for farmers, if cattle had strayed onto their land, to report it to the police, who acted as a clearing house. On the day in question the Pearson family had found that some cattle had strayed onto the land and Dick Pearson went into the local town to report this fact. Unknown to them the local IRA had intended to blow up a bridge as an ambush for Black and Tans. But they didn't arrive, and Dick Pearson in particular was blamed, and his family was blamed by association, for passing information that he may have got.

CU ...photo of ..Cecil Pearson...

Ws...cattle straying across avenue

Ws..... of bridge in town..

Archive ....shots of Auxies

> ******* COMMENT 24[Pat Muldowney]:
> This 'new information' was emphasized by RTÉ in pre-broadcast publicity. It is flimsy second generation hearsay. No credence can be attached to this fable as it lacks any factual substance. There was no RIC presence in the nearby village of Kinnity. The unoccupied police barracks was burned in 1920. It further underlines the absence of any consultant historian to ensure accuracy and quality control for the programme.

Narrator....[V/O]... In the aftermath of the incident it seemed any rumour about the Pearsons was readily believed. There was even speculation that they were running an underground militia from their home.

> ******* COMMENT 25:[PM]
> Comment 23 shows that the Narrator has no grounds for the first sentence. It is empty rhetoric. The second sentence mentions "underground militia", implying this is paranoid fantasy. But Alan Stanley's own account of his father's

423

loyalist activities in Luggacurran (which he learned from his uncle as William Stanley had concealed it from his son) cannot be dismissed as a far-fetched conspiracy theory. Many of the Luggacurran planters' had Ulster origins and some were also members of the Orange Order, including William's father.

Paddy Heaney...[V/O].. I do believe that the Pearsons were spies. Everything added up, that the Pearsons were involved in an underground movement. And people knew that.

Ws....of men striding purposefully through woods with guns...

******* COMMENT 26:[PM]
The previous statement by the Narrator has already planted the idea that what Paddy Heaney is saying here is paranoid fantasy. So it is rebutted editorial before it is even spoken (- "pre-buttal").

[spacey mood music]

CU...lad walks in wood in a hurry...

Philip McConway...[V/O].. According to local speculation British Army soldiers worked undercover as farm labourers and during the night the Pearsons would help pinpoint where the IRA Volunteers lived.

CU McConway

******* COMMENT 27:[PM]
The Narrator has already planted the idea editorially that none of this could conceivably be true – "pre-buttal".

[mood music]

Narrator....[V/O]... At a time of war local speculations could have serious consequences. In other parts of the country, notably Cork, alleged informers were shot without much hard evidence. But did the local IRA have more on the Pearsons?

various CU's...[actors] conspiratorial lads around a table looking tense....dragging on fags...meaningfully..

******* COMMENT 28:[Pat Muldowney]
The narrator chips in with a reference to Cork, a murky situation where lists of Protestant informers were found in an RIC station when the RIC were stood down. Similar lists were found in other vacated RIC stations, indicating there may have been a "dirty tricks" operation. In Co. Cork there is debate about who actually carried out these shootings, and it is possible that the "dirty tricks" operation extended to carrying out the shootings themselves. The only thing that is certain about the Cork case is that nothing is as it seems, certainly not the trite and bogus theory of sectarian 'massacre' proposed by historian Peter Hart. Hart's claims are repeated ad nauseam by Alan Stanley in his book and also by Eoghan Harris in his journalism. These views are parroted here by the Narrator. Hart was disgraced when a "witness" he said he'd interviewed for claims he made about the Kilmichael ambush was found to be dead at the time of the supposed interview! See the article in this book by Brian Murphy.

CU's.....
...more of same....

******* COMMENT:
The visual prompts show the Pearsons going about their farming work peacefully and innocently, while ominous, militaristic stuff is afoot all around them.

Prof. Rich. English….[V/O].. I've seen no evidence that would persuade me that the Pearsons were running an underground militia from the farm, or passing on information about the local IRA. I think it's a convenient claim, because if you can present them as being effectively a militia force, then taking violent action against the Pearson brothers would seem to be more an act of legitimate war between combatant groups.

CU's….
…even more conspiring…heavy smoking….

Cu….English

> ******* COMMENT 29:[Pat Muldowney]
> The final part of this sequence has Prof. Peter English rebutting Heaney and McConway, using the by-now-discredited words "underground militia", so he may either have been shown their statements or had the statements relayed to him for more focused contradiction. This is followed (below) by further statements of Heaney and McConway, which show no evidence of them knowing how English responded to them. Superficially they seem to have the last word, but it is done in such a way that their argument is weakened even further by the editorial methods of the documentary.
>
> Had Prof. English examined the *King's County Chronicle* which documented the arrests of John Dillon and J.J. Horan after the mass path dispute, fermented by Richard Pearson, he might not have been so dismissive of the latter's role as an informer. Prof. English also conveniently airbrushes out the Lugaccuran connection of Stanley and his role as a member of an armed loyalist group. When it comes to understanding militant loyalism, Luggacurran and Coolacraese are inextricably linked.

Paddy Heaney [V/O] The Pearsons weren't innocent and the research I carried out talking to a lot of those fellows who were involved in that period - they were spies and informers. That's my opinion. I documented it in my local history. I stand over it.

CU…..archive….Pearso Bros

CU……Heaney

Philip McConway…[V/O]… A British army deserter, who used to drive staff officers to Coolacrease - he deserted to join the IRA - he said the Pearsons had very close contacts with British army soldiers at the time and they were passing on information. There is no documentary information to support that, but it is a reasonable conclusion to make.

CU……..archive
        British soldiers

CU McConway

Alan Stanley…[V/O]… It's very easy to create an enemy. You just find a way of antagonising him and then you have an enemy.

[blast of music]

425

******* COMMENT 30:
The last word is again given to the Pearson side. The British Army deserter was Charlie Chidley, an Englishman and a Protestant. Chidley's military skills were much appreciated by the IRA.

CU.........fields

J.J. Dillon....[V/O]... Well, it probably started over a pathway to Cadamstown. People used to call it the mass path.

Narrator...[V/O].. The path was strategically important to the IRA. Crossing the Pearsons' land, it was being used by IRA men moving between hideouts in the mountains and their targets in the villages below. In the Spring of 1921 it would become the flashpoint for all the bitter divisions over land and religion.

WS......a "mass" path

[piano music]

WS.........man walks over mountain.....watched by Dick Pearson

******* COMMENT 32:[PM]
The first sentence of the Narrator is complete invention. As is the second sentence. The "bitter divisions" of the third sentence concerned politics, not land and religion, and the programme did not produce the slightest shred of evidence to the contrary. It simply depended on persuading the audience of this fiction by repeated assertion and nothing else.

******* COMMENT 31:
The scene is open, desolate country bearing absolutely no resemblance to the actual mass-path which is sheltered and runs through a narrow tree-growing strip of ground.

J.J. Dillon...[V/O]... The Pearsons didn't want people who they thought were IRA people using this pathway. My father onetime was coming down the pathway and he met Dick Pearson. He told him they had no right to cross their land. They had a heated discussion. It was always said he was carrying a gun that day 'cos he expected confrontation, I think, and he simply wasn't prepared to back off.

CU's........actors...enact the incident on mountain

Narrator..[V/O].. But the story that spread in the community cast the Pearsons in a strongly sectarian light.

******* COMMENT
The local IRA Volunteers were not living in hideouts. They lived openly in their own homes, where many of them were arrested immediately following incidents involving the Pearsons. The McRedmonds, Joe O'Carroll, Tom Donnelly JJ Horan lived adjacent to to the Pearsons. It was not the IRA, but the Crown forces, who had to take precautions when moving around the area

******* COMMENT 33:[PM]
The evidence, reinforced by the early history of Cooneyism, shows that the Pearsons actually were strongly sectarian at this time. John Dillon and J.J. Horan, District Councillor for Birr, were arrested after this incident. In a letter to the Broadcasting Complaints Commission, RTÉ stated that they had found no evidence for the arrest of Dillon and Horan. RTÉ claimed to have travelled to the Kew Archives in London to examine interment lists. The arrests were in fact reported in the *King's County Chronicle*. This was brought to the producer's attention by credited researcher Philip McConway, but ignored by the producer. Dillon and Horan feature in the photograph of the Cadamstown prisoners broadcast by the programme. Though the photograph itself was evidence of the Pearsons' informing activities, no explanation of who the internees actually were accompanied

The impression is given here that, in the mass path dispute, the Pearsons responded to some external factor,

426

the shot of the photograph.

Philip McConway.....[V/O].. They prevented local Catholics from accessing a traditional mass path in the area when people were coming home from mass. The Pearson brothers would ride horses to disperse Catholics from the road, in what was tantamount to religious bigotry on the Pearsons' part.

Alan Stanley: I find that unbelievable. That wasn't their way. Their Christian way was not to stop anyone going to church. There was something else going on...

> ******* COMMENT 34:[Pat Muldowney]
> Rebuttal again awarded editorially to the Pearson side. The wording shows that Stanley has either heard or seen the McConway statement, and is offered an opportunity to deny it. There is no indication that any such advantage was given to the other side at any point in the programme. Regarding the substantive point, early twentieth century Cooneyites were notorious for unseemly sectarian squabbling.

Narrator...[V/O].. Another time the conflict over the mass path might have died away. But in April 1921 the subject of Offaly was on the agenda of the IRA GHQ.

Murphy, Mater Dei..[V/O].. The IRA are under extraordinary pressure in Offaly. They are regularly being arrested. Their own community is under pressure and GHQ has finally decided the Offaly IRA didn't know how to run their own affairs and they needed to be shaken up.

> ******* COMMENT: [PM]
> "Their own community"? Does he mean religious community? Or political community? Are we supposed to assume the two are the same? Does he think the audience is a bunch of simple-minded fools?

Prof. Rich English...[V/O]... What often happened when an area was seen to be inactive was that an organizer would be sent to chivy them along, to organise them and get them into higher gear if you like, and an organizer was sent in Spring of 1921 to Offaly

Murphy ...[V/O] Tom Burke was a trusted organizer, well known in GHQ. Upon his arrival you can see a significant change in Offaly.

---

challenge or provocation. But every account of this subject shows that the Pearsons took the initiative.

CU.......McConway

CU...yellow cornfields...black crow flies across it...
CU Stanley

WS......yellow cornfields......gurgling stream

CU.......IRA document....

CU Murphy
CU.......IRA document
CU.....C.O.S. Gen. Richard Mulcahy inspects his troops in the field...[archive]

CU.......Richard Mulcahy inspecting IRA troops in field

CU.............IRA organizer......TOM

427

******* COMMENT: [PM] Yes, the Dublin organizer arrives and we get the Kinnitty ambush and the execution of the Pearsons. So where does this leave the local land hunger and sectarian hostility theory?	BURKE
At least two GHQ organisers were sent to south Offaly in 1921. In the eyes of Richard Mulcahy both were seen as ineffective and were recalled. The 'significant change' occurred when Burke became O/C South Offaly No. 2 Brigade not while he was an organizer and leader of a flying column. There were seven killings under his command: 2 RIC Constables at the Kinnity ambush, 2 informers, 1 spy and the 2 Pearson militant loyalists. Before his arrival there was just one enemy combatant fatality, RIC Sergeant Denis McGuire.	WS...Slieve Blooms
Prof. Richard English...[V/O]... It's been claimed that the rise of IRA activity in Offaly before the Treaty reflects the desire to settle some scores, and to do some ... housecleaning, if you like.	
******* COMMENT 35:[PM] Or could it simply be exactly what it says on the tin – that there was a war on, and every effort had to be made to resist the occupying terror forces and their collaborators, especially since the intensification of the English war effort since January 1921? Also, the ominous "housecleaning" reference is preparing the ground for the programme's claims of ethnic cleansing. At this stage, the local IRA was subject to an increasingly centralised command, and had less not more control before the Truce.	[burst of choral music] WS....various.....SLIEVE BLOOM CU........typing...
Murphy ...[V/O]... There was a considerable number of shootings of spies in Offaly between May and July 1921. On 17th May, the Offaly IRA pulled off one of its biggest coups. It was the Kinnitty ambush. They succeeded in killing two RIC men in Kinnitty. The Kinnitty action was extremely significant. It provoked a reaction from the British Army. There were reprisals, widespread arrests, escalation of violence.	CU.......RIC man outside barracks CU...photo of Pearsons.... Police, document being typed
Prof. Rich. English...[V/O].. So those who were seen as closer to the British forces would have been at greater risk at this point in summer 1921.	CU English
******* COMMENT 36:[PM] As were those who were actually in collaboration with the imperial terror. To be 'at risk' from the Offaly IRA depended on actions not political outlook. The sequence of contributions above is designed to give the impression that the trouble that befell the Pearsons was not of their making, but was a consequence of how Mulcahy and Burke amended	

their strategy in Offaly in 1921.

Narrator...[V/O]... There were deadly whispers in the wind. At this point an event occurred which sealed the fate of the Pearsons.

CU.......big ominous night sky.....

[blast of gothic choral music]

> ******* COMMENT 37:[PM]
> The wording is prejudicial. To balance this, there would need to be some statement that what happened to the Pearsons was the result of actions they carried out entirely on their own initiative.

Murphy ...[I/V].. One night in June 1921, the local IRA embarked on an activity that was typical of that period, blocking roads.

CU.......Murphy

CU's......lads in woods with guns

Paddy Heaney...[V/O] They chose a tree on Pearsons' land. Seven or eight of them went out there at 11.30 pm and they began to cut down the tree.

[dramatic music]

Michael Donnelly...[V/O].. My uncle Tom Donnelly and another man were providing armed cover. Both of them were armed.

CU's.......men in woods

Alan Stanley...[V/O].. Old William Pearson was away at the time, so Richard was left in charge. And when he sees these men cutting the trees without a by-your-leave, my father told me he confronted the tree-fellers. He said: *"Aren't ye the brave lads with all your guns"*, and fired over their heads.

CU ....Stanley

CU,S....men shouting at each other

Dick Pearson: *"Who goes there?"* IRA man: *"Mind your own business, Pearson."* D.P.: *"You have no right to be on this land."* D.P. points gun upwards. Gun fired upwards into the air.

> ******COMMENT:[Pat Muldowney]
> This is the crux of the whole Coolacrease story. To understand it, the location and topography must be grasped. The Pearsons' house stands about a hundred metres off the Birr-Tullamore road. In 1921 it was surrounded by trees. The location of the roadblock was several hundred metres back along the road in the direction of Birr, about half-way between the Pearsons house and the village of Cadamstown (see the maps in the Appendices of this book). A single tree on the roadside was being cut down to make a roadblock, as part of county-wide manoeuvres in support of a proposed ambush of Crown forces near Birr. The purpose of the Cadamstown roadblock was to hinder the movement of Crown forces from Tullamore to Birr. The tree was at the point on the roadside where the Pearsons' land adjoined the farm of JJ Horan, an IRA member who had been arrested and jailed following the confrontation with the Pearsons over the mass path. It was not "the Pearsons' tree". It was a considerable distance from their house. Retired RIC man Bert Hogg visited the Pearsons regularly, and on that particular evening was arrested by the roadblock party as he

******COMMENT:
This is one of many notable instances of the documentary reversing situations from the way they are actually reported. There are only two detailed accounts of the roadblock incident, Paddy Heaney's and Alan Stanley's. The *"Who goes there?"* comment is reported by Paddy Heaney, not by Alan Stanley. But in Paddy Heaney's account, this warning or challenge is given, not by Richard Pearson but by Vol.

made his way home towards Lackamore on the far side of Cadamstown. (As a loyalist, he could not be relied on.) There was no prior confrontation or conversation with Richard Pearson. About ten minutes after the arrest of Hogg, the Pearsons arrived at the roadblock, walking along the public road. Mick Heaney was on sentry duty on that side of the roadblock. When he challenged them they shot him in the stomach and neck. Tom Donnelly was on sentry duty on the Cadamstown side of the roadblock, and he ran towards Mick Heaney and fired at the Pearsons. They fired again and wounded Donnelly in the head, and Hogg in the leg and back as he tried to run away towards Cadamstown. According to the RIC report, the Pearsons mistakenly thought they had killed one of the IRA men.

Mick Heaney

******* COMMENT 39:
The reconstruction affirms Ala Stanley's father's version of th (Amish-like!) Pearsons firing into the air. So maybe Mick Heaney just had a bad fall off his bicycle

Prof. Rich. English....[V/O] The Pearsons are merely doing what any law abiding citizen should do and legally they are within their rights to defend their land and as they would see it, to protect it against terrorist activity.

CU's......scene in woods acted out.

******* COMMENT 38:[PM]
The British and loyalist interpretation of the context is provided here. Nowhere in this sequence is the Irish view given of a citizen V/Olunteer defence force bravely risking their lives against terrible odds on behalf of the legitimate, democratically elected government.

CU........Donnelly

MICHAEL Donnelly...[V/O] My uncle Tom Donnelly returned fire. He wounded one of the Pearsons, but he was also wounded himself.

CU.... Man firing gun horizontally

Paddy Heaney...[V/O] Mick Heaney, on the first blast of the shotgun, the lead embedded in the scarf around his neck and he was shot also in the stomach.

CU......Heaney

Sen. Eoghan Harris....[I/V] I dunno if they hit anybody or not. Paddy Heaney says they did. I dunno. When Paddy Heaney tells me things like that I want documentary corroboration in evidence.

CU......Harris

******* COMMENT 40:[PM]
Is it possible that a whole community without exception could conform to a lie, that Mick Heaney could simulate his crippled condition for five years, and that he could conveniently die prematurely just to give the appearance of truth to this invention? And that this lie could be upheld for generations?

Paddy Heaney...[V/O] Those men who were there that night, and I spoke to most of them, they all maintain that the Pearsons deliberately shot at Mick Heaney and Tom Donnelly that night.

Narrator...[V/O] Sometime later the local police inspector did report the allegation that the Pearson had shot and wounded two local IRA men. However, there was no official investigation into what actually happened that night. Both sides do agree that there were no fatalities. But the incident would be used to justify what was to come.

******* COMMENT 41:[Pat Muldowney]
The "local police inspector" was the County Inspector of Queen's County RIC – a very senior official. The British Court of Inquiry file includes: *"It is said by the C.I. Queens County that the two Pearson boys a few days previously had seen two men felling a tree on their land adjoining the road. Had told the men concerned to go away, and when they refused had fetched two guns and fired and wounded two Sinn Feiners, one of whom it is believed died."* The wording is of a fact, not an allegation. The Irish military also conducted an official investigation. The RIC had the Pearsons in their custody and could question them at their convenience. A retired RIC officer, Ian Hogg, had been shot (by the Pearsons) at the roadblock. In the circumstances of war the incident was justification for *"what was to come."* Having both conducted official investigations both the RIC and IRA were unequivocal as to the motive for the execution. William Pearson and his son, Sidney, were in Mountmellick, Co. Leix at the time of the execution, coming from a religious meeting at Carrick House. While there they were taken into protective custody, which is why the rport is from the C.I. Queen's County (Laois) rather than King's County (the authority for Cadamstown). It is not credible that they were not questioned by the Mountmllick RIC as to the motive for the execution.

Murphy..[V/O] It allowed the local IRA to express the fears they had about the Pearsons. It justified their paranoia. It justified their social resentment at their landholding. And now they had a reason.

******* COMMENT 42:[PM]
This rhetoric re-states the earlier, unfounded speculation, indeed fancy, about land envy. It is entirely one side of the argument, and is not backed up by any evidence or balanced by any rebuttal or relevant balancing contribution. It trivializes the military challenge that the Pearsons presented to the authority of the legitimate, elected Dáil.

CU........woods scene....
Pearson aiming shotgun horizontally. Gun fired horizontally (shooter not shown).

CU.....woods scene

CU...Portion of page of contemporary document shown, the words *"Revenge by I.R.A."* visible. (The document is not identified, but it is from the British Commander's report of "Possible Motives" for the executions, among the papers of the British Military Courts of in Lieu of Inquests.)

CU......Group of young peasant men sit around table in cottage.....conspiring...

CU....Heaney

Paddy Heaney...[I/V] T'was coming to them. The writing was on the wall for the Pearsons. If they'd kept their heads down and kept with the local people they'd still be there today.

[blast of music]

> ******* COMMENT 43:[PM]
> Paddy Heaney is given the appearance of having the last word, but the words are in no way a rebuttal or debunking of the previous rhetoric – a rebuttal which would have been very easy for him to do if the programme had been inclined to give him any such opportunity.

[END OF PART ONE]

End of part one

[Picture / soundtrack]

THE KILLINGS AT COOLACREASE

PART TWO

[Interview/Voice over]

CU.....men sitting around Table ....conspiring

Alan Stanley... (VO) It's very hard not to wonder if somebody who knew that truce was imminent did not decide, *"Well look lads, there's some nice pickings here, lets go for it."* I know it's very dangerous to say that... but the land... of course... the land... of Ireland for the people of Ireland.

CU....faces looking tense
CU....Stanley

CU ....men around table

JJ Dillon... (VO) In conflict those things occur. Like hatred comes into it, revenge comes into it.

> ******* COMMENT 44:[PM]
> JJ Dillon's pacifist, anti-war words could relate to any side in any war. In no way are they balance or rebuttal to the very specific speculative allegations just made by Stanley.

[eerie music]

CU ....mountains

Narrator... (VO) Days after the shoot out on the Pearsons' land the local IRA met to decide the fate of the Pearson family. For IRA commander Tom Burke, there was now no going back, no second chances.

CU......hand stubs out

Actors Voice…(reading statement of Tom Burke): " C Company, the 3rd Battalion, reported to me on the 26th of June 1921 that some of their men had been fired on a few nights previously, whilst engaged in a road blockade operation, by three men armed with shot guns. As a result, one of their men was somewhat seriously injured.".	cigarette CU….men around table CU….McConway
Ph. Mc Conway (VO)… If the local IRA were to be criticised, it was that they were too lenient and that they showed consistent restraint, given the provocation by the Pearsons. And that restraint almost cost the lives of two Volunteers.	[doomy music] CU….men around table
Actors Voice (reading statement of Tom Burke)(VO): "The Pearsons had always displayed open hostility towards the IRA and have been active in promoting the Ulster Volunteer movement in their district in which there are a number of Planters. There are good grounds for suspecting the family of transmitting information".	CU ….hard faced men [actors]…around table.

> ******* COMMENT 45:[PM]
> Comment 22 above, about William Stanley, the Luggacurran Planters, and their Ulster connections, shows how Tom Burke's words have substance. The term 'planters' should be explained, but of course isn't. To a modern audience it seems to be a sectarian term. But it did not refer to Protestants in general or Protestant farmers in particular. It referred to people who had been planted on the land of evicted tenant farmers in the current generation, and was also a term used by the RIC in its reports of these incidents. The term 'local IRA' used by the narrator is also intentionally misleading, and is used to support the thesis that local people were involved for land-grabbing purposes. It was not the 'local IRA' which decided these things, but an Officers' Council of the South Offaly Brigade, commanded by Tom Burke, who was from Galway. Only Brigade Commanders had the authority to authorize an execution, which had to conform to strict guidelines issued by IRA GHQ (Mulcahy).

	CU…..English
Prof. Rich. English.. (I/V)… It's quite comforting if you do target people, afterwards to build up as much justifications as possible. I think the real justification lay in the fact that the IRA and their authority in the area had been challenged in an unacceptable way and in order to show who is boss in the area they had to teach the Pearsons a lesson. You can exert your authority and in the long run you can also maximise access to land.	CU….men around table [mood music]

> ******* COMMENT 46:[PM]
> The IRA Court of Enquiry, or Officers' Battalion Council, was held before the executions. English has no grounds for supposing that Thomas Burke invented the reasons

supposing that Thomas Burke invented the reasons retrospectively in order to justify the executions. English offers no valid reasons for doubting the validity of this official Enquiry. Instead he attempts to muddy the waters by suggesting there were multiple justifications for the execution. There was only one reason cited for the execution: the three eldest Pearson brothers' armed attack on local Volunteers. This was the sole 'justification'. The allegation repeated here again about an intention to *"maximise access to land"* is a pure fantasy on English's part. It is given apparent credibility by the narrator's references to the *"local IRA"* meeting to *"decide the fate of the Pearsons."*

Actors Voice (reading statement of Tom Burke)(VO)... *"Having satisfied myself by enquiries that there was no doubt about the identity of the men who fired, I ordered that these men be executed and their houses destroyed."*

Ph. Mc Conway (VO)... Ultimately it was the senior IRA leadership who took the decision to execute. In the context of the times it was a necessary military action to protect and safeguard local republicans.

P. Heaney (I/V)... And when they got their orders, it had to be carried out. They had no choice. No, indeed.

Stanley (VO)... The warning came from a person in the community. By giving the warning he put himself at great risk. The postman came and said to Mrs. Pearson. *"Get your sons out of here. I am in the IRA myself,"* he said. *"I was at a meeting . It was decided they would be shot,"* he said. *"I don't have a stomach for it."* That's all I remember my father saying.

P. Heaney (VO)... No, the family never were tipped off. It wasn't possible for the Pearsons to be tipped off by anybody local. It couldn't be possible. It didn't happen.

********COMMENT:[Pat Muldowney]
[Pages 36, 37 and 68 of Alan Stanley's book *I met Murder on the way,* 2nd edition, 2005: *"The postman* [Delahunty, page 68] *came to deliver the mail. ... he said he had attended an [IRA] meeting at which the decision had been made to kill Richard, Abe and* [William Stanley/Jimmy Bradley]." In a startling omission from the 3rd edition of Alan Stanley's book, Delahunty is excised from the text. This is a tacit acknowledgement by Stanley that his account is incorrect hence no reference to Delahunty. The cornerstone of his warning theory revolves around Delahunty. With this significant omission the validly of the warning theory collapses. Jimmy Delahunty was Quartermaster of the

CU...fields...
[music]
CU... blue cigarette smoke
.....snakes up slowly

CU McConway.....
CU ...face looks out cottage window
[mood music]

CU...Heaney
[dramatic burst of music]
CU...conspirators...shotgun being loaded
CU.....bicycle on road...
CU ..Postman on bike..
CU...agitated postman..
[mood music]
CU....scared postman knocks on door...door opens...

WS... postman on bike cycling ...then he "vanishes"

collapses. Jimmy Delahunty was Quartermaster of the Cadamstown IRA and was one of the IRA party attacked by the Pearsons-Stanley/Bradley at the road-block a week earlier. He was arrested and jailed in the round-up following the attack on the road-block, before the Pearsons were executed, and the photograph of Cadamstown prisoners in Rath Camp shown on the programme includes Delahunty. His father Tim Delahunty had been postman; he died in 1919. Tim's sister Bess Grennan was the acting postman during 1919-24. No letters were delivered to the Pearsons' house; they collected their post themselves from McAllister's Post Office.

(If they were communicating with the British military, this would be a more secure way of dealing with correspondence. The statement in question is by William Stanley; a similar statement was made by David Pearson in 1983 (pages 46, 48). He said that his father William Pearson and brother Sydney left Coolacrease House after this information was received as *"they felt they had done nothing to provoke the IRA,"* and he argues that if they really were spies and informers they would have gone to the police. But spying/informing are quite different from seeking protection against a death threat. If they were innocent they can hardly be criticised now for seeking out whatever protection that could be provided, from any source, against an unwarranted threat. In fact, in his application to the Irish Grants Committee, William Pearson later claimed that when the executions took place he and Sidney were away seeking help from the RIC. In fact they were Mountmellick, returning from a religious convention in Carrick House)

Jim Delahunty became postman in 1923. From 1982 Alan Stanley consulted Tom Mitchell of Kinnitty, who lived next door to Jimmy Delahunty, still alive at that time. Yet Stanley neglected to interview this crucial witness. Just as he did not publish his version until all the volunteer soldiers who defended the democratically elected government against military dictatorship were dead and safely out of the way, unable to contradict him or to defend their reputations against slander. (For details see Stanley, page 68.)]

Prof. R. English (VO)... It's claimed that the Pearsons got a warning on the day of the 30th of June 1921. The family, it appears, thought that this was just a warning that was intended to frighten them out. William Pearson and one of his sons, Sidney, were away from the estate leaving the two boys, Richard, who was 24, and Abraham, who was 19, on their own in terms of protection, and leaving the rest of the family, the women, effectively defenceless.

Heaney (VO)... I suppose the Pearsons were marked men. They were very arrogant, we are told, and they brought that

WS/CU,S...various...fields
..
CU,S..Pearson boys pitching hay in sunny field

CU...English

....CU...Haymaking

WS...men running through woods with guns

435

on themselves because, speaking to Protestant people who knew the Pearsons well, they were told to keep their heads down. But they didn't listen to those people.	CU …Pearson boy and Wm Stanley…[actors]
	[mood music build up with slashing fx]
P. Mc Conway (VO)… They were extremely arrogant towards their neighbours, they had a profound disdain for local Republicans, including the Irish Volunteers, whom they openly antagonised and provoked.	CU…Pearsons pitching hay
Alan Stanley (VO)… My father was aware of the warning and he thought the warning was genuine. He had his eyes peeled. He was the first to see them. He told the two boys to run for their lives. He himself ran. He was a very good runner.	[build up …mood music…] CU…Wm Stanley pitching hay..[actor]…. ..WS….Posse of IRA men appear over brow of hill..
P. Heaney (VO)… He ran zig zag down across the field. The local OC with the column, ordered a couple of men down to fire on him.	CU….Stanley runs off.
Stanley (VO)… He actually called out a second time for the boys to run but they were rooted to the spot.	CU..Pearsons.."rooted to the spot"
Heaney (VO)… Then the Pearsons were brought up to the house, the Pearson family was there. The girls were very aggressive, more aggressive than the brothers, or their parents.	CU…IRA give chase…Capture the Pearsons… CU…Heaney
	CU…IRA men attack Pearsons house… CU… wedding photo. Pearsons
Olive Boothman, Grandniece/Susan Pearson(I/V)… My mother was there. They were told the house was going to be burnt and they were all brought out into the yard including Aunt Susan.	CU…. Boothman
P.McConway (VO).. According to IRA regulations at the time any Loyalist who attempted to resist the IRA forfeited their property to the Irish state. That included burning the house down.	CU's….IRA taking Family out of house…..setting house alight…. CU….McConway CU,S…military archive statement…1712…. Michael Cordial… Kinnity..Co Offaly.
P. Heaney (VO)… Well, reading Michael Cordial's report… Michael was involved with the local IRA. He gave the report that when the house was fired the roof lifted off from explosions. Well, it was known locally that the Pearsons had ammunition stored in their house.	CU….Heaney
Narrator (VO)… What Michael Cordial's statement actually said is that heavy explosions were heard when the house was burning. One possible explanation for the explosion was later accounted by IRA commanding officer on the day, Joe Connolly.	CU's…various… Pearsons house burning…. CU's…archive… Pearson's house burnt out

******* COMMENT 47:[Pat Muldowney]
Nobody denies that the Pearsons had guns and ammunition in the house. They attacked the roadblock with them (or, if we are to believe the version of the Luggacurran loyalist paramilitary, William Stanley, they "fired in the air", leaving unexplained the gunshot wounds suffered by Mick Heaney, Tom Donnelly, and retired RIC man Bert Hogg). The only question is about the quantity of armaments they held. Michael Cordial's Bureau of Military History Witness Statement says: *"Heavy explosions were heard while the house was burning which indicated that a large amount of ammunition was stored in it."* To start a fire in a house you need inflammable material such as hay, which, even in summer, can usually be found in a farmyard. Did the IRA party, travelling on foot from distant parts (the local IRA had largely been arrested the week before), bring enough petrol – a barrel, say – to cause *"several heavy explosions"*? It is likely they brought a can or two, which if poured or splashed carelessly on burning hay would ignite and possibly engulf the person holding the can. That is what the following statement by Michael Connolly indicates. It does not explain several large explosions.

Michael Connolly (Son of Joe Connolly) (I/V)... Daddy got petrol and threw it in on the floor and there was an explosion once it lit up and he was thrown back into the yard.	CU....archive.., Joe Connelly...[in free state uniform..]
Ruth Kelly (VO).... It exploded when it was set alight. But of course it exploded!! They filled it with petrol!!	CU's...house burning...

******* COMMENT:[PM]
As usual, the Pearson side is given the opportunity to debunk the case against them. But this advantage is not reciprocated. Even though it is quite easy to debunk the latter remark. There is a great difference between a small amount of petrol bursting into flame - which might cause somebody close by to be thrown backwards - and a quantity of ammunition blowing the roof off a house. The latter would kill anyone nearby, not throw them off their feet. It is also significant that the RIC County Inspector's report on the incident states that *"It is further rumoured when the Farm house was burning, two guns fell out of the roof."*

Alan Stanley (VO)... The women were all brought out into the court yard. The two boys were stood against the wall.	CU,S...various....women and men being roughly manhandled in yard and men being put up agains

******* COMMENT 48:[Pat Muldowney]
According to the evidence given by Ethel Pearson to the British Military Court of Inquiry in Lieu of Inquest held in Birr on 2nd July 1921: *"My mother who was in a fainting condition was carried by my two brothers into a little wood we call the Grove and we all went with her by the order of the raiders."* So according to this the women were not taken to the yard, but to a place from where the interior of the enclosed yard was not visible. She does NOT say they were taken to the yard. She does say the following: *"I saw the raiders search my brothers and place them against the wall of the barn and shoot them",* even though this was physically impossible from the Grove. The atrocity myths devised by the Pearsons began very quickly and grew ever more fanciful and outlandish with time. William Pearson's 1927 version has 500 IRA raiders descending on the house and shooting his daughter as she tried to save her brothers from being shot. The statements of the Pearsons (and of William Stanley) have to be taken with great caution. There is no indication that the Hidden History programme used any critical judgement in assessing them. This contrasts with the automatic scepticism with which any evidence from Republican sources is treated by the programme. The fact there was a British Court of Inquiry was not disclosed, and no balancing views were expressed.

Heaney (VO)... The Court Martial was read out.

Stanley (VO)... They were told, apparently, that they had been sentenced to death, making it all nice and legal and proper, of course.

P. Heaney (VO).... The executions were duly carried out.

Stanley (VO)... They were shot first of all with numerous rounds aimed to the groin area. They had turned their backs as we all might do. Then there was more fire.

******* COMMENT 49:[PM]
The Court of Inquiry shows that the men received mostly superficial gunshot wounds all over their bodies, only one of them to the (right) groin of one of the men. The programme, in a calculated decision according to Philip McConway, scrupulously excluded all reference to this evidence. No counter-balancing contributions were provided to Stanley's and Harris's outrageous statements on this point.

Stanley (VO)... Richard died seven and three quarter hours later. Abraham fourteen hours later. In fact Abraham died the following day, so I imagine that they would have been in

wall...with 5 (!) adult women watching. (There were 4 adult women present on the actual occasion.)

CU...HEANEY

CU ...FIRING SQUAD
CU... TWO PEARSON BOYS' FACES... THE FIRING SQUAD SHOOTS....

CU...PEARSONS FALL SCREAMING...CLUTCHING GROINS...

WS...firing squad fires again with five (!) adult women in background looking on

CU.....woman's face in horror...
CU...more firing...
Then....

[angelic choral music]...

CU......Pearsons in slow

438

unbelievable pain.

Prof. Richard English (VO)... The details of the killing, dying slowly while bleeding to death, made this a particularly ghastly episode, even if one were broadly sympathetic with IRA Republicanism.

       ******* COMMENT 50:[PM]
       Assuming the Pearsons were innocent of the roadblock attack, this statement would be fair. The programme was not entitled to make that assumption on behalf of the viewers, and therefore not entitled to leave this statement without an accompanying statement based on the opposite assumption. Their deaths, however tragic, were no more 'ghastly' than many others in Co. Offaly. In terms of prolonged pain, far worse and more harrowing cases exist. IRA Lieutenant Matthew Kane, shot in the stomach by the RIC, bled to death in a field while alone and without medical attention. Liam Dignam shot by the Black and Tans in Clara fell in writhing in agony and died months later. The programme isolated the Pearson killings, providing no context.

JJ Dillon (VO)... It was crazy. It was brutal. It was wrong. Even in death a person is entitled to dignity.

       ******* COMMENT 51:[PM]
       This is not a balancing statement. It is in the broadly anti-war spirit of JJ Dillon's earlier statement *"In conflict those things occur. Like hatred comes into it, revenge comes into it."*
From this point of view, the blame lies with the party which instigated the war. And the programme made no effort to give a balanced explanation of the political context out of which the war came.

P. Heaney (VO)... People resented, I suppose, the way they were shot, but they were executed and that was it.

       ******* COMMENT 52:[PM]
       This is not a balancing contribution giving the just and legitimate war-time reasons for the executions. Any number of Paddy Heaney's statements explaining these could have been inserted here. Editorially, the programme chose a statement which does not include such a reason. The viewers thus get an impression of a hard, unfeeling person who needs no reason for such a measure.

Sen. Eoghan Harris (VO)... That's not an execution. That's an atrocity. Shooting them very deliberately, in the genitals, in

---

motion... falling to ground...much blood...

CU,....,,Richard on ground writhing in pain being attended by girls...
CU......Abraham bleeding on ground...

[angelic mood music]

CU'S....women attending Pearson boys on ground yard
CU'S.......women attending boys in yard ...t mood music

CU...DILLON
[mood music]..

CU's......bodies on ground..

CU's .....bleeding boys being attended to by women on ground.....

CU....Bodies on ground..
CU...Heaney

CU.........Harris...
CU...... bloodied boys again..

439

their sexual parts, in their sexual organs, what it really says is you are The Other, you are an outsider, we hate you, go away and die.

CU....HARRIS

[mood music]

******* COMMENT 51:[PM]
This statement is contrary to the evidence that the Pearsons were guilty of what they were charged with, and contradicts the medical evidence. It unjustly charges those involved in the executions with attitudes, and with a crime, for which there is no evidence. This statement is the most highly charged part of the programme, and was the basis of the resulting frenzied propaganda in the media. If the programme was fair, impartial and objective, it would have provided an examination of the evidence from the medical reports, which is very precise.

[fade to black]

Philip Mc Conway (VO)... The IRA botched the execution in that they didn't finish them off with head shots. In hindsight it was wrong for the IRA to allow the mother and sisters to witness the executions. But the female members of the Pearsons were deemed to be as hostile as their brothers to the local volunteers.

CU...McConway...

CU...archive...Pearson women...[.plus angelic music]... and re-enactment of firing squad once again
...

******* COMMENT 52:[PM]
This does not provide balance or rebuttal (for which there is plenty of evidence well known to the programme makers) to the preceding statement of Harris. Harris was facilitated by the programme in making his powerful, but unjustified, case. Philip McConway has explained that the programme makers knew before broadcast that new evidence had caused him to change his opinion on whether the Pearson women had seen the executions. The programme knowingly and consciously misrepresented him.
The execution party – from the Active Service Unit of the Kilcormac Battalion IRA - had limited combat experience and were not battle hardened veterans. Unsuccessful executions were not uncommon. At Coolacrease it was wrongly assumed the first volley of shots would be fatal.

JJ Dillon (VO)... A lot of their people, they weren't trained to kill. They were overawed, frightened, they were victims as well in a different kind of way, probably haunted by it, maybe for the rest of their lives.

CU's....individual members of firing squad...
they fire their guns yet again....[actors]...
.[angelic music]

******* COMMENT 53:[Pat Muldowney]
This is a broad anti-war statement similar to those expressed earlier by JJ Dillon. Having allowed Harris to make an unchallenged allegation of atrocity, this statement of JJ Dillon's is not a counter-statement, it actually reinforces

*******COMMENT:[PM]
The gory execution scene is played over and over again. This is the focus and fulcrum of the

440

Harris's position. JJ Dillon's humanitarian, anti-war sentiment is used to buttress the political position of Harris. This would not have been possible if the case had been made for the guilt of the Pearsons, and their complicity in the imperial onslaught against Irish democracy. Responsibility for the war, and the consequent horrors, lie with the side which resorted to force to overturn the democratically expressed choice of the voters by making the country ungovernable by the legitimate, elected government programme and its political propaganda. It is a powerfully contrived emotional blast. Ther is not even a gesture towards balance. Feelings of sympathy are artfully evoked in order to overwhelm any remaining faculty of judicious rationality in the viewers. But war consists of combatants on each side attacking and killing combatant on the other side. The moral guilt resides with the authority which caused the war. The human and personal consequences are experienced by everyone involved. The Pearsons chose to get involved in violent conflict with the democracy, when they could very easily have kept out of it. They were not innocent victims Any violent incident in any war could be presented in a way which focuses on the personal suffering involved, without offering any explanation of the why's and wherefore's. But this documentary was advertised as providing an explanation of what happened in Coolacrease. It did exactly the opposite. These scenes are the high point of the programme's propaganda

Edna Black...[I/V]..[grand daughter/Wm./Susan Pearson]
I myself lost a son. It was after his death that I sort of thought of my grandmother losing two sons in a tragedy. It's hard just to enter into the depth of sorrow that she was asked to face into that day by her own fellow countrymen, which is even sadder.

CU....Black...
CU.....Susan Pearson..

******* COMMENT 54:[PM]
Those attacked by the Pearsons were also afflicted. That aspect should have been included in the summing up. The points made by JJ Dillon could easily have been developed in this direction, instead of being misused to buttress the Harris position.

Sen. Eoghan Harris...[I/V].. Even if there were shots fired, even if there were rows over mass rocks and rights of way...nothing...nothing...can disturb the starkness of 30 or 40 men going to a farmhouse, pulling two young men, Abe and Richard, out of a field, standing them against a wall,

CU...Sen. Harris
CU...IRA going into house...firing squad fires yet again....

CU...Harris

441

shooting them in the groin, then shooting them in the ass when they turned round in pain and horror and then leaving them to bleed to death. Nothing can disturb that image in the public mind. And I believe that the plain people of Ireland have a good idea that something evil was done that day.

[silence...pause]

******* COMMENT 55:[PM]
This dramatic, rhetorical conclusion, reiterating earlier unfounded statements, is given powerful, unchallenged and unbalanced display.

Narrator...[V/O].. A few days later Richard and Abraham Pearson were buried without ceremony in an unmarked grave in Co. Laois, almost 30 miles from their home.

Jenny Turnidge..[I/V].. They couldn't be buried in their local area. They had to be taken out of the area and they had to be buried without a name.

******* COMMENT 56:[PM]
All graves are unmarked at time of burial. It was up to the Pearsons themselves to mark the graves subsequently. William Pearson was diligent in attending to many other things, coming and going to his property at Coolacrease over the following two years, and he could hardly plead poverty! The brothers were buried in Killermogh, in the Aghaboe area where they had lived the earlier part of their lives, where they came from only ten years earlier, the area where their ancestors had lived and died. Newspapers of the time report that issues and disputes tended to arise in burials of Cooneyites. For one thing, they did not have formal church buildings or formal burial grounds of their own. And since Cooneyism only began around 1900, the only mainstream congregation the Pearsons would have been connected with would have been in the place they resided before Cooneyism came into the picture. So it is quite understandable that they were taken to that area, that church, and that graveyard for burial.

Alan Stanley..[V/O]... I spoke to a man who witnessed the burials. He said that as they came out of the church two Crossley type tenders pulled up to the gate .He then saw two soldiers remove two coffins. Two young women followed weeping bitterly. They saw coffins being lowered and instantly the graves being filled and they were gone almost as soon as they arrived.

Paddy Byrne...[Cadamstown resident]... I asked an old woman, she was an old woman, where were they buried and

CU......Pearson family...outside burnt out house

[.fade to black...]

CU.....laneway...flowers i foreground.

CU......flowers...

CU ...Turnidge

CU....Killermogh church i Co Laois

.CU.....inside empty church..

C U....Byrne

442

she said, if they were buried in the bog it would be too good for them. There was bitterness everywhere.

WS...church..

CU...flowers...

******* COMMENT 57:[PM]
By juxtaposing these two statements, the deliberate (though unfounded) impression is created that the local people somehow were instrumental in unseemly and undignified interment. Burial arrangements had to made from Crinkle Military Barracks in Birr, and had nothing to do with the local people. If we allow the possibility that the Pearsons were guilty of a violent and unprovoked attack on members of the volunteer citizen army defending the elected government, after they had been welcomed only a few years earlier into the bosom of the local community, then the bitter sentiments reported by Paddy Byrne are perfectly understandable.

Sen. Harris...[V/O].. It was only a few days before the Truce. Everybody knew there was going to be a Truce...there was no need for this...

Archive...B&W shots of Truce...
CU...Harris...

Prof. Rich. English....[I/V]... There is a particular poignancy in the Pearsons' story, as I think there is in other conflicts, insofar as immediately before a ceasefire, or before a Truce, it becomes to look increasingly futile when you look back at it through the lens of the Peace which is about to emerge.

CU...English

******* COMMENT 58:[PM]
More irrelevant anachronisms from Prof. English. The Truce was eleven days away at the time of the executions, and there was no atmosphere as yet of a truce being imminent. The war was most intense at that point, when the Pearsons decided to become active combatants. What happened to Mick Heaney, and to the others who were wounded and imprisoned because of the Pearsons, was also very unfortunate and poignant.
This should also have been pointed out by the programme, in the interests of fairness and balance.

Narrator...[V/O] After burying their sons, the Pearsons decided to remain on at Coolacrease, living in the coach house behind the ruin of their former home.

CU....burnt out house...Pearson family in foreground...

******* COMMENT 59:[PM]
According to Alan Stanley's book, and according to William Stanley's 1927 Grants Committee application, William Stanley moved his family to Wales and England, and stayed in the coach house himself during his subsequent visits to Offaly.

£5,000, the Land Commission paid an exorbitant price to Pearson, probably because he extorted it by holding out and, in effect, leaving an economic resource unworked, unlet, unsold and uncultivated. After the prosperous Great War years, and not having had to employ many locals, he had accumulated £6,000 (the price of three Coolacreases) in the bank, according to his Grant application. So he could afford to put the squeeze on the Land Commission. Dooley's statement is quite ludicrous. The Percy letter is an obvious fraud (as is another sham valuation of £17,000 put forward by Pearson) – and was probably recognised as such by the Grants Committee. But the Committee seemed to swallow the by now rampant Pearson atrocity propaganda, and latched on to the Percy letter as a device to compensate Pearson, not for his farm (for which he was excessively paid by the Land Commission) but for his cleverly spun and highly imaginative atrocity tale.

Narrator...[V/O]... There was some consolation for the family. The Irish Grants Committee, a British agency, established to compensate loyalists who had lost out during the war, granted William Pearson 7,500 pounds

CU......Irish Grants Committee Doc.

******* COMMENT:[PM]
Which, in addition to the compensation from the King's County Court, the money from the Land Commission and the income from the auction of stock and machinery, brings the total amount that Pearson came away with to well over £15,000.

Dr. W. Murphy ..[V/O]... Pearson describes himself as an ardent loyalist, but he does so in the context of applying for compensation from the British Government for his sufferings. Therefore, at that time, it is going to be in his interest to describe himself as an ardent loyalist.

CU...Murphy

******* COMMENT 61:[Pat Muldowney]
Here is how Pearson describes himself: *"I was always known as a staunch Loyalist and upholder of the Crown. I assisted the Crown Forces on every occasion."* Using misdirection and evasion, Murphy addresses the first part of this and ignores the second part. It was perfectly obvious he was a loyalist, he had nothing to prove on this score. Anyway, Murphy accepts him as a loyalist earlier, so why the back-tracking and quibbling about it now? The Pearsons crime was not loyalism, but engaging in armed combat against the elected government.

Narrator..[V/O]... In 1911, the Pearson family had bought the

CU...red poppies in field of

444

Dr Terence Dooley...[I/V]... William Pearson had lost his two eldest sons who he had used to run the farm. Essentially he couldn't get others from the local community to work for him. Raids continued on his property, and his attempts to sell...his cattle were boycotted by the locals. He couldn't sell his farm because any potential buyer was put off, e.g. William Percy,"*The price I offered was 10,000 and I might have gone higher only the people would not allow any outsider to purchase the land. I was not allowed to close the bargain.*" So he was becoming squeezed all the time. What he attempted to do was cut his losses by actually selling the land to the Land Commission for around 5000 pound.

CU.....Dooley..
CU.....farm..
CU......cows, sheds, cattle
CU...Advert in paper to sell farm...
CU......letter...Wm Percy
CU......Dooley...
CU... archive...Irish Land Registry document, showing purchase price of £2000 for Coolacrease in 1911.

******* COMMENT 60:[Pat Muldowney]
The first sentence is incorrect. They were not his two eldest sons. Sidney, 20, was the second eldest and was away with his father at the time of the execution. Richard Pearson, 24, was the eldest. Abraham was aged 19. Regarding the second sentence, the *King's County Chronicle* of 13th October 1921 quotes William Pearson as saying that his two boys had spared him the expense of employing a lot of workmen every year, as one man interested in the work would be worth six who were not. In other words, William Pearson was never too keen on employing locals, locals who could not afford to be choosy about any kind of paid employment. (The same newspaper records the steadily developing atrocity stories being peddled by the Pearsons – no talk now of being moved to the shelter of the Grove; ALL the women, including the mother who was carried to the Grove in a faint, were FORCED to watch the executions in the yard.)

The next three sentences of Dooley's statement are based on Pearson's 1927 application to the British Government's Grants Committee for loyalists who suffered injury or damages. That document is riddled with lies (the 500 raiders, the shooting of his daughter, about half of the items claimed for turned down as implausible or too obviously unjustified. The Grants Committee papers note that he had sold his farm equipment by public auction and received fair prices for it. The *Midland Tribune* of August 27 1921 reported that he had refused all bids for his farm when it was put up for public auction on 23rd August. The papers of William Pearson's application to the Grants Committee record that he auctioned his farm equipment and received fair prices for it.

The Land Commission document shown on screen at this point on the programme gives the 1911 purchase price of Coolacrease as £2,000, a reasonable price for rather poor land between the bog and the mountain. Land prices went through the floor after the Great War agricultural boom. At land at Coolacrease. Now, just under a decade later, they were leaving, never to return.

Paddy Heaney [V/O].... When the land was divided by the Irish Land Commission, I think two, maybe three whose people were involved in the IRA received parcels of land there ....

CU ...Heaney..

CU ......Poppies in field

> ******* COMMENT 62:[Pat Muldowney]
> Paddy Heaney's position, well known to the programme, is and always has been the opposite of what editorial chicanery is ascribing to him here. His position is that the Pearson place was divided by the Land Commission, and the first three people to be allocated land were ex-British soldiers. People excluded at the initial meetings mostly by the machinations of the anti-Republican parish priest, Fr Houlahan, protested and some later were allocated land. Two or three ex-IRA people got land there subsequently. A number of people failed to farm successfully, because of the high repayments to the Land Commission resulting from the price extorted from them by William Pearson. There is no evidence of Land Commission complicity in a land grab by Republicans, or that there was any such land grab by anyone at all. If there had been such complicity, it would make for a new and sensational story, as it would fly in the face of the reputation of Land Commission officials for scrupulous adherence to procedure. They have never before been tarred with such an accusation.

Prof. Rich. English....[V/O] You can justify killing someone on the grounds that they are an enemy of the war for freedom. But it could also be that in this case they own a large farm ...as in this case.... It is divided up amongst the local people. This was an attack not just on the Pearson boys who were actually killed. It was an attack which drove effectively the Pearsons out.

CU ....English...

CU ......archive... photo of Pearsons.

> ******* COMMENT 63:[Pat Muldowney]
> Having deliberately distorted Paddy Heaney's words and meaning into the opposite of what the programme knew he meant, English is allowed to expand on his unfounded speculations. English's comments suggest that Paddy Heaney was providing actual evidence for his speculations - not a shred of which English could produce himself.

CU ......Newspapers...
[1]......"widespread expulsion of Protest..."
[2]"terrible double tragedy: two farmers shot dead"
[3] "County Wicklow JP shot dead.. Son seriously wounded"
[4] "terrible night inWest Cork:further shootings over a wide area"

Sen. Harris ...[V/O]... 60,000 Protestants were driven from the South of Ireland. They usually scattered, in the night, grabbing what belongings they could. As time passed the usual mist and fog that descends over any incident.... descended.

CU...Harris...

******* COMMENT 64:[Pat Muldowney]
This is the ethnic cleansing theory signalled in RTÉ's presentation on 30th May 2007 at Clontarf Castle, and repeated in supporting commentaries at the time of broadcast in the *Sunday Independent* on 21st October 2007 and on RTÉ Radio's 'Tubridy Show' on 22nd October 2007. There is no evidence to corroborate the sensationalist land grabbing and ethnic cleansing claims of the programme. The Pearson were executed as a result of their participation in the war as combatants, thereby forfeiting their civilian status. They attacked an IRA roadblock and wounded two Volunteers. Separate investigations by the RIC and IRA show this to have been the motive for the execution. British loyalists were expelled from the British colonies in America after its War of Independence and British people in India had the option of taking Indian citizenship, but almost all of them left. In Ireland nobody was compelled to give up British citizenship, and the newly formed Senate was practically a preserve of Unionists. No historian, not even Peter Hart, has openly espoused the ethnic cleansing theory implied by Eoghan Harris and explicitly trumpeted by RTÉ.

********COMMENT: Without actually uttering the loaded words *"Ethnic Cleansing"* which RTÉ used in its internal 30th May meeting in Clontarf Castle, the viewers are presented with the unfounded propaganda of the period. No counter-balancing visuals are presented.[Pat Muldowney]

Narrator…[V/O] In 1922, the Pearsons joined this exodus leaving first for England, and, some years later, for a new life in Australia.

CU ..passport..Pearson and sons
CU……steamer ship and passengers.

Sen. Harris…[I/V]… The Pearsons became true forgotten ones. They became, literally, the disappeared of history.

CU… Harris [catch in voice]

******* COMMENT 65:[pm]
Balance would require some corresponding emotional display on behalf of those who suffered because of the Pearson engagement on the imperial side. No proof was given in the programme that the Pearsons were innocent of what the official Irish Military Court of Enquiry found.

Jenny Turnidge ..[V/O].. This family had nowhere to go, no one to turn to. I really admire the fact that they effectively walked away, because I don't know that I could.

CU…Susan Pearson
CU……..Pearsons in front of burn out house…
CU……Turnidge…

******* COMMENT:[PM]
According to Alan Stanley's book, from the mixed bogland and mountain of Coolacrease they were able to buy a 200-acre farm in the Home Counties (Suffolk) – and that was BEFORE the massive award received from the Irish Grants Committee, when they went on to purchase farms and businesses in Australia.

CU…Newspaper, Jan. 17, 1930.. [Sidney Peewspaper, "Irish

Voiceover...Actor....[reading diary: Jan. Fri. 17 1930] *"watch ship coming up river into harbour....look out for our people...see them waving to us...Interviewed by pressman. Have our photo taken, to be put into paper..."*	loyalists to settle here. Two sons killed by rebels in 1921" CU...Pearson
Vernon Pearson...[I/V]... They arrived in Australia from an English winter and when he arrived in that he said ...the sweat, what on earth...he wondered what they were coming to...	CU...fields..
Narrator...[V/O].. The Pearsons reached Australia in 1930. After a short period in Melbourne they went back to farming and bought land in South Gipsland, Victoria...	CU...fields..
Mervyn Pearson..[Grandson...Wm./susan Pearson]..[I/V]... My grandfather William and Susan settled here with their son Sid and my dad settled further over there where he bought his own property and that's where he settled. The original house here...[points]...would have been where that new house is being built at the moment. ...that's where the original house would have survived until two years ago, I believe, where it was burnt...	CU...Mervyn Pearson.. CU...fields
Vernon Pearson...[V/O] They had a big battle, 'cos the conditions in Australia were so different to the conditions they had in Ireland and a lot of them took a long time to get into a place where...y'know.. they could say they were comfortable.	CU Vernon CU...house.. CU......Photos of Pearsons
Mervyn Pearson [V/O] I saw the results of what had happened in their lives. They were all affected by it by the time their life was over	CU... House
Edna Black..[granddaughter of Wm./Susan Pearson] Grandma Pearson, I sort of remember her sitting beside her window, and the blind would be drawn and very little light, sitting there...and she seemed to be sitting there with her eye on the window just wondering what could happen again.	Photo William Pearson CU...grandma Pearson CU...window
Ruth Kelly..[V/O]... Aunty Ethel...she was very security conscious...oh so many padlocks,...and the windows were all pasted over with brown paper, y'know, she was just terrified.	CU.... Aunt Ethel CU ...house..
Doris Turnidge... [granddaughter] [V/O]... Tilly was definitely the strongest one. But it hit her the hardest. She would sort of stamp her feet a little and her husband would say *"Its all right Tilly...its all right now...you're here in Australia, you're fine"*...but it effected her quite badly nerves wise..	CU...Tilly.. CU......Doris Turnidge
Edna Black....[V/O]... The tragedy really did shatter the family and it was a life time sentence really to the whole	Archive photos........Pearson

family....

Narrator...[V/O] In the early 1930,s William Pearson's health began to fail. He and Susan left the farm in Gipsland and travelled north to the sun settling in the mining town of Bendigo

Doris Turnidge...[V/O]... Grandfather used to say to them prior to all of that, *"No problems, I'll die amongst the gold"* and they used to laugh at him...but actually, he did ...he died in Bendigo..

Narrator [V/O]... Susan Pearson moved to Melbourne to live closer to her daughter Tilly until her death in 1947. She never returned to Ireland. Some of her children eventually made the trip back.

Doris Turnidge....[V/O].. We walked up the avenue, right to the front door. Some of the glass was still in the windows. The memories flooded back. She was home. That's the point. But she would never go and live in Ireland because of fear. I can understand that.

Vernon Pearson....[V/O] My father went back to Ireland in 1975. Well, he went back to look at the old areas where he saw the troubles and he couldn't get out quick enough.

Olive Boothman, Grand-niece...[I/V].. I came upon it unexpectedly. I found myself in Cadamstown and I drove out the road and saw Coolacrease.. the ruins... and trees growing out of it and I just said ...no way would I walk down to the house...you didn't want to disturb it in some way, y'know, you didn't feel you had any right to tread on the ground, then you kind of shook your head and drove on. ...It lives on... and it's not a good memory ...

Narrator....[V/O] When the ruins of Coolacrease House finally fall asunder the last physical connection between family and community will disappear ...land ...religion ... and politics ... separated the Pearsons from their friends and neighbours. They will, however, always be bound by what happened on that day at Coolacrease...

family in Australia...plus Aussie flag...
WS.......Aussie town...[Gipsland/Bendigo.

WS........Wm Pearson..
CU....golden sunset.
CU ...... Doris Turnidge

CU......Tilly Pearson...
CU......... Doris Turnidge

CU.......windows..

CU........ Offaly

CU........photo ..old Pearsons..
WS ...ruined house in Offaly...

CU........ various shots of ruined house...

CU...........Pearson Gran daughter/niece..

CU..........ruins..
CU ....poppies...
CU ....graves

[mood music]..

******* COMMENT:[Pat Muldowney]
The incident in Coolacrease was a relatively unimportant one, and had fallen into oblivion. But not in the local area, where the pro's and con's were keenly debated and digested down the generations. It was NOT the dark and guilty secret that 'Hidden History'/RTÉ trumpeted in their propaganda and advertising, to be opened up to the bright light of day by the sharp sword of truth wielded by their fearlessly self-

449

regarding reporters. The local community was way ahead of them. The first published account of the incident was produced in 2002 in the village of Cadamstown itself by Paddy Heaney, in his book *At the Foot of Slieve Bloom*. And as more light is shed on the incident, his accuracy, authority and spirit of generous forgiveness are evident.

Sen. Harris ...[V/O] Yeats said it, he said...."Though gravediggers toil be long.... Sharp their spades and muscles strong... *They will thrust their buried men .. Into the public mind again....*"
The more you try to put them down ... the more they come back up. The Pearsons of Coolacrease is a good place to start to look at what happened in the War of Independence. It wasn't all heroism. It wasn't all "Four Glorious Years," and a lot of the stuff that our grandfathers and uncles and cousins did wouldn't bear looking at in the light of day..

> ******* COMMENT: [Pat Muldowney]
> So how come the Senator has lapsed into relative silence, after his initial bluster about the Pearsons was challenged and exposed? Has he bottled out? Does he want to bury the Pearsons' story again? Or could it be that his version of the story *"won't bear looking at in the light of day"*?
> But he can rest assured that it will definitely be *"thrust ... into the public mind again"* – as a caution against revisionist fantasy!

Alan Stanley....[V/O]... I don't harbour bitterness ... but it's not quite as simple as that. There has to be a sort of cleansing from some source, from somewhere, so that we can look back and say...*"how was it that we acted that way, thought that way, behaved that way."* Perhaps it's more than we can deal with in some cases, I suppose...

Paddy Heaney...[V/O] Speaking to people who were involved at that time, they regretted a lot of things ... that happened .... and maybe that shouldn't have happened. But that's what happens when you have a War of Independence. It's part of our history. We can't change it and we're not responsible for it...

Edna Black....[V/O] Ye can't change the past, can ye, but ye'd like to think that what was left on record, whether it be history, or what would be a truthful, honest, and correct interpretation of what happened.....

CU............grave..
CU............Harris..

{mood music}.

CU.......Pearsons..on front out of burnt house...
CU........gurgling stream..
CU.......archive..cheering crowds..
CU.........old photo..

CU............waterfall
CU..........Stanley
CU............cheering crowd...
CU..............river

CU..............cheering crowds
CU............stream
{mood music}
CU..............flag..
CU..............stream

[mood music]

CU............stream...
WS..............Pearson boys walk down the road with scythe...look back at camera...walk over hill out

******* COMMENT 66:[Pat Muldowney]
Harris's and Stanley's summing up on the basis of assumed Pearson innocence needed to be balanced by some overview predicated on the much more likely scenario that the Pearsons were combatants. This balance is NOT provided by the remarks of Paddy Heaney, which are true of any side in any war, and have no special relevance to the Coolacrease incident

A fair and balanced programme would have included the subsequent human and family history of the people who suffered injury and imprisonment because of the Pearsons. The final contributions are chosen and combined in a way which suggests strongly, contrary to the actual evidence, that the Pearsons were innocent victims of an atrocity.

of sight....

[music swells to finis and fades.]

SOME CREDITS

NARRATOR : ORLA BRADY

SCRIPT CONSULTANT : PAT SAMMON

RESEARCH :PAUL ROUSE

PHILIP McCONWAY

VIDEO EDITOR : RAY ROANTREE

PRODUCED AND DIRECTED: NIAMH SAMMON

Appendix 10

List of Documents (Appendixes 2-8)

1. Procedures for reprisals: IRA G.H.Q. Order, 22nd June 1921
2. Report by Thomas Burke, O/C Offaly No. 2 Brigade IRA, on the execution of the Pearson brothers
3. Witness Statement of Michael Cordial, Formerly Quartermaster, 3rd Battalion, Offaly No. 2 Brigade IRA
4. Extract: Report of 3rd Battalion (Kilcormac), Offaly No. 2 Brigade IRA on activities in June 1921
5. Map of Birr-Cadamstown area
6. Map of Cadamstown-Coolacrease with locations of 1921 events
7. Map and scene of the Pearson Execution
8. Proceedings of the British Military Courts of Inquiry in lieu of Inquests into the deaths of Richard and Abraham Pearson, 2nd July 1921 (Transcript)
9. Original of the Proceedings of the Court of Inquiry in lieu of Inquest into the death of Abraham Pearson, Crinkle Barracks, 2nd July 1921
10. Distribution of the proceedings of the "Court of Inquiry in lieu of Inquest" up the British chain of command
11. Dublin Castle Statement on the Pearson executions, 9th July 1921
12. Note on 'Possible Motives' circulated by the British command
13. British GHQ to Under Secretary, Dublin Castle, 27th July 1921: Note on "Possible Motives"
14. Land Registry Folio 1863. Record of registered title of the Pearson Farm 1909-1930

15. Letter, Melanie Hall, Keeper of Records, Land Services Division, Department of Agriculture, to Pat Muldowney, 13th March 2008

16. Order vesting the Pearson Farm in the Land Commission, 2nd August 1923

17. Land Commission map: Sub-division of the Pearson Farm

18. Land Commission. Pearson Estate: 'Schedule of Areas'

19. Land Commission. Pearson Estate: "Schedule giving Particulars of Division."

20. Land Commission allocations, Pearson Estate: Inspector T.H. Blackall to Commissioner Hogan, 18th September 1923

21. Resolving allocation issues: letter, Bernard (Brian) Heaney, Cadamstown, to Land Commission, 28th September 1923

22. Purchase agreement for the allocation to Bernard (Brian) Heaney 12th September 1923 (extracts)

23. Land Commission: consolidation of holdings from the Pearson Estate, 1929

24. Valuation Office: Birr 1 1857-1934 Book A: Coolacrease 1909

25. Valuation Office: Birr 1 1857-1934 Book D: Coolacrease 1912-34

26. Valuation Office: Birr I 1934-69, Bk 23, Co. Offaly, RD Birr No. 1

27. Land Registry Folio 7911 (Extract): Land allocated to John Multany

28. Land Registry Folio 7399 (Extract): Land allocated to Jim Delahunty

29. Land Registry Folio 7400 (Extract): Allocation to Martin Egan

30. Land Registry Folio 7405 (Extract): Allocation to Jim McCormack

31. Request by Sidney Pearson to the Irish Grants Committee to lodge a claim, 25th October 1926

32. Application by Sidney Pearson to Irish Grants Committee, 28th October 1926

33. Reference from Rev. Robert E. Weir of Mountrath, Co. Kildare, with Sidney Pearson's application, 1st December 1926

34. Irish Grants Committee: Correspondence on Sidney Pearson's claim

35. Cover letter from Major White, Southern Irish Loyalists Relief Association, accompanying William Pearson's application to the Irish Grants Committee, 24th May 1927

36. William Pearson's application to the Irish Grants Committee, 24th May 1927 (original document)

37. Transcript of William Pearson's claim to the Irish Grants Committee, 24th May 1927

38. Schedule A – Schedule Showing Value of Losses and Compensation Claimed and Received (attachment to William Pearson's application to the Irish Grants Committee, 24th May 1927)

39. Schedule B: Schedule of Losses for which no Compensation was Paid (attachment to William Pearson's application to the Irish Grants Committee, 24th May 1927)

40. Response of the Irish Grants Committee to Southern Irish Loyalists Relief Association on William Pearson's application, 1st June 1927

41. Major White, Southern Irish Loyalists Relief Association, to Alan Reid Jamieson, Secretary, Irish Grants Committee, 11th June 1927

42. Correspondence between Major White and Alan Reid Jamieson on William Pearson's claim.

43. Major White, Southern Irish Loyalists Relief Association, to Alan Reid Jamieson, Secretary, Irish Grants Committee, 25th January 1928

44. Note, Telford's of Birr, valuing the Pearson farm, 6th October 1927

45. Note on William Percy's alleged offer for the farm. n.d.

46. Report by Alan Reid Jamieson, Secretary, Irish Grants Committee, on Franks assessment of the Pearson claims, n.d.

47. Decision of the IGC on the Pearson application, February 1928

48. Notes by M.J. Drayson and Sir Harry Batterbee (Dominions Office) on the IGC decision, n.d.

49. Under Secretary Sir H. Batterbee orders payout of the full claim award to William Pearson, 2nd March 1929

50. Extract from *The Gadfly*, by E.L. Voynich

51. Eoghan Harris, 'This tree has rotten roots and bitter fruit', *Sunday Independent*, 9/10/2005

52. 'Atonement: Ethnic Cleansing in the Midlands, 1922': slide show by Kevin Dawson, 30th May 2007 and RTÉ Announcement of Autumn 2007 Schedules

53. Niamh Sammon, 'A true history of violence', *The Irish Times*, 20/10/07

54. David Adams, 'Diehards reveal true colours', *The Irish Times*, 9/11/07

55. John Martin (*Irish Political Review*), 'Disarray', *Indymedia*, 11/11/2007

56. Pat Muldowney, 'Evidence excluded from Pearsons programme: The Pearson brothers sided with the British and forfeited their civilian status', *The Irish Times*, 27/11/07

57. Tommy Graham. Editorial – 'Let's hear him deny it', *History Ireland*, vol. 16, no. 1, Jan-Feb 2008

58. Brian Hanley, 'Platform', *History Ireland*, vol. 16, no. 1, 2008

59. RTÉ Announcement: Summer 2008 Schedules, Feb. 2008

Index

Abbot, Richard 239
Adams, David 228, 260, 388, 390, 398, 400-1, 455
Aghaboe 9, 108, 413, 417, 423, 442
"Agrarian outrages" 71, 98, 114-5, 216
Ahern, Bertie 226
All-For-Ireland League 184, 215
Amery, Sir Leopold 135, 141, 156, 158, 382
Amish 3, 108, 144-151, 227, 269, 287, 292, 405, 410, 430
Amritsar 208
An tÓglach 93
Anabaptists 10, 108, 109, 149-150
Anderson, Sir John 154, 292
Anglican Church 9, 14, 252, 287
Anglo-Irish Agreement (1938) 118, 382
Annan Bryce, John 179
Annuities 63, 657, 107-9, 112, 117-9, 127-8, 131-3, 340, 343-6, 362
Anti-Sinn Fein Society 159
Ashton family 9, 13, 27, 33, 62, 112, 290
Asquith, George 187
At the Foot of Slieve Bloom 32, 89, 94, 95 , 114, 117, 217, 294
Athlone 83
Aubane Historical Society 2, 6, 159-160, 220, 228, 246, 316, 389, 399-400
Austria 184, 186, 210
Australia 7, 8, 24, 29, 32, 59, 61, 67-8, 126, 128, 146, 148-9, 151, 217-8, 255-6, 341, 379, 396, 404-6
Auxiliaries 19, 26, 28, 30, 32, 35, 75-6, 81, 86, 87, 90, 94-6, 113, 163-4, 166-9, 219, 223, 291, 293, 414, 422

Ballygeehan 409, 411
Bandon 173, 175, 179, 207, 400
Bantry 179
Barry, Tom 163, 166-7, 170, 172, 234
Barton, Robert 177, 180
Basra 89
Batterbee, Sir Harry 140, 381-2, 455
Battles, Jan 390
Beak, Captn. D.M.W. 87, 292, 308, 310, 311
Béal na Blath 196
Béaslai, Piaras 170, 298
Belfast 86, 98, 199, 203, 235, 294, 397, 420
Bennett, Louie 179
Benwell family 9, 10, 31, 106-110, 124, 131, 133, 322, 337, 412
Bernard family 72, 78
Beresford Ellis, Peter 88
Bew, Lord Prof. Paul 115
Biddulph family 9, 14, 27, 33, 77, 112, 272, 290
Biggs, G.W. 179
Birkenhead, Lord 155, 185
Black, Edna 410, 441, 448, 450
Black-and-Tans 19, 75, 83, 86, 88, 223, 234, 299, 397, 421, 423, 439
Blackall, T.H. 65-6, 121, 123, 329, 332-4, 453
Blair, Tony 183
Blakemore family 30, 113
Boer War 17, 186
Boland, W. M. 158
Boothman, Olive 408, 436, 449
Borgonovo, John 159
"botched execution" 262, 385-7, 405, 440
Boycott 8, 56-7, 61, 97, 99-106, 139, 348, 357, 362, 370, 373, 377
Brady, Orla 407, 451

456

"Bradley, Jimmy" (= William Stanley) 26-7, 40, 59, 108, 288, 421, 434

British Army 5, 14, 16, 19-20, 48, 68, 70, 73, 84, 86-96, 122, 124-5, 128-130, 165, 169, 173-4, 186, 191, 208, 243, 266-7, 273, 285, 292, 293, 316, 321, 330, 340, 344, 358, 363, 418, 420-424, 425, 428 (see also Crown Forces and individual regiments - Connaught Rangers, Irish Guards, Royal Dublin Fusiliers, "Irish" Regiments, Leinster Regiment, Royal Irish, Royal Scots Fusiliers)

British Cabinet 86, 134, 154, 187

British Empire 15, 17-18, 21, 22, 34, 59, 84, 89-90, 156, 183, 186, 196, 207-210, 215, 383-4

British Government 9, 15-16, 18-19, 22, 24, 27, 32, 50, 52, 111, 122, 128, 134-5, 137, 140-1, 152-8, 170, 173, 182-216, 222, 242-4, 271, 279, 343, 349, 352, 360, 363, 382, 399, 402, 403, 416, 444-445

Broadcasting Complaints Commission 3, 63, 100, 101, 104, 181, 229-231, 232, 258-278, 372, 426

Brodrick, Alibinia 178

Brophy, Jack 20, 36, 38, 60, 73, 81, 114, 130, 320

Brophy, Katie 74

Brophy, Tim 84

Brown, Dr. 38, 47

Brown, Major E.H. 78

Browne, Major G.W. 48, 50, 87, 91, 305, 308, 311

Browne, Vincent 227-8

Brugha, Cathal 59, 79, 160, 300

Brunyate, Sir James 135, 157

Bruton, John 194

Budenny, Marshal 90

Bureau of Military History 160, 216, 219, 279, 300

Burke, Edmund 183

Byrne, Paddy 413, 442-443

Burke, Commandant Thomas (Tom) 22-3, 26, 29, 35-36, 39, 49, 52, 59-60, 91-2, 113, 244, 250, 282, 298-9, 401, 427, 428, 432, 433-434, 452

Bury, Robin 153, 392

Byrne, Elizabeth 68, 129

Byrne, RIC Sgt. 76

Cadamstown 2-143 *passim*, 217, 219, 231, 272, 280-3, 286-7, 290, 299-300, 302, 305, 307, 309, 317, 332, 333, 363, 396-7, 405, 413, 415, 417, 421, 426, 429-431, 435, 442, 449-450, 452-3

Cadamstown Scarifier 72

Cafferty, Brendan 236, 246, 250-252, 390, 391

Carlow 32, 172, 218, 393

Carrick House 144, 149, 356, 431, 435

Carroll, John 44, 68, 82, 111, 128, 331, 340

Carroll, Jim 75

Carroll, Joe 36, 37, 60, 73, 77, 82, 114, 130, 281, 413, 426

Carroll, John 44, 68, 82, 111, 128, 281

Carroll, Mick ("Mick the Yank") 67, 111, 126, 330, 340

Carroll, Mick (IRA Vol.) 60-1, 68, 126

Carroll, Mrs. 72, 74, 83, 84, 280

Carroll, Patrick 20, 73, 78, 130

Carson, Edward 155, 185, 187

Castlebernard Estate 78

457

Castlerea 298
Cavendish-Bentinck, W. 158, 179
Chamberlain, Joseph 185
Chamberlain, Neville 155
Chidley, Charlie 23, 425
Childers, Erskine 170, 174, 177
Church & State 153, 220, 259
Church of Ireland 9, 14, 178
Churchill, Sir Winston S. L. 86, 88, 135, 157-8, 192, 195, 291
Civil War 25, 38, 56, 59, 60, 85, 114, 117, 124, 126, 127, 129, 184, 185, 196, 222, 240, 283, 285
Clanrickard Estate 124
Clara 418, 439
Clareen 79
Clarendon, Lord 156
Clarke, Basil 161-3, 168-9
Clissman, Inge 259
Cloghan 74, 298
Clonaslee 67, 74, 79, 128, 363
Clontarf Castle 97, 212, 295, 388, 394
Coach house (Coolacrease) 10, 27, 30, 31, 36, 37, 52, 69, 113, 128, 285, 443
Coffey, Leigh-Ann 34-5, 102, 222
Collins, Michael 59, 170, 192, 195-8
Colonial Office 153-6
Condemnation of Fermanagh 145, 147, 287
Connaught Rangers 88
Connolly, James 183
Connolly, Joe 79, 282, 437
Connolly, Michael 437
Connolly, Nora 212-3
Connolly, Seán 391
Connors, RIC Constable 80
Conscription 18, 122, 204, 211
Cooney, Edward 144-151, 287, 392, 410-411
Cooneyism/Cooneyites 6, 7, 9-11, 30, 108-9, 144-151, 222, 237, 246, 256, 269, 273, 287, 392, 396, 404-5, 410-1, 414, 420, 4-427, 442
Cope, Andy 161
Corcoran, Farrel 230
Cordial, Michael 47, 53, 59-60, 219, 281-2, 300-1, 421, 436-437, 452
Cork 20, 33, 59, 93, 110, 159, 286, 291, 392-3, 424, 446
Cork Brigade IRA 33, 73, 163, 165, 166, 170, 179, 195, 196-8, 239, 246, 253, 256, 272, 286
Cosby Estate 103-4, 106
Coughlan, James 68, 111, 125, 129, 331, 341
County Court (Offaly) 31, 52, 63, 115, 142
County Inspector (R.I.C.) 49, 91, 93, 95, 115, 320, 365, 401, 431, 437
Court of Enquiry (Irish) 299, 431, 433, 447 (see also Officers' Battalion Council)
Court of Inquiry in lieu of Inquest (British Military) 42, 44-8, 50, 52, 87, 91, 137, 168, 220, 222-4, 227, 261, 291-2, 305-11, 402, 431, 438, 452
Courts, Republican 23, 56, 76, 114-5, 180, 241, 270, 417
Cowan, W.H. 189
Crinkle Barracks (Birr) 5, 14, 23, 30, 43, 45-7, 54, 75-6, 87, 89, 90, 113, 116, 125, 285, 293, 305, 307-11, 314, 401, 443, 452
Cromer, Lord 208-210
Crotty, Dr. Raymond 109, 118, 130-1
Crown Forces 22-3, 27-8, 32, 35, 36, 39, 44, 86-96, 137, 163-4, 169, 180, 226, 234, 237, 247, 251, 271-3, 358, 363, 417-418, 422, 426, 429, 445 (see also 'British Army')
Crozier, General F.P. 87, 96, 160, 170,

291, 293
Crutchley, E. 137, 154, 292
Cullen, Prof. Louis 131
Cumann na mBan 2, 20, 37, 38, 74-5, 77-8, 85, 383
Cumann na nGaedhal 32
Cunningham, Thomas 298
Curragh Camp 21, 48, 60, 68, 74, 82-4, 87, 91, 95, 96, 113-4, 281, 283, 308, 310
Curragh Mutiny 191
Curtis, Lionel 153, 156, 160, 170, 178
Curzon, Lord 88
Cush Bog 40
Czechoslovakia 210
Dáil Éireann 6, 19, 22, 23, 82, 86, 99, 100, 120-1, 131-2, 157, 168, 170, 174, 175, 177-8, 180, 200, 204, 235, 237-8, 241-3, 252, 270, 383, 408, 411, 431
Daly, Luke 20, 73, 74, 81, 130
Danesfort, Lord 155-6
Darling, Cpt. William 96, 293
Davis, Richard 212
Davis, Thomas 212
Davis, Tommy 71, 124
Dawson, Kevin 87, 221, 295, 388, 394, 455
De Valera, Eamon 33, 119, 133, 140, 192, 197, 343-5, 382
Deasy, Pat 163, 166-7
Deegan, Denis (Din) 13, 62, 81, 110, 112, 412
Deegan, Sr. 79
Deerpark 13, 37, 62, 74, 81, 413
Delahunty, James (Jimmy) 19, 20, 28-9, 36, 37, 60, 65, 66-8, 73, 77, 82, 111, 114, 122, 124, 125, 127, 130, 280, 281, 283, 330, 332, 344, 434-435, 453
Deniken, General 90

Department of Agriculture 4, 64, 101-2, 104-6, 120, 177, 231, 325, 453 (see also Records Branch)
Department of Industry and Commerce 118, 132
Dermody, Paddy 415
Derry 218, 397
Derrylea 107, 323
Devlin M.P., Joseph 199, 201
Dignam, Liam 439
Dillon, James 111
Dillon, John (Cadamstown) 20, 23, 36, 73-5, 78, 80-83, 113, 130
Dillon, John (Irish Parliamentary Party) 187, 190-2
Dillon, John Joe 261-4, 270, 272, 281, 284, 425-426
Dillon, J. J. (son of above) 408, 413, 415-418, 425, 432, 439-441
Dillon, Mary Ellen 74, 284
Dillon, Pat 67, 74, 95
Dillon, Tom 111, 128, 331, 340
Dominion Status 21-2, 59, 412
Dominions Office 135, 140, 156-7, 380-2, 455
Donnelly, Brian 13, 62, 81, 112, 412
Donnelly, Joe 13
Donnelly, Michael 429
Donnelly, Sr. 79
Donnelly, Sis 74-5
Donnelly, Thomas (Tom) 19-20, 36-8, 60, 73, 78, 81-2, 112, 114, 130, 280, 281, 283, 320, 412, 426, 429, 430-431, 437
Dooley, Jack 20, 73, 77, 130
Dooley, Dr. Terence 61-3, 69, 98-105, 107-8, 114, 115, 117, 120, 122, 132, 177, 179, 202, 216, 227, 231, 271, 274, 335, 343, 411-5, 416, 443-5
Doran, RIC Constable 80
Douglas, James 178

459

Downey, Dan 66-7, 69, 117, 122, 128, 133, 303, 330
Doyle, Frank 38
Drayson, M. J. 381
Drought Cptn., family 9, 14, 20, 27, 33, 68, 72, 77-8, 112, 129, 272, 290, 360, 413
Drumcullen 78-9, 82, 283, 421
Dublin 12, 18, 22, 27, 33, 60, 72, 77, 79, 84, 92, 96, 97, 101, 102, 106, 110, 120, 136, 155, 160, 169, 179, 184, 196-7, 222, 232, 234, 241, 242, 254, 255, 257, 291, 297, 383, 392, 393, 401, 403
Dublin Castle 47, 52, 78, 80, 82, 95, 101, 115, 137, 154, 161, 165, 180, 291-2, 316, 317-8, 321, 365, 374-5, 452
"Dublin Four" 216, 231-2
Dublin Opinion 216
Duffy, Joe 177, 182, 204, 228, 240-8, 253-5, 257
Dulanty, John 382
Dum-dum bullets 29-30, 218
Dunedin, Lord 156
Dunmanway 163, 233-4, 250
Dunne, RIC Constable 80
Egan, Kathleen 127
Egan, Martin 67, 111, 127, 330, 340, 345, 453
Egan, Mary 125, 285
Egan, Mick 71
Eglish 39, 82
Egypt 88, 89, 91, 207, 209
Election (1918) 5, 19, 74, 86, 182-3, 192, 194, 199-204, 205-9, 214-5, 270, 277, 290, 296, 383-4, 403
Elections (other) 178, 184, 189-192, 195, 214
Elections (uncontested seats) 213-4
English, Jim 38
English, Prof. Richard 62, 98-9, 146, 202, 204-6, 211-6, 269-270, 274, 408, 411, 413-414, 417, 421, 424-425, 427-428, 430, 433-435, 439, 443, 446, 448
Enniskillen 9, 148, 151
Ethnic cleansing 6-7, 15-16, 24, 33, 34, 61, 70, 97-8, 103, 155, 189, 218, 221, 226-7, 234, 238, 260, 268, 295, 388, 389, 393, 394, 400, 402, 404, 422, 428, 446, 447, 455
Excommunication 21, 48
Faith Missions 9
"false surrender" 164, 170
Famine (1846-51) 14, 15, 71, 86
Farmers' Association (King's County) 11, 27, 48, 109, 421
Feeney, Peter 261-5, 276
Fehery, Jack (John) 37, 65-7, 125-6, 330, 332, 344
Fermanagh 9, 145-8, 150, 254, 287
Festing, FM Sir Francis W. 92
Fianna Fáil 117-8, 157, 203
Fine Gael 32, 33, 59
First World War 125, 131, 242, 416 (see also 'Great War')
Fitzgerald, RIC Constable 80
Fitzpatrick, Prof. David 174, 203
Flannery, Noel 390
Fleming, Judge 52, 56, 116, 361
Flying Column (IRA) 20, 39, 40, 76, 80, 83, 84, 163, 165-7, 169, 303
Folley, Nick 4, 97, 227, 233, 251, 257
Foster, Prof. Roy 202-3
France 12, 66, 87, 88, 125, 126, 128, 148, 183, 210, 292, 293, 331
Frankford 46, 100, 116, 138, 294, 307, 309, 373 (see also Kilcormac)
Franks, Harry 138, 139, 155, 370, 371, 374-5, 378, 380, 454
Free State 21, 25, 31, 32, 34, 37-8, 48, 59, 60-1, 67, 85, 103, 108, 117, 118, 120, 121, 123, 127, 130, 134,

460

152, 153, 156-7, 158, 178, 196, 197, 206, 233, 252, 282, 411, 412, 437
French Estate 331
French, Lord Lieutenant 122
French Revolution 183
G.A.A. 72, 125, 280
Gaelic League 72
Galway 12, 22, 60, 92, 124, 179, 281
Gallipoli 88
Genitals (Harris wound allegations) 8, 47, 146, 176, 249, 260-4, 312, 399-402, 405, 439
Geraghty family 74
Gilfoyle, J.J. 334-5
Gillespie, Dr. Raymond 145, 410
Ginty, Niall 246, 249, 250, 253, 389
Gipsland 448-449
Gladstone, Sir William 24, 215
Glenleitir/Glenlitter 37, 67, 74, 81, 126, 127, 333, 341
Glenn, Mary 37, 285, 340
Glenn, Pat 127, 285
Glenn, William (Bill) 20, 36, 37, 60, 68-9, 73, 111, 112, 114, 124, 127, 130, 285, 330, 340
Graham, Tommy 391
Grammar Of Anarchy, The 200
Grant-Taylor, Lieutenant 94
"Great War" 18-19, 20, 21, 54, 56, 63, 78, 87, 88-90, 125, 130-131, 183, 185, 196, 200, 206, 208-210, 213, 215, 290, 292, 384, 416, 444-445
Griffith, Sir John 178
Griffiths, Sir Richard 109
Griffiths Valuation 109, 117-8, 130
Grogan, John 40, 66, 74, 111, 125, 330, 340
Grove (at Pearson farm) 41, 42-3, 46, 47, 51, 53-4, 223-4, 303, 304, 307, 309, 313, 403

Guerin, Niall 4
Guerin, Claire 245-6
Guinan, Kate 74
Guinan, Martin 19, 73, 130
Guinan, Michael 20, 73, 130
Hapsburg Empire 210
Haldane, Lord 155, 191
Hall, Melanie 102, 104, 325, 453
Hanley, Brian 171, 391
Harris, Senator Eoghan 33, 49, 61, 69, 92, 97, 105, 121, 135, 136, 141, 143, 144, 145-6, 150, 172, 175-8, 181, 194-6, 198, 203, 215-6, 217, 221, 226, 227-8, 249, 250, 253-7, 2605, 267, 268, 272, 275, 287, 312, 314, 335, 388-90, 391, 400-2, 408-411, 418-420, 424, 430, 438-441, 443, 446-447, 449-451, 455
Hart, Peter 32, 159, 162-5, 167-177, 179-181, 202-3, 233-236, 249, 250, 400
Hartnett, Mossie 234
Hayden, Gerard 390
Heaney, Bernard (Glenlitter) 20, 66-7, 74, 81, 111, 127, 331, 333, 341
Heaney, Bernard Brian (Cadamstown) 64, 66-7, 68, 111, 126-7, 286, 294, 453, 330-4, 340
Heaney, Joseph 20, 73, 130
Heaney, Mick 19, 20, 36-40, 47, 54, 55, 60-1, 66-8, 73, 77-8, 81, 114, 126, 127, 130, 150, 275, 280, 283, 301, 320, 341, 408, 429-431, 437, 443
Heaney, Paddy 4, 5-6, 32, 40, 58, 64, 69, 89-90, 94-5, 100-101, 102, 104, 107, 111, 114, 117, 122, 125, 126, 130, 143, 217-224, 229, 245-7, 250-2, 255, 257, 266-8, 269, 275, 279, 294, 389-91, 408-409, 413, 415, 418-420,

461

423-425, 429-431, 434-439, 445-446, 450-451, 453
Heaney, Séamus 218
Heaney, William 20, 73, 130
Hemmende M.P., E.G. 190
Herzog, Dr. Chaim 178
"*Hidden History*" 5, 35, 58, 61, 63, 69-70, 97, 100, 103-5, 109, 113, 114, 117, 119-121, 123, 138, 144, 145, 152, 159, 172, 175-7, 180-1, 216, 223-232, 233, 236-241, 244-7, 252, 258-278, 287, 321, 325, 373, 384, 388, 389, 391, 395-404, 407, 438, 449
History Ireland 171, 174, 176, 236, 388, 391, 403-4, 455
Hitler, Adolf 156, 199
Hoare, Sir Samuel 153
Hogan, Land Commissioner 332, 334
Hogg, Bert 38, 49, 81, 275, 320, 429-431, 437
Home Rule 16-18, 23, 34, 72, 73, 87, 184-193, 200-201, 207-216
Honan, Joseph 20, 73, 130
Honan, Patrick 20, 73, 130
Horan, Mary Anne 111, 341
Horan, Johanna 74
Horan, John Joe 13, 20, 23, 36, 62, 73, 76, 78, 81-2, 112, 113, 130, 281, 284, 412, 426, 429
Horan, Thomas (Tom) 13, 20, 36, 37, 62, 73, 82, 114, 130, 281
Houlahan, Fr. (Kinnity) 48, 65-9, 78, 117, 121-2, 124-8, 266, 446
Hourihane, Ann Marie 180, 228, 388-90
House of Lords 135, 140-1, 155, 158, 190, 382
Howard, Patricia 252, 257
Hume, John 195
Hyde, Douglas 178
I Met Murder on the Way 24-6, 32, 51, 62, 68, 94, 98, 108, 113, 120, 144, 172, 217, 222, 273, 314, 388
Iley, Cpl.Robert William 242
Impartial Reporter, The 147-8, 150
Imperial War Museum 279
Independence, Declaration of 5
India 24, 87-9, 91, 135, 156, 157, 158, 207-8, 447
"Indian Mutiny" 87, 208
Indymedia 98, 101, 119, 159, 162, 163, 167, 171, 220, 225-8, 229, 232, 257, 384, 388, 390-1, 400, 455
Informers 22, 146, 159, 173, 225, 227, 234, 250, 256, 277, 389, 397-8, 405-6
Inniskeen 216
IRA – see Irish Republican Army
Iraq 88-9, 207
Irish Bulletin 168-9
Irish Government 5, 19, 27, 31, 33, 113, 119, 120, 134, 153, 154, 211, 241-4, 270, 279, 402 (see also Free State, De Valera)
Irish Distress Committee 134, 153-5
Irish Examiner 177, 180, 391
Irish Grants Committee 27, 32, 50, 52-3, 55-8, 62-3, 97, 99, 100, 101-3, 109, 112, 116-7, 119, 132, 134-143, 152-158, 222, 273, 276, 288, 289, 292, 314, 337, 347, 352, 360-382, 416, 418, 435, 443-445, 447, 453, 454
Irish Guards Rgt. 66, 89, 125, 126, 330
Irish Land Commission 6, 7, 16, 31, 37, 38, 56, 60, 62-70, 97, 99-143 *passim*, 216, 230-1, 266-8, 271, 283, 284, 295, 301, 322, 324-335, 338, 342, 344-6, 348, 361, 362, 367, 369, 377, 412, 444-446, 453
Irish Land Finance Co. 136
Irish Land League 72, 351
Irish Office 153, 162, 168, 375
Irish Parliamentary Party (Irish Party) 72, 88, 187, 188, 192,

204, 206 (see also John Redmond, Joe Devlin, Redmondites)
Irish Political Review 171, 251, 259, 389, 399, 400, 455
"Irish" Regiments (British Army) 87-90, 185-8
Irish Republic 18, 19, 32, 33, 59, 76, 86, 152, 175, 183, 195-7, 199, 212, 241, 242-3, 252, 258, 296, 297, 391
Irish Republican Army (IRA) 5, 7, 19-23, 26-28, 32-3, 25-44, 47-52, 55-6, 59-60, 65, 68, 70, 71-96, 97, 99-101, 113-4, 116, 122, 124, 126-130, 144, 146, 150, 159, 162-8, 171-3, 175-7, 181, 195, 197, 202, 206, 211, 218-9, 233-5, 237-8, 241-5, 248-251, 254-5, 257, 262, 266-7, 270, 272-5, 280-8, 295, 297-301, 303, 313-4, 318, 320, 349, 383, 389-91, 393, 395, 398-401, 404-6, 452 (see also Cork, Offaly, Tipperary Brigades, Volunteers, Flying Column)
Irish Republican Brotherhood (IRB) 71
Irish Times, The 61, 86, 87, 97-8, 125, 152, 164, 165, 171, 179, 180, 195, 227, 228, 231, 232, 236, 251, 259, 260, 318, 384, 388-90, 391, 393, 395-8, 400-1, 455
Irvine, William 146, 148
Jackson, Albert 13, 14, 33, 54, 62, 66, 112, 128, 137, 290, 303, 363
Jaenen, C. J. 151
Kane, Lt. Matthew 439
Kavanagh, James 26, 34
Keating, Sean 198
Kee, Robert 214
Kehoe, Emmanuel 145, 148, 389

Kelleher, Dr. Jeremiah 168
Kelly, Ruth 410, 419-420, 437, 448
Kemmy T.D., Jim 198
Kemp, Colonel J. C. 92, 281
Kilcormac 38, 40, 43, 76, 78, 79, 80, 83, 100, 116, 137, 282, 283, 294, 301, 373, 440, 452 (see also Frankford)
Kildare 21, 74, 80, 82, 108, 323, 351, 389, 454
Kilkenny 24, 248
Killermogh 30, 57, 442
Killings at Coolacrease, The 8, 31, 35, 61, 98, 145, 229, 231, 258-262, 264, 274, 295, 388, 389-91, 395-6, 398-9, 404, 405, 407 (see also *"Hidden History"*)
Killoughey Company (IRA) 79, 80
Kilmichael 162-170, 178, 202, 291
Kilnaparson 13, 62, 66, 112, 128, 290, 363
King, RIC Sgt 298
King's County Chronicle 49, 52, 62, 113, 115-6, 314, 425, 426, 444
Kingston, Lieut. 87, 305, 308, 310, 311
Kinnear, Michael 215
Kinnity 8, 38, 44, 48, 60, 113, 284, 298-9, 301-2, 305, 313, 401-2, 421, 423, 428, 436
Kinsale, Battle of 13, 218
l'Estrange Malone, Rev. Saville 106, 124, 321-2, 332, 336
Lackaroe 40
Langton, Lawrence (Lar) 73-6, 90
Land Acts 7, 106-7, 109, 117-8, 124, 126, 130, 178, 330, 334, 411, 412
Land Commission – see Irish Land Commission
"Land hunger" 61, 91, 103, 107, 145, 266-9, 397, 405
"*Land Grab*" 6, 7, 25, 30-31, 34-5, 39, 58, 61-4, 70, 97-8, 100, 102-3, 105,

463

117, 120-1, 130, 134, 141, 143,
201, 216, 226-7, 230, 248, 267,
269, 272, 274-7, 295, 325, 329,
333-5, 397, 400, 403, 433, 446-7
Land Registry Office (Dublin) 4, 63,
65, 69, 97, 101, 106, 125-7, 133,
141, 143, 231, 322-4, 343-6, 443-
444, 452, 453
Land War 16-17, 24-5, 72, 96, 124,
293
Landlords 9, 14, 16-17, 25, 61, 71-2,
98, 103-4, 106-7, 117-8, 124,
132, 177, 271, 322, 332, 338,
411-412
Lane, Jack 4, 6, 220, 241, 243, 254,
389, 391
Lane, Timothy 279
Lansdowne (Lord, Marquis of) 24,
102-4, 155, 189, 218
Laois (Leix, Queen's) County 11-13,
15, 24, 30, 35, 39, 49, 67, 87, 89,
91, 102, 103, 108, 128, 136, 137,
149, 155, 218, 282, 320, 350,
356, 363, 409, 422, 431, 442
Leeson, David 159-165, 167
Leinster Regiment (British Army)
75-6, 87-90, 293, 305, 308, 311
Lewis, Jon E. 242
Liberal Party 24, 184-7, 189, 191,
200-1
'Limerickman' 384, 390
Lipsett K.C., L.R. 136, 139, 156,
354, 368, 370, 380
Liveline (RTÉ chat show) 58, 228,
240-1, 243-8, 254 (see also Joe
Duffy)
Lloyd George, David 201
Loach, Ken 4, 115, 231, 396
Loyalists 23-4, 26-7, 32, 34-5, 39,
50, 52, 57, 70, 78, 80, 98, 102,
108, 134-8, 142, 147, 153-8, 175,
178, 218, 222, 233, 235-8, 273,

276, 288, 301, 317, 351, 358, 363,
389, 393, 401, 414, 418, 422-423,
425, 429-430, 436-437, 444-447
(see also Southern Irish Loyalists
Relief Association)
Luggacurran 24-35, 39, 41, 50, 58-9,
70, 98, 102-4, 108, 113, 149, 155,
189, 218-9, 222, 291, 422-423,
424-425, 433, 437
Lynn, Dr. Kathleen 178
Lyons, Prof. F.S.L. 187-8
Lyons, Peter 283, 421
Lyons, Sean 390
McAllister family 9, 14, 27, 29, 33, 435
McArdle, Dorothy 241, 297
McCarthy, Michael 166
McConway, Philip 4, 55, 64, 93-4,
105, 115, 176, 222, 262, 301, 389,
390, 400, 407, 408, 415, 424, 425-
427, 433-436, 438, 440, 451
McCormack, James (Jim) 68, 77, 94,
111, 128, 133, 284, 331, 346, 453
McCormack, Michael 282
McDonnell, Michael 20, 73, 130
McDowell, Prof. R.B. 136, 152-3, 155,
157, 350
McGouran, Seán 4, 153, 222-3
McGrath-Guerin, Claire 4
McIntyre family 74
McKee T.D., Richard 291
McNeill M.P., Ronald 190
McRedmond, John Joe (J.J.) 20, 69, 73,
82, 111, 112, 114, 126, 130, 281,
330, 339, 340, 413, 426
McRedmond, Michael (Mick) 19, 36-7,
62, 73, 112, 114, 130, 413, 426
McRedmond, William 111
McVeagh M.P., Jeremiah 190
Macready, General 169
Macroom 163, 168
Magherabawn 37
Maher family 10, 30

464

Mahon family 41, 107
Mahon, Commandant Seán 92
Malone Estate 106, 124, 332, 336
Maloney family 74
Manifold, Ann 74
Manifold, John 19, 20, 23, 36, 37, 60, 73, 114, 130
Manifold, Joseph 19, 60, 73, 130
Manifold family 20, 72, 290
Mansergh T.D., M. 391, 393, 399
Martin, John 86, 390, 400, 455
Martin, Pierce 390
Marxism 194, 197-8
'Mass path incident' 36, 50, 81, 113, 146, 223, 284, 303, 425-427, 429
Mater Dei Institute of Education 62, 99, 202
Matthew, St. 144, 148-9, 150
Mayne, Erskine 207
Maynooth (University) 98, 102, 145, 202, 410
Medical evidence 44-7, 261-5, 268, 440 (see also Wounds, Court of Inquiry in lieu of Inquest)
Melbourne 126, 448
Meehan, Niall 179-180, 253-4, 257, 390
Methodism 145-7
Midland Tribune 62, 114, 116, 444
Military Archives (Irish) 4, 160, 219
Milner, Lord 153, 156
Mitchell, Herbert 20, 257, 272, 286
Mitchell, Tom 20, 73, 435
Mitchell, Walter 20, 73, 272, 286
Monasterevin 108
Month, The 170-1
Moorehead, Alan 15
Morning Post 155
Morton, Dr. 43
Mountbolus 41
Mountmellick 10, 43, 49, 149, 431
Mountrath 136, 155

Moylan, Seán 160
Mulcahy, General Richard 21-2, 59, 92, 416, 418, 427-428, 433
Muldowney, Pat 6, 64, 100-1, 104-5, 119, 202, 232-3, 243-4, 253-5, 268-9, 272, 275-7, 389-91, 400, 401, 408-451 *passim*, 453, 455
Mullins, David 34
Mullins, Francis 34
Multany, Jack 66, 111, 125, 128, 133, 331, 340, 343, 453
Murphy osb, Dr. Brian P. 96, 154, 159, 161, 163, 167, 168, 171, 316, 391, 424
Murphy, Prof. John A. 194-5, 198
Murphy, Dr. William 62, 69, 99, 202, 227, 273-4, 276, 414, 417-418, 427-429, 431, 445
Myers, Kevin 194-6, 251
National Archives 4, 101, 159-160, 162, 279, 305, 398
National Land Bank 178, 180
National Library of Ireland 298
New History Of Ireland 187, 213
1916 Rising 18-20, 33, 73, 74, 88, 160, 164, 172, 183-4, 193-4, 196, 199, 204, 206, 212, 242, 251, 257, 272, 296, 383
Nolan, Tim 13-4, 38, 47, 54, 62, 74, 76, 112, 303
Northern Ireland 28, 30, 113, 134, 153, 175, 194-5, 198, 206, 218, 289
Northumberland, Duke of 153, 155-6
O'Brien, Fergal 78
O'Brien, Nellie 74
O'Brien, Paddy 166
O'Brien, Tom 68, 111, 129, 331, 340-1
O'Carroll, Joseph (Joe) 13, 20, 62, 112
Ó Ceallaigh, President Seán T. 292
O'Connell, Daniel 15, 212-3
O'Connell, Tim 166
O'Connor, John 20, 73, 130

465

O'Connor, Philip 64, 102, 279
O'Donnell (Hugh) 13
O'Donovan T.D., D. J. 291
O'Donovan, Pat 166
O'Dwyer, Sir Paul 208
Ó hAilbhe, Daithí 389
O'Neill (Hugh) 12, 71, 218
O'Malley, Ernie 84, 391
O'Rourke, Bernard 216
O'Sheil, Judge Kevin 115
O'Sullivan, Garóid 298
O'Sullivan, Jim 166
Oakley, Sir John 135, 157
Offaly (King's) County 5, 7, 8-9, 12-13, 15, 16, 20, 21-22, 35, 36, 39, 55, 56, 59, 61, 70-93, 110, 113, 115, 130, 132, 141-5, 217-220, 222, 226, 239, 248-250, 255-7, 258, 270-2, 280, 292, 391, 293, 298-304, 320, 342, 350, 360-3, 373, 389-91, 395-405 *passim*, 407-451 *passim*, 452-3
Offaly Brigade IRA (Offaly No. 2) 22, 35, 39, 73, 75-6, 79, 82, 84, 92-3, 113, 144, 272, 280-2, 286, 298-301, 416-451 (see also Irish Republican Army, Officers' Battalion Council)
Offaly Heritage Journal 218, 389
Offaly Historical and Archaeological Society 4, 218, 222, 279, 389
Offaly Independent 226
Officers' Battalion Council (IRA) 22, 39, 299, 402, 433-4 (see also Court of Enquiry)
Ogden, Perry 220
Orange Order 24, 34, 108, 298, 424
Oxford 33, 162, 187, 203, 233
Pale 12, 232
Pearse, Patrick 183, 196-9, 209
Palestine 88, 91
Parnell, Charles Stewart 72, 214-5

Parker, Doug and Helen 150-1
Peace Process 195, 393
Peace with Ireland Council 179
Pearson, Abraham (Abe) 7, 8, 10, 19, 22, 28-30, 39-46, 54, 70, 144, 222, 261-4, 288, 301, 305-10, 311, 312, 315, 395-9, 401-2, 404-5, 410, 421, 434-438, 441-444, 452
Pearson, Cecil 35
Pearson, Cyril 423
Pearson, David 10, 29-34, 42-3, 50-2, 54-9, 113, 252, 289
Pearson, Emily 10, 29-32, 59, 113, 289
Pearson, Ethel 10, 29-30, 33, 42-3, 45, 51-2, 66, 91, 113, 289, 306, 309, 312, 313, 399, 402
Pearson, Matilda 10, 29-30, 46, 113, 177, 181, 289, 307, 309, 313, 420
Pearson, Mervyn 448
Pearson, Richard (Dick) 7, 8, 19, 22, 28-30, 39-46, 54, 70, 80, 144, 146, 222, 261-4, 272, 288, 301, 305-10, 311, 312, 315, 395-9, 401-2, 404-5, 415, 421, 425, 429-410, 434-435, 438, 441-442, 444, 452
Pearson, Richard (Rathdowney) 108
Pearson, Roger 255-6
Pearson, Sidney (Syd) 10, 22, 28, 30-1, 39, 43, 49-50, 53, 56, 58-9, 101, 112-3, 116, 119, 136, 144, 149, 320, 347, 350, 352, 353, 354, 374, 396, 399, 453-4
Pearson, Susan 10, 29-30, 42, 44, 46-7, 57, 68, 113, 149, 307-10, 314, 406, 408-410, 419, 436, 441, 447-409
Pearson, Tilly 392, 419-420, 448-9
Pearson, Vernon 410, 413-414, 448-9
Pearson, William 11, 27-8, 30-32, 36, 43, 48, 52-8, 61-3, 69, 70, 98-101, 107-8, 110, 113, 115, 117, 119-120, 123, 136, 139, 141-3, 271, 289, 320, 323, 351, 354, 356, 360-

466

4, 371, 400, 408-21, 423, 429,-31, 435, 438, 442, 444-51, 454-5
Pearsons *passim*
Percy, Lord Eustace 153, 155-6
Percy, William 62, 99, 100, 116, 119, 137-8, 141, 373, 444, 454
Petty-Fitzmaurice, Charles Henry 24
Phillips, Alison 169
Phoenix magazine 226-8, 389
Plantation 8, 106, 136, 155, 189, 218
Planters 24-7, 34-5, 39, 58, 102-3, 222, 299
Plunkett, Sir Horace 178
Police Cadets - see Auxiliaries
Pollard, Cpt. H.B.C. 168
Pollock, H.M. 237
Portland, Duke of 158
Portumna 22, 60, 124, 282
Presbyterians 145, 236, 391
Protestants *passim*
Punch 235
Purcell, Mick 71
Purcell, Pat 81, 95
Queen's County – see Laois
R.I.C. – see Royal Irish Constabulary
Repeal Association 212
RIC *Weekly Summary* 96, 293
Rahan 20, 73, 286
Rangoon 90-1
Rath 76, 91, 96, 408, 435
Rathdowney 103-4, 108, 149
Records Branch, Land Services Division 4, 64, 101-6, 120-1, 231, 325
Redmond, John 88, 184-8, 192, 213, 215
Redmond, William 199
"Redmondites" 73, 121, 189
Reform Group 143, 176, 181
Reid Jamieson, Alan 135, 138-140, 153, 157, 352-3, 370, 374-5, 379, 454

Reilly, Michael 298
Rent 14, 63, 79, 103, 109, 117-8, 131, 340
Refugees 134, 153, 155-6, 347
Reprisals 22, 91, 93-4, 96, 255, 291, 293, 297-8, 320, 452
Republic – see Irish Republic
Republicans 18, 34, 35, 50, 56, 60-1, 67-8, 70, 95, 117, 121-2, 125-6, 129-130, 136, 143, 174-6, 196-7, 235, 238, 251, 284-5, 293, 333, 341, 352, 357, 361-2, 365, 392-3, 396, 408, 417, 419, 421, 422, 434, 438, 439, 446
Restoration of Order in Ireland Act 180
Reviews in History 159
Revisionism, revisionists 97, 182, 188-9, 194-6, 203, 205-6, 209, 213-6, 233, 235-6, 248, 253, 403
Roadblock (at Coolacrease) 5, 22-3, 28, 32, 36-9, 47-51, 56-60, 65-6, 68, 70, 82, 91, 95, 99, 113-4, 124, 126, 129, 150, 219-220, 223-6, 245, 174-5, 280, 282-3, 288, 303, 320-1, 341, 344, 391, 405, 415, 419, 429-31, 437, 439, 447
Roantree, Ray 451
Roberts, Patricia 151
Robinson, Mary 194
Roscomroe 20, 73, 286
Roscrea 74-5
Round Table Group 153, 156, 170
Rouse, Dr. Paul 105, 125, 230, 276, 407, 451
Rowe, Patrick 67, 111, 128, 331, 340
Royal Dublin Fusiliers 88-9
Royal Irish Constabulary (R.I.C.) 14, 16, 19, 20, 22-3, 26, 33, 35-6, 38-9, 41, 43, 48-9, 55, 73, 78, 80-1, 83, 86-7, 89-91, 93-6, 115, 124, 158, 220, 223-4, 235, 239, 257, 272,

467

275, 291, 293, 298, 303, 318, 320, 365-6, 384, 399, 401, 411, 418, 420,423-424, 428, 429-431, 433, 435, 437, 439, 447 (see also Black-and-Tans, Auxiliaries)
Royal Irish Regiment 88-9
Royal Irish Guards 88
Royal Irish Rifles 88
Royal Munster Fusiliers 88
Royal Scots Fusiliers 50, 87, 90-95, 281, 292-3, 311, 318, 319, 421
Russia 87, 292
RTÉ 5, 6, 7, 31, 35, 49, 58, 61, 63-4, 70, 97-8, 104-7, 136, 145, 150, 172, 175-181, 182, 194, 201, 204, 216, 220-222, 226-232, 233, 236, 239, 241, 243, 247, 253, 258-9, 261-5, 276-8, 295, 325, 335, 356, 384, 388, 389-91, 394, 395, 398-401, 403, 405, 407, 416, 423, 426, 446-7, 449, 455
Russell (AE), George 178
Ryan, Meda 163, 166, 171, 202, 234-5, 250
Salisbury, Marquess of 155
Sammon, Niamh 61, 63-4, 69, 92, 97-8, 100-101, 105-6, 119, 121, 128, 135-6, 143, 145, 147, 176, 179-181, 216, 220-1, 223-232, 236, 239-240, 247-250, 263-4, 266-8, 275-6, 314, 326, 333, 335, 372, 384, 388, 389-90, 395-7, 407, 413, 451, 455
Sammon, Pat 407, 451
Sarkisyanz, Dr. Manuel 156
Savarkar, V.D. 208
Scotland 28, 34, 37, 90, 103, 108, 148
Scully, Bernard 68, 129
Scully, Margaret 68, 111, 129, 331, 341
Sectarianism 6-7, 34, 36, 61, 70, 97-8, 100, 104-5, 120-1, 130, 137, 141-3,
150-1, 171–181, 198, 223, 226-8, 231, 233-6, 238, 246, 248-9, 253-5, 257, 268-9, 271-2, 277, 295, 325, 335, 388-91, 393, 397-8, 400-4, 412-4, 424, 426-8, 433
Seskin 74, 81
Silver River 40, 68-9, 111, 123, 126, 141, 328
Sinclair-Poulton, Clive 236
Sinn Féin 48, 52, 76, 88, 95, 120, 126, 154, 159, 169-170, 194-9, 204, 206, 211, 213-4, 216, 237, 241, 243, 257, 270, 279, 284, 286, 383, 399, 401, 416, 431 (see also Republicans)
Skinner, Col. P.C.B. 91, 308, 310, 319
Slieve Bloom mountains 8, 13-14, 21, 23, 71, 74, 83, 85, 294, 302, 396, 409, 428, 450 (see also *At the foot of Slieve Bloom*)
Smith, F.E. 185 (also Lord Birkenhead)
Smith Gordon, Lionel 177
Somme, Battle of the 20, 37, 60, 69, 125, 128, 285, 340
South Africa 17
Southern Irish Loyalists Relief Association 135-8, 142, 155-8, 350, 354, 360, 374, 400, 454
Spies 22, 94, 96, 146, 159, 225, 227, 234, 240, 250-1, 298-9, 389, 397, 405-6
Spink Hill 79, 332
Squatting 8, 31, 56-7, 70, 112-7, 120
Stanley, Alan 24-6, 29-35, 41, 50-1, 55, 57-70, 94, 98, 108, 112-3, 116, 120, 144, 172-3, 175-6, 181, 217-220, 222-6, 231, 252, 260-1, 269-270, 273, 275, 279, 314, 388, 391-2, 395-6, 401
Stanley, Edward 34
Stanley, Frank 26, 422
Stanley, Henry 24-5, 34, 55, 113

Stanley, Hilary 32, 50, 252
Stanley, Oliver
Stanley, Violet 26
Stanley, William 26-31, 34-5, 39-41, 50, 55, 58-60, 98, 102, 108, 113, 217-8, 220, 222-3, 273, 288-9, 291, 420-424, 431, 434-438, 443 (see also ("Jimmy Bradley"))
Stone, Joseph 34
Stone, Philip 34
Stopford Green, Alice 178
Stradbally 218
Street, Major C.J.C. 160, 162, 168
Strickland Papers 163-4
Strong, Lt. Kenneth 94, 420-421
Stuart-Menzies, Mrs. 155
Sturgis, Mark 137, 153-4, 292
Suffolk 32, 56, 63, 350, 352, 359-60, 379, 447
Sunday Business Post 145, 389
Sunday Independent 97, 144, 175-7, 180, 217, 221, 228, 259, 268, 389-91, 400, 447, 455
Sunday Times, The 194, 249, 390
Syngfield 75
Sythes, George 34
Tasmania 15
Telfords 119, 139, 343, 372, 454
Templemore 291
Tenants 9, 14, 24-5, 34, 79, 103-4, 106-7, 117-8, 122, 124, 130, 132, 322, 412, 422
Thomas, J. H. 382
Thurles 72, 125
Time magazine 158
Times, The (London) 15, 18, 24, 107, 134, 156, 157
Tipperary 10, 40, 74-5, 88, 144, 239, 242, 393
Tipperary Brigade (IRA) 40, 75
Tormey, Jim 83
Townshend, Caroline Mary 179

Townshend, Prof. Charles 154, 203
Treaty (1921) 22, 25, 32, 33, 49, 59, 60, 65, 66, 67, 85, 89, 96, 116, 128, 134, 152-3, 155, 196, 233
Trinity College 152, 169, 203, 222
Trotter, Rev. I.C. 179
Truce (1921) 19, 56, 84, 98, 136, 140, 152, 154, 254, 269, 301, 363, 370, 381, 391-2, 396, 428, 432, 443-4
'Truth about Ireland League' 155
Tubridy, Ryan 61, 98, 204, 227, 236, 239-240, 247-9, 268, 413, 417, 447
Tullamore 8, 14, 22, 28, 30, 33, 38, 41, 42, 43, 47, 76-7, 81, 82, 87, 113, 115, 223, 302, 318, 390, 416, 429
Tullamore Jail 79, 82, 91, 94-5, 284, 389, 408
Tullamore Tribune 115, 279, 389-90
Turkey 88, 184, 186-7
Turnidge, Jenny 409, 414-5, 442, 447-9
Ulster 13, 18, 24, 34, 73, 89, 103, 108, 196, 203
Ulster Unionists 18, 185, 198, 203, 206, 422, 424, 433
Ulster Volunteer Force (U.V.F.) 19, 23, 26, 35, 39, 299, 433
Uncontested Seats 213-4
Union Jack 17, 21, 129, 414
Unionist Party (British) 184-5, 201, 206
United Irish Society 71, 183
United Kingdom (UK) 9, 18, 137, 193, 204, 214, 223, 235, 239, 242, 363
United States of America (USA) 12, 24, 87, 103
Valuation (land) 57, 109, 110-112, 117-8, 130, 132-3, 139, 274, 330, 336-7, 340, 342, 352
Valuation Office (Dublin) 4, 65, 69, 97, 106, 109, 125, 126, 128, 129, 133, 141, 143, 336-340, 453
Value (of Pearson farm) 8, 47, 69, 97, 100, 109-112, 116, 119-120, 130-2,

469

136-143, 271, 276, 444
Verisimilitude 161-2, 168-9
Versailles Conference and Treaty 19, 206, 210-211, 242
Village magazine 227-8, 389
Volunteers (Irish) 18-20, 23, 26, 36-7, 39, 72-3, 74-5, 78-84, 114, 166, 196, 242-3, 300--4, 384
Volunteers (National) 18-19, 72-3, 186
Volunteer Dependents Fund 74
Voynich, E.L. 383, 390
Wales 25-30, 41, 55, 58, 87, 113, 218, 443
Walsh, John 68, 127, 332, 344
Walsh, J.E. 155
Watson (RIC Sgt.) 75
Westmeath 83
Weir, Rev. Robert A. 136, 155, 350-1, 374, 454
Westminster 72, 184, 186, 188, 200
Wexford 71, 252, 289
Wilson, F.M. Sir Henry 88
Wilson, President Woodrow 242
White, J. 50
White, Major 138-140, 156, 368-73, 380, 454
Williams, Basil 179
Wind that Shakes the Barley 4, 115, 231, 396, 413
Winters, Dr. Jane 160
Witness, The 236-8
Witness Statement 47, 60, 160, 219, 282, 300, 315, 395, 437, 452
Wolfe Tone, Theobald 72
Wood Renton, Sir Alexander 135, 153, 157, 353
Woods, C.R., Lt. Col. RAMC 45, 402, 308, 402
Woods, Dr. Frederick W. 44-5, 305-6, 402
Wounds (Pearson brothers') 30, 38, 42-7, 54-5, 137, 249, 261-2, 306-7, 310, 312, 315, 402, 439, 416, 438-441 (see also 'medical evidence', 'genitals allegation', 'Court of Inquiry')
Wounds (Volunteers') 22, 38-9, 60, 75, 81, 85, 90, 114, 126, 129, 146, 166-7, 219, 226, 283, 341, 408, 430, 439
Wynne, Sir Henry 156
Yeats, W.B. 178
Young, Joe 68, 129
Young, Ned 166
Yugoslavia 210
Ziehr, Wilhelm 15

Other titles available:

Sean Moylan. *In His Own Words.* His memoir of the War of Independence, with a selection of his speeches and poems. 3rd edition with Introduction by *Éamon Ó Cuív*, Preface: *Jack Lane*, Epilogue: *Brendan Clifford*. 234pp. Index. ISBN 1 90349715 9 (3rd edn). AHS, 2004.

Myths From Easter 1916, by *Eoin Neeson*. Index. 222pp. ISBN ISBN 978-1-903497-34-0. AHS. 2007.

An Answer To Revisionists—Éamon Ó Cuív TD and others launch *Seán Moylan In His Own Words:* Includes 1st pub. of Moylan-McGarritty corresponddence, Michael O'Riordan's review of the Moylan *Memoir*, and materials added to various editions of Moylan's Memoir. 116pp, Index. 1 903497 18 3. AHS, 2004.

Seán O'Hegarty, O/C First Cork Brigade, Irish Republican Army by *Kevin Girvin*. Index. 248pp. ISBN 978-1-903497-30-2. AHS. 2007.

Batt O'Connor: *With Michael Collins In The Fight For Freedom.* With *Mrs. O'Connor's Statement* to the BMH. Introduction: *B. Clifford*. 142pp. Index. ISBN 1 90349717 5. AHS, 2004

Six Days Of The Irish Republic (eyewitness account of 1916), by *L.G. Redmond-Howard*. Contains a profile of Roger Casement, written during his trial; the Irish Case for the League of Nations; and a play written jointly with Harry Carson (the Ulster leader's son). Intro. by *Brendan Clifford*. Index. 256pp ISBN 1 903497 27 2. AHS, March 2006.

The Origins and Organisation of British Propaganda in Ireland 1920 by *Brian P. Murphy osb*. Foreword: *Prof. David Miller*. ISBN 1 903497 24 8. 100pp, Illus. Bibliog. Index. AHS + Spinwatch., Feb. 2006.

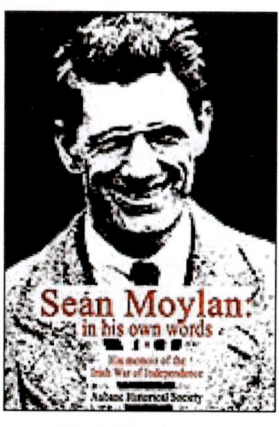

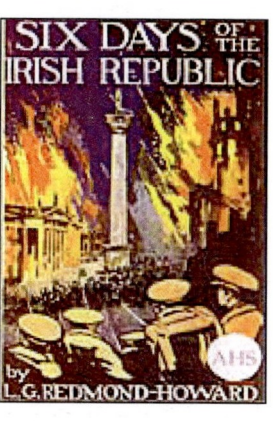

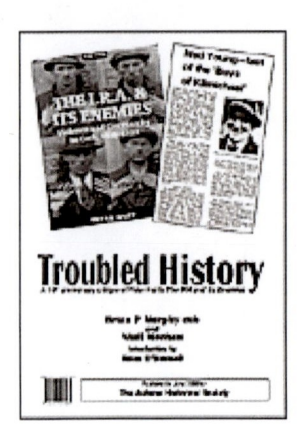

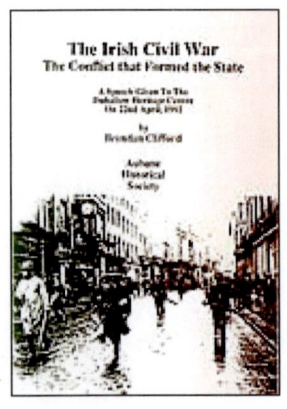

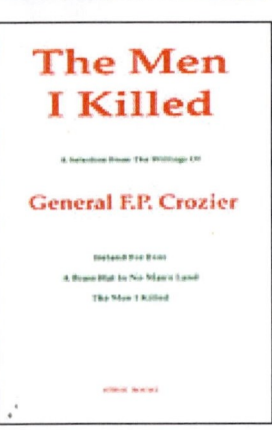

Troubled History: A 10th Anniversary Critique Of *The IRA & Its Enemies* by *Brian Murphy osb and Niall Meehan*. Introduction *Dr. Ruan O'Donnell*. 48pp. ISBN 978-1-903497-46-3.

The Irish Civil War, The Conflict That Formed the State by *B. Clifford*. 22pp. 0 9521081 00 0.

Joe Devlin: **What Now?**, *His Confrontation of the British Parliament, After The 1918 Election*. Edited by *Brendan Clifford*. 48pp. 978-1-874158-19-6. A Belfast Magazine No. 32. Oct. 2007.

Kilmichael: The False Surrender: a discussion by *Peter Hart, Padraig O'Cuanachain, D.R. O'Connor Lysaght, Dr. Brian Murphy, & Meda Ryan*, with: **Why The Ballot Was Followed By The Bullet** by *J. Lane & B. Clifford*. 48pp. ISBN 1 903497 00 0. Nov. 1999.

The 'Boys' of the Millstreet Battalion Area—Some personal accounts of the War of Independence *by veterans of the Battalion*. 63pp (A4). 1 903497 12 4.

The Burning Of Cork (1920),—An Eyewitness Account by *Alan Ellis*, and other items. 44pp (A4). 1 903497 116 7.

Michael Collins. *Some Documents In His Own Hand*. Introduced by *Dr. Brian P. Murphy osb*. 40pp A4. ISBN 1 90349719 1. July 2004.

General F.P. Crozier: *The Men I Killed* (1937), *Irish Memoirs* &other writings. Introduction by *B. Clifford*. 152 pp. ISBN 0 85034 085 3. AB, 2002.

Contact us for a full list: Aubane Historical Society, Aubane, Millstreet, Co. Cork

www.aubane.org
Orders: jacklaneaubane@hotmail.com